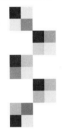

A First Look at ASP.NET v. 2.0

- **Alex Homer**
  Dave Sussman
  Rob Howard

♦♦ Addison-Wesley

Boston • San Francisco • New York • Toronto • Montreal
London • Munich • Paris • Madrid
Capetown • Sydney • Tokyo • Singapore • Mexico City

The publisher offers discounts on this book when ordered in quantity for bulk purchases and special sales. For more information, please contact:

U.S. Corporate and Government Sales
(800) 382-3419
corpsales@pearsontechgroup.com

For sales outside of the U.S., please contact:

International Sales
(317) 581-3793
international@pearsontechgroup.com

Visit Addison-Wesley on the Web:
www.awprofessional.com

Library of Congress Cataloging-in-Publication Data
Homer, Alex.
  A first look at ASP.NET v. 2.0 / Alex
Homer, Dave Sussman, Rob Howard.
    p. cm.
  Includes bibliographical references and index.
  ISBN 0-321-22896-0
    1. Active server pages. 2. Microsoft.NET. 3. Web sites—design. 4. Web site development. I. Sussman, David. II. Howard, Rob. III. Title.

TK5105.8885.A26H6598 2003
006.7'6—dc22

                                    2003062966

ISBN: 0-321-22896-0
Text printed on recycled paper
1 2 3 4 5 6 7 8 9 10—CRS—0706050403
First printing, October 2003

A First Look at
ASP.NET v. 2.0

Microsoft .NET Development Series

John Montgomery, *Series Advisor*
Don Box, *Series Advisor*
Martin Heller, *Series Editor*

The **Microsoft .NET Development Series** is supported and developed by the leaders and experts of Microsoft development technologies including Microsoft architects and DevelopMentor instructors. The books in this series provide a core resource of information and understanding every developer needs in order to write effective applications and managed code. Learn from the leaders how to maximize your use of the .NET Framework and its programming languages.

Titles in the Series

Brad Abrams, *.NET Framework Standard Library Annotated Reference Volume 1*, 0-321-15489-4

Keith Ballinger, *.NET Web Services: Architecture and Implementation*, 0-321-11359-4

Don Box with Chris Sells, *Essential .NET, Volume 1: The Common Language Runtime*, 0-201-73411-7

Mahesh Chand, *Graphics Programming with GDI+*, 0-321-16077-0

Anders Hejlsberg, Scott Wiltamuth, Peter Golde, *The C# Programming Language*, 0-321-15491-6

Alex Homer, Dave Sussman, Mark Fussell, *A First Look at ADO.NET and System.Xml v. 2.0*, 0-321-22839-1

Alex Homer, Dave Sussman, Rob Howard, *A First Look at ASP.NET v. 2.0*, 0-321-22896-0

James S. Miller and Susann Ragsdale, *The Common Language Infrastructure Annotated Standard*, 0-321-15493-2

Fritz Onion, *Essential ASP.NET with Examples in C#*, 0-201-76040-1

Fritz Onion, *Essential ASP.NET with Examples in Visual Basic .NET*, 0-201-76039-8

Ted Pattison and Dr. Joe Hummel, *Building Applications and Components with Visual Basic .NET*, 0-201-73495-8

Chris Sells, *Windows Forms Programming in C#*, 0-321-11620-8

Chris Sells and Justin Gehtland, *Windows Forms Programming in Visual Basic .NET*, 0-321-12519-3

Damien Watkins, Mark Hammond, Brad Abrams, *Programming in the .NET Environment*, 0-201-77018-0

Shawn Wildermuth, *Pragmatic ADO.NET: Data Access for the Internet World*, 0-201-74568-2

Contents

Figures

Tables

Foreword

ASP.NET IS THE FASTEST-GROWING Web development platform in the world today. It powers some of the biggest Web sites and applications in the world—a shortlist of well-known customers include: Dell Computer, Merrill Lynch, the London Stock Exchange, NASDAQ, JetBlue Airways, USA TODAY, Home Shopping Network, Weight Watchers, Bank One, and Century 21.

Every day thousands of new developers begin learning ASP.NET for the first time—supported by an incredible developer community of books (170+ different ASP.NET books have been printed), user groups (more than 150+ worldwide), forums (300,000+ registered users on the www.asp.net public forums), e-mail-based listservs, and Web logs.

Our goal while building ASP.NET version 2.0 has been not only to develop a product that makes this developer community proud but also to build a platform that defines a new level of rich features and functionality against which all Web development is measured.

Specifically, we've focused our work on ASP.NET 2.0 around three core themes:

Developer productivity: Our goal with ASP.NET 2.0 is to enable developers to build full-featured Web applications faster than ever before. We've spent countless hours talking with developers and looking at existing applications to identify the common features, patterns, and code that Web developers build over and over today. We've then worked to componentize and include these features as built-in functionality of ASP.NET. For example, ASP.NET 2.0 now includes built-in support for Membership (username/password credential storage) and Role Manager services out of the box. The new Personalization service enables quick storage and retrieval of user settings and preferences—facilitating rich customization with minimal code. Master pages enables flexible page UI inheritance across sites. The navigation system enables developers to quickly build menu-associated link structures. Themes enable flexible UI skinning of controls and pages. And the new Web Parts framework enables rich portal-style layout and end user customization features that would otherwise require writing tens of thousands of lines of code.

Augmenting all these great infrastructure features are more than 40 new server controls in version 2.0 that enable powerful declarative support for data access, security, wizard navigation, menus, tree views, portals, and more. For example, building a page with a DataGrid in ASP.NET 1.0 that was filtered using a drop-down list, while also supporting paging and sorting and editing, would have required approximately 100 lines of code (and probably a few trips to the help documentation). In ASP.NET 2.0, this scenario can be accomplished with not a single line of procedural code (the new data controls do all the work)—and literally can be built in seconds using the new edition of Visual Studio development tools.

The collective arsenal of features now available to developers in ASP.NET 2.0 is truly awesome. With it, projects that used to take days or weeks can now be done in as little as a few hours.

Administration and management: Our goal with ASP.NET 2.0 is to ensure that administrators love ASP.NET as much as developers do today. This means building features that further enhance the deployment, management, and operations of ASP.NET servers.

In ASP.NET 2.0 we've built new configuration management APIs—enabling users to programmatically build programs or scripts that create, read, and update `web.config` and `machine.config` configuration files. And we've provided a new comprehensive administration tool that plugs into the existing IIS Administration MMC and enables an administrator to graphically read or change any setting within our XML configuration files.

ASP.NET 2.0 will ship with a new application deployment utility that will enable both developers and administrators to pre-compile a dynamic ASP.NET application prior to deployment. This pre-compilation automatically identifies any compilation issues anywhere within the site and also enables ASP.NET applications to be deployed without any source being stored on the server (even the content of .aspx files is removed as part of the compile phase).

We are also providing new health monitoring support to enable administrators to be automatically notified when an application on a server starts to experience problems. New tracing features will enable administrators to capture runtime and request data from a production server to better diagnose issues.

Speed and performance: ASP.NET is already the world's fastest Web application server. Our goal with ASP.NET 2.0 is to make it even faster.

ASP.NET 2.0 is now 64-bit enabled, meaning it can take advantage of the full memory address space of new 64-bit processors and servers. Developers can simply copy existing 32-bit ASP.NET applications onto a 64-bit ASP.NET 2.0 server and have them automatically be JIT compiled and executed as native 64-bit applications (no source code changes or manual recompile are required).

ASP.NET 2.0 also now includes automatic database server cache invalidation. This powerful and easy-to-use feature allows developers to aggressively output cache database-driven page and partial page content within a site—and have ASP.NET automatically invalidate these cache entries and refresh the content whenever the back-end database changes.

At the same time that we've focused efforts on making ASP.NET even better, we have also made significant improvements to the Web development support within Visual Studio. This includes much better WYSIWYG designer support—to avoid any HTML reformatting of source, to provide full XHTML compliance of markup, and to provide a WYSIWYG designer for the new ASP.NET 2.0 master pages feature. It includes major project system enhancements—the FrontPage Server Extensions are no longer required to create, edit, and run applications (just point at a file system directory and you can begin editing). It includes improvements to the code editing and code separation models—making code behind much more elegant and robust. And it includes rich support for data access—leveraging the new ASP.NET 2.0 data controls features to enable easy and powerful data UI generation with no code required. The combination of ASP.NET 2.0 and the new Visual Studio development tool features compliment each other perfectly, enabling developers to quickly and easily build applications like never before.

This book is the first to guide developers toward all of the amazing functionality that will be available with this new generation of products. It provides an overview of the most important of the new features and helps explain how to begin using them with the ASP.NET 2.0 alpha release.

Some details will change as ASP.NET 2.0 progresses further (we won't start locking everything down until the beta release of the product), but you'll be able to use this book now as a valuable resource to gain insight into the new features coming—and to recognize just how much easier and better Web development will be when ASP.NET 2.0 is released.

Scott Guthrie
Product Unit Manager
ASP.NET and Visual Studio Web Tool Teams
Microsoft Corporation

■ 1 ■

An Introduction to ASP.NET 2.0

W HEN MICROSOFT RELEASED the .NET Framework 1.0 Technology Preview in July 2000, it was immediately clear that Web development was going to change. The company's then current technology, Active Server Pages 3.0 (ASP), was powerful and flexible, and it made the creation of dynamic Web sites easy. ASP spawned a whole series of books, articles, Web sites, and components, all to make the development process even easier. What ASP didn't have, however, was an application framework; it was never an enterprise development tool. Everything you did in ASP was code oriented—you just couldn't get away without writing code.

ASP.NET was designed to counter this problem. One of its key design goals was to make programming easier and quicker by reducing the amount of code you have to create. Enter the declarative programming model, a rich server control hierarchy with events, a large class library, and support for development tools from the humble Notepad to the high-end Visual Studio .NET. All in all, ASP.NET was a huge leap forward.

What's Wrong with ASP.NET 1.x?

So if ASP.NET 1.0 and 1.1 are so great, what's wrong with them? Well, nothing, actually, but when developing software there is always a trade-off between how much can be done, how many resources you have, and how much time you have to do it. There is an almost never-ending supply of features you can add, but at some stage you have to ship the product. You cannot doubt that ASP.NET 1.0 shipped with an impressive array of features, but the ASP.NET team members are ambitious, and they not only had plans of their own but also listened to their users.

ASP.NET 2.0, code-named "Whidbey," addresses the areas that both the development team and users wanted to improve. The aims of the new version are listed below.

- **Reduce the number of lines of code required by 70%.** The declarative programming model freed developers from having to write reams of code, but there are still many scenarios where this cannot be avoided. Data access is a great example, where the same `Connection`, `DataAdapter`/`DataSet`, and `Command`/`DataReader` code is used regularly.

- **Increase developer productivity.** This partly relates to reducing the amount of code required but is also affected by more server controls encompassing complex functionality, as well as providing better solutions for common Web site scenarios (such as portals and personalized sites).

- **Use a single control set for all devices**. Mobile devices are becoming more pervasive, with an increasing number of new devices. Many of the server controls render appropriately for small screens, but there are two major problems with the current support for mobile devices: (1) having a separate set of server controls purely for mobile devices is not only confusing but also costly, and (2) adding support for new devices requires additional development work and maintenance. ASP.NET 2.0 will provide a single set of controls and an extensible architecture to allow them (and other controls) to support multiple devices.

- **Provide the fastest Web server platform.** Although ASP.NET 1.0 offers a fast server platform, ASP.NET 2.0 will improve areas such as application start-up times and provide better application tracing and performance data. Innovative caching features will enhance application performance, especially when SQL Server is used.

- **Provide the best hosting solution**. With the large number of Internet applications being hosted, it's important to provide better solutions for hosters. For example, better management features to identify and stop rogue applications will give hosters more control over their current environment. More control can also be given to hosted companies by use of the new Web-based administration tool, allowing users to easily control the configuration of applications remotely.

- **Provide easier and more sophisticated management features**. Administration of ASP.NET applications under version 1.x required manual editing of the XML configuration file, which is not a great solution for administrators. Version 2.0 brings a graphical user interface–based administration tool that is integrated with the Internet Information Services (IIS) administration tool.

- **Ease implementation of entire scenarios.** The better management features are built on top of a management application programming interface (API), allowing custom administration programs to be created. Along with application packaging this will provide support for easily deployable applications, with or without source.

Even from this broad set of aims you can see that ASP.NET 2.0 is a great advance from 1.x for both developers and administrators.

New Features

This chapter isn't an in-depth look at any specific feature—instead we are going to give you a taste of what's to come so you can see how much easier Web development is going to be. For this outlook we've broken down the new features into rough end-to-end scenarios.

Templates for a Consistent Look and Feel

ASP.NET 1.x provides an easy way to develop Web sites, but one thing that has become apparent is the lack of an architecture for applying a consistent look and feel. Several workaround techniques emerged:

- Creating a custom class object that inherits from `Page` and having this custom page preload controls
- Creating a templated server control, where the templates provide the layout areas for each page, and using this control on every page
- Having User Controls for common areas of the site, such as headings, menus, and footers

Of these, the first two require knowledge of creating server controls, and while this is a topic most ASP.NET developers could master, it may not be one they've had experience with. Therefore a solution using custom server controls tends to be avoided. The last option, though, is a simple solution, easy to create and implement. User Controls were created to provide reusable functionality, and this is a great use for them. However, to apply a consistent look and feel you need to first place the User Controls on each page, then ensure that they are placed in the same place on each page. In other words, you really need a page template, and in reality this manifests itself as an ASP.NET file that you simply copy for each new page. The danger of this approach is that it's too easy to modify a page and change the layout for that single page.

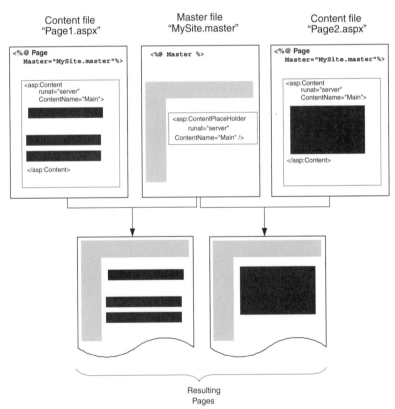

FIGURE 1.1. Combining a master page and a child page

To provide a templating solution, ASP.NET 2.0 has the concept of master pages, which provide a template for the look and implementation of a page. A **master page** is an ASP.NET page that provides a template for other pages, giving shared page-level layout and functionality. The master page defines placeholders for the content, which can be overridden by child pages. The resultant page is a combination of the master page and the child page, as shown in Figure 1.1.

Master pages are covered in Chapters 2 and 5.

Styles for Controls

The second major feature of ASP.NET 2.0 that deals with the look and feel of a site is that of themes. Theming, or skinning, has become very popular, allowing users to create a customized look for applications. On the Windows desktop two of the most popular themed applications are audio players (WinAmp and Windows Media Player), and with some additional software, even Windows XP can be themed.

The popularity of theming is due to the nature of humans—we like to choose the way things look, and we like to express our individuality. This is easy on the desktop, where users generally have a single machine each. With Web sites, however, theming becomes a harder issue because of the number of users. Tracking which users have which themes and managing those themes becomes an overhead that site administrators don't want to get involved with.

Some Web sites provide forms of theming, but these are relatively limited in terms of customization, perhaps allowing only a choice of color scheme. Other sites provide a selection of stylesheets for users to pick from, assuming their browsers support this feature, or alternatively change the stylesheet on the server. This allows not only color schemes to be selected but also complete style choices, such as fonts, style of borders, and so on.

In ASP.NET 2.0 the goals for theming are quite simple.

- Make it simple to customize the appearance of a site or page, using the same design tools and methods used when developing the page itself. This means there's no need to learn any special tools or techniques to add themes to a site.

- Allow themes to be applied to controls, pages, and even entire sites. For example, this allows users to customize parts of a site while ensuring that other parts (such as corporate identity) aren't customized.
- Allow all visual properties to be customized, thus ensuring that when themed, pages and controls can achieve a consistent style.

The implementation of this in ASP.NET 2.0 is built around two areas: skins and themes. A **skin** is a set of properties and templates that can be applied to controls. A **theme** is a set of skins and any other associated files (such as images or stylesheets). Skins are control specific, so for a given theme there could be a separate skin for each control within that theme. Any controls without a skin inherit the default look. The implementation is simple because a skin uses the same definition as the server control it is skinning, and themes are just a set of files in a directory under the application root. For example, consider the sample directory structure shown below:

```
default.aspx
\Themes
  \MyTheme
    MySkin.skin
  \YourTheme
    YourSkin.skin
```

Each theme consists of a directory under the `Themes` directory. Within each theme there is a file with a `.skin` suffix, which contains the skin details for that theme. For example, `MySkin.skin` might contain:

```
<asp:Label SkinID="Normal" runat="server"
  Font-Bold="True" BackColor="#FFC080" />
<asp:Label SkinID="Comic" runat="server"
  Font-Italic="True" Font-Names="Comic Sans MS" />
```

This defines two skins for the `Label` control, each with different visual properties. The theme can be chosen by setting a page-level property, and the skin is chosen by setting a control-level property, as demonstrated below.

```
<%@ Page Theme="MyTheme" %>

<form runat="server">

  <asp:Label SkinID="Comic" Text="A Label" />

</form>
```

Both of these can be set at runtime as well as design time, so this provides an extremely powerful solution, especially when connected with the new Personalization features.

Personalization and themes are covered in Chapter 7.

Securing Your Site

With the large amount of business being done on the Web, security is vitally important for protecting not only confidential information such as credit card numbers but also users' personal details and preferences. Thus you have to build into your site features to authenticate users. This was easy to do in ASP.NET 1.x, although you still had to write code. Security was created by picking your preferred security mechanism (most often Forms Authentication) and then adding controls to your page to provide the login details—user name, password, "remember me" checkbox, and so on. There was no built-in mechanism for storing personal details, so this was a roll-it-yourself affair.

With ASP.NET 2.0, the pain has been taken out of both areas. For login functionality, there is now:

- A `Login` control, providing complete functionality for logging into a site
- A `LoginStatus` control, which indicates the login status and can be configured to provide automatic links to login and logout pages
- A `LoginName` control to display the current (or anonymous) name
- A `LoginView` control, providing templated views depending on the login status
- A `PasswordRecovery` control, encompassing the "I forgot my password" functionality

For example, to add login features to your page all you need to do is add the following code:

```
<form runat="server">
  <asp:Login runat="server" />
</form>
```

Log In

User Name: _____
Password: _____
☐ Remember me next time.
[Log In]

FIGURE 1.2. The Login control

This gives us the simple interface shown in Figure 1.2.

This could be achieved easily in previous versions of ASP.NET, but not with such simplicity. You needed labels, text entry boxes, buttons, and validation, whereas it's now all rolled into one control. Sure it looks raw, but this is the basic unformatted version. Using the design tool Visual Studio .NET (more on that in Chapter 2), you can auto-format this for a better look. You can also skin the interface, as shown in Figure 1.3, or even template it to provide your own customized look. Along with the other login controls you get a complete solution for handling user logins.

The user interface isn't the only part of logging into a site; there's also the code needed to validate the user against a data store. With ASP.NET 1.x this required not only code to be written but also knowledge of what that data store was and how it stored data. ASP.NET 2.0 introduces a new Membership API, whose aim is to abstract the required membership functionality from the storage of the member information. For example, all of the data handling we'd have done in previous versions to validate a user can now be replaced with the code shown in Listing 1.1.

LISTING 1.1. Validating User Credentials

```
Sub Login_Click(Sender As Object, E As EventArgs)

  If Membership.ValidateUser(Email.Text, Password.Text) Then
    FormsAuthentication.RedirectFromLoginPage(Email.Text, False)
  Else
    LoginMessage.Text = "Invalid credentials. Please try again."
  End If

End Sub
```

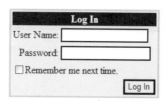

FIGURE 1.3. A skinned Login control

What's even better is that when using the `Login` control you don't even have to do this—the control handles it for you.

The great strength of the `Membership` API is that it is built on the idea of Membership Providers, with support for Microsoft SQL Server and Access supplied by default. To integrate custom membership stores you simply need to provide a component that inherits from the Membership interface and add the new provider details to the configuration file.

The Membership API has some simple goals.

- Offer an easy solution for authenticating and managing users, requiring no knowledge of the underlying storage mechanism.
- Provide support for multiple data providers, allowing data stored about users to come from different data stores.
- Provide comprehensive user management in a simple-to-use API, giving an easy way for developers to store and access user details.
- Give users a unique identity, allowing integration with other services such as the Personalization and Role Manager features.

Security, membership, and role management are covered in Chapter 6.

Personalizing Your Site

One of the areas driving changes on the Internet is that of communities. People like to belong, and the Internet is a big, lonely place. Community sites give you a home, a sense of belonging. Part of that comes from being in contact with like-minded people, and part comes from the features some of these sites offer. Our houses are decorated to our style, and many of us customize our Windows desktop, so why shouldn't our favorite Web sites offer the same opportunity?

Hand in hand with the Membership API lie the Personalization features. These provide a simple programming model for storing user details (including those of anonymous users), with easy customization. Like Membership, Personalization can be configured to work with multiple data providers and provides an easy way to define custom properties for each user. This leads to a user profile with strong types, allowing easy access within ASP.NET pages. For example, you can create a profile with `Name`, `Address`, and `Theme` as properties and a page that allows the user to update them, as shown in Listing 1.2.

LISTING 1.2. Using the Profile Custom Properties

```
<script runat="server">

  Sub Page_Load(Sender As Object, E As EventArgs)

    Name.Text = Profile.Name
    Address.Text = Profile.Address
    Theme.Text = Profile.Theme

  End Sub

  Sub Update_Click(Sender As Object, E As EventArgs)

    Profile.Name = Name.Text
    Profile.Address = Address.Text
    Profile.Theme = Theme.Text

  End Sub

</script>

<form runat="server">
  Name:      <asp:TextBox id="Name" runat="server" /> <br />
  Address:  <asp:TextBox id="Address" runat="server" /> <br />
  Theme:     <asp:TextBox id="Theme" runat="server" /> <br />
  <asp:Button Text="Update" onClick="Update_Click" runat="server" />
</form>
```

The simplicity of this method means we only have to deal with the user profile. We don't need to know how it stores the data—we just deal with the properties each profile has. This personalization also allows us to easily use the theming capabilities, changing the theme when the page is created, as demonstrated below.

```
Sub Page_PreInit(Sender As Object, E As EventArgs)

  Me.Theme = Profile.Theme

End Sub
```

To ensure that the theme customization is applied before the controls are created we use the new PreInit event.

Personalization is covered in Chapter 7.

Creating Portals

As if customization of a site's look weren't enough, ASP.NET 2.0 also brings a way to alter the structure with its new portal framework.

The success of the ASP.NET IBuySpy portal application and its off-shoots shows that customized sites are popular. The trouble has always been how to provide a consistent look while still allowing user customization not only of the style but also of the content and placement of content. Microsoft has already implemented solutions to provide this functionality, including SharePoint Server and Outlook Web Parts.

In ASP.NET 2.0, Web Parts become the underlying technology for all Microsoft portal applications, allowing a single easy-to-use, extensible framework. The concept revolves around two key controls—the `WebPartZone` and the `WebPart`. The `WebPartZone` identifies areas on the page in which content can be changed, and the `WebPart` identifies the part (or module) within the zone. There are different types of `WebPart` controls for different purposes, for example:

- `ContentWebPart`, for arbitrary controls and content
- `CatalogPart`, which contains a catalog of parts not currently on the page
- `EditorPart` controls, such as `AppearanceEditorPart` and `LayoutEditorPart`, allowing customization of the parts

For example, consider an intranet site that needs a selection of areas of content—links, announcements, and so on. Figure 1.4 shows a sample site.

This site has two main areas of content—the left area with the welcome message and the announcements, and the right area showing weather and links. Each of these main areas is a `WebPartZone` and the content with them a `ContentWebPart`. The code for this page appears in Listing 1.3.

Listing 1.3. Sample Intranet Site Using Web Parts

```
<table>
  <tbody>
    <tr>
      <td valign="top" align="left">
      <asp:WebPartZone id="LeftZone" runat="server"
          Title="Left Zone" partFrameType="TitleOnly"
          lockLayout="False" borderColor="White">
      <ZoneTemplate>
        <asp:ContentWebPart id="ContentWebPart1"
            title="Welcome" runat="server">
        <ContentTemplate>
```

continues

```
          This project …
      </ContentTemplate>
      </asp:ContentWebPart>
      <uc1:Announcements id="Announcements1" runat="server" />
    </ZoneTemplate>
    </asp:WebPartZone>
  </td>
    <td valign="top" align="left">
      <asp:WebPartZone id="RightZone" runat="server"
        title="Right Zone" width="100%"
        partFrameType="TitleOnly" lockLayout="False"
        borderColor="White">
       <ZoneTemplate>
       <sample:WeatherWebPart runat="server" id="WeatherWebPart"
          Title="My Weather" width="250px" />
        <uc1:dailylinkswebpart id="DailyLinksWebPart1"
           runat="server" title="Daily Links" />
      </ZoneTemplate>
      </asp:WebPartZone>
  </td>
    <td valign="top" align="left">
    </td>
  </tr>
  </tbody>
</table>
```

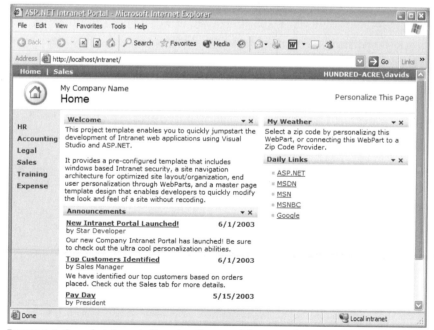

FIGURE 1.4. Sample intranet site using the portal framework

Here you can see two `WebPartZone` controls separating the left and right content. Within each there is a mixture of content, including static text, user controls, and custom server controls.

At first glance this doesn't look like much improvement over existing layout methods such as user controls—in fact, it looks more complex. However, the framework on which Web Parts is built is great for developers and users alike. Developers only have to drop user controls or server controls into a `ZoneTemplate` to automatically receive Web Parts functionality. To enhance this functionality you can add verbs to the `WebPartZone` to indicate which features the framework should add to each part within the template. Listing 1.4 shows an example.

Listing 1.4. Web Part Verbs

```
<WebPartCloseVerb checked="False"
   imageUrl="images/CloseVerb.gif"
   enabled="True" text="Close"
   description="Closes the WebPart"
   visible="True" />

<WebPartRestoreVerb checked="False"
   imageUrl="images/RestoreVerb.gif"
   enabled="True" text="Restore"
   description="Restores the WebPart"
   visible="True" />

<WebPartMinimizeVerb checked="False"
   imageUrl="images/MinimizeVerb.gif"
   enabled="True" text="Minimize"
   description="Minimizes the WebPart"
   visible="True" />

<WebPartHelpVerb checked="False"
   enabled="True" text="Help"
   description="Shows help for the WebPart"
   visible="True" />

<WebPartEditVerb checked="False"
   imageUrl="images/EditVerb.gif"
   enabled="True" text="Edit"
   description="Edits the WebPart"
   visible="True" />
```

Here there are verbs that allow minimizing and maximizing the `WebPart` controls, editing, help, and so on.

For the user, the Personalization features allow each `WebPart` to be moved to other `WebPartZone` controls or edited. For example, moving a

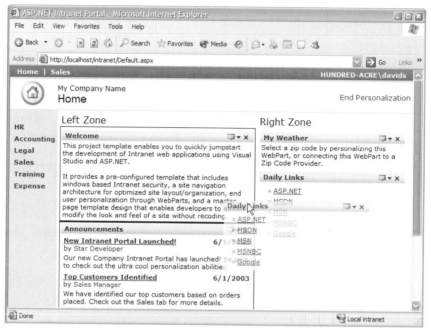

Figure 1.5. Dragging a *WEBPART* to another location

WebPart is simply a matter of drag and drop, as shown in Figure 1.5, where the Daily Links section is being moved to the Left Zone.

Editing of WebPart controls is also part of the portal framework, where by default the user can alter the title, height, width, and frame style. Each WebPart can also provide custom properties that can be edited. For example, the WebPart for the My Weather section allows the zip code to be set, upon which the weather for that zip code is displayed. Editing of WebPart controls is provided by the inclusion of an EditorZone, which details what can be edited. For example, for our sample intranet site, the EditorZone might include the code shown in Listing 1.5.

Listing 1.5. Adding Editor Parts to an EditorZone

```
<asp:EditorZone id="EditorZone1" title="Edit WebParts"
  runat="server" partFrameType="TitleOnly"
  cssClass="EditorZoneBody">
  <ZoneTemplate>
  <asp:AppearanceEditorPart id="AppearanceEditorPart1"
    runat="server" font-size="8pt" font-bold="true" />
  <asp:PropertyGridEditorPart id="PropertyGridEditorPart1"
    title="Custom Settings" font-size="8pt" runat="server" />
```

```
    </ZoneTemplate>
</asp:EditorZone>
```

FIGURE 1.6. Editing the My Weather *WEBPART*

This indicates that there are two editor parts—one for the appearance, and one for the property grid—for properties of the `WebPart` that are marked as personalizable. Selecting the edit button invokes the editing features and the `EditorZone` is made visible, as shown in Figure 1.6. Once edited for zip code 02116, the `WebPart` shows the weather for Boston (Figure 1.7).

The portal framework is covered in Chapter 8.

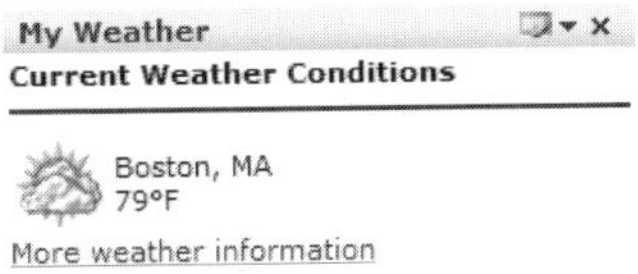

FIGURE 1.7. The My Weather *WEBPART*

Setting Up and Managing Your Site

ASP.NET 1.x made deployment of Web sites easy with its xcopy deployment model. This removed the need for some administrative tasks, such as registering COM components, but still left other tasks, such as site administration, as more manual affairs. The XML-based configuration file obeyed the xcopy rule, but there are three major problems with it. First, there is no easy-to-use administration tool, meaning you must have knowledge of the

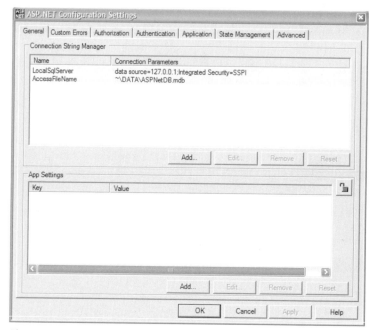

Figure 1.8. ASP.NET Configuration MMC Snap-in

XML schema before you can modify it. Second, you need some way to actually fetch the file, edit it, and then upload it. This is a problem particularly for hosted scenarios, where users are always remote, and administration of many sites can become a management nightmare. Finally, you cannot create a Web Application, which is required for sites that require security.

Three features in ASP.NET 2.0 help solve these issues. The first is the Microsoft Management Console (MMC) Snap-in for configuration, as shown in Figure 1.8.

The second feature is a Management API, providing a programmable interface to manage a site. For example, Listing 1.6 sets the authorization mode using the API.

Listing 1.6. Setting the Authorization Mode

```
Dim cfg As Configuration
Dim ms As AuthenticationSection

cfg = Configuration.GetConfigurationForUrl(Request.ApplicationPath)
ms = CType(cfg.GetConfigurationSection("system.web/authentication"),
    AuthenticationSection)
ms.Mode = HttpAuthenticationMode.Windows
cfg.Update()
```

The Management API provides access to all areas of the configuration, both at the machine level (`machine.config`) and the application level (`web.config`). This allows utilities to be written not only to manage a single site but also to manage all sites.

The third aspect of site management is the creation of a Web-based tool, wrapping much of the Management API. This provides a simple way to remotely administer a site, as shown in Figure 1.9.

FIGURE 1.9. The Web management tool

Here you have a simple Web interface that allows configuration of all aspects of a site. The interface is designed to be customized, so corporations and hosts can give it a company look.

Administration is covered in Chapter 13.

Using Images on Your Site

Using images isn't a particularly difficult area of site design, but their use has been eased with two new server controls. First, the `ImageMap` control provides easy support for image maps, as demonstrated on the next page.

```
<asp:ImageMap runat="server"
    onClick="Map_Click"
    ImageUrl="images/states.jpg">
  <asp:CircleHotSpot X="100" Y="100" Radius="25"
      Value="Other State" />
  <asp:RectangleHotSpot Top="200" Left="150" Right="200" Bottom="150"
      Value="More State"/>
  <asp:PolygonHotSpot Coordinates="3,4, 15,18, 45,18, 15,70, 3,4"
      Value="State 1" />
</asp:PolygonHotSpot>
```

The detection of the hot spot is handled in the postback event:

```
Sub Map_Click(Sender As Object, E As ImageMapEventArgs)

  Select Case e.Value
  Case "State 1"
    ' ...
  Case "Other State"
    ' ...
  Case "More States"
    ' ...
  End Select

End Sub
```

The second new image-handling feature is that of dynamic images, designed specifically to render images appropriate to the calling browser. This is necessary because images displayed in Web browsers generally aren't suitable for smaller devices, such as PDAs or phones. The new DynamicImage control uses an HttpHandler to sniff the browser type and render the appropriate image. For example, consider the following code:

```
<form runat="server">
  <asp:DynamicImage DynamicImageType="ImageFile"
                    ImageFile="car.gif" runat="server" />
</form>
```

For a standard Web browser the image is rendered as expected, but for a Wireless Access Protocol (WAP) phone, the image is rendered as a Wireless Bitmap (WBMP). This removes any need for the developer to specifically target images to browser types.

Images are covered in Chapter 12.

Using Data on Your Site

It's probably no exaggeration to say that most, if not all, Web sites use some form of data to drive them. Whether XML files, a database, or another dynamic form of storage, the data allows a site to respond to the user and to be up to date. ASP.NET 1.x provided some great data binding capabilities, but they always involved code, often the same code used over and over. One of the key goals of ASP.NET 2.0 is to reduce code and to ease the use of databases, especially for beginner programmers. To achieve this a new set of data controls has been introduced, removing the need for in-depth knowledge of ADO.NET.

Data source controls provide a consistent and extensible method for declaratively accessing data from Web pages. There are several data source controls, including AccessDataSource, SqlDataSource, XmlDataSource, and ObjectDataSource, and it's likely that others (perhaps for Excel and Exchange Server) will appear as ASP.NET 2.0 nears release, along with third-party data sources. The use of data controls is simple, as shown below.

```
<asp:SqlDataSource id="ds1" runat="server"
  ConnectionString="localhost;database=pubs;Trusted_Connection=True"
  SelectCommand="SELECT * FROM authors"/>

<asp:DataGrid DataSourceId="ds1" runat="server" />
```

This just encapsulates the code everyone used to put in the Page_Load event—it connects to the database, fetches the data, and binds the grid. The contents of the SelectCommand can be a stored procedure as well as a SQL command, thus preserving the separation of data access from the page itself. There are commands for updating, inserting, and deleting.

This model is extended by use of a parameter collection, allowing parameters to be passed into the command from a variety of sources. For example, the code in Listing 1.7 automatically takes the value from the TextBox control txtState and feeds this into the parameter @state.

Listing 1.7. Using a ControlParameter

```
<asp:SqlDataSource id="ds1" runat="server"
  ConnectionString="localhost;database=pubs;Trusted_Connection=True"
  SelectCommand="SELECT * FROM authors WHERE state=@state">
  <SelectParameters>
    <ControlParameter name="@state" ControlID="txtState" />
  </SelectParameters>
</asp:SqlDataSource>

<asp:TextBox id="txtState" runat="server" />

<asp:DataGrid DataSourceId="ds1" runat="server" />
```

There are also other parameter types, allowing parameter information to be taken directly from Session variables, Cookies, the Request (QueryString), and the HTML Form.

Data Binding

Data binding in ASP.NET 1.x was simple, but it did cause confusion in some areas. For example, should you use early binding, for which you have to know the underlying data structure? Or should you take the development shortcut and use late binding, like this:

```
<%# DataBinder.Eval(Container.DataItem, "au_lname") %>
```

With ASP.NET 2.0 this syntax has been simplified:

```
<%# Eval("au_lname") %>
```

There is also an equivalent XPath syntax for XPath expressions when binding to XML documents:

```
<%# XPath("@au_lname") %>
```

Binding to Objects

One of the most requested features has been the ability to bind data directly to objects. Good design dictates that you separate your data access layer from your presentation layer, and this is often done as a set of classes. The new `ObjectDataSource` allows you to simply bind directly to existing objects, such as classes, thus allowing you to have a strongly typed data layer but still participate in the easy data binding that ASP.NET 2.0 brings.

Data source controls and data binding are covered in Chapter 3.

Adding Mobility Support

Mobile devices are becoming more pervasive. It seems everyone has a mobile phone, many people have PDAs, and some great devices now combine the functionality of both. From the development perspective the problem with these devices is their screen size and rendering capabilities. Not only do many of them not accept HTML, but with their tiny screens some also can't display images, tables, and so on.

In ASP.NET 1.x, the Microsoft Mobile Internet Toolkit (MMIT in version 1.0 and ASP.NET Mobile Controls in version 1.1) provided this support, including separate controls for building Web pages suitable for small-screen browsers. In ASP.NET 2.0, the MMIT is no longer required because mobile support is built into all controls. This reduces not only the amount of code required but also the need for specialist knowledge about mobile platforms. This might seem relatively unimportant while the number of sites that target mobile browsers is small, but this is bound to increase as the features of small devices improve and prices drop.

The really important part of the changes is to the infrastructure of the ASP.NET server controls. All controls are now built on a control adapter architecture, where there is an adapter for each specific device. The adapters have knowledge of each device and perform the rendering appropriate for its markup language and screen size. Since the controls are derived from adapters, they don't need to perform any special action to choose what to render—the adapter intelligently renders the appropriate content based on the calling device. New devices are easily supported because they require only the addition of an adapter, which the controls can then take advantage of.

Device Filters

This architecture is taken further by allowing adapter-specific attributes for controls, enabling the page designer to provide different content for specific devices. For example, the following code shows how different text and cascading style sheet (CSS) styling can be defined for a mobile device.

```
<asp:Label id="MyLabel" runat="server"
           Text="Welcome to our site"
           Nokia:Text="Time to upgrade your Nokia phone!"
           cssClass="StandardStyleClass"
           Nokia:cssClass="SpecialNokiaStyleClass" />
```

Device Templates

Along with modified attributes, we also have the ability to provide templates for specific devices. We know that mobile devices have a small screen size, so repeated controls such as grids and lists either aren't appropriate or need different output. By using specific templates for devices we can now provide different content to different devices, as shown in Listing 1.8.

Listing 1.8. Filtered Templates for Mobile Devices

```
<asp:Repeater runat="server" ..>

  <HtmlBrowsers:HeaderTemplate>
    <table>
      <tr><td>UserName</td><td>Address</td><td>Phone</td></tr>
  </HtmlBrowsers:HeaderTemplate>

  <HtmlBrowsers:ItemTemplate>
    <tr>
      <td><%# Container.DataItem("UserName") %></td>
      <td><%# Container.DataItem("Address") %></td>
      <td><%# Container.DataItem("Phone") %></td>
    </tr>
  </HtmlBrowsers:ItemTemplate>

  <WmlBrowsers:ItemTemplate>
    <asp:Panel runat="server">
      <%# Container.DataItem("UserName") %>
      <%# Container.DataItem("Phone") %>
    </asp:Panel>
  </WmlBrowsers:ItemTemplate>

  <HtmlBrowsers:FooterTemplate>
    </table>
  </HtmlBrowsers:FooterTemplate>

</asp:Repeater>
```

These mechanisms provide a way for developers to override the built-in rendering for mobile devices. Along with automatic mobile support with the standard controls, there are controls specifically designed for mobile devices, such as `PhoneLink` (to launch a phone call) and `Pager` (to provide paging support). Standard controls also support the `SoftKeyLabel` attribute to allow specific text to be targeted to soft keys on phones.

Mobility is covered in Chapter 10.

Compilation and Deployment

Since the release of ASP.NET 1.0 there's been a fairly standard approach to Web site architecture. In general there has been a separation of business logic into separate assemblies, often in a separate directory with a make file. Using Visual Studio .NET 1.0 and 2003 for this approach is fine since it provides the compilation step for you, but stand-alone tools (such as Web Matrix) don't, so you have to handcraft a batch file to make your assemblies.

ASP.NET 2.0 provides automatic compilation for satellite code by supporting a **code** directory. All files within this directory will be compiled on the first run, thus removing the need for separate compilation scripts. Files within the code directory don't have to be just pure code, such as Visual Basic .NET or C# files. Support is also included for Web Services Description Language (WSDL) files and strongly typed DataSets (XSD) files. For WSDL files the proxy will automatically be created, and for XSD files the appropriate classes will be created.

Along with automatic compilation comes pre-compilation—an entire site (Web pages and code) can be pre-compiled. This not only provides a way to deploy compiled applications but also removes the performance hit taken by the compilation process on the first run. In addition, since only compiled files are deployed, intellectual property is protected.

Another automatic feature is that of resources, such as those used for globalization. The **resources** directory provides a place for these, which are included as part of the compilation process.

Compilation is covered in Chapter 2.

Development Tools

Having a whole raft of new features in ASP.NET is great, but what about design tools? Version 2.0 of the .NET Framework will introduce the latest version of Visual Studio .NET—Visual Studio .NET "Whidbey." When ASP.NET 1.0 was released it quickly became apparent that a development tool targeted at Web developers was required. Visual Studio .NET provides great project and design features targeted at corporate developers. Web Matrix was released to appeal to ASP.NET developers who don't have access to Visual Studio .NET. It's a small stand-alone tool, specifically targeted at ASP.NET development, and provides some features that aren't in Visual Studio .NET.

With ASP.NET 2.0, Visual Studio .NET "Whidbey" has undergone some major enhancements and now provides a far superior environment for developing Web applications than previous versions. While the design environment is very familiar, the feature set has improved, making it a premier Web development tool.

Key design features for Visual Studio .NET "Whidbey" include the following:

- Traditional in-line coding approach, plus a new code-behind model
- Support for all managed languages
- Ability to edit any file anywhere (FTP, File System, Front Page Extensions, and so on)
- Support for data controls, drag and drop, and database access, with a rich design surface
- Support for visual inheritance through master pages
- No project files, allowing projects to be manipulated outside of the tool
- Integrated Web Administration Tool
- IntelliSense included
- Debugging support
- No "build" step—ability to compile on first run

This feature set is really a combination of features from Visual Studio .NET and Web Matrix.

Visual Studio .NET "Whidbey" is covered in Chapter 2.

SUMMARY

Of course, there are many changes within ASP.NET 2.0—too many to mention in this introduction, although some highlights were covered in this chapter. The remainder of the book covers these changes (including items such as changes to existing controls, changes to page attributes, new controls, and so on) in detail.

It's important to remember that this is a preview technology, still evolving and still in testing. Despite that, the initial feature set is extremely impressive and provides a leap in productivity for Web site developers.

2

Tools and Architecture

IN THE PREVIOUS CHAPTER we gave a brief outline of some of the new and exciting features in ASP.NET 2.0, and now it's time to dig into them a bit deeper. In this chapter we're going to look at how development has been eased in two main areas. The first is the design time experience. With ASP.NET 1.x you had the choice of Visual Studio .NET or Web Matrix for development. With ASP.NET 2.0 this is still the case, but Visual Studio .NET "Whidbey" ("Whidbey" is the code name for the .NET Framework 2.0) is greatly improved for ASP.NET developers.

The second main area we'll cover is compilation. It may not seem like much of a burden in the current release, especially when using Visual Studio .NET, but there are several ways in which compilation has been improved, including a better model for code separation, centralized code directories with automatic compilation, and pre-compilation of sites to improve speed and deployment.

Visual Studio .NET "Whidbey"

You may wonder about the confusion over development tools and which tool a developer should use for which purpose. After all, no matter what type of development is being done, many of the requirements are the same. However, there are differences in the ways developers work in different types of applications, especially Web applications. To understand those differences you have to look at both the history of ASP development and the current tools. ASP rapidly rose to success, with a very diverse set of developers, ranging from corporate teams to home hobbyists. Despite its widespread use there was no dedicated development tool. There were plenty of editors with which ASP could work (Visual InterDev, Front Page, and so on), but nothing specific. Visual Studio was purely a Windows development tool.

With the release of .NET 1.0, Visual Studio became Visual Studio .NET and was enhanced to allow Web development. The real trouble with this approach wasn't with Visual Studio .NET itself but more with the completely different way of working from that previously used by most ASP developers. For example, the code-behind model was alien to ASP scripters, who were used to having all of their code within the same file, and the whole idea of a project didn't relate well with people who were used to just dealing with files in a directory.

Another issue was that Visual Studio .NET is a professional development tool and therefore commands a professional price. A large amount of Web development is done by amateurs, for whom the price of this tool is too high. Enter Web Matrix, a small, easy-to-use, and (most importantly) free development tool. Web Matrix is aimed only at ASP.NET developers and also has become a test bed for new ideas and features that weren't in Visual Studio .NET. There wasn't a tool that had everything a developer needed—until now.

The latest version, Visual Studio .NET "Whidbey," is not only a combination of the best bits of both Visual Studio .NET 2003 and Web Matrix but also the next step upward. Along with great design features such as support for drag and drop, Visual Studio .NET "Whidbey" also brings the following benefits.

- There are no project files, thus existing sites can simply be opened from their locations.
- Support for code in-line, or the new code-separation model, allows files created with other editors to be easily imported.
- Multiple ways to access Web sites, such as through the file system, IIS, FTP, and SharePoint, are available.
- The Data Explorer integrates a data editing tool and allows drag and drop of tables onto the design grid.
- Support for the new data binding models allows easy design of data-driven pages.
- Visual inheritance with master pages eases site design.

- Full IntelliSense in HTML and code views enables quicker code development.
- A built-in Web Server allows development and testing without IIS.
- The ability to import and export user settings allows you to easily configure other installations of Visual Studio .NET "Whidbey" with your favorite preferences.
- Sample projects help developers create out-of-the-box sites with little or no extra work required.

In this chapter we'll look at some of these features and see how some of the new architectural changes to ASP.NET integrate with Visual Studio .NET "Whidbey" and make development easier.

Project-less Development

There are two very good reasons why moving to a project-less system is a good choice. First, it makes team development simpler. For teams using a source code control system the project file becomes a blocking point. All files checked into and out of the project require the project file to be checked in and out. With multiple people editing multiple files, the project file can easily be locked by another person. Second, a project-less system is easier for sites designed with other development tools—the absence of a project

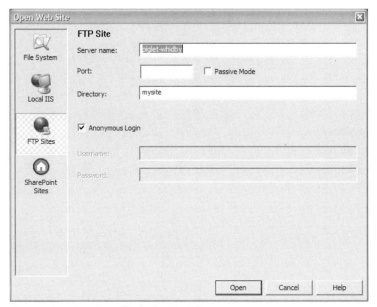

FIGURE 2.1. Opening a Web site via FTP

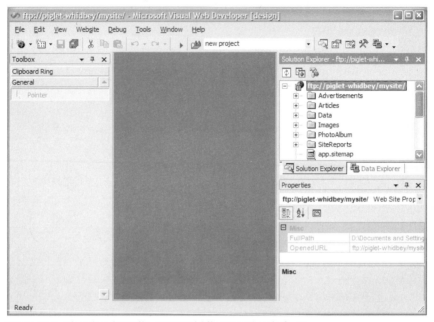

FIGURE 2.2. The Visual Studio .NET "Whidbey" main windows

system means sites can be easily accessed directly. For example, Figure 2.1 shows the Open Web Site dialog when selecting FTP as the mechanism.

If an existing site was not created with Visual Studio .NET "Whidbey," it will be upgraded in place, so be careful if you plan to open existing Web sites. (You will see a warning.) Whichever method of opening a site you use, or when creating new sites, you will see a familiar layout (Figure 2.2).

Although this is a new tool you can see it looks very similar to both Visual Studio .NET 1.0/2003 and Web Matrix, thus ensuring that developers can work in a familiar environment. When you work within it, though, you will soon realize that there are many more features.

FIGURE 2.3. The Solution Explorer

The Solution Explorer

The Solution Explorer is almost the same as in previous versions of Visual Studio .NET, although it has been simplified. There are no longer two buttons for opening Web pages, one for design view and one for code view. (How often did you double-click to open the file only to have it open in design view rather than code view?) Visual Studio .NET "Whidbey" supports both in-line code and the new code-separation model, where files show in the Solution Explorer as two files (Figure 2.3).

Here you can see that both the user-interface (UI) file and the code-behind file are separate items. Double-clicking opens the file in the design window.

The Toolbox

The Toolbox is the same as in previous versions of Visual Studio .NET, although there are more tabs, with controls split into logical groups:

- Core, for the core server controls such as `TextBox`, `Label`, and so on
- Data, for the `DataSource` and grid controls
- Personalization, for the `WebPart` controls
- Security, for the login controls
- Validation, for the field validator controls
- Navigation, for navigation controls, such as `SiteMapPath`
- HTML, for the HTML controls

Of course, the Toolbox is customizable, not only by adding local components but also by adding components from Web sites by use of the Control Gallery, as shown in Figure 2.4. This means that it's going to become easier to find additional components.

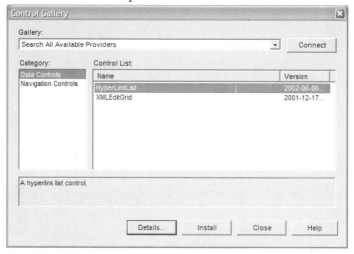

Figure 2.4. Adding components from the Control Gallery

The Design Window

The design window is similar to that in previous versions of Visual Studio .NET, although there are a number of important differences. The first thing to note is that the default layout mode is flow, not absolute; the second is the different views you get within the editor. Figure 2.5 shows the design window with two files open: `Authors.aspx` and its associated code-behind file, `Authors.aspx.vb`.

At the bottom of this window there are three buttons to switch between the design view, the entire source view, and the code view. All three of these apply to the same file but show a different view.

- **Design** is the standard design surface.
- **Source** is the entire source code for the file, including the UI section and in-line code.
- **Server Code** is just the in-line code.

It is important to realize that ASP.NET pages can have code both in-line and in the code-behind file, as seen in Figure 2.5, although it's best to keep

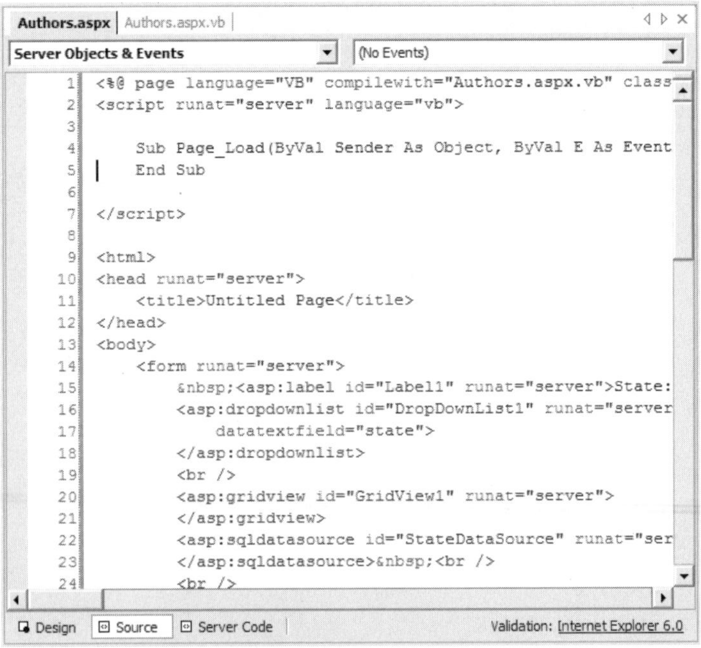

```
Authors.aspx  Authors.aspx.vb                                    ◁ ▷ ×
Server Objects & Events              ▼   (No Events)                ▼
 1  <%@ page language="VB" compilewith="Authors.aspx.vb" class
 2  <script runat="server" language="vb">
 3
 4      Sub Page_Load(ByVal Sender As Object, ByVal E As Event
 5      End Sub
 6
 7  </script>
 8
 9  <html>
10  <head runat="server">
11      <title>Untitled Page</title>
12  </head>
13  <body>
14      <form runat="server">
15           <asp:label id="Label1" runat="server">State:
16          <asp:dropdownlist id="DropDownList1" runat="server
17              datatextfield="state">
18          </asp:dropdownlist>
19          <br />
20          <asp:gridview id="GridView1" runat="server">
21          </asp:gridview>
22          <asp:sqldatasource id="StateDataSource" runat="ser
23          </asp:sqldatasource> <br />
24          <br />
```
Design   Source   Server Code   Validation: Internet Explorer 6.0

FIGURE 2.5. The design window

code in one location only. Here there is a `Page_Load` event in-line with the server control, and yet there is also a code-behind file. For code-behind files, creating an event with Visual Studio .NET "Whidbey" (either by double-clicking or from the Properties window) for a control with a code-behind file will switch to the code-behind file and create the event procedure there. For code-in-line files, the event procedure will be created in-line. We'll look at the structure of this in more detail later in the chapter.

Another addition to the source view is that the Toolbox isn't disabled because drag and drop is fully supported in the source editor. This prevents having to switch to the design view to add new controls—they can simply be dragged from the Toolbox and dropped into the source file. Better support for the code editor has also been provided by enabling the Properties window to track the cursor so that the properties reflect the object the cursor is currently on. Both of these features are attractive to developers who prefer to work in source view rather than design view.

The Design Surface

The design surface works exactly the same as in previous versions of Visual Studio .NET except that it's more context sensitive (e.g., the right-mouse click generally has more features) and supports common tasks for many controls. For example, consider Figure 2.6, where a `GridView` has been added to the page. Selecting the `GridView` shows an additional icon, like a SmartTag in Office.

Upon selecting this tag, a Common Tasks panel is displayed (Figure 2.7), showing the most common tasks applicable to the object. Some of these are also available from the context menu, thus giving you different ways to set the properties for an object.

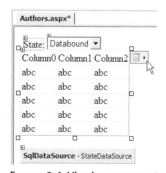

FIGURE 2.6. Viewing common tasks for a GridView

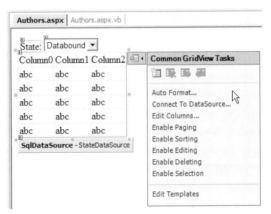

FIGURE 2.7. The GridView common tasks

The Data Explorer

A new feature that comes from Web Matrix is the Data Explorer, which allows connections to data stores to be set up. For example, Figure 2.8 shows a connection to a SQL Server. With the Technology Preview release, the only supported provider from the Data Explorer is OleDb, but future revisions will support all providers.

Once connected, you have a great range of features to control your data source—in fact, the Data Explorer is almost a mini SQL Server Enterprise Manager. For example, you can create new objects (including database diagrams and functions), edit existing ones, edit data, export data, and so on. The great advantage of having so much power in the Data Explorer is that

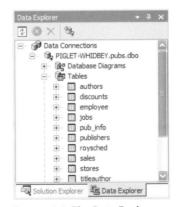

FIGURE 2.8. The Data Explorer

au_id	au_lname	au_fname	phone	address	city
Databound	Databound	Databound	Databound	Databound	Databc
Databound	Databound	Databound	Databound	Databound	Databc
Databound	Databound	Databound	Databound	Databound	Databc
Databound	Databound	Databound	Databound	Databound	Databc
Databound	Databound	Databound	Databound	Databound	Databc

SqlDataSource - SqlDataSource2

FIGURE 2.9. A database table dropped onto a page

you don't have to load an additional tool—everything you need is right within your development environment. In fact, it's better than Enterprise Manager because the stored procedure editor isn't modal!

Another great feature links two windows, allowing you to drag tables from the Data Explorer and drop them onto the design surface. When you do this a `DataSource` and `GridView` are automatically created and formatted, as shown in Figure 2.9, where the authors table has been dropped onto the page.

The `SqlDataSource` is automatically configured, and the commands used to fetch and update data are populated. To edit the properties of the `DataSource` control you can select Configure DataSource from the Common Tasks menu, which displays the window shown in Figure 2.10. Here you see the currently selected connection (from the Data Explorer) and the provider details. These cannot be changed here, but if you do need to edit

Configure DataSource - SqlDataSource2

Choose a connection
Select a connection to use in this data source.

Choose a data connection:

PIGLET-WHIDBY.pubs.dbo ▼   New...

Data connection details
Provider:

System.Data.OleDb

Connection string:

Provider=SQLOLEDB.1;Integrated Security=SSPI;Persist Security Info=False;Initial Catalog=pubs;Data Source=;Use Procedure for Prepare=1;Auto Translate=True;Packet Size=4096;Workstation ID=PIGLET-WHIDBY;Use Encryption for Data=False;Tag with column collation when possible=False

Previous   Next   Finish   Cancel

FIGURE 2.10. Configuring a DataSource

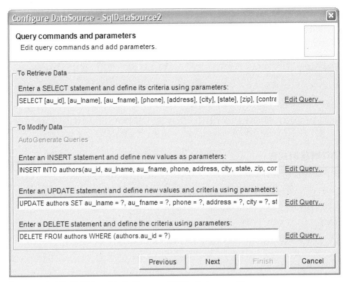

FIGURE 2.11. Editing DataSource SQL statements

them (e.g., to pick another provider), you can edit the connection details manually in the properties for the DataSource.

Clicking the Next button allows you to edit the SQL statements used to fetch and update data, as shown in Figure 2.11. By default these are built as direct SQL strings, but they can just as easily be stored procedures.

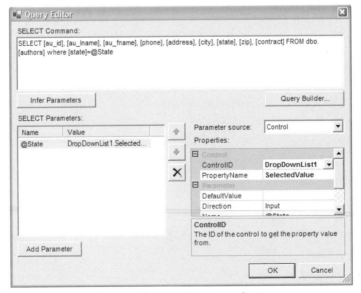

FIGURE 2.12. Configuring the SELECT command

You can fine-tune the commands by selecting the Edit Query link, which displays the window shown in Figure 2.12.

Here you can edit the query, add parameters, and specify the source of the parameter—in this case it's set to the value of a drop-down list. This allows you to easily build commands based on values external to the data source, such as control values, form fields, query string values, and so on. This technique allows you to build powerful pages without any code at all.

Visual Inheritance

In Chapter 1 we briefly looked at how a single site-wide style could be applied to all pages through the use of master pages. Visual Studio .NET "Whidbey" fully supports this model. It allows the creation of master pages and the linking of standard pages to a master, and it shows the visual inheritance of the master. For example, Figure 2.13 shows a master page that defines the menu on the left and the logo and login details along the top.

The important aspect of this page is the ContentPlaceHolder, which defines the area where child pages can add their content, as shown in Figure 2.14. Here all of the content from the master page shows on the screen but is disabled. Thus you can edit content only in the area allowed by the master page.

FIGURE 2.13. A master page

FIGURE 2.14. A child page that uses a master

Master pages are covered in more detail in Chapter 5.

Built-in Administration

Administration of Web sites has been improved by building in support for the Web Administration Tool. From the Website toolbar there is an ASP.NET Configuration option, which launches the Web Administration Tool within a window within Visual Studio .NET "Whidbey", allowing you to configure your site without leaving the editor.

This same menu will also have the capability to publish an entire site to a remote location, allowing you to easily work on a local copy and deploy it when ready.

Code Separation

We saw earlier that files created with code separation now show in Visual Studio .NET "Whidbey" as two files. In ASP.NET versions 1.0 and 1.1, the code-behind model allowed separation of code from content, and in ASP.NET 2.0 this model has been changed to simplify development. Instead of the content page inheriting from the code-behind page, we now specify which code-behind file is to be compiled with the content file. That may seem like just a change in semantics, but it's actually a more fundamental change, made at the Common Language Runtime (CLR) level.

Version 2.0 of the CLR provides support for **partial classes**, where the same class can span multiple files. This allows the code-separation page to be far simpler than in previous versions because it can be part of the same class as the content page, meaning no more public variables are required to reference the controls on a page.

The implementation of this is easy. Consider the page for Authors.aspx (Listing 2.1).

Listing 2.1. Using Code Separation—the ASP.NET Page

```
<%@ Page compileWith="Authors.aspx.vb"
         className="ASP.authors_aspx" %>


<form runat="server">

  <asp:Button runat="server" onClick="button_Click" />
  <asp:Label runat="server" id="Message" />

</form>
```

Because of partial classes, the code-separation file (Authors.aspx.vb) is simple, as shown in Listing 2.2.

Listing 2.2. Using Code Separation—the Code-Behind File

```
Namespace ASP

  Expands Class Authors_asp

    Sub button_Click(Sender As Object, E As EventArgs)
      Message.Text = "You pressed the button"
    End Sub

  End Class

End Namespace
```

Partial classes have introduced the new Expands keyword, indicating that this class is not self-contained and is part of the Authors_asp class. For the content page, the compileWith attribute defines the physical file containing the code to compile along with the content page, and the className attribute indicates the name (including the namespace) of the class. When the `className` attribute of the content file and the namespace and `Class` of the code file match, code for both files is compiled into a single class.

Dynamic Compilation

ASP.NET 1.x already supports **dynamic compilation** of pages and user controls (`.aspx` and `.ascx` files), eliminating the need for an explicit compilation step. Pages are compiled the first time they are requested by a user, when they are changed, or when any of their dependencies (such as `web.config` or `global.asax`) are changed. Files with no explicit dependency, however, do not trigger this compilation. This includes components (assemblies in the `\bin` folder and their source), resource files, Web Services, and so on. Not only do they not trigger their target ASP.NET pages to be compiled, but they also aren't compiled automatically. They require a manual compilation stage, which invariably means a batch file to compile them or the use of a make system.

ASP.NET 2.0 improves dynamic compilation by supporting an increased number of files. Stand-alone classes, Web Services, typed data sets, master pages, and themes can now be automatically compiled without the need for manual intervention. There are two real benefits to this approach. First, developers can concentrate on just coding. Saving your files to the appropriate folder means your Web applications will always be up to date. Second, when using Visual Studio .NET "Whidbey" there's no need for an intermediate compile stage—you don't have to build the application to use it, you can just hit the Refresh button in the browser.

New Folders for Dynamic Compilation

Developers tend to follow the same style for laying out the folders in Web applications—an \Images folder for all of the site images, perhaps a \Components folder to store user controls or source for data layers, and so on. The expansion of dynamic compilation introduces some fixed folders.

- The **\Code** folder is for storage of class files (`.cs` or `.vb`), WSDL (`.wsdl`) files, and typed data sets (`.xsd`). Placing files of these type in the \Code folder will enable them for automatic compilation.
- The **\Resources** folder is for storage of globalization resources (`.resx` and `.resources`). Resource files can also be stored in the \Code folder.
- The **\Themes** folder is for storing themes and skins (`.skin`).

FIGURE 2.15. Creating classes in the \Code folder

Using these fixed folders allows the ASP.NET compilation process to automatically compile files as part of its normal compilation of ASP.NET pages.

Using the \Code Folder in Visual Studio .NET "Whidbey"

The \Code folder is fully supported in Visual Studio .NET "Whidbey", and its use is simply a matter of creating the folder. Code classes can be added, as shown in Figure 2.15.

A great use of the \Code folder's automatic compilation is for placement of business objects. For example, consider Listing 2.3, which shows a class to handle data from an authors table (`Authors.vb`).

Listing 2.3. A Simple Business Component

```
Imports System
Imports System.Web
Imports System.Data
Imports System.Data.SqlClient

Namespace Pubs
  Public Class Authors

    Public Function GetAuthors() As DataSet
      Dim conn As New _
        SqlConnection("server=.;database=pubs;Trusted_Connection=True")
      Dim da As New SqlDataAdapter("select * from authors", conn)
      Dim ds As New DataSet

      da.Fill(ds, "Authors")

      Return ds
    End Function
  End Class
End Namespace
```

We can simply use this code from within our existing pages, perhaps by using an `ObjectDataSource` to bind directly to the class, and then by using a grid to bind to the data source, as shown in Figure 2.16.

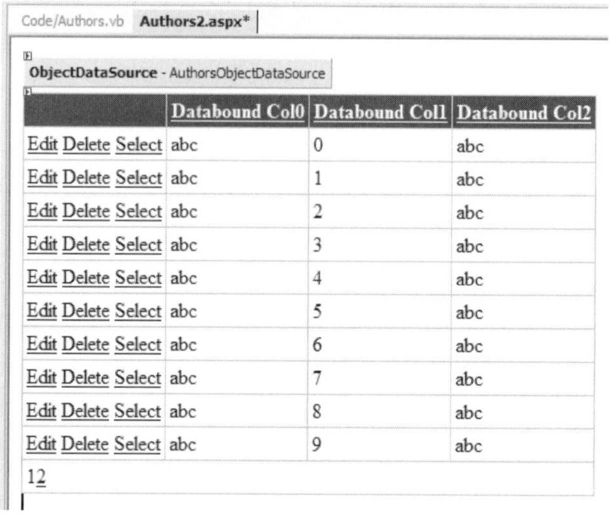

Code/Authors.vb	**Authors2.aspx***	

ObjectDataSource - AuthorsObjectDataSource

	Databound Col0	**Databound Col1**	**Databound Col2**
Edit Delete Select	abc	0	abc
Edit Delete Select	abc	1	abc
Edit Delete Select	abc	2	abc
Edit Delete Select	abc	3	abc
Edit Delete Select	abc	4	abc
Edit Delete Select	abc	5	abc
Edit Delete Select	abc	6	abc
Edit Delete Select	abc	7	abc
Edit Delete Select	abc	8	abc
Edit Delete Select	abc	9	abc
1 2			

FIGURE 2.16. Binding an ObjectDataSource

Folder Hierarchy

The hierarchy of these folders can be configured depending on requirements, but there are some rules. At the top level the names cannot change, and they must be underneath the application root. Within the folders, though, there are some options.

The \Code Folder

There is no restriction on creating subfolders to organize your code. For example, consider the following application structure:

```
c:\Inetpub\wwwroot
  Default.aspx
  \Code
    Authors.vb
    \Utilities
      Tools.vb
```

Here we have `Authors.vb` at the top level of the \Code folder and `Tools.vb` under the \Utilities folder. Both files will be dynamically compiled and linked to the target assembly. This means that types within these classes are automatically available from any other page within the application. You therefore don't have to use namespaces and import them in your ASP.NET pages, meaning new code files can just be dropped into the \Code folder for them to become available for use.

Supporting Multiple Languages. By default the \Code folder supports only a single language (since everything is compiled into a single assembly), no matter what the hierarchy of subfolders. However, this behavior can be configured through the application configuration file, as demonstrated in Listing 2.4.

Listing 2.4. Configuring Compilation Directories

```xml
<?xml version="1.0" encoding="UTF-8" ?>

<configuration>
  <system.web>
    <compilation>
      <codeSubDirectories>
        <add directoryName="vb_code" />
        <add directoryName="cs_code" />
      </codeSubDirectories>
    </compilation>
  </system.web>
</configuration>
```

This instructs the compilation system to produce separate assemblies for files under the two directories, and therefore they can contain different languages (although they are still restricted to a single language per directory). For example, our folder hierarchy could now become:

```
c:\WebSites\MySite
  Default.aspx
  \Code
    \vb_code
      Authors.vb
      \Utilities
        Tools.vb
    \cs_code
      Interop.cs
```

Folders added to the `codeSubDirectories` section of the configuration file are only a single layer deep. Thus you cannot code:

```
<add directoryName="vb_code\utilities" />
```

You can, however, have a deep hierarchy underneath the top level, but all code files will be built into a single assembly for that folder.

The assemblies created are not placed in the \bin directory—indeed, with this system there is no need for a \bin folder, although the \bin folder is still supported and should be used for scenarios where dynamic compilation is not required or supported. Automatically compiled assemblies are placed in a folder managed by ASP.NET, so you don't even have to worry about where they are. If deployment is intended, then pre-compilation is required, and that is covered a little later in the chapter.

Web Services. In ASP.NET 1.x, Web Service proxies had to be manually created, usually by use of the `wsdl.exe` tool, or by including a reference in Visual Studio .NET. In ASP.NET 2.0, Web Services are catered for by including WSDL files in the \Code folder. With automatic compilation, a proxy class is automatically built from the WSDL file and linked to the default assemblies, and the service can be called directly from ASP.NET pages.

Typed Data Sets. Typed data sets provide strongly typed access to data, either from XML files or `DataSets`. Like Web Services, in version 1.x these had to be manually generated (using `xsd.exe`), but they follow the same pattern as WSDL files in version 2.0. All that's required is for the XSD file to be placed in the \Code directory, and the proxy will be generated automatically.

The \Resources Folder

The \Resources folder allows for easy globalization of applications. Under ASP.NET 1.x, resource files were manually compiled and placed in the \bin folder, under subfolders named for the culture of the resource.

In ASP.NET 2.0, resources can be placed into the \Resources folder, where they are then compiled as part of dynamic compilation.

The \Themes Folder

As mentioned in Chapter 1, themes provide a way to supply different UI styles to controls. Since themes can be set at runtime they are late compiled when required. A local themes file is used only for local themes—site-wide themes, such as those supplied by standard in ASP.NET 2.0, are held in a central location.

Themes are covered in detail in Chapter 7.

Configuring Compilation Options

The dynamic compilation system allows configuration through `web.config`. Earlier we talked about the `codeSubDirectories` section allowing configuration of folders and target assemblies. Table 2.1 shows that there are also batch options available as attributes to the `compilation` element.

TABLE 2.1. Compilation Configuration Options

Attribute	Default Value	Description
batch	true	Indicates whether or not batch compilation takes place.
batchTimeout	15	The number of seconds for compilation to take place. An exception is thrown if this time is exceeded.
maxBatchSize	1000	The maximum number of pages/classes compiled into a single batch.
maxBatchGeneratedFileSize	3000K	The maximum size (in kilobytes) of an assembly.

Custom Builds. Like much of ASP.NET, the build process is extensible, using build providers targeted at specific file extensions. These are configured by default in machine.config and can be added there or within web.config. For example, the <compilation> section could look like Listing 2.5.

Listing 2.5. Configuring Build Providers

```
<configuration>
  ...
  <buildProviders>
    <add extension="*.aspx" appliesTo="Web"
        type="System.Web.Compilation.PageBuildProvider" />
    <add extension="*.wsdl" appliesTo="Code"
        type="System.Web.Compilation.WsdlBuildProvider" />
  </buildProviders>
</configuration>
```

Build providers are also inferred from the compilers section of the configuration, so there are no explicit build providers for code files. The extension applies to the folder in which dynamic compilation applies. The appliesTo attribute indicates the folder in which the build provider applies, where Web indicates general Web folders. Multiple folders for build providers are supported by simply separating the folders in the appliesTo attribute with a comma.

This system allows custom providers to be built for types not known to ASP.NET, allowing specification of selected directories for those files.

Build Order and Life Cycle Dynamic compilation builds automatically; therefore, understanding the build order is important to ensure that dependencies are not missed. The build order is as follows:

- The \Resource folder and other resource files
- The \Code folder and other code files
- Global.asax
- Resource files outside of the \Resource and \Code folders
- Individual Web files, such as ASP.NET pages of Web Services

The life cycle of pages and the application is also affected by dynamic compilation because updating a file can result in more than just a single page hit. Table 2.2 details what happens when files are changed, whether recompilation takes place, and whether the Application Domain is restarted. Recompilation will also take place if the <pages> and <compilation> sections of web.config are changed.

Pre-compilation of Applications

Dynamic compilation is targeted at reducing the number of manual steps developers have to perform while constructing a site. **Pre-compilation,** on the other hand, targets two issues with ASP.NET 1.x: (1) the compilation delay when first hitting a site or page, and (2) the hosting scenario, where source code must be present on the server. For intellectual property reasons this isn't always an acceptable situation.

Both of these issues are tackled individually by a pre-compilation system. Part of this functionality will not be in place for the initial Technology Preview release but will be available in later betas and the final release.

In-place Pre-compilation

While ASP.NET performs extremely well, the hit taken while a site initially compiles can be quite large. To avoid this, some developers have built tools to hit every page to ensure it is compiled. In ASP.NET there is support for in-place compilation, which does just that—it compiles every file within an application root. This mechanism is done by navigating to the special URL:

http://applicationDirectory/precompile.axd

TABLE 2.2. Compilation Life Cycle

Scenario	Pages and Themes	\Resources Folder	\Code Folder	Global .asax	Personalization	Restart Application Domain?
Modify .aspx, .asmc, mascx	Compile as necessary					No
Modify Global .asax	Compile			Compile		Yes
Modify source files in \Code	Compile		Compile	Compile	Compile	Yes
Modify Web. config	Compile	Compile	Compile	Compile	Compile	Yes
Modify \Bin	Compile	Compile	Compile	Compile	Compile	Yes
Modify \Resources	Compile	Compile	Compile	Compile	Compile	Yes
Add .resx anywhere	Compile	If referenced	If referenced			No
Add source files anywhere	Compile		If referenced			No
Change themes	Late bound compile of themes only if referenced					Yes
Personalization	Compile			Compile	Compile	Yes

The precompile.axd URL is handled by an HttpHandler, which pre-compiles the entire site, thus avoiding the compile delay during the first hit. There is no overhead if the URL is called multiple times because only changed files are recompiled. Global dependencies, such as changes to global.asax and web.config, are obeyed, and all source files will be marked as out of date, triggering a complete compilation if requested.

Errors that occur during pre-compilation will halt the entire process. These appear in the browser window exactly as they would if the page in error had been hit directly.

Pre-compilation for Deployment without Source

Being able to pre-compile to a target directory without the source is a great way to not only deploy ready-to-go applications but also to protect intellectual property. Pre-compilation is achieved by use of the aspnet _compiler.exe tool, whose syntax is shown below:

```
aspnet_compiler.exe [-m metabasePath |
                     -c virtualPath
                     [-p physicalPath]]
                     [targetDirectory]
```

where:

- metabasePath is the full IIS metabase path of the application.
- virtualPath is the virtual path of the application.
- physicalPath is the physical path of the application.
- targetDirectory is the target directory for the fully compiled application.

If the target directory is not supplied, the application is pre-compiled in place and the source is left where it is. When a target directory is specified, the target will contain no source code after the compilation. A text file is placed at the top-level directory indicating that the site has been pre-compiled. All of the source files are compiled into assemblies, and the source files have all content removed and remain simply as markers so that IIS can find the physical files.

Pre-compilation does not compile static files, such as HTML files, web.config, XML files, and so on. These are just copied to the target directory. If you wish to keep the contents of HTML files from being readable in the target directory, you could rename them to .aspx so they will take part in the pre-compile. This isn't recommended, however, because it loses the benefits of IIS being able to serve HTML pages efficiently, and the performance loss may not be acceptable. Assemblies in the \Bin directory of the source application are also preserved and copied directly to the target directory.

Once an application has been pre-compiled in this manner, changes (e.g., additions to the source directory) will not trigger a recompilation. Compilable files (such as .aspx files) cannot be added to the target directory once it has been generated. They must be added to the source directory and recompiled to the target.

Pre-compilation for Deployment with Source

As mentioned above, dynamic files cannot exist in a pre-compiled target directory, so it is not possible to deploy a pre-compiled application with the source intact. This is a feature that is being investigated for later releases, but for the time being the standard deployment and in-place pre-compilation is a great model to work with.

The Compilation API

The technology underlying the pre-compilation system is the Client BuildManager, which also provides an API, allowing custom tools to be built. Listing 2.6 shows how this can be achieved.

Listing 2.6. Using the Compilation API

```
Imports System.Web.Compilation

Public Sub BuildApplication

  Dim src As String = "C:\Development\WebSites\MySite"
  Dim vdir As String = "/MySite"
  Dim tgt As "C:\InetPub\WWWRoot\MySite"

  Dim bmgr As New ClientBuildManager(src, vdir, tgt, vbNull)

  bmgr.PrecompileApp()

End Sub
```

SUMMARY

In this chapter we've looked at the new design tool, Visual Studio .NET "Whidbey," and some of the great features it offers, including some data binding scenarios, support for master pages, connections to databases, and so on. Rather than list all of the new features, we've concentrated on the ones that will have the most dramatic effect on development, making sites easier and quicker to construct.

The second topic of this chapter was compilation and the underlying changes to ASP.NET. We've seen how the compilation system can free you from the "make file nightmare," allowing you to just save files and browse the application. Pre-compilation brings improvements in two areas: (1) performance, by compiling in-place to avoid the first-hit compilation, and (2) protection of intellectual property, by removing the source code.

Now it's time to start looking in depth at the ASP.NET 2.0 features, starting with data source controls and binding.

3

Data Source Controls and Data Binding

O NE OF THE FEATURES of ASP.NET 1.0 that so excited developers was the introduction of server-side data binding. This had probably the greatest effect of all the new features in reducing the code required to build data-driven pages, when compared with previous versions of ASP (and other dynamic Web page technologies). No longer do you need to write masses of intermingled markup, literal text, and code to build HTML tables in your pages to display data. And, as an added advantage, data binding usually provides improved performance as well.

ASP.NET 2.0 continues the process of reducing the requirements for code and developer effort. It provides new controls that remove the need to write those almost identical chunks of data access code that fetch the data you need from the data store. And it also considerably simplifies the previously cumbersome syntax for server-side data binding.

In this chapter and the next, we look at the main areas where ASP.NET 2.0 changes the data access, data binding, and data output models used in ASP.NET 1.x. In this chapter we'll cover the following:

- An overview of "code-free" data binding and data updating techniques

- The new data source controls that expose data without requiring any data access code

There is also a new feature in the .NET Framework that can be useful when working with data in your Web pages and applications: a facility to add data source connection strings to a new section of a web.config file, which allows them to be encrypted for security purposes. This topic is covered, along with other configuration topics, in Chapter 13.

Meanwhile, we start off in this chapter with a brief "wow factor" look at just how easy it is to display and edit data using the combination of a data source control and a GridView control. This will also give you a good overview of the new controls and techniques that are explained in more detail throughout the rest of this chapter and the next.

Code-Free Data Binding

One of the major goals of ASP.NET since version 1.0 has been to allow developers to achieve more while writing less code. Server controls such as the DataGrid, as well as the rest of the ASP.NET page architecture and postback mechanism, remove the need for code that iterates through rowsets, generates HTML table elements, and manages the values of controls between postbacks.

However, one area that seems to have been ignored until now is data access. In ASP.NET 1.x, you still have to create functions or routines that connect to the data store, extract the rows or values, and then expose them to the server controls in the page. OK, so that's generally not difficult, and it does provide plenty of flexibility. But it's still effort you have to put in when building the pages.

In ASP.NET 2.0, Microsoft has added new controls that take away the need for this code. Data source controls allow declarative definition of all the information required to extract the data from the data source, and they react to events within the page framework to fetch this data and display it in other data-bound controls to which they are attached.

Displaying Data with a Data Source Control

As a simple example and a dramatic indication of how easy it is to do, Listing 3.1 shows the complete declaration of the <form> section of a page that displays rows from a database. This is all you need—there is no server-side code in the page at all.

LISTING 3.1. Displaying Data with a Data Source Control

```
<form runat="server">

<asp:SqlDataSource id="ds1" runat="server"
   ConnectionString="server=localhost;database=Northwind;uid=x;pwd=x"
   SelectCommand="SELECT ProductID, ProductName, QuantityPerUnit,
                   UnitPrice, UnitsInStock, Discontinued FROM Products"
/>

<asp:GridView id="grid1" DataSourceID="ds1" runat="server" />

</form>
```

The SqlDataSource control uses a connection string and a SQL statement (or a stored procedure name), plus sensible default settings, to connect to a database and extract the data rows. It reacts to the page-level events that occur when the page is requested and internally builds the usual ADO.NET objects it needs (either a Connection, DataAdapter, and DataSet or a Connection, Command, and DataReader). If you think about it, when you create these objects yourself all you start out with is the connection string and a SQL statement!

The other control, the GridView, displays the data. The GridView is a new version of the DataGrid from ASP.NET 1.0, enhanced with a lot of new features. Notice how it is connected to the data source control using the DataSourceID attribute. All ASP.NET server controls that support data binding expose this attribute in version 2.0, so they can be used interchangeably with any data source control.

The screenshot in Figure 3.1 shows the result of the code in Listing 3.1. You can see that it looks rather like the output you would get from the version 1.0 DataGrid control. It displays all the rows from the Products table in the Northwind database, just as specified in the SQL statement. Notice the Discontinued column, however. This is a Boolean field in the table, and the control automatically displays it using read-only (disabled) checkboxes.

Adding Row Sorting Capabilities

Another example of the power of the GridView control can be seen when you want to allow the user to sort the rows in the grid. In ASP.NET 1.0, with the DataGrid, this was relatively easy. It meant adding a couple of attributes to the control declaration and writing a dozen or so lines of code. However, with the GridView, all you need to do is add the AllowSorting attribute to the control declaration:

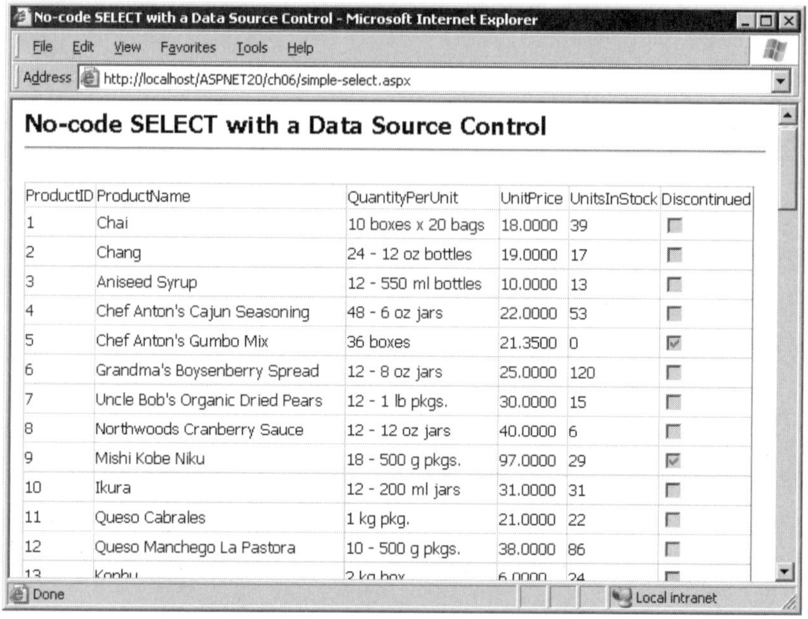

FIGURE 3.1. Displaying data with a data source control

```
<asp:GridView id="grid1" DataSourceID="ds1" runat="server"
        AllowSorting="True" />
```

There's no code to write, no events to handle, and nothing more to do. The control looks after everything for you. Of course, you can provide custom sorting features if you want, but it's not a requirement.

Adding Row Paging Capabilities

Another common requirement, which was a little more difficult to do in version 1.0 with the DataGrid, is to add "paging" so that only a specific number of rows are shown each time and the display provides links to go to other pages. Again, with the GridView, it's just a matter of adding one attribute to the control declaration:

```
<asp:GridView id="grid1" DataSourceID="ds1" runat="server"
        AllowSorting="True"
        AllowPaging="True" />
```

As before, there's no code to write. It just works. The screenshot in Figure 3.2 shows the result of adding the attributes that enable sorting and paging to the basic GridView declaration.

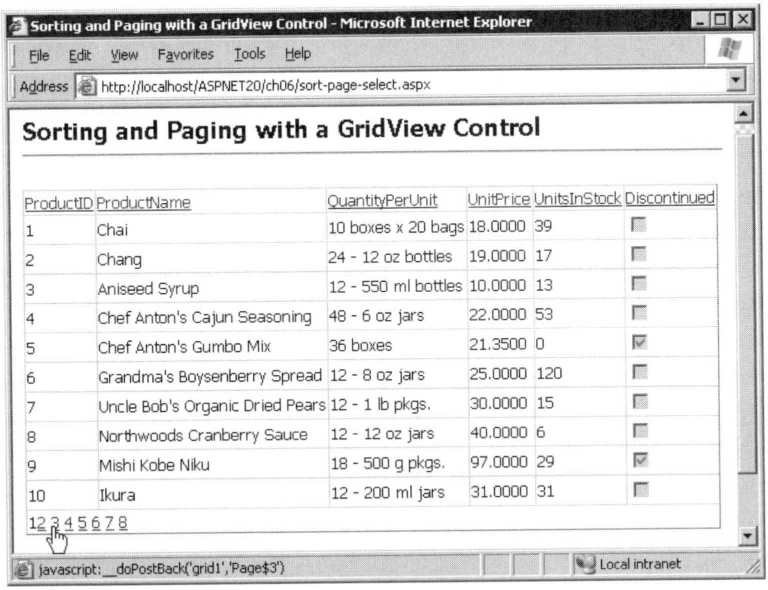

FIGURE 3.2. Paging with a `GridView` control

You can see that only ten rows are displayed by default, and the paging controls at the bottom of the window provide links to the other pages. Also notice that the column headings are now hyperlinks—the grid now supports sorting as well. The screenshot in Figure 3.3 shows the result of clicking the

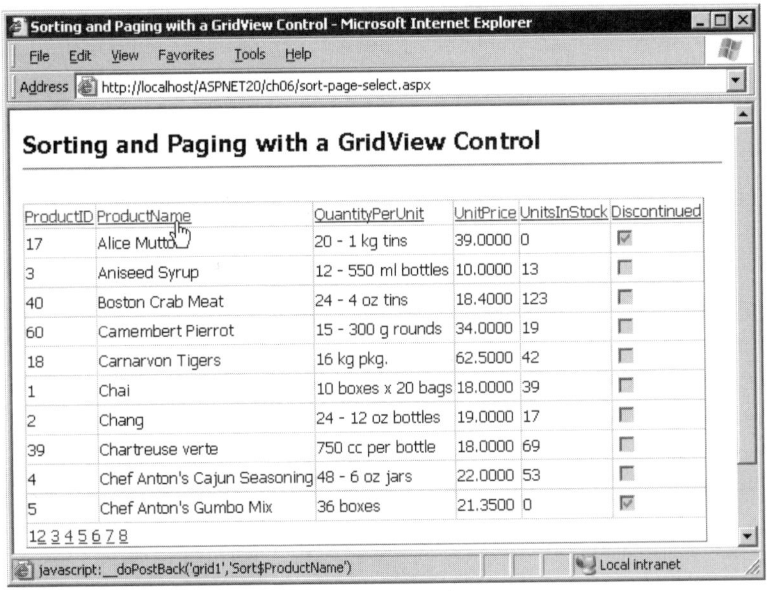

FIGURE 3.3. Sorting with a `GridView` control

ProductName heading. Repeated clicks alternate between ascending and descending sort order.

Built-in Small-Screen and Mobile Device Support

The GridView control is part of the unified control architecture we discuss in more detail in Chapter 10, using an adapter to generate the appropriate device-dependent markup for clients that load the page. Tables and grids are notoriously difficult for small-screen devices to display, and Microsoft has addressed this issue by creating two different modes for displaying data in a table: summary view and details view.

The GridView control supports this approach automatically. If you open the page shown in Figure 3.2 in a suitable mobile device or device emulator, you'll see that the control renders the content using these two views. Figures 3.4 and 3.5 show the kind of output you can expect, though it does of course differ depending on the device.

In Figure 3.4 the grid is in summary view. You can see the ProductName column heading and below it the values from that column. All of these are links. Selecting the column heading link causes the data to be sorted on the values in the column. Each product name below the column heading provides a link to display more details about that product (the other values from that row in the table).

Figure 3.5 shows the output after selecting a product in the previous screen. The grid is now in details view, and the values of the selected product are shown. Notice how the checkbox for the Discontinued column is rep-

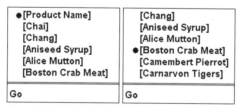

FIGURE 3.4. Mobile device output in summary view

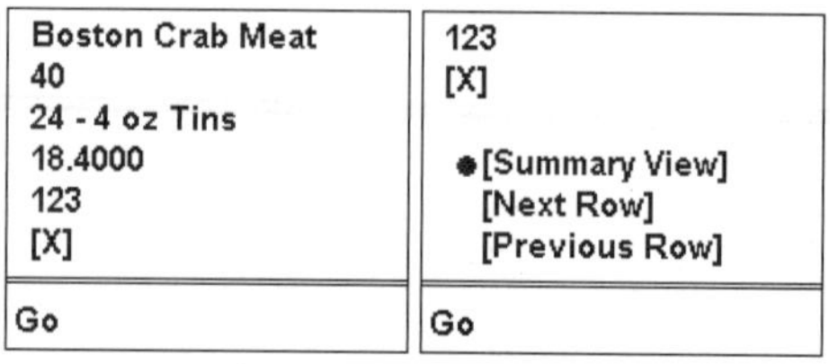

FIGURE 3.5. Mobile device output in details view

resented in a way that suits the device. Following all the values are the links to switch back to summary view or to move to the next or previous row.

Specifying the Summary View Column

All this output is created automatically and does not require any developer effort. However, one point worth bearing in mind is that by default the summary view will display the first column. In the figures we showed the second column (the product name) as the summary column. To achieve this, just add the `SummaryViewColumn` attribute to the declaration of the `GridView` control and specify the column name:

```
<asp:GridView id="grid1" DataSourceID="ds1" runat="server"
    AllowSorting="True"
    AllowPaging="True"
    SummaryViewColumn="ProductName" />
```

It's worth adding this attribute every time you use a `GridView` so that small-screen devices see the most useful column. It doesn't affect the display for "normal" devices in any way.

Linking Page Controls and Data Source Control Parameters

A regular requirement for pages that display data is to include one or more controls that can be used to select or filter the rows displayed. For example, you may display a list of countries and then show only the rows from a table of customer details for that country. The data source controls can be used to fill both the list of countries and the rows for a particular country when the user makes a selection.

The example in Listing 3.2 uses two data source controls. The first, with ID value `ds1`, retrieves a list of the countries in the rows of the Customers table using the `DISTINCT` keyword in the SQL statement. These rows are then displayed in an ASP.NET `DropDownList` control by assigning the data source control to the `DataSourceID` property of that control and specifying the column to be displayed as the `DataTextField` attribute. Notice also that the `DropDownList` control has `AutoPostback` set to `True`, so selecting a country will cause a postback to the server.

LISTING 3.2. Linking Data Source Control Parameters

```
<asp:SqlDataSource id="ds1" runat="server"
  ConnectionString="server=localhost;database=Northwind;uid=x;pwd=x;"
  SelectCommand="SELECT DISTINCT Country FROM Customers
```

continues

```
                    ORDER BY Country"
   EnableCaching="True" CacheDuration="300" />

<asp:DropDownList id="lstCountry" DataSourceID="ds1"
  DataTextField="Country" AutoPostback="True" runat="server" />
...
```

One extremely useful feature of the data source controls is the ability to cache the data they retrieve, thus reducing server loading and improving performance in cases where the data is not expected to change between postbacks. The EnableCaching and CacheDuration attributes are discussed later in this chapter, along with the ability to link the cache to the original data source so that changes to the data will invalidate the cache.

Specifying and Using the Country Parameter

The next section of code in this page declares the second data source control and the GridView control (see Listing 3.3). The data source control ds2 has a SQL statement for the SelectCommand attribute that contains the parameter WHERE Country = @Country. There is also a SelectParameters section within the data source control declaration. This declares a ControlParameter named Country that takes its value from the Selected Value property of the control named lstCountry (the data-bound DropDownList populated with the country names that is declared in Listing 3.2). Finally, a GridView control is bound to the ds2 data source.

LISTING 3.3. Linking Data Source Control Parameters

```
...
<asp:SqlDataSource id="ds2" runat="server"
  ConnectionString="server=localhost;database=Northwind;uid=x;pwd=x;"
  SelectCommand="SELECT * FROM Customers WHERE Country = @Country">

  <SelectParameters>
    <asp:ControlParameter Name="Country" ControlID="lstCountry"
                          PropertyName="SelectedValue" />
  </SelectParameters>

</asp:SqlDataSource>

<asp:GridView id="grid1" DataSourceID="ds2" runat="server" />
```

FIGURE 3.6. Using control parameters with a data source control

When the page is executed, the `ControlParameter` is populated with the value currently selected in the `DropDownList` control, then this parameter is added to the data source control's `Parameters` collection before the SQL statement is executed. All this happens automatically, and no code is required. The data source control then selects only the rows that satisfy the parameter value and displays these in the `GridView` control. You can see the result in the screenshot in Figure 3.6.

Editing Data with a GridView and a Data Source Control

As a final example of the power of the new combination of data source controls and the `GridView` control, this section looks at in-line editing of the data within a `GridView` control. And, like all of the previous examples, no code is required to make it work.

In fact, there is a small section of code in this example, which we discuss when we look at how you can react to events raised by the `GridView` control in Chapter 4, but this is not usually required for the simple editing and deleting of rows demonstrated here.

To enable in-line editing of rows, the declaration of the data source control must include a value for the `UpdateCommand` attribute, and to allow rows to be deleted, the `DeleteCommand` attribute must be defined. In Listing 3.4, both are SQL statements including parameters that will be populated from the `GridView` control automatically in response to `Update` and `Delete` commands. The automatic parameter population also gives a useful extra benefit by helping to protect against SQL scripting attacks that can occur if you use values typed in by users.

The `GridView` control declaration also requires a few "extra" attribute values to be defined. You must specify the `DataKeyNames` attribute value as a comma-delimited list of primary key column names so that the control can locate the correct values for the key in the table and prevent editing of the key values. In this case it's just `ShipperID`. And, so that the Edit, Update, and Delete links will appear in the grid, you must set the `AutoGenerate` `EditButton` and `AutoGenerateDeleteButton` attributes to `True`.

LISTING 3.4. A Data Source Control with Edit Commands

```
<asp:SqlDataSource id="ds1" runat="server"
  ConnectionString="server=localhost;database=Northwind;uid=x;pwd=x;"
  SelectCommand="SELECT * FROM Shippers"
  UpdateCommand="UPDATE Shippers SET CompanyName=@CompanyName,
                  Phone=@Phone WHERE ShipperID=@ShipperID"
  DeleteCommand="DELETE FROM Shippers WHERE ShipperID=@ShipperID" />

<asp:GridView id="grid1" DataSourceID="ds1" runat="server"
  DataKeyNames="ShipperID"
  AutoGenerateEditButton="True"
  AutoGenerateDeleteButton="True" />
```

And that is all that is required to make it work. The screenshot in Figure 3.7 shows the grid with all the rows in normal mode, as it appears when first loaded. The Edit and Delete links appear in the first column.

Clicking an Edit link switches that row in the grid to edit mode, and the value of the non-key columns can be edited (see Figure 3.8). Notice that the ShipperID column, the primary key specified in the `DataKeyNames` attribute, is not editable.

After editing the values, the Update link pushes the changes back into the database using the SQL statement specified for the `UpdateCommand`, while the Cancel link just switches the row back to normal mode without persisting the changes to the row values. Likewise, the Delete link uses the

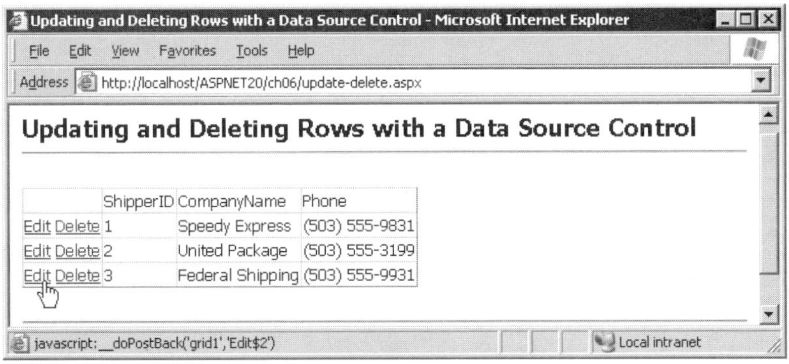

FIGURE 3.7. Selecting a row to edit with a data source control

SQL statement specified as the `DeleteCommand` to remove the row that contains the link.

> However, because the table has linked child rows in the Products table, you can't actually delete a row with this example. Instead, the page handles the delete action and displays a message. You'll see more about this in Chapter 4 in the subsection Handling a GridView Event.

So, having seen just how powerful this new approach to data access, display, and editing is, and how easy it is to achieve, the remaining sections of this chapter and all of the next chapter look in more depth at the

FIGURE 3.8. Updating a row with a data source control

controls themselves and the more advanced techniques that you can take advantage of when working with them.

The DetailsView Control

All of the examples shown previously in this chapter use a `GridView` control to display the data rows. The `GridView` provides the ubiquitous "grid" layout that is so familiar with controls such as the `DataGrid` in version 1.x. However, often you want to display data so that only one "row" or "record" is visible, allowing users to scroll through the rows—and perhaps to edit the values as well. The second of the new data-bound controls in ASP.NET, the `DetailsView` control, does just that.

We'll be looking in more depth at the `GridView` and `DetailsView` controls in Chapter 4. However, just to complete this first look at the controls, the screenshot in Figure 3.9 shows the `DetailsView` control in action. You'll see how this works in the next chapter.

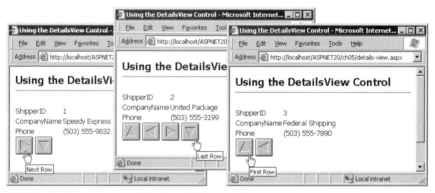

FIGURE 3.9. Viewing rows with a DetailsView control

Data Source Controls

In essence, a data source control simply replaces the data access code you create in ASP.NET 1.x to generate the rowset of data that you want to use in your page. Instead of writing a function that returns (for example) a `DataSet` loaded with the data rows you want to display, you just place a data source control on the page and set the properties to define the data you want. When a control such as a `GridView` or a `DropDownList` renders the data, it uses the data source control to fetch the data and expose it for data binding.

Therefore, when adding a control that supports data binding to the page, you don't have to write any code at all. And the new `GridView` and

`DetailsView` controls can automatically provide features to update the data as well—again without requiring you to write any code. Meanwhile, you *can* still write code to interact with the controls if you want to, and you can perform customized data binding or manipulate the data directly. However, in the vast majority of cases the controls will do all the work for you.

The aims of the data source controls (combined with the new `GridView` and `DetailsView` controls and data binding) are to provide the following.

- **Data binding without requiring any code to be written**. You can display, edit, and sort data with little or no code required. A data source control has the same kind of simple declarative persistence format, using HTML-like elements, as other ASP.NET server controls. Where code is required, the data source controls make it intuitive and concise.

- **A consistent declarative and programming model**, regardless of the type of data source or data provider. Developers use the same syntax irrespective of the data source, and control authors have a common interface to implement in their custom data source controls.

- **A self-describing interface** that makes it easy to discover the capabilities of the control. `Boolean` properties indicate whether `SELECT`, `INSERT`, `UPDATE`, `DELETE`, and sorting operations are supported for the data source. Code in the page can test for these capabilities, and custom control authors can implement automatic behavior when certain capabilities are available.

- **A richer design-time experience**. Development tools can make it easier to generate instances of the controls and the data binding statements, perhaps using drag-and-drop design techniques. The controls can use a schema to display the data at design time in a way that more closely resembles the runtime appearance.

- **The same flexibility as in version 1.0**, by allowing developers to take full control of the data binding process and react to events (though there should be far less need to do so).

- **Performance equal to or exceeding that of version 1.0** when retrieving data and displaying it through data binding.

To connect a data source control to a server control that will display the data, you use the `DataSourceID` attribute of the data-bound server control—setting it to the `id` attribute value of the data source control. All the

controls in the `System.Web.UI.WebControls` and `System.Web.UI.Html`
`Controls` namespaces that already support server-side data binding now
accept the `DataSourceID` attribute.

One important point to note is that the data source controls in the Technology Preview release are not designed to support ADO.NET data row
paging. Paging is available in the `GridView` control (as in the `DataGrid`
control in version 1.x) but is implemented within the `GridView` control and
not by the underlying data source control. In future releases the relational
data source controls such as `SqlDataSource` will take advantage of
ADO.NET paging features to improve performance.

> ADO.NET 2.0 itself now supports paged results sets, so if you need to
> use paging with a large number of rows you may prefer to use this
> technique rather than a data source control. See the companion book
> to this one, *A First Look at ADO.NET and System.Xml v. 2.0* (Boston,
> MA: Addison-Wesley, 2004, ISBN 0-321-22839-1) for more details.

Types of Data Source Controls

Data source controls fall into different classes, depending on the type of
data source they will be used to access. All data source controls live in the
`System.Web.UI.WebControls` namespace of the .NET Framework class
library, and all implement one or both of the `IDataSource` and
`IHierarchicalDataSource` interfaces. The data source controls are listed
below.

- The `SqlDataSource` control is the one you'll use for most of your
  relational database access requirements. It can be used with a database through the SQL Server provider (using the classes from the
  `SqlClient` namespace), through OLE-DB, or through ODBC.
- The `AccessDataSource` control makes it easy to connect to a Microsoft Access database. This is just one of the database-specific controls;
  other types of data sources can be accessed through specific data
  source controls that are under development at the time of writing.
- The `XmlDataSource` control can expose hierarchical XML documents
  and XML data for data binding to controls such as a `TreeView`, as
  well as exposing the data as an `XmlDataDocument`.

- The `DataSetDataSource` control exposes nonhierarchical XML as a rowset for data binding, as well as exposing the data as an ADO.NET `DataSet` and an `XmlDataDocument`.

- The `ObjectDataSource` control allows developers to interact with a data access layer consisting of suitable classes, rather than directly with the database.

In forthcoming releases of ASP.NET you can expect to see more new data source controls such as the `WebServiceDataSource`, `Excel DataSource`, and `IndexServiceDataSource`. A list of the proposed data source controls appears near the end of this chapter.

Here, we'll look at each of the data source controls in the Technology Preview version individually. We'll start with the `SqlDataSource` control and then see how the other data source controls differ from it.

The SqlDataSource Control

For most relational database access tasks, the `SqlDataSource` control is the obvious choice. By default it will use a SQL Server–specific connection, but by simply changing the connection string you can use any of the databases for which a provider is available, without having to rewrite your code or change the page in any other way.

Declaring a SqlDataSource Control

All data source controls can be instantiated through declarative elements in the page, and their properties set using attributes, just as you declare any other ASP.NET server control. The complete set of attributes you can use in a `SqlDataSource` control declaration is shown in Listing 3.5.

LISTING 3.5. Declaring a SqlDataSource Control

```
<asp:SqlDataSource id="String" runat="server"
  ConnectionString="String"
  ProviderName="String"
  DataSourceMode="[DataSet|DataReader]"
  SelectCommand="String"
  InsertCommand="String"
  UpdateCommand="String"
  DeleteCommand="String"
  FilterExpression="String"
  EnableCaching="[True|False]"
  CacheDuration="Integer"
  SqlCacheDependency="String"
```

continues

```
CacheExpirationPolicy="[Absolute|SlidingWindow]"
OnSelecting="SqlDataSourceCommandEventHandler"
OnSelected="SqlDataSourceStatusEventHandler"
OnUpdating="SqlDataSourceCommandEventHandler"
OnUpdated="SqlDataSourceStatusEventHandler"
OnInserting="SqlDataSourceCommandEventHandler"
OnInserted="SqlDataSourceStatusEventHandler"
OnDeleting="SqlDataSourceCommandEventHandler"
OnDeleted="SqlDataSourceStatusEventHandler"
OnDataSourceChanged="EventHandler" >

    <SelectParameters>
        [<System.Web.UI.WebControls.Parameter ...>]
    </SelectParameters>
    <UpdateParameters>
        [<System.Web.UI.WebControls.Parameter ...>]
    </UpdateParameters>
    <InsertParameters>
        [<System.Web.UI.WebControls.Parameter ...>]
    </InsertParameters>
    <DeleteParameters>
        [<System.Web.UI.WebControls.Parameter ...>]
    </DeleteParameters>
    <FilterParameters>
        [<System.Web.UI.WebControls.Parameter ...>]
    </FilterParameters>

</asp:SqlDataSource>
```

The attributes in the opening element tag correspond in a one-to-one fashion to the properties of the control listed in the next subsection, which details the complete control interface. The **content** of the `<asp:SqlData Source>` element is a series of parameter declarations that define how the control should select and filter the data and how it will update the data when changes are pushed back into the database. We'll look at these parameter declarations later in this chapter.

Like all server controls, the `SqlDataSource` exposes an interface that you can access programmatically. When the control is inserted into the page, ASP.NET instantiates the control and uses the attributes you specify to set the properties without requiring any code to be written in the page. Of course, you can read and set the properties in code as required.

SqlDataSource Properties and Attributes

Table 3.1 lists the properties and attributes shown in the declaration of the control in Listing 3.5. In general, you must set at least the `Connection String` and `SelectCommand`. If you are *not* accessing SQL Server, you must also set the `ProviderName` to the namespace of the classes in the .NET Framework library that correspond to the type of data source and data access method you are using.

TABLE 3.1. The SqlDataSource Class Properties and Attributes

Property/Attribute	Description
`ConnectionString`	Sets or returns the connection string that the control uses to access the database as a `String` value. The format of the string must match the requirements of the database provider specified for the `ProviderName`. If no `ProviderName` is specified, the control assumes that SQL Server TDS will be used. For security reasons, the `ConnectionString` property is not stored in the view-state of the page.
`ProviderName`	Sets or returns the namespace that contains the data provider used by the control as a `String`. The default is `System.Data.SqlClient`. The providers that are available are listed in the `<providerConfiguration>` section of the `<system.data>` element in `machine.config`.
`DataSourceMode`	Sets or returns the type of object that the control will use to access the database as a value from the `SqlDataSourceMode` enumeration. The available values are `DataSet` and `DataReader`. A `DataReader` provides better performance but does not allow for caching, filtering, or sorting within the control. The default is `SqlDataSourceMode.DataSet`.
`SelectCommand`	Sets or returns a `String` that specifies the SQL statement or stored procedure name that will be used to extract the data from the database. Parameters are passed to the SQL statement or stored procedure by using a `<SelectParameters>` element or by assigning values at runtime to the `SelectParameters` property (discussed later in this chapter).
`InsertCommand`	Sets or returns a `String` that specifies the SQL statement or stored procedure name that will be used to insert rows into the database. Parameters are passed to the SQL statement or stored procedure by using an `<InsertParameters>` element or by assigning values at runtime to the `InsertParameters` property (discussed later in this chapter).

continues

TABLE 3.1. The SqlDataSource Class Properties and Attributes (continued)

Property/Attribute	Description
UpdateCommand	Sets or returns a `String` that specifies the SQL statement or stored procedure name that will be used to update existing rows within the database. Parameters are passed to the SQL statement or stored procedure by using an `<UpdateParameters>` element or by assigning values at runtime to the `UpdateParameters` property (discussed later in this chapter).
DeleteCommand	Sets or returns a `String` that specifies the SQL statement or stored procedure name that will be used to delete rows from the database. Parameters are passed to the SQL statement or stored procedure by using a `<DeleteParameters>` element or by assigning values at runtime to the `DeleteParameters` property (discussed later in this chapter).
FilterExpression	Sets or returns a `String` that contains the expression to be used to filter the data specified in the `SelectCommand` property. It is valid only when the `DataSourceMode` is `DataSet`. The syntax of the filter expression is the same as that used in the `RowFilter` property of an ADO.NET `DataView`. Parameters should be prefixed with the @ character (or a character specific to the database). For example: `"FieldName1=value1, FieldName2='value2'"` `"FieldName=@param"`
EnableCaching	Sets or returns a `Boolean` value that specifies whether caching will be applied to the data selected in the control. It is valid only when the `DataSourceMode` is `DataSet`. When `True`, the data is cached and used in subsequent `Select` operations. The default is `False`.
CacheDuration	Sets or returns the number of seconds that data is cached when `EnableCaching=True`, as an `Integer`. The `CacheExpirationPolicy` property determines whether this is an absolute or sliding window value. If not specified, the data is cached for all subsequent `Select` operations.
CacheExpirationPolicy	Sets or returns a value from the `DataSourceCache Expiry` enumeration that specifies the expiry policy for the cache, as defined in the `CacheDuration` property. Valid values are `Absolute` or `SlidingWindow`. The default is `DataSourceCacheExpiry.Absolute`.

TABLE 3.1. The SqlDataSource Class Properties and Attributes (continued)

Property/Attribute	Description
SqlCacheDependency	Sets or returns an optional cache dependency as a `String`. The syntax is of the form `connection:table-name`. The `connection` refers to a named entry within the `<cache>` section of `machine.config` or `web.config`. The `tablename` refers to the name of the table in the database. Multiple dependencies can be delimited with a semicolon, for example: `connection:table1;connection:table2`. The database must be configured to support SQL cache invalidation.

Specifying Parameters for the SqlDataSource Control

To be able to use a control to access (and update) data, there has to be a way to pass parameter values to the SQL statements or stored procedures it uses under the hood. Otherwise the value of the `SelectCommand` would need to be changed each time the control is required to extract a different set of rows (or to perform different updates to the database tables).

So that you don't have to write code to set these parameter values, the `SqlDataSource` control exposes the parameters in a way that allows them to be set declaratively by referencing dynamic values that are part of the page request or the control tree.

For a stored procedure, parameters are defined as part of the procedure definition within the database itself. For a SQL statement, parameters are specified using placeholders, for example:

```
"SELECT * FROM Customers WHERE Country='@Country'"
```

At runtime, the control replaces the `@Country` placeholder with the specific value of the parameter.

The values that are passed to the SQL statement or stored procedure can be taken directly from:

- The value of a server control within the page, using a `ControlParameter` control
- A name/value pair that appears in the `Request.QueryString` collection, using a `QueryStringParameter` control
- A value from a control that appears in the `Request.Form` collection, using a `FormParameter` control

- A value stored in the user's ASP.NET session, using a `SessionParameter` control
- A value in a cookie sent by the browser with the request, using a `CookieParameter` control

These controls are declared within the `SqlDataSource` control element as a set of optional nested elements. As well as the parameters for the `Select`, `Update`, `Insert`, and `Delete` operations, there is an optional element that can be used to filter the rows returned by a `Select` operation (see Listing 3.6).

LISTING 3.6. Parameter Outline for a SqlDataSource Control

```
<asp:SqlDataSource id="String" runat="server"
  ... >

    <SelectParameters>
        ... one or more xxxParameter elements here ...
    </SelectParameters>

    <UpdateParameters>
        ... one or more xxxParameter elements here ...
    </UpdateParameters>

    <InsertParameters>
        ... one or more xxxParameter elements here ...
    </InsertParameters>

    <DeleteParameters>
        ... one or more xxxParameter elements here ...
    </DeleteParameters>

    <FilterParameters>
        ... one or more xxxParameter elements here ...
    </FilterParameters>

</asp:SqlDataSource>
```

At runtime, ASP.NET creates a separate `ParameterCollection` for each of the sections that appear within the declaration of the control and populates these collections using the `Parameter` elements in each section. The `ParameterCollection` instances are then applied to the properties of the `SqlDataSource` control. These properties are shown in Table 3.2.

TABLE 3.2. The ParameterCollection Class Properties

Property	Description
SelectParameters	Returns a reference to the ParameterCollection containing the parameters for the Select operation.
UpdateParameters	Returns a reference to the ParameterCollection containing the parameters for the Update operation.
InsertParameters	Returns a reference to the ParameterCollection containing the parameters for the Insert operation.
DeleteParameters	Returns a reference to the ParameterCollection containing the parameters for the Delete operation.
FilterParameters	Returns a reference to the ParameterCollection containing the parameters used to filter the rows returned by a Select operation.

Parameter Properties and Attributes. The five types of parameter that you can use within the parameter sections of the SqlDataSource control are descended from the common base class System.Web.UI.WebControls .Parameter. This class exposes five properties that are inherited by all of the parameter types (see Table 3.3).

TABLE 3.3. The Parameter Class Properties and Attributes

Property/Attribute	Description
Name	Sets or returns the name of the parameter as a String, corresponding to the parameter in the SQL statement or stored procedure to which it will be applied. Note that the @ prefix should not be included in the name.
Direction	Sets or returns the "direction" for the parameter, as a value from the System.Data.Parameter Direction enumeration. Valid values are: • Input: The parameter carries an input value for the query. • Output: The parameter collects an output value from the query. • InputOutput: The parameter carries an input value for the query and returns with the value updated by the query. • ReturnValue: The parameter carries the value specified by a RETURN statement in a stored procedure.

TABLE 3.3. The Parameter Class Properties and Attributes (continued)

Property/Attribute	Description
`DefaultValue`	Sets or returns the default value of the parameter as a `String` representation of that value.
`Type`	Sets or returns the data type that the value and the `DefaultValue` represent, using a standard .NET `TypeCode` value such as `String`, `Int16`, or `Decimal`.
`TreatEmptyStringAsNull`	Sets or returns a `Boolean` value that indicates whether an empty `String` for the value will be treated as `null` when the SQL statement or stored procedure is executed.

The five specific parameter classes expose at least one additional `String` property, depending on the parameter type (see Table 3.4). These properties are used to specify how the value for the parameter is selected from all the values available in the set of controls on the page, in the `QueryString` or `Form` collection, in the session, or in the cookies sent from the client.

TABLE 3.4. The Five Parameter Section Types

Parameter Control	Properties
`ControlParameter`	`ControlID`: The `id` of the control containing the value to use. `PropertyName`: The name of the control property that contains the value, for example, `Text` for the `Text` property of a `Textbox` control.
`QueryStringParameter`	`QueryStringField`: The name of the name/value pair that contains the value to use, for example, `UserID`, where the query string contains `UserID=smithron`.
`FormParameter`	`FormField`: The name of the control on the page that contains the value to use. It does not have to be a server control. Corresponds to the `name` attribute of the control within the HTML source of the page.
`SessionParameter`	`SessionField`: The name of the key used to store the value in the user's ASP.NET session, for example, `UserID`, where the value was stored using `Session("UserID") = "smithron"`.
`CookieParameter`	`CookieName`: The name of the key used to store the value in the cookie.

Listing 3.7 shows an example of the ways that the parameter controls can be used. Each of the properties of the SqlDataSource can be set with any of the five different parameter types or with a mixture of different types.

LISTING 3.7. Parameter Details for a SqlDataSource Control

```
<asp:SqlDataSource id="String" runat="server"
  ... >

    <SelectParameters>
      <asp:ControlParameter Name="UserID"
          ControlID="txtUserID" PropertyName="Text" />
      <asp:ControlParameter Name="UserName"
          ControlID="lstName" PropertyName="SelectedValue" />
    </SelectParameters>

    <UpdateParameters>
      <asp:FormParameter Name="Country" FormField="CountryBox" />
    </UpdateParameters>

    <InsertParameters>
      <asp:QueryStringParameter Name="UID" QueryStringField ="uid" />
      <asp:SessionParameter Name="Page" SessionField ="PageName" />
    </InsertParameters>

    <DeleteParameters>
      <asp:ControlParameter Name="UserID"
          ControlID="txtUserID" PropertyName="Text" />
      <asp:FormParameter Name="Country" FormField="CountryBox" />
      <asp:CookieParameter Name="CheckVal" CoookieName="CheckSum" />
    </DeleteParameters>


</asp:SqlDataSource>
```

Remember that you need to set only the SqlDataSource properties that correspond to the operations you'll be carrying out. In other words, if you are just displaying data—and not updating it—you can omit the UpdateParameters, InsertParameters, and DeleteParameters sections.

Applying a Dynamic Filter Expression with Parameters. The same approach is taken if you want to specify a filter that will be applied to the results of the SelectCommand. For example, the code in Listing 3.8 specifies the Text value of a Textbox control that has the ID txtFilterExpr. This value is used as a filter against the column named *table-column-name* within the results set—in effect setting the FilterExpression to *table-column-name=value-of-textbox.*

LISTING 3.8. Using FilterParameters with a SqlDataSource Control

```
    . . .
<FilterParameters>
  <asp:ControlParameter Name="table-column-name"
        ControlID="txtFilterExpr" PropertyName="Text" />
</FilterParameters>
    . . .
```

Working with the SqlDataSource Control at Runtime

The combination of the `SqlDataSource` control and data-bound controls (such as the new `GridView` and `DetailsView` controls) is designed to remove the need for you to write runtime code to create output in the page. However, there are still occasions where you may want to interact with a data source control directly, for example, to modify the output based on the content of the data rows by reacting to an event that the control (or some other control on the page) raises. The next subsections list the remaining members of the interface for the `SqlDataControl`.

SqlDataSource Control Methods. The `SqlDataSource` control exposes four methods that you can call to perform data access operations through the control. Each method uses the appropriate command specified in the `SelectCommand`, `DeleteCommand`, `InsertCommand`, or `UpdateCommand` property of the control and takes into account any parameters defined for the `SelectParameters`, `DeleteParameters`, `InsertParameters`, or `UpdateParameters` properties, respectively. The four methods are shown in Table 3.5.

SqlDataSource Control Events. The `SqlDataSource` control raises various events as it operates on the data source or when its methods are called. The event handlers that will respond to these events can be specified within the declaration of the `SqlDataSource` control or added to the control at runtime by using the `AddHandler` method in Visual Basic .NET or by appending them to the event property in C# in the usual way. The events are shown in Table 3.6.

TABLE 3.5. The SqlDataSource Control Methods

Method	Description
Select()	Returns all the rows specified by the `SelectCommand` and the values in the `SelectParameters` collection from the data source or from the cached `DataSourceView` that contains the rows. Returns a `System.Data.DataView` instance if the `DataSourceMode` property is set to `DataSet`, or a `DataReader` if the `DataSourceMode` property is set to `DataReader`. The `DataReader` must be explicitly closed after use.
Delete()	Deletes the row(s) specified by the `DeleteCommand` and the values in the `DeleteParameters` collection from the data source. Returns an `Integer` that is the number of rows deleted from the data source.
Insert()	Inserts a new row into the data source using the `InsertCommand` and the values in the `InsertParameters` collection. Returns an `Integer` that is the number of rows inserted into the data source table.
Update()	Updates rows in the data source using the `UpdateCommand` and the values in the `UpdateParameters` collection. Returns an `Integer` that is the number of rows updated in the data source.

TABLE 3.6. The SqlDataSource Control Events

Event	Description
Selecting	Raised before the `Select` method is executed. A `SqlDataSourceCommandEventArgs` instance passed to the event handler exposes a single property: • `Command`: A reference to the provider-specific `Command` instance that will be used to execute the operation. The current operation can be canceled by returning `False` from the event handler.
Selected	Raised after the `Select` method completes. A `SqlDataSourceStatusEventArgs` instance passed to the event handler exposes three properties: • `OutputParameters`: Returns an ordered dictionary of the parameters from the command (usually a stored procedure) where the parameter has a `Direction` property value of `Output` or `InputOutput`. • `ReturnValue`: Returns the value of the parameter from the command (usually a stored procedure) where the parameter has a `Direction` property value of `ReturnValue`. • `RowsAffected`: Returns the number of data rows affected by this operation.

TABLE 3.6. The SqlDataSource Control Events (continued)

Event	Description
`Deleting`	Raised before the `Delete` method is executed. A `SqlDataSourceCommandEventArgs` instance is passed to the event handler (see the `Selecting` event for details).
`Deleted`	Raised after the `Delete` method completes. A `SqlDataSourceStatusEventArgs` instance is passed to the event handler (see the `Selected` event for details).
`Inserting`	Raised before the `Insert` method is executed. A `SqlDataSourceCommandEventArgs` instance is passed to the event handler (see the `Selecting` event for details).
`Inserted`	Raised after the `Insert` method completes. A `SqlDataSourceStatusEventArgs` instance is passed to the event handler (see the `Selected` event for details).
`Updating`	Raised before the `Update` method is executed. A `SqlDataSourceCommandEventArgs` instance is passed to the event handler (see the `Selecting` event for details).
`Updated`	Raised after the `Update` method completes. A `SqlDataSourceStatusEventArgs` instance is passed to the event handler (see the `Selected` event for details).
`DataSourceChanged`	Raised when the contents of the `SqlDataSourceView` for this control change, and causes any data-bound controls to rebind.

SqlDataSource Constructors. You can create an instance of a `SqlData-Source` control and add it to the `Controls` collection of the page by using one of the constructors. You also need to set the property values and then call any methods you need (such as `Select` or `Update`). The constructors are shown in Table 3.7.

TABLE 3.7. The SqlDataSource Constructors

Constructor	Description
`SqlDataSource()`	Creates a new `SqlDataSource` instance with the default values for all the properties.
`SqlDataSource (connect-string, select-command)`	Creates a new `SqlDataSource` instance with the specified values for the `ConnectionString` and `SelectCommand` properties. All other properties are set to the default value. As the `Provider` property defaults to `SqlClient`, this only allows access to SQL Server via TDS unless you set this property to another provider namespace.

The Parameter and ParameterCollection Interfaces A `Parameter` for use with the `SqlDataSource` control can be created by using one of the three constructors. It has a single method (see Table 3.8).

TABLE 3.8. The Parameter Class Interface

Constructors	Description
`Parameter()`	Creates a new `Parameter` instance with the default values for all the properties.
`Parameter(name, value-name)`	Creates a new `Parameter` instance with the specified value for the `Name` property (as a `String`) and the specified *value-name* (as a `String`) for the type-specific property that identifies the source of the value (i.e., `ControlID`, `FormField`, `CookieName`, and so on).
`Parameter(name, type-code, value-name)`	Creates a new `Parameter` instance with the specified value for the `Name` property (as a `String`), the specified data type (as a value from the `TypeCode` enumeration), and the specified *value-name* (as a `String`) for the type-specific property that identifies the source of the value.
Method	
`ToString()`	Returns the value of the `Parameter` as a `String`. If the value is specified as representing a different data type, the `String` representation of the value is returned.

The `ParameterCollection` class holds a collection of `Parameter` instances, as assigned to one of the *xxx*`Parameters` properties of the `Sql-DataSource` control (e.g., the `SelectParameters` or `FilterParameters` property)—see Table 3.9.

TABLE 3.9. The ParameterCollection Class Interface

Constructor	Description
`ParameterCollection()`	Creates a new empty `ParameterCollection`.
Properties	
`Count`	Returns the number of parameters in the collection as an Integer.
`Item(name)`	Returns a reference to a parameter within the collection specified by its name as a `String`.
`Item(index)`	Returns a reference to a parameter within the collection specified by its index as an Integer.
Methods	
`Add(param)`	Adds the specified `Parameter` instance to the collection. Returns the index of the parameter within the collection as an Integer.
`Add(name, value)`	Adds a `Parameter` with the specified (`String`) name and specified (`String`) value to the collection. Returns the index of the parameter within the collection as an Integer.
`Add(name, type, value)`	Adds a `Parameter` with the specified (`String`) name, the specified (`TypeCode`) data type, and the specified (`String`) value to the collection. Returns the index of the parameter within the collection as an Integer.
`GetValues(section)`	Returns an ordered dictionary containing the name/value pairs for the parameters for a specified section of the `SqlDataSource` control, for example, the `SelectParameters` or `UpdateParameters` section.
`Insert(index, param)`	Inserts the specified `Parameter` instance into the collection at the specified zero-based Integer index. No return value.
`Remove(param)`	Removes the specified `Parameter` instance from the collection. No return value.

TABLE 3.9. The ParameterCollection Class Interface (continued)

Constructor	Description
RemoveAt(index)	Removes the parameter at the specified zero-based Integer index position within the collection. No return value.
UpdateValues(section)	Updates the parameters for a specified section of the SqlDataSource control with the values returned by executing the operation for that section. No return value.

Event	
ParametersChanged	Raised when the value of a parameter in the collection changes (e.g., following a Select method call), when a value is changed in code, or when a parameter is added to or removed from the collection.

The SqlDataSourceView Interface

Every data source control exposes the data it selects from its corresponding data store as a DataSourceView. The SqlDataSource control exposes a SqlDataSourceView instance. The data-bound controls in the page then consume the SqlDataSourceView and display the data rows it contains.

Of course, if you are simply declaring the SqlDataSource and GridView controls on your page and not interacting with them in code, you don't need to worry about the SqlDataSourceView itself. However, it is useful when you want to access rows and individual values in, say, an event handler. The SqlDataSourceView has a single constructor (see Table 3.10) and exposes broadly the same set of properties, methods, and events as the SqlDataSource control itself.

TABLE 3.10. The SqlDataSourceView Constructor

Constructor	Description
SqlDataSourceView(owner, name)	Raised when the value of a parameter in the collection changes (e.g., following a Select method call), when a value is changed in code, or when a parameter is added to or removed from the collection.

SqlDataSourceView Properties. The `SqlDataSourceView` exposes the same `SelectCommand`, `SelectParameters`, `UpdateCommand`, `UpdateParameters`, `InsertCommand`, `InsertParameters`, `DeleteCommand`, `DeleteParameters`, `FilterExpression`, and `FilterParameters` properties as the `SqlData Source` control. Additionally there are properties that provide information about the `SqlDataSourceView`'s capabilities, set the sorting order, and expose the name of the `SqlDataSourceView` instance (see Table 3.11).

TABLE 3.11. The SqlDataSourceView Properties

Property	Description
Name	Returns the name of this `SqlDataSourceView` instance as a `String`.
CanDelete	Returns a `Boolean` value that indicates whether rows can be deleted from this `SqlDataSourceView` instance. Returns `False` if the `DeleteCommand` property is empty.
CanInsert	Returns a `Boolean` value that indicates whether rows can be inserted into this `SqlDataSourceView` instance. Returns `False` if the `InsertCommand` property is empty.
CanUpdate	Returns a `Boolean` value that indicates whether rows can be updated within this `SqlDataSourceView` instance. Returns `False` if the `UpdateCommand` property is empty.
CanSort	Returns a `Boolean` value that indicates whether the rows in this `SqlDataSourceView` instance can be sorted. Returns `False` if the `DataSourceMode` property of the owning `SqlDataSource` control property is not set to `DataSet`.
SortExpression	Sets or returns a `String` that defines the sort order for the rows in this `SqlDataSourceView` instance. This is a comma-delimited list of column names, each optionally suffixed with `DESC` for a descending sort. This property applies only when the `DataSourceMode` property of the owning `SqlDataSource` control is set to `DataSet`.

SqlDataSourceView Methods. The `SqlDataSourceView` exposes the same `Delete`, `Insert`, `Select`, and `Update` methods as the `SqlDataSource` control, plus three methods that operate directly on rows within this `SqlDataSourceView` instance (see Table 3.12).

SqlDataSourceView Event. The `SqlDataSourceView` exposes the same `Selected`, `Selecting`, `Updated`, `Updating`, `Deleted`, `Deleting`, `Inserted`, and `Inserting` events as the `SqlDataSource` control, plus one other event (see Table 3.13).

TABLE 3.12. The SqlDataSourceView Methods

Method	Description
Delete(parameters)	Deletes row(s) using the parameters specified as a dictionary of name/value pairs. Returns the number of rows deleted as an Integer.
Insert(values)	Inserts a new row using the values specified as a dictionary of name/value pairs. Returns the number of rows inserted as an Integer.
Update(parameters, values)	Updates row(s) using the parameters specified as a dictionary of name/value pairs, and the values specified as a dictionary of name/value pairs. Returns the number of rows updated as an Integer.

TABLE 3.13. The SqlDataSourceView Event

Event	Description
DataSourceViewChanged	Raised when the contents of the SqlDataSourceView change, which raises the DataSourceChanged event for the owner DataSourceControl and causes any data-bound controls to rebind.

The AccessDataSource Control

The AccessDataSource control inherits from SqlDataSource and carries a few extra interface members that make it easier to work with Access database files. The abridged declaration of the control shown in Listing 3.9 highlights the extra properties of this control.

LISTING 3.9. Declaring an AccessDataSource Control

```
<asp:AccessDataSource runat="server"
  DataSourceMode= "SqlDataSourceMode"
  DataFile="String"
  ShareMode="FileAccess"
  UserID="String"
  Password="String"
  SelectCommand="String"
  InsertCommand="String"
  UpdateCommand="String"
  DeleteCommand="String"
  ...
  </asp:AccessDataSource>
```

TABLE 3.14. The AccessDataSource Control Properties

Property	Description
DataFile	Sets or returns the relative path to the `.mdb` database file as a `String` and is used in place of the `ConnectionString` property. The value is passed to the `Server.MapPath` method to convert it to a full physical path before appending it to the `ConnectionString`.
ShareMode	Sets or returns a value from the `System.IO.FileAccess` enumeration that specifies the way the database file is accessed. Valid values are `Read`, `ReadWrite`, and `Write`. The default is `Read`. The account you specify for access to the file, or the anonymous process account under which ASP.NET is running if you don't specify a `UserID` and `Password`, must have the appropriate permission to access the file in the specified mode.
UserID	Sets or returns the user ID under which the database file is accessed as a `String`. Optional; added to the `ConnectionString` if a value is provided.
Password	Sets or returns the password that will be used to access the database file as a `String`. Optional; added to the `ConnectionString` if a value is provided.

The four attributes highlighted in Listing 3.9 correspond to the four properties used to construct the connection string that the `AccessDataSource` will use to access the database file (see Table 3.14).

The XmlDataSource Control

The data source controls we've looked at so far connect to a relational database and extract data as a series of rows and columns. However, it's becoming increasingly common to encounter data that is persisted or exposed as XML. There are two data source controls in the Technology Preview release of ASP.NET 2.0 that are designed to work with XML data:

- The `XmlDataSource` control, which is designed to expose hierarchical XML and is ideal for binding to controls such as a `TreeView`, which can display nested data
- The `DataSetDataSource` control, which works only with nonhierarchical ("flat") data structures such as a single data table

We look at the `XmlDataSource` control in this subsection and the `DataSetDataSource` control in the following subsection.

The `XmlDataSource` control loads an XML document and exposes the data it contains. If the XML has nested elements, giving a hierarchical structure, the control exposes the data in this way. The result is that data cannot then be bound to controls that accept only flat data structures such as a table or array—for example, the ordinary "list" controls. However, controls such as the `TreeView` expect to receive hierarchical data, and for these the `XmlDataSource` control is the obvious choice.

Declaring an XmlDataSource Control

Since it inherits from the base `DataSource` class, the `XmlDataSource` class inherits all of the same interface members as `SqlDataSource`. This means that attributes you use with the `SqlDataSource` control (such as `Enable Caching` and `CacheDuration`) apply equally to the `XmlDataSource` control. However, the control accesses an XML document (a disk file or a resource that dynamically creates and returns XML), so there are different attributes that specify how to load the XML document, plus a series of nested elements that allow the source data to be declared in-line (see Listing 3.10).

LISTING 3.10. Declaring an XmlDataSource Control

```
<asp:XmlDataSource id="String" runat="server"
  DataFile="String"
  ReadOnly="[True|False]"
  SchemaFile="String"
  TransformFile="String"
  AutoSave="[True|False]"
  XPath="String"
  UniqueID="String"
  EnableCaching="[True|False]"
  CacheDuration="Integer"
  CacheExpirationPolicy="[Absolute|SlidingWindow]"
  OnDataSourceChanged="EventHandler"
  OnTransforming="EventHandler" >

    <Data>
      [...Inline XML Data...]
    </Data>
    <Schema>
      [...Inline XML Schema...]
    </Schema>
    <Transform>
      [...Inline XSL/XSLT Transform...]
    </Transform>

</asp:XmlDataSource>
```

The attributes highlighted in Listing 3.10 are those that have not been discussed previously in this chapter. The others behave exactly as described earlier in this chapter for the `SqlDataSource` control.

The XmlDataSource Control Interface

The attributes and nested elements shown highlighted in Listing 3.10 correspond to the properties in Table 3.15.

TABLE 3.15. The XmlDataSource Control Properties

Property	Description
DataFile	Sets or returns the relative or absolute path to the XML data file to use as input. This property accepts a `String` value.
ReadOnly	Sets or returns a `Boolean` value that indicates whether the XML document will be opened in read-only mode. The default is `True`. When set to `False`, the XML document is opened in read-write mode and the `CanInsert`, `CanUpdate`, and `CanDelete` properties of the `DataSetDataSourceView` will return `True`.
SchemaFile	Sets or returns the relative or absolute path to a schema that defines the structure of the XML. This property accepts a `String` value.
TransformFile	Sets or returns the relative or absolute path to an XSL or XSLT document that will be used to transform the XML data before it is exposed by the control. This property accepts a `String` value.
AutoSave	Sets or returns a `Boolean` value that indicates whether changes to the data will be saved back to the XML disk file automatically, as soon as a change is made. The default is `True`. When set to `False`, the `Save` method must be called to update the XML disk file. This can be used to reduce disk accesses.
XPath	Sets or returns a `String` containing an XPath statement that filters or selects elements from the source document. Has the same kind of effect as applying a `FilterExpression` with the `SqlDataSource` control.
UniqueID	Returns a `String` value that acts as a unique identifier for the document.

TABLE 3.15. The XmlDataSource Control Properties (continued)

Property	Description
Data	Sets or returns the XML content that will be used as the source data, as a `String`. This property can be set declaratively using the `Data` child element within the main `XmlDataSource` element. The `DataFile` property must be empty in this case.
Schema	Sets or returns the schema content that defines the data structure, as a `String`. This property can be set declaratively using the `Schema` child element within the main `XmlDataSource` element. The `SchemaFile` property must be empty in this case.
Transform	Sets or returns the XSL or XSLT document that will be used to transform the data before it is exposed by the control, as a `String`. This property can be set declaratively using the `Transform` child element within the main `XmlDataSource` element. The `TransformFile` property must be empty in this case.
TransformArgumentList	Gives a reference to an `XsltArgumentList` instance containing the arguments that will be used in the transformation process when using the `TransformFile` or `Transform` properties to specify an XSLT stylesheet. This property should be set in the `OnTransforming` event to ensure that the arguments are available when the transformation is applied.

The `XmlDataSource` control exposes two methods you can use to interact with the control at runtime (see Table 3.16).

Finally, there are two events you can handle to interact with the process (see Table 3.17 on the next page).

TABLE 3.16. The XmlDataSource Control Methods

Method	Description
GetXmlDataDocument()	Returns a reference to an `XmlDataDocument` instance that contains the XML representation of the source data from the control.
Save()	Persists the current values in the control to the XML disk file.

TABLE 3.17. The XmlDataSource Control Events

Event	Description
OnTransforming	Raised before the control applies any XSL or XSLT stylesheet to the XML source data. Useful if you need to provide an XsltArgumentList reference to the control before the data is bound to other controls in the page.
OnDataSourceChanged	Raised when the data source for the control changes, allowing data-bound controls to rebind to the data source control.

The DataSetDataSource Control

The second data source control designed to handle XML data is the DataSetDataSource control. It is very similar in both declaration and interface to the XmlDataSource. Two properties are omitted, and there is one extra method.

One interesting possibility for manipulating XML data is to store it in and expose it through a DataSet. And, more than that, the nature of the DataSet allows it to move between a relational and an XML-based view of that data. In effect, the DataSetDataSource control provides an interface to an instance of a DataSet and implements the same processes as other data source controls such as the SqlDataSource to support automated server-side data binding—as well as features that allow the XML source data to be updated. The DataSetDataSource also allows runtime code to access the data directly as a DataSet or as an XmlDataDocument instance, giving almost ultimate flexibility in working with the data.

Declaring a DataSetDataSource Control

The declaration of a DataSetDataSource control is almost identical to the XmlDataSource control, but without the XPath and UniqueID attributes. Again, optional nested elements can be used to declare the data, schema, and XSL/XSLT stylesheet in-line if required (see Listing 3.11).

LISTING 3.11. Declaring a DataSetDataSource Control

```
<asp:DataSetDataSource id="String" runat="server"
  DataFile="String"
  ReadOnly="[True|False]"
  SchemaFile="String"
  TransformFile="String"
  AutoSave="[True|False]"
```

```
EnableCaching="[True|False]"
CacheDuration="Integer"
CacheExpirationPolicy="[Absolute|SlidingWindow]"
OnDataSourceChanged="EventHandler"
OnTransforming="EventHandler" >

    <Data>
      [...Inline XML Data...]
    </Data>
    <Schema>
      [...Inline XML Schema...]
    </Schema>
    <Transform>
      [...Inline XSL/XSLT Transform...]
    </Transform>

</asp:DataSetDataSource>
```

The DataSetDataSource Control Interface

As mentioned, the `DataSetDataSource` does not have the `UniqueID` and `XPath` properties, but otherwise the list of properties is identical to the `XmlDataSource` control shown earlier in this chapter. There is one extra method available on the `DataSetDataSource` that is not implemented by the `XmlDataSource` control. It can be used to directly access and manipulate the `DataSet` that is holding the source data (see Table 3.18).

TABLE 3.18. The DataSetDataSource Control Method

Method	Description
GetDataSet()	Returns a reference to the `DataSet` that is the source of the data from the control.

The ObjectDataSource Control

All of the data sources covered so far encourage a "two-tier architecture" approach to building applications. They directly access the data store (the data layer), be it a relational database or an XML document. However, the `ObjectDataSource` control allows developers to work with three-tier or n-tier architectures by exposing data access layer and/or custom business objects in a way suited to declarative server-side data binding. Like the other data source controls, simply declaring the `ObjectDataSource` control on the page and linking it to a suitable data-bound control can provide "no-code" data binding—and even editing capabilities.

The only limitations are that the objects the ObjectDataSource control will access must be stateless, must expose a default constructor, and must have methods that can be directly and individually mapped to the Select, Update, Insert, and Delete actions of the control (although a subset of these can be supported if not all types of update actions are required, e.g., an application may be designed to support inserting of objects but not updates to them).

Data access to objects revolves around methods that the objects expose, so ordinary SQL statements cannot be used to select or update them. Instead, the objects themselves take care of extracting values from their own data store, exposing the values, and persisting changes where appropriate. This means that a data source control that accesses objects has to provide an interface that can be used to define the processes required to extract and update data. It does this by referencing the methods within the objects that perform these processes.

Declaring an ObjectDataSource Control

The ObjectDataSource control exposes many of the same properties as the SqlDataSource control we examined earlier in this chapter. The main difference is that the operations on the data must be specified as methods of the objects referenced by the control. The differences in the declaration of the control compared to a SqlDataSource control are highlighted in Listing 3.12.

LISTING 3.12. Declaring an ObjectDataSource Control

```
<asp:ObjectDataSource id="String" runat="server"
  ClassName="String"
  SelectMethod="String"
  UpdateMethod="String"
  InsertMethod="String"
  DeleteMethod="String"
  FilterExpression="String"
  EnableCaching="[True|False]"
  CacheDuration="Integer"
  CacheExpirationPolicy="[Absolute|SlidingWindow]"
  SqlCacheDependency="String"
  OnSelecting="ObjectDataSourceMethodEventHandler"
  OnSelected="ObjectDataSourceMethodExecutedEventHandler"
  OnUpdating="ObjectDataSourceMethodEventHandler"
  OnUpdated="ObjectDataSourceMethodExecutedEventHandler"
  OnInserting="ObjectDataSourceMethodEventHandler"
  OnInserted="ObjectDataSourceMethodExecutedEventHandler"
  OnDeleting="ObjectDataSourceMethodEventHandler"
  OnDeleted="ObjectDataSourceMethodExecutedEventHandler"
  OnObjectCreated="ObjectDataSourceObjectEventHandler"
  OnObjectDisposing="ObjectDataSourceObjectEventHandler" >
```

```
    <SelectParameters>
        [<System.Web.UI.WebControls.Parameter ...>]
    </SelectParameters>
    <UpdateParameters>
        [<System.Web.UI.WebControls.Parameter ...>]
    </UpdateParameters>
    <DeleteParameters>
        [<System.Web.UI.WebControls.Parameter ...>]
    </DeleteParameters>
    <InsertParameters>
        [<System.Web.UI.WebControls.Parameter ...>]
    </InsertParameters>
    <FilterParameters>
        [<System.Web.UI.WebControls.Parameter ...>]
    </FilterParameters>
</asp:ObjectDataSource>
```

The ObjectDataSource Control Interface

The highlighted sections of Listing 3.12 of the `ObjectDataSource` control show the attributes, and hence the properties, that are different from the `SqlDataSource` control. These are listed in Table 3.19.

TABLE 3.19. The ObjectDataSource Control Properties

Property	Description
ClassName	A String that contains the type name of the object to create. This can be a partially qualified name such as MyClass or a fully qualified name such as MyNamespace.MyClass.
SelectMethod	The method of the object to invoke for a SELECT operation. Any parameters required can be defined as the SelectParameters property or in the nested SelectParameters element of the control declaration.
UpdateMethod	The method of the object to invoke for an UPDATE operation. Any parameters required can be defined as the UpdateParameters property or in the nested UpdateParameters element of the control declaration.
InsertMethod	The method of the object to invoke for an INSERT operation. Any parameters required can be defined as the InsertParameters property or in the nested InsertParameters element of the control declaration.
DeleteMethod	The method of the object to invoke for a DELETE operation. Any parameters required can be defined as the DeleteParameters property or in the nested DeleteParameters element of the control declaration.

TABLE 3.20. The ObjectDataSource Control Events

Event	Description
ObjectCreated	Raised immediately after the object specified by ClassName has been created. Can be used to set properties on the object instance or to call methods to prepare it for use if required.
ObjectDisposing	Raised just before the object specified by ClassName is disposed. Can be used to clean up before the object is destroyed or to call other methods on the object if required.

The ObjectDataSource exposes the same events as the SqlDataSource, though these accept different types of "argument" classes. The events that occur before an operation on the data (i.e., Selecting, Inserting) pass an instance of the ObjectDataSourceMethodEventArgs class to the event handler. The events that occur after an operation on the data (i.e., Selected, Inserted) pass an instance of the ObjectDataSourceMethodExecuted EventHandler class to the event handler. Both of these argument classes expose a reference to the method that was called as a MethodInfo instance.

There are also two extra events for the ObjectDataSource, which are invoked after an instance of the class that the data source will use is created and before it is disposed, respectively. Both events pass an ObjectDataSourceEventArgs instance as an argument to the event handler, which exposes the ObjectInstance property containing a reference to the object instance just created or disposed (see Table 3.20).

Possible Forthcoming Data Source Controls

More data source controls are planned for future releases of ASP.NET, and the following may well find their way into the final release version:

- A WebServiceDataSource control to allow you to work with data exposed by Web Services
- An ExcelDataSource control to allow access to Excel worksheet files
- An OracleDataSource control to allow manipulation of data in an Oracle database without using OLE-DB or ODBC directly
- An IndexServiceDataSource control that will allow the Indexing Service catalog to be queried
- A SharePointDataSource control that will allow interaction with the database of resources maintained in Microsoft SharePoint

SUMMARY

This is the first of two related chapters that look at how ASP.NET 2.0 changes the way data can be accessed, displayed, and updated—without requiring any code to be written (or at least considerably reducing the code requirements) in almost all cases. The combination of a data source control and server-side data binding, especially when matched up with a `GridView` or `DetailsView` control, provides a powerful new technique for working with data in your Web pages and Web applications.

In this chapter we started off with a brief look at what the new controls can achieve. The "no-code" examples we used show just how powerful the new approach is and how quickly and easily you can build pages that are attractive and highly interactive.

Then we moved on to look in more depth at the data source controls that power the process. The most commonly used is likely to be the `SqlDataSource` control, and we concentrated mainly on this in the chapter and the examples. However, we also looked at the other data source controls that are included in the Technology Preview release and those that may appear as the product moves toward final release.

In the next chapter we continue on the same theme and complete the discussion of accessing, displaying, and manipulating data through the new controls. In particular, we look in depth at the new `GridView` and `DetailsView` controls and the new simplified syntax for data binding.

4

The GridView and DetailsView Controls

THIS IS THE SECOND in a two-chapter look at the new approach to accessing, displaying, and manipulating data introduced with ASP.NET 2.0. This new approach is based around the concept of data source controls and the new `GridView` and `DetailsView` bound controls. The previous chapter gave a brief overview of the process, demonstrated the ease with which it can be accomplished, and examined the data source controls in depth.

In this chapter we'll build on what you've seen so far by looking in more detail at the two new controls for displaying rowset data—the `Grid View` and `DetailsView` controls. These powerful yet easy-to-use controls include a wide range of features that make building even the most complex types of data-bound page a lot easier than it was in ASP.NET 1.x.

The topics we'll be covering include the following:

- The new `GridView` control for displaying rowset data as a table
- The new `DetailsView` control for displaying rowset data as individual pages
- The simplified syntax for data binding expressions and the new XML binding syntax
- How to build data-bound pages with Microsoft Visual Studio .NET "Whidbey"

We start with a detailed look at the `GridView` control. You saw some examples of this control at the start of Chapter 3, but here you'll see how flexible it is and how easily it can be declared and used in even quite complex scenarios.

The GridView Control

One of the most useful controls introduced with ASP.NET 1.0 is the `Data Grid`. This control makes it easy to display rowsets of data, provides plenty of opportunities for formatting the output, and even supports in-line editing of the data. However, to use a `DataGrid` you still have to write code that generates the rowset and then bind it to the `DataGrid` control at runtime.

As you saw in Chapter 3, the new data source controls in ASP.NET 2.0 remove the need to write data access code and can also expose various kinds of data as rowsets suitable for data binding to any of the ASP.NET server controls. However, to take maximum advantage of these data source controls, Microsoft added a new grid control in version 2.0. The `GridView` control enables data to be displayed, sorted, and edited without having to write any code at all. It can even provide a paging facility and—when combined with the `DetailsView` control that you'll read more about later in this chapter—enables you to create pages that allow new data rows to be inserted.

An Overview of the GridView Control

In basic terms, the `GridView` is similar to the version 1.0 `DataGrid` (which is, of course, still provided within the Framework). It exposes many of the same features for formatting the data content using style attributes and templates. However, it also adds a few extra features, such as support for multiple primary keys, extra opportunities for customizing the appearance, and new column types and templating options. There is also a new model for handling or canceling events. The aims of the `GridView` and `DetailsView` control combination are the following:

- To support the new data source controls by exposing a binding model that allows developers to display data without the need to write any code
- To provide features such as sorting, paging, editing, and updating of the data without requiring any code to be written
- To support the adaptive page rendering approach used in other controls in version 2.0, providing output that is compatible with mobile devices and other user agents

- To add features requested by users of the version 1.0 `DataGrid` control, such as multiple-field primary keys, hyperlink columns that have more than one data field, columns with checkboxes, and columns with standard buttons
- To provide better templating options to support custom paging and better support for null values

While the `GridView` control does have an object model similar to that of the `DataGrid`, it is not 100% backward compatible. You can't just switch from a `DataGrid` to a `GridView` in your pages without some reworking of the attributes and code. In general, you may find that it's better to use the `GridView` when you build new pages that take advantage of its capabilities, rather than trying to retrofit it into existing pages.

Also note that the `GridView` does not support automatic insert operations for new rows. The associated `DetailsView` control is used to provide this feature, and—in some cases—you have to write at least a few lines of code to achieve this.

Declaring a GridView Control

The `GridView` is obviously quite a complex control and has a correspondingly large number of properties and events. Listing 4.1 shows the general declaration of a `GridView` control and the types of values used for the attributes. The tables in the following subsections list and describe all of the properties, except for the generic styling properties (which are familiar from the `DataGrid` control).

LISTING 4.1. The General Declaration of a GridView Control

```
<asp:GridView id="String" runat="server"
  DataSourceID="String"
  DataKeyNames="[column-name[,column-name]]"
  AutoGenerateColumns="[True|False]"
  RowStyle-[PropertyName]="[value]"
  AlternatingRowStyle-[PropertyName]="[value]"
  AllowSorting="[True|False]"
  AllowPaging="[True|False]"
  PageSize="Integer"
  PageIndex="Integer"
  PagerStyle-[PropertyName]="[value]"
  AutoGenerateSelectButton="[True|False]"
  SelectedIndex="Integer"
  SelectedRowStyle-[PropertyName]="[value]"
  AutoGenerateDeleteButton="[True|False]"
  AutoGenerateEditButton="[True|False]"
  EditIndex="Integer"
```

continues

```
EditRowStyle-[PropertyName]="[value]"
ShowHeader="[True|False]"
HeaderStyle-[PropertyName]="[value]"
ShowFooter="[True|False]"
FooterStyle-[PropertyName]="[value]"
SummaryViewColumn="String"
SummaryTitleStyle-[PropertyName]="[value]"
DetailNextRowText="String"
DetailPreviousRowText="String"
DetailSummaryText="String"
DetailLinkStyle-[PropertyName]="[value]"
DetailTitleStyle-[PropertyName]="[value]"
NullText="String"
BackImageUrl="String"
CellPadding="Integer"
CellSpacing="Integer"
Enabled="[True|False]"
GridLines="[Both|Horizontal|Vertical|None]"
HorizontalAlign="[Center|Justify|Left|Right|NotSet]"
OnRowDeleting="GridViewDeleteEventHandler"
OnRowDeleted="GridViewStatusEventHandler "
OnRowUpdating="GridViewUpdateEventHandler"
OnRowUpdated="GridViewStatusEventHandler"
OnRowEditing="GridViewEditEventHandler"
OnRowCancellingEdit="GridViewCancelEditEventHandler"
OnPageIndexChanging="GridViewPageEventHandler"
OnPageIndexChanged="EventHandler"
OnSelectedIndexChanging="GridViewSelectEventHandler"
OnSelectedIndexChanged="EventHandler"
OnSort="GridViewSortEventHandler"
OnRowCommand="GridViewCommandEventHandler"
OnRowCreated ="GridViewRowEventHandler"
OnRowDataBound="GridViewRowEventHandler" >

  <[...TableItemStyle...] />

  <[...Style...] />

  <PagerStyle />

  <PagerSettings />

  <ColumnFields>
    <...[column-definition]... />
  </ColumnFields>

</asp:GridView>
```

As with the DataGrid control, the GridView contains nested elements that further define the appearance and behavior of the control. We'll examine these later.

The Properties and Attributes of the GridView Control

The attributes shown in Listing 4.1 are documented in Tables 4.1, 4.2, and 4.3. These attributes set the corresponding properties of the control, though (as with other server controls) you can read and set these properties at runtime as well. Table 4.1 lists the properties that correspond to attributes in the same order as in the control declaration shown in Listing 4.1. (Note that style-related properties and attributes are not included in this table.)

The attributes shown in Listing 4.1 that do not appear in Table 4.1, such as RowStyle-[*PropertyName*] and PagerStyle-[*PropertyName*], are used to specify the style of various sections of the output generated by the GridView. As with other Web Forms controls, the attribute sets a property of the object that generates that specific section of the output. For example, the following code sets the foreground color of the rows in the output to red:

```
RowStyle-ForeColor="Red"
```

TABLE 4.1. The Properties and Attributes of the GridView Control

Property/Attribute	Description
DataSourceID	Sets or returns a String value that is the id of the data source control that supplies the data for the GridView and through which any updates will be processed.
DataKeyNames	Sets or returns a String Array that specifies the primary key fields/columns for the rows. It is set in a control declaration attribute as a comma-delimited list. These keys are used to uniquely identify each row when performing updates or deletes in the source data. By default, the specified columns are displayed as read-only when in edit mode.
AutoGenerateColumns	Sets or returns a Boolean value that specifies whether the control should create columns based on the structure of the source rows (True, the default) or use the column definitions declared in a <ColumnFields> element (False).
AllowSorting	Sets or returns a Boolean value that indicates whether the grid will support sorting and display the column headings as hyperlinks. The default is False. If the CanSort property of the data source is True, the sorting process is handled automatically.
AllowPaging	Sets or returns a Boolean value that indicates whether the grid will support paging and display controls for navigating from one page to another. The default is False. A SqlDataSource must have its DataSource Mode property set to DataSet for this to work.

continues

TABLE 4.1. The Properties and Attributes of the GridView Control (continued)

Property/Attribute	Description
AllowPaging	Sets or returns a `Boolean` value that indicates whether the grid will support paging and display controls for navigating from one page to another. The default is `False`. A `SqlDataSource` must have its `DataSourceMode` property set to `DataSet` for this to work.
PageSize	Sets or returns an `Integer` value that indicates the number of rows to be displayed on each page when paging is enabled.
PageIndex	Sets the current page number for the grid to display, or returns the current page number as an `Integer` value, when paging is enabled for the grid. This is the ordinal index of the page, starting from `0`.
AutoGenerateSelectButton	Sets or returns a `Boolean` value that indicates whether a column containing a **Select** button will appear in the output.
SelectedIndex	Sets or returns the index of the row that will be displayed in selected mode as an `Integer` value.
AutoGenerateDeleteButton	Sets or returns a `Boolean` value that indicates whether a column containing a **Delete** button will appear in the output.
AutoGenerateEditButton	Sets or returns a `Boolean` value that indicates whether a column containing an **Edit** button will appear in the output.
EditIndex	Sets or returns the index of the row that will be displayed in edit mode as an `Integer` value.
ShowHeader	Sets or returns a `Boolean` value that indicates whether a header row will be included in the output from the control.
ShowFooter	Sets or returns a `Boolean` value that indicates whether a footer row will be included in the output from the control.
SummaryViewColumn	Sets or returns a `String` value that indicates the name of the column that will be shown when the control renders output to a mobile device. By default this is the first column. See Chapter 3 for more details of how tables are displayed on mobile devices.
DetailNextRowText	Sets or returns a `String` value that is the text to display for the link to the next column when the control renders output to a mobile device. The default is **Next Row**.

TABLE 4.1. The Properties and Attributes of the GridView Control (continued)

Property/Attribute	Description
DetailPreviousRowText	Sets or returns a String value that is the text to display for the link to the previous column when the control renders output to a mobile device. The default is **Previous Row**.
DetailSummaryText	Sets or returns a String value that is the text to display for the link from details view back to summary view when the control renders output to a mobile device. The default is **Summary View**.
NullText	Sets or returns a String value that will appear in the output of the control where a null value occurs in the source data.

The GridView also supports theming, so it accepts attributes and exposes properties such as SkinID and EnableTheming that you can use to specify the theme for the control. See Chapter 7 for more details of the themes feature in ASP.NET 2.0.

Declarative and Dynamic Version 1.x–Style Data Source Assignment

Two properties of the GridView control can be used to specify data binding to a rowset that you generate in code, in the same way that you had to do with the DataGrid and other list controls in ASP.NET 1.x (see Table 4.2). You won't use these properties if you take advantage of the no-code approach to displaying data—you'll just use the DataSourceID instead.

Read-Only Properties. The GridView exposes a series of properties that are read-only at runtime and can be used to get information about the control or to get a reference to the various objects that together generate the control output (see Table 4.3). Again, if you use the no-code approach you won't need to access these properties.

TABLE 4.2. Data Binding Properties and Attributes of the GridView Control

Property/Attribute	Description
DataSource	Sets or returns a reference to an Object that exposes the data rows or collection members that the GridView control will display.
DataMember	Sets or returns a String value that indicates the specific item within an IListSource instance that will be used as the data source for the control. For example, when the DataSource is a DataSet (which could contain more than one table), this property is the table name.

TABLE 4.3. The Read-Only Properties of the GridView Control

Property/Attribute	Description
BindingContainer	Returns a reference to the `Control` instance that represents the control performing the binding of the values.
DataKeys	Returns a `DataKeyArray`, which is a collection of `DataKey` instances—one for each row in the `GridView`. Each `DataKey` instance contains a name/value pair for each key listed in the `DataKeyNames` property and the corresponding value for the current row. In other words, it exposes the primary key value(s) for each row in the grid.
SelectedDataKey	Returns a `DataKey` instance that exposes the primary key values for the row that is in selected mode.
SelectedValue	Returns an `Object` containing the current value of the `DataKey` for the current row.
SortExpression	Returns a `String` value that contains the current sort expression for the control.
SortDirection	Returns a value from the `SortDirection` enumeration that indicates the direction of the current sort expression. Valid values are `Ascending` or `Descending`.
PageCount	Returns an `Integer` value that indicates the number of pages available when paging is enabled, based on the number of rows in the data source and the setting of the `PageSize` property.
ColumnFields	Returns a `DataControlFieldCollection` that represents all of the columns (all the *xxx*`Fields`) in the grid control.
Rows	Returns a `GridViewRowCollection` that represents all of the data-bound rows in the grid control, excluding any header, footer, or pager rows and excluding the null row if the data source returns no rows.
SelectedRow	Returns a reference to the `GridViewRow` instance that represents the row in the grid control output that is currently in selected mode.
HeaderRow	Returns a reference to the `GridViewRow` instance that represents the header row of the grid control output.
FooterRow	Returns a reference to the `GridViewRow` instance that represents the footer row of the grid control output.
TopPagerRow	Returns a reference to the `GridViewRow` instance that represents the row at the top of the grid control output that contains the pager controls.

TABLE 4.3. The Read-Only Properties of the GridView Control (continued)

Property/Attribute	Description
BottomPagerRow	Returns a reference to the GridViewRow instance that represents the row at the bottom of the grid control output that contains the pager controls.
PagerSettings	Returns a reference to the PagerSettings instance that represents the appearance of the pager rows. The PagerSettings options are described later in this chapter.

The DataBind Method of the GridView Control

When a data source control and a GridView are combined (as shown in Chapter 3), there is no need to write code to initiate data binding, as you would with other data-bound controls such as the DataGrid. The Data Bind method of the GridView is called automatically. However, this method is also declared as Public and so is exposed for use in your own code if required. If you bind a GridView to a source of data other than a data source control, using the DataSource and DataMember properties, you must call the DataBind method yourself.

The Events of the GridView Control

The GridView control raises a series of events as it binds to a data source, generates the output, and in response to user interaction (see Table 4.4). You can handle these events to provide custom output, interact with the output process, and execute code in response to user actions.

Handling a GridView Event

The example of editing rows shown at the start of Chapter 3 (Listing 3.4) contains a Delete link for each row displayed in the GridView control. However, in the sample Northwind database that the page uses, rows cannot be deleted from the Shippers table because there are related child rows in other tables. As an example of handling the events raised by the GridView control, the page prevents these existing rows from being deleted by checking the value of the primary key.

The declaration of the GridView includes the OnRowDeleting attribute, which specifies that an event handler named CheckDelete will be executed when the RowDeleting event is raised (see Listing 4.2). This occurs just before the GridView control instructs the data source control to delete the row. There is also a Label control on that page where the event handler will display any error message.

TABLE 4.4. The Data Binding Events of the GridView Control

Event	Description
PageIndexChanging	Raised when a pager navigation control is activated, before the grid changes to the new page. Passes a GridView PageEventArgs instance to the event handler, which exposes the following properties: • Cancel: A Boolean property that can be set to True to prevent the page changing. • NewPageIndex: An Integer that is the ordinal index of the page that will be shown next.
PageIndexChanged	Raised when a pager navigation control is activated, after the grid has displayed the new page. Passes a standard EventArgs instance to the event handler.
RowCancellingEdit	Raised when the Cancel command is activated for a row that is in edit mode. Passes a GridViewCancelEditEventArgs instance to the event handler, which exposes the following properties: • Cancel: A Boolean property that can be set to True to prevent the edit operation from being canceled. • RowIndex: An Integer value indicating the index of the row within the data source.
RowCommand	Raised when a control in the rows of the grid causes a postback. This command may be one of the predefined buttons such as **Edit, Cancel, Delete,** or **Update,** or it may be a custom command. Passes a GridViewCommandEventArgs instance to the event handler, which exposes the following properties: • CommandArgument: The value of the Command Argument property of the button that raised the event. • CommandName: The value of the CommandName property of the button that raised the event. • CommandSource: A reference to the button that raised the event.
RowCreated	Raised when a new row is created in the source rowset for the grid. Passes a GridViewRowEventArgs instance to the event handler, which exposes the Row property that returns a reference to the new row.
RowDataBound	Raised for each row in the grid after it has been bound to its data source row, allowing the output for the row to be modified. Passes a GridViewRowEventArgs instance to the event handler, which exposes the Row property that returns a reference to the row.
RowDeleting	Raised before the data source control deletes a row in the data source. Passes a GridViewDeleteEventArgs instance to the event handler, which exposes the following properties:

TABLE 4.4. The Data Binding Events of the GridView Control (continued)

Event	Description
	• `Cancel`: A `Boolean` property that can be set to `True` to cancel the delete operation. • `Keys`: An `IOrderedDictionary` instance containing the primary key values for the row. • `RowIndex`: An `Integer` value indicating the index of the row within the data source rowset. • `Values`: An `IOrderedDictionary` instance containing the values currently in the row. These values will not be passed to the `DataSource` control unless you move them into the `Keys` `IOrderedDictionary`.
`RowDeleted`	Raised after the data source control has deleted a row from the data source. Passes a `GridViewStatusEventArgs` instance to the event handler, which exposes the `AffectedRows` property, indicating the number of rows affected by the delete operation.
`RowEditing`	Raised when an `Edit` command in the grid is activated, before a row changes into edit mode. Passes a `GridViewEditEventArgs` instance to the event handler, which exposes the following properties: • `Cancel`: A `Boolean` property that can be set to `True` to prevent the row from entering edit mode. • `NewEditIndex`: An `Integer` you can set to the index of the row that will be placed in edit mode, or –1 if no row will be in edit mode.
`RowUpdating`	Raised before the data source control updates a row in the data source. Passes a `GridViewUpdateEventArgs` instance to the event handler, which exposes the following properties: • `Cancel`: A `Boolean` property that can be set to `True` to cancel the update operation. • `CommandArgument`: The value of the `Command` `Argument` property of the button that raised the event. • `Keys`: An `IOrderedDictionary` containing the primary key values for the row. • `NewValues`: An `IOrderedDictionary` containing the values that will be placed into the row. • `OldValues`: An `IOrderedDictionary` containing the values currently in the row. These values will not be passed to the `DataSource` control unless you move them into the `Keys` `IOrderedDictionary`.
`RowUpdated`	Raised after the data source control has updated a row in the data source. Passes a `GridViewStatusEventArgs` instance to the event handler, which exposes the `AffectedRows` property, indicating the number of rows affected by the update command.

continues

TABLE 4.4. The Data Binding Events of the GridView Control (continued)

Event	Description
SelectedIndexChanging	Raised when a Select command in the grid is activated, before the row is placed into selected mode. Passes a GridViewSelectEventArgs instance to the event handler, which exposes the following properties: • Cancel: A Boolean property that can be set to True to prevent the row from being placed into selected mode. • NewSelectedIndex: An Integer you can set to the index of the row that will be placed in selected mode, or −1 if no row will be in selected mode.
SelectedIndexChanged	Raised after a row has been placed into selected mode. Passes a standard EventArgs instance to the event handler.
Sorting	Raised when a column heading is activated to sort the rows in the grid. Passes a GridViewSortEventArgs instance to the event handler, which exposes the following properties: • Cancel: A Boolean property that can be set to True to prevent the sort. • SortExpression: A String containing the sort expression that will be applied.
Sorted	Raised after the sorting process has completed. Passes a standard EventArgs instance to the event handler.

LISTING 4.2. Using the RowDeleting Event

```
<asp:GridView id="grid1" DataSourceID="ds1" runat="server"
    DataKeyNames="ShipperID"
    AutoGenerateEditButton="True"
    AutoGenerateDeleteButton="True"
    OnRowDeleting="CheckDelete" />

<asp:Label id="lblError" EnableviewState="False" runat="server" />
```

The event handler is shown in Listing 4.3. It simply extracts the value of the primary key from the Keys array passed to the event handler within the GridViewDeleteEventArgs instance—there is only one column in the primary key, so the code just accesses Keys(0). Then, if this key value is less than 4 (in other words, this is one of the existing rows in the table), it sets the Cancel property to True to prevent the GridView from continuing with the delete operation, and it displays a message in the Label control.

LISTING 4.3. The Event Handler for the RowDeleting Event

```
<script runat="server">
Sub CheckDelete(oSender As Object, oArgs As GridViewDeleteEventArgs)
  Dim iKey As Integer = oArgs.Keys(0)
  If iKey < 4 Then
    oArgs.Cancel = True
    lblError.Text = "Cannot delete the original rows from the table"
  End If
End Sub
</script>
```

Figure 4.1 shows the result. An attempt to delete the first row causes the event handler to display the error message below the grid. If you want to try deleting a row, use Enterprise Manager or type a SQL statement into Query Analyzer to insert a new row into the Shippers table, then run the page to delete the new row.

The Nested TableItemStyle Elements

You can optionally include, within the declaration of a GridView control, nested elements that define the style for various sections of the output generated as HTML table rows. The general declaration of these elements is shown in Listing 4.4.

LISTING 4.4. The Nested TableItemStyle Elements

```
<[TableItemStyle]
  BackColor="Color"
  BorderColor="Color"
  BorderStyle="[Solid|Dashed|Dotted|Double|Groove|
               Ridge|Inset|Outset|None|NotSet]"
  BorderWidth="Unit"
```
continues

FIGURE 4.1. Handling the RowDeleting event for a GridView control

```
CssClass="String"
Font-[Bold|Italic|Name|Names|Overline|Size|
                    Strikeout|Underline]="[value]"
ForeColor="Color"
Height="Unit"
Width="Unit"
HorizontalAlign="[Center|Justify|Left|Right|NotSet]"
VerticalAlign="[Bottom|Middle|Top|NotSet]"
Wrap="[True|False]" />
```

The seven types of elements you can use (replacing `[TableItemStyle]` in the preceding declaration are shown in Table 4.5.

The Nested Style Elements

Another type of nested element that you can optionally include within the declaration of a `GridView` control is one that defines the style for the text and links that appear only when the grid is rendered on a small-screen or mobile device, where the output is displayed as separate summary and details views. The general declaration of these elements is shown in Listing 4.5.

LISTING 4.5. The Nested Style Elements

```
<[TextStyle]
  BackColor="Color"
  BorderColor="Color"
```

TABLE 4.5. The TableItemStyle Element Types

TableItemStyle	Description
RowStyle	Sets the style and appearance for the data-bound rows within the grid.
AlternatingRowStyle	Sets the style and appearance for alternate data-bound rows within the grid.
SelectedRowStyle	Sets the style and appearance for the selected row within the grid.
EditRowStyle	Sets the style and appearance for the row that is in edit mode within the grid.
NullRowStyle	Sets the style and appearance for data-bound rows that contain `null` values.
HeaderStyle	Sets the style and appearance for the header row of the grid.
FooterStyle	Sets the style and appearance for the footer row of the grid.

TABLE 4.6. The Style Element Types

TextStyle	Description
SummaryTitleStyle	Sets the style and appearance of the title text displayed when the grid is displaying the data in summary view.
DetailTitleStyle	Sets the style and appearance of the title text displayed when the grid is displaying one of the rows in details view.
DetailLinkStyle	Sets the style and appearance of the links included in each row when the grid is displaying the data in summary view.

```
BorderStyle="[Solid|Dashed|Dotted|Double|Groove|
              Ridge|Inset|Outset|None|NotSet]"
BorderWidth="Unit"
CssClass="String"
Font-[Bold|Italic|Name|Names|Overline|Size|
               Strikeout|Underline]="[value]"
ForeColor="Color"
Height="Unit"
Width="Unit" />
```

The three types of elements you can use (replacing [TextStyle] in the declaration above) are shown in Table 4.6.

How the GridView Appears on Small-Screen and Mobile Devices. As you will surmise from the previous subsections, the GridView control automatically changes the way it renders the data when viewed on a small-screen or mobile device. When the page first loads, only the column specified by name as the SummaryViewColumn property is displayed. Each value in this single column is a link that changes the display to show all the column values for just that row (see Figure 4.2). These are the summary view and details view mentioned in the property descriptions in this chapter and demonstrated at the start of Chapter 3.

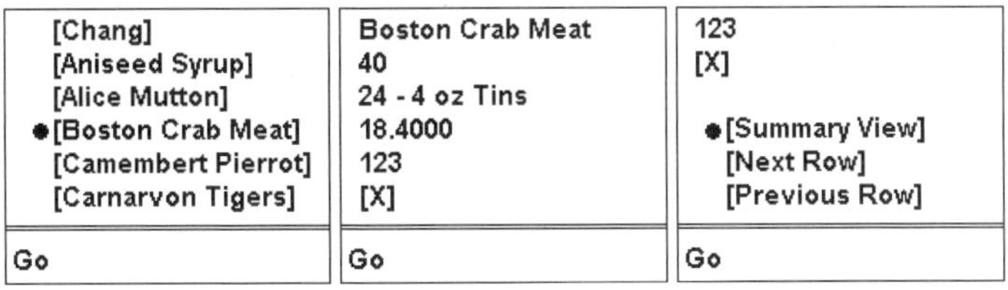

[Chang] [Aniseed Syrup] [Alice Mutton] ●[Boston Crab Meat] [Camembert Pierrot] [Carnarvon Tigers]	Boston Crab Meat 40 24 - 4 oz Tins 18.4000 123 [X]	123 [X] ●[Summary View] [Next Row] [Previous Row]
Go	Go	Go

FIGURE 4.2. The GridView control on small-screen devices

The Nested PagerStyle and PagerSettings Elements

If you specify that the `GridView` will support paging by including the `AllowPaging="True"` attribute in the declaration, you can optionally specify in more detail how the section of the output that includes the page navigation controls will appear. You include a nested `PagerStyle` element, and/or a nested `PagerSettings` element, within the declaration of the `GridView` control.

The `PagerStyle` element is identical to the `TableItemStyle` elements shown earlier, with one extra attribute supported that indicates where row(s) containing the pager controls will appear:

```
Position="[Bottom|Top|TopAndBottom]"
```

The `PagerSettings` element defines the appearance of the paging controls in more detail. It allows you to use images, text links, or page numbers for the navigation controls. The general declaration of this element is shown in Listing 4.6.

LISTING 4.6. The PagerSettings Element

```
<PagerSettings
  Mode="[NextPrevious|NextPrevFirstLast|Numeric|NumericFirstLast]"
  FirstPageText="String"
  PrevPageText="String"
  NextPageText="String"
  LastPageText="String"
  FirstPageImageUrl="url"
  PrevPageImageUrl="url"
  NextPageImageUrl="url"
  LastPageImageUrl="url"
  PageButtonCount="Integer" />
```

Defining the Columns in a GridView Control

The `GridView` control can automatically generate the columns required to display the contents of the source data rows, just as the ASP.NET 1.0 `Data Grid` control does. The default for the `AutoGenerateColumns` property is `True`, indicating that an `AutoGeneratedField` bound column will be generated for each column in the data rows.

However, as with the `DataGrid`, you can set this property to `False` and specify the columns you want instead. This is useful if you want to use any of the special column types, other than the default type that displays the value as a text string (or in a `TextBox` control when the row is in edit mode) or as a `CheckBox` control (if the data is a `Boolean` or bit field).

Compared with the `DataGrid` control, there are some interesting new column types available for the `GridView` control.

The GridView Column Types

The `GridView` control supports a range of column types, allowing you to display the data within each column in a range of ways. Note that the controls are named as *xxx*`Field`, in order to differentiate them from the *xxx*`Column` controls used in a `DataGrid` control.

- The `AutoGeneratedField` column, the default column type, is used when the `AutoGenerateColumns` property is set to `True`. It acts like both a `BoundField` column and a `CheckBoxField` column. If the data is `Boolean`, a disabled `CheckBox` control appears with its `Checked` property signifying the value of the `Boolean` data. When the row is in edit mode, the `CheckBox` becomes enabled and the user can check or uncheck the `CheckBox` to change its value. If the data is of any other type, the value is displayed as text (in a `TextBox` control when in edit mode). However, note that the `AutoGeneratedField` column type should *not* be declared directly and is used only when the `Auto` `GeneratedFields` property is `True` for the `GridView` control.

- The `BoundField` column works like that in the existing version 1.x `DataGrid` control. It displays the value from this column for each row as a text string (or in a `TextBox` control when the row is in edit mode).

- The `ButtonField` column displays a `Button` control in each row of this column. It can be rendered as a standard HTML button, a text `LinkButton`, or a clickable image. The caption, text, or URL can be set to the value from this column for each current row.

- The `CheckBoxField` column displays a `CheckBox` control in this column of each row. This column type is usually bound to a column in the data source that contains `Boolean` or bit values, and the checkbox sets or reflects the value of this column for each row.

- The `HyperLinkField` column displays a `HyperLink` control in this column of each row. The value of the column, or other static values, can be used to set the `Text` and `NavigateUrl` properties of each `HyperLink` control.

- The `TemplateField` column provides a free-form section where the developer specifies all the details of the required user interface. A range of templates can be specified to display different controls depending on the current mode of the row. This type of column is useful when you need to include validation controls as well as interactive UI controls.

• The CommandField column displays a series of text links, HTML buttons, or clickable images used to change the mode of the current row for editing. Depending on the current mode and the property settings for the column, these buttons can include Select, Edit, Delete, Insert, and Cancel (or equivalent images provided by the developer).

Other types of columns are scheduled for development with the final release version of ASP.NET 2.0. These include the ImageField and Drop DownListField, whose names are self-explanatory.

Declaring a BoundField Column

In a BoundField column, the value in the column is displayed as text, except when the row is in edit mode, in which case it is displayed in a standard ASP.NET TextBox control. The DataFormatString property takes a String value that includes the placeholder {0} where the value should be inserted. And you can add one of the standard formatting characters, for example, using {0:C} to display the value as currency. The outline declaration of a BoundField is shown in Listing 4.7.

LISTING 4.7. Declaring a BoundField Column

```
<asp:BoundField
  DataField="String"
  DataFormatString="String"
  TreatEmptyStringAsNull="[True|False]"
  NullDisplayText="String"
  ReadOnly="[True|False]"
  InsertVisible="[True|False]"
  Visible="[True|False]"
  SortExpression="String"
  ShowHeader="[True|False]"
  HeaderText="String"
  HeaderStyle-[PropertyName]="[value]"
  HeaderImageUrl="String"
  ItemStyle-[PropertyName]="[value]"
  FooterText="String"
  FooterStyle-[PropertyName]="[value]" />
```

The attributes shown in Listing 4.7 correspond to the properties in Table 4.7.

TABLE 4.7. The Properties and Attributes of the BoundField Control

Property/Attribute	Description
DataField	Sets or returns a `String` that is the name of the column in the source rows that will provide the data to display in this column of the grid.
DataFormatString	Sets or returns a `String` that contains the formatting details for the value displayed in this column.
TreatEmptyStringAsNull	Sets or returns a `Boolean` value that indicates whether an empty string in this column should be treated as `null`. This is useful when editing the data if the data source expects `null` values to be used when no value is present.
NullDisplayText	Sets or returns a `String` that is the text to display in the grid for rows that have a `null` value in this column.
ReadOnly	Sets or returns a `Boolean` value that indicates whether the values in this column can be edited. If `True`, the column will not display a `TextBox` in edit mode.
InsertVisible	Sets or returns a `Boolean` value that indicates whether this column will be displayed when inserting a new row into the source rowset.
Visible	Sets or returns a `Boolean` value that indicates whether this column is visible within the output generated by the grid control.
SortExpression	Sets or returns a `String` that defines the sort expression for this column, as a comma-delimited list of column names.
ShowHeader	Sets or returns a `Boolean` value that indicates whether the header for this column will be displayed.
HeaderText	Sets or returns a `String` that is the text to display in the header row for this column.
HeaderStyle	Returns a reference to a `TableItemStyle` instance that describes the style and formatting of the header for this column. The `TableItemStyle` properties were described earlier in this chapter.
HeaderImageUrl	Sets or returns a `String` that is the relative or absolute URL of an image to display in the header row for this column.

continues

TABLE 4.7. The Properties and Attributes of the BoundField Control (continued)

Property/Attribute	Description
ItemStyle	Returns a reference to a TableItemStyle instance that describes the style and formatting of the values in the data-bound rows in this column.
FooterText	Sets or returns a String that is the text to display in the footer row for this column.
FooterStyle	Returns a reference to a TableItemStyle instance that describes the style and formatting of the footer for this column.

Declaring a ButtonField Column

A ButtonField is used when you want each row in the output to include a button or a clickable link that causes a postback, perhaps to display more details of the row or to open an image or other resource. It can display the link as a standard HTML button control (an <input type="submit"> element), a clickable image (an <input type="image"> element), or a text link (an <a> element with some client-side script to submit the page). The outline declaration of a ButtonField is shown in Listing 4.8.

LISTING 4.8. Declaring a ButtonField Column

```
<asp:ButtonField
  ButtonType="[Button|Image|Link]"
  CommandName="String"
  DataTextField="String"
  DataTextFormatString="String"
  CausesValidation="[True|False]"
  ValidationGroup="String"
  Text="String"
  ImageUrl="String"
  Visible="[True|False]"
  SortExpression="String"
  ShowHeader="[True|False]"
  HeaderText="String"
  HeaderStyle-[PropertyName]="[value]"
  HeaderImageUrl="String"
  ItemStyle-[PropertyName]="[value]"
  FooterText="String"
  FooterStyle-[PropertyName]="[value]" />
```

TABLE 4.8. The Properties and Attributes of the ButtonField Control

Property/Attribute	Description
ButtonType	Sets or returns a value from the ButtonType enumeration (Button, Image, or Link) that specifies the type of control to create in each row of this column. The default is Link.
CommandName	Sets or returns a String value that is the CommandName property of the button in each row of the output.
DataTextField	Sets or returns a String that indicates the name of the column within the source data that will supply the value for the Text property of the control (the caption of a button or the text of a link).
DataTextFormatString	Sets or returns a String that contains the formatting information for the value in the row. Uses the same syntax as the DataFormatString property described for the BoundField control, using {0} as a placeholder.
CausesValidation	Sets or returns a Boolean value that indicates whether the button will cause any validation controls in the page to validate their values and report any errors. The default is True.
ValidationGroup	Sets or returns a String that is the name of the group of validation controls this button will initiate. See Chapter 9 for more details about validation groups.
Text	Sets or returns a String that will be used in place of DataTextField, in other words, the static value for the caption or text of the link that is the same for every row.
ImageUrl	Sets or returns a String that is the relative or absolute URL of the image to display when the ButtonType property is set to Image.

The attributes shown highlighted in Listing 4.8 correspond to the properties in Table 4.8. The rest are the same as those listed for the BoundField control in Table 4.7.

Declaring a CheckBoxField Column

A CheckBoxField is used when you want every row to display a checkbox in this column, with the checkbox setting reflecting the value in the row. Because an HTML checkbox can be only on or off, this column type really only works with columns in the source data rows that contain `Boolean` or bit values. The outline declaration of a `CheckBoxField` is shown in Listing 4.9.

LISTING 4.9. Declaring a CheckBoxField Column

```
<asp:CheckBoxField
  DataField="String"
  ReadOnly="[True|False]"
  Text="String"
  InsertVisible="[True|False]"
  Visible="[True|False]"
  SortExpression="String"
  ShowHeader="[True|False]"
  HeaderText="String"
  HeaderStyle-[PropertyName]="[value]"
  HeaderImageUrl="String"
  ItemStyle-[PropertyName]="[value]"
  FooterText="String"
  FooterStyle-[PropertyName]="[value]" />
```

The attributes shown highlighted in Listing 4.9 correspond to the properties in Table 4.9. The rest are the same as those listed for the `BoundField` control in Table 4.7.

Declaring a HyperLinkField Column

A `HyperLinkField` is used to display a clickable link in each row by inserting a standard `<a>` element into the output. The control allows you to set the text content of the `<a>` element and the `href` attribute as either

TABLE 4.9. The Properties and Attributes of the CheckBoxField Control

Property/Attribute	Description
DataField	Sets or returns a `String` that is the name of the column in the source rows that will provide the data to determine the settings of the checkbox.
ReadOnly	Sets or returns a `Boolean` value that indicates whether the values in this column can be changed.
Text	Sets or returns a `String` that will be used as the `Text` property of the `CheckBox` control.
InsertVisible	Sets or returns a `Boolean` value that indicates whether this column will be displayed when inserting a new row into the source rowset.

static values or as values from the source data row. You can also specify a value for the target window name, though this can be only static text and not a bound value. The outline declaration of a `HyperLinkField` is shown in Listing 4.10.

LISTING 4.10. Declaring a HyperLinkField Column

```
<asp:HyperLinkField
  DataTextField="String"
  DataTextFormatString="String"
  Text="String"
  DataNavigateUrlField="String"
  DataNavigateUrlFormatString="String"
  NavigateUrl="String"
  Target="String"
  Visible="[True|False]"
  SortExpression="String"
  ShowHeader="[True|False]"
  HeaderText="String"
  HeaderStyle-[PropertyName]="[value]"
  HeaderImageUrl="String"
  ItemStyle-[PropertyName]="[value]"
  FooterText="String"
  FooterStyle-[PropertyName]="[value]" />
```

The attributes shown highlighted in Listing 4.10 correspond to the properties in Table 4.10. The rest are the same as those listed for the `Bound Field` control in Table 4.7.

TABLE 4.10. The Properties and Attributes of the HyperLinkField Control

Property/Attribute	Description
DataTextField	Sets or returns a `String` that indicates the name of the column within the source data that will supply the value for the `Text` property of the control (the visible text of the link).
DataTextFormatString	Sets or returns a `String` that contains the formatting information for the bound value that is applied to the `Text` property of the link.
Text	Sets or returns a `String` that will be used in place of `DataTextField`, in other words, the static value for the text of the link that is the same for every row.

continues

TABLE 4.10. The Properties and Attributes of the HyperLinkField Control (continued)

Property/Attribute	Description
DataNavigateUrlField	Sets or returns a String that indicates the name of the column within the source data that will supply the value for the NavigateUrl property of the control (the href attribute of the resulting <a> element).
DataNavigateUrlFormatString	Sets or returns a String that contains the formatting information for the bound value that will be applied to the NavigateUrl property.
NavigateUrl	Sets or returns a String that will be used in place of DataNavigateUrlField, in other words, the static value for the href of the link that is the same for every row.
Target	Sets or returns a String that is the name of the target window for the link and will be used as the target attribute of the resulting <a> element.

Declaring a TemplateField Column

When you need to provide output that is not supported by any of the standard column types, you can use a TemplateField. This works just as in the DataGrid from version 1.0 of ASP.NET and is the same approach to generating list output as used by other controls such as the Repeater and DataList. You specify all the content that you want to be output for the column within one or more templates nested within the TemplateField declaration (or added at runtime in code). The control selects the appropriate template depending on which mode the row is currently in. The outline declaration of a TemplateField is shown in Listing 4.11.

LISTING 4.11. Declaring a TemplateField Column

```
<asp:TemplateField
  Visible="[True|False]"
  SortExpression="String"
  ShowHeader="[True|False]"
  HeaderText="String"
  HeaderStyle-[PropertyName]="[value]"
  HeaderImageUrl="String"
  ItemStyle-[PropertyName]="[value]"
  FooterText="String"
  FooterStyle-[PropertyName]="[value]" >
```

```
<HeaderTemplate>...</HeaderTemplate>
<ItemTemplate>...</ItemTemplate>
<AlternatingItemTemplate>...</ AlternatingItemTemplate>
<SelectedItemTemplate>...</SelectedItemTemplate>
<EditItemTemplate>...</EditItemTemplate>
<FooterTemplate>...</FooterTemplate>
```

```
</asp:TemplateField>
```

All the attributes of the control are the same as those listed for the `BoundField` control in Table 4.7. The six kinds of templates that you can specify, highlighted in Listing 4.11, are documented in Table 4.11.

Declaring a CommandField Column

The final column type for the `GridView` control is the `CommandField` column. This is used to switch the row between modes and to confirm updates to the values. When the row is not in edit mode, the column displays one or more of the Select, Insert, Edit, and Delete buttons, depending on the values you've specified for the `ShowxxxButton` properties of the `GridView` control. When the row is in edit mode, it displays Update and Cancel buttons, again depending on the property settings you make for the `GridView` control.

TABLE 4.11. The Templates of the TemplateField Control

Template	Description
HeaderTemplate	The markup, text, controls, and other content required to generate the entire content for the header of this column of the grid.
ItemTemplate	The markup, text, controls, and other content required to generate the entire content for this column in data-bound rows within the grid.
AlternatingItemTemplate	The markup, text, controls, and other content required to generate the entire content for this column in alternating data-bound rows within the grid.
SelectedItemTemplate	The markup, text, controls, and other content required to generate the entire content for this column in the row within the grid that is in selected mode.
EditItemTemplate	The markup, text, controls, and other content required to generate the entire content for this column in the row within the grid that is in edit mode.
FooterTemplate	The markup, text, controls, and other content required to generate the entire content for the footer of this column of the grid.

Clicking on the buttons raises an event that is automatically handled by the data source control to which the GridView is connected, though you can also respond to the events in code yourself by handling the RowCommand event. The outline declaration of a CommandField is shown in Listing 4.12.

LISTING 4.12. Declaring a CommandField Column

```
<asp:CommandField
   ButtonType="[Button|Image|Link]"
   UpdateText="String"
   UpdateImageUrl="String"
   ShowCancelButton="[True|False]"
   CancelText="String"
   CancelImageUrl="String"
   ShowSelectButton="[True|False]"
   SelectText="String"
   SelectImageUrl="String"
   ShowInsertButton="[True|False]"
   InsertText="String"
   InsertImageUrl="String"
   ShowEditButton="[True|False]"
   EditText="String"
   EditImageUrl="String"
   ShowDeleteButton="[True|False]"
   DeleteText="String"
   DeleteImageUrl="String"
   CausesValidation="[True|False]"
   ValidationGroup="String"
   Visible="[True|False]"
   SortExpression="String"
   ShowHeader="[True|False]"
   HeaderText="String"
   HeaderStyle-[PropertyName]="[value]"
   HeaderImageUrl="String"
   ItemStyle-[PropertyName]="[value]"
   FooterText="String"
   FooterStyle-[PropertyName]="[value]" />
```

The attributes shown highlighted in Listing 4.12 correspond to the properties in Table 4.12. The rest are the same as those listed for the Bound Field control in Table 4.7.

Using a Mixture of Column Types

To demonstrate some of the column types available for the DataGrid control, Listing 4.13 shows a GridView control that extracts some rows from the Northwind database Products table and displays them with sorting and

TABLE 4.12. The Properties and Attributes of the CommandField Control

Property/Attribute	Description
ButtonType	Sets or returns a value from the ButtonType enumeration (Button, Image, or Link) that specifies the type of controls to create in each row of this column. The default is Link.
UpdateText	Sets or returns a String value that is the caption for the button that causes an update process to occur. The default is **Update**.
UpdateImageUrl	Sets or returns a String that is the relative or absolute URL of the image to display in place of a text **Update** link.
ShowCancelButton	Sets or returns a Boolean value that indicates whether a **Cancel** button will be displayed in this column when the row is in edit mode.
CancelText	Sets or returns a String value that is the caption for the button that cancels an update process. The default is **Cancel**.
CancelImageUrl	Sets or returns a String that is the relative or absolute URL of the image to display in place of a text **Cancel** link.
ShowSelectButton	Sets or returns a Boolean value that indicates whether a **Select** button will be displayed in this column.
SelectText	Sets or returns a String value that is the caption for the button that causes the row to be shown in selected mode. The default is **Select**.
SelectImageUrl	Sets or returns a String that is the relative or absolute URL of the image to display in place of a text **Select** link.
ShowInsertButton	Sets or returns a Boolean value that indicates whether an **Insert** button will be displayed in this column.
InsertText	Sets or returns a String value that is the caption for the button that inserts a new row into the grid. The default is **Insert**.
InsertImageUrl	Sets or returns a String that is the relative or absolute URL of the image to display in place of a text **Insert** link.
ShowEditButton	Sets or returns a Boolean value that indicates whether an **Edit** button will be displayed in this column.
EditText	Sets or returns a String value that is the caption for the button that causes the row to be shown in edit mode. The default is **Edit**.
EditImageUrl	Sets or returns a String that is the relative or absolute URL of the image to display in place of a text **Edit** link.
ShowDeleteButton	Sets or returns a Boolean value that indicates whether a **Delete** button will be displayed in this column.

continues

TABLE 4.12. The Properties and Attributes of the CommandField Control (continued)

Property/Attribute	Description
DeleteText	Sets or returns a `String` value that is the caption for the button that deletes a row. The default is **Delete**.
DeleteImageUrl	Sets or returns a `String` that is the relative or absolute URL of the image to display in place of a text **Delete** link.
CausesValidation	Sets or returns a `Boolean` value that indicates whether the button will cause any validation controls in the page to validate their values and report any errors. The default is `True`.
ValidationGroup	Sets or returns a `String` that is the name of the group of validation controls this button will initiate. See Chapter 9 for more details about validation groups.

paging enabled. The data source control declaration contains the commands required to allow updating of the data in the table and caches the data for five minutes to improve performance when just reading the rows.

LISTING 4.13. Using a Mixture of Column Types

```
<asp:SqlDataSource id="ds1" runat="server"
  ConnectionString="server=localhost;database=Northwind;uid=x;pwd=x;"
  SelectCommand="SELECT ProductID, ProductName, QuantityPerUnit,
                Discontinued, UnitPrice FROM Products"
  UpdateCommand="UPDATE Products SET QuantityPerUnit=@QuantityPerUnit,
                Discontinued=@Discontinued
                WHERE ProductID=@ProductID"
  DeleteCommand="DELETE FROM Products WHERE ProductID=@ProductID"
  EnableCaching="True" CacheDuration="300" />

<asp:GridView id="grid1" runat="server" DataSourceID="ds1"
  AllowSorting="True" AllowPaging="True" PageSize="5"
  DataKeyNames="ProductID"
  AutoGenerateColumns="False" OnRowCommand="ShowDetails">

  <ColumnFields>
    ... column definitions shown later ...
  </ColumnFields>

</asp:GridView>

<asp:Label id="lblInfo" EnableViewState="False" runat="server" />
```

The RowCommand event is raised when any control other than a standard Edit, Delete, Update, or Cancel link in the grid causes a postback. Code in the page will handle this event and display details about a row in a Label control (declared at the end of Listing 4.13) when a button in that row is clicked. The screenshot in Figure 4.3 shows the result; the custom column declarations the `GridView` uses are discussed afterward.

The `GridView` control shown in Listing 4.13 and Figure 4.3 contains the attribute `AutoGenerateColumns="False"`, so it will not automatically generate the columns based on the structure of the data rows. The columns are declared individually within the `<ColumnFields>` element. The next sections describe each of the columns we've used.

The ButtonField Column

The first column is a `ButtonField` column that displays a button with the row ID as the caption. The `DataTextField` attribute causes the values from the `ProductID` column to be used for the `Text` property of the button in each row, and the `SortExpression` attribute allows the rows to be sorted using the values in this column (see Listing 4.14). A header row is displayed for this column, containing the text "ID", and it is styled as bold Verdana font. Finally, the `CommandName` attribute causes the `CommandName` property of each button to be set to `MyRoutine`. This is required to be able to identify which control caused the postback when we handle the `RowCommand` event.

LISTING 4.14. Declaring the ButtonField Column

```
<asp:ButtonField ButtonType="Button" DataTextField="ProductID"
    SortExpression="ProductID" ShowHeader="True" HeaderText="ID"
    CommandName="MyRoutine" HeaderStyle-Font-Name="Verdana"
    HeaderStyle-Font-Bold="True" />
```

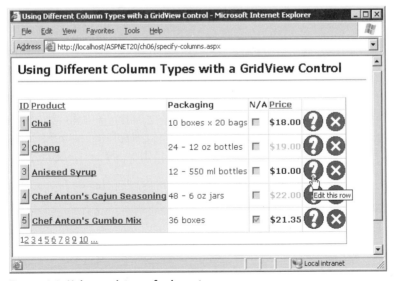

FIGURE 4.3. Using a mixture of column types

The HyperLinkField Column

The next column is a `HyperLinkField`, bound to the `ProductName` column. The `Text` property of each hyperlink is set to the value in each row of the `ProductName` column by the `DataTextField` attribute (see Listing 4.15). The `NavigateUrl` (`href`) of each hyperlink is set to a string value such as `http://www.mysite.com/products?product=3` by the combination of the `DataNavigateUrlField` attribute (which specifies the `ProductID` column) and the `DataNavigateUrlFormatString` attribute (which supplies the format string with the placeholder `{0}` for the value from each row).

LISTING 4.15. Declaring the HyperLinkField Column

```
<asp:HyperLinkField DataTextField="ProductName"
    ShowHeader="True" HeaderText="Product"
    DataNavigateUrlField="ProductID"
    DataNavigateUrlFormatString=
                    "http://www.mysite.com/products?product={0}"
    SortExpression="ProductName" HeaderStyle-Font-Name="Verdana"
    HeaderStyle-Font-Bold="True" ItemStyle-Font-Name="Verdana"
    ItemStyle-Font-Bold="True" ItemStyle-BackColor="Yellow" />
```

The BoundField Column

Next comes a `BoundField` column, bound to the `QuantityPerUnit` column. It too has a header, and both this and the "item" rows are styled using attributes in the column declaration (see Listing 4.16).

LISTING 4.16. Declaring the BoundField Column

```
<asp:BoundField DataField="QuantityPerUnit" ShowHeader="True"
    HeaderText="Packaging" HeaderStyle-Font-Name="Verdana"
    HeaderStyle-Font-Bold="True" ItemStyle-Font-Name="Verdana" />
```

The CheckBoxField Column

The `Discontinued` column in the data rowset is a `Boolean` type, so the ideal representation is a checkbox. This is the default for this type of data column anyway. The `CheckBoxField` column is bound to the `Discontinued` column in the data rows and the header "N/A" (not available) declared for it (see Listing 4.17).

LISTING 4.17. Declaring the CheckBoxField Column

```
<asp:CheckBoxField DataField="Discontinued" ShowHeader="True"
    HeaderText="N/A" HeaderStyle-Font-Name="Verdana"
    HeaderStyle-Font-Bold="True" />
```

The TemplateField Column

The most complex column type is the `TemplateField`, and this cannot be bound directly to a column in the source data rowset. Instead, it contains individual templates that define the output to be displayed depending on the row location and which mode the row is in. You can see that the eample contains an `ItemTemplate` and an `AlternatingItemTemplate`, each containing a `Label` control that displays the value from the `UnitPrice` column in each row—and with alternating foreground colors (see Listing 4.18).

LISTING 4.18. Declaring the TemplateField Column

```
<asp:TemplateField ShowHeader="True" HeaderText="Price"
      SortExpression="UnitPrice" HeaderStyle-Font-Name="Verdana"
      HeaderStyle-Font-Bold="True" ItemStyle-Font-Name="Verdana"
      ItemStyle-Font-Bold="True">
  <ItemTemplate>
    <asp:Label runat="server"
            Text='<%# Eval("UnitPrice", "${0:F2}") %>' />
  </ItemTemplate>
  <AlternatingItemTemplate>
    <asp:Label runat="server" ForeColor="DarkGray"
            Text='<%# Eval("UnitPrice", "${0:F2}") %>' />
  </AlternatingItemTemplate>
</asp:TemplateField>
```

It's possible to include an `EditItem` template that defines the appearance of the row when it is in edit mode, but because this column type cannot be bound to a column in the source data it is not possible to achieve the "no-code" updates we've seen earlier when using a `TemplateField`. Instead you have to write code that is executed in response to the `Row Updating` event and add the value(s) of the fields in the `TemplateField` to the `NewValues` dictionary of the `GridViewUpdateEventArgs` using the value in the column in this case.

The CommandField Column

The final column displays the images for switching to edit mode, updating a row, canceling the changes, and deleting the row. The `CommandField` column declaration specifies that the links should be images and also declares the relative URL of the images and the text to use as the `alt` attribute of these images (see Listing 4.19).

LISTING 4.19. Declaring the CommandField Column

```
<asp:CommandField ButtonType="Image"
     UpdateImageUrl="i.gif" UpdateText="Apply these changes"
```

continues

```
ShowCancelButton="True" CancelImageUrl="s.gif"
CancelText="Cancel this update"
ShowEditButton="True" EditImageUrl="q.gif"
EditText="Edit this row"
ShowDeleteButton="True" DeleteImageUrl="x.gif"
DeleteText="Delete this row" />
```

As we've seen earlier, the `GridView` control manages all the mode switching and updates automatically, without requiring any code to be written. The screenshot in Figure 4.4 shows the grid with the third row in edit mode. Notice that the `HyperLinkField` column does not allow the value to be edited, while the `BoundField` column does. The `CheckBox Field` column automatically enables the checkbox in this row to allow the value to be changed. Meanwhile the `CommandField` column displays the Update and Cancel images. All this happens automatically with the column declarations we used, without any code required.

Handling the RowCommand Event

The first column (a `ButtonField` column) contains buttons that raise the `RowCommand` event when clicked. The declaration of the `GridView` control includes the attribute `OnRowCommand="ShowDetails"`, which will execute the only code in the page—an event handler named `ShowDetails` (see Listing 4.20)—when any one of the buttons is clicked.

Figure 4.4. Editing a row with custom column types

However, the `RowCommand` event is also raised for some other actions that cause a postback, including the pager links at the bottom of the grid. So, before processing the row values, the event handler has to check whether it was in fact a button in the first column that caused the postback. The `ButtonField` column declaration contains the attribute `Command Name="MyRoutine"`, so the event handler can check the `CommandName` property of the `GridViewCommandEventArgs` instance passed to it. If this is a button from the first column, a reference to it is obtained from the `CommandSource` property of the `GridViewCommandEventArgs` instance, and the `Text` property contains the value from the current row.

LISTING 4.20. The Event Handler for the RowCommand Event

```
Sub ShowDetails(oSender As Object, oArgs As GridViewCommandEventArgs)
   If oArgs.CommandName = "MyRoutine" Then
     lblInfo.Text = "More details here for product " _
               & oArgs.CommandSource.Text
   End If
End Sub
```

The code in Listing 4.20 simply displays the text "More details here for product x" but could easily go off and query the database or fetch an image of the product to display more information as required. The result of clicking one of the buttons in the first column is shown in Figure 4.5.

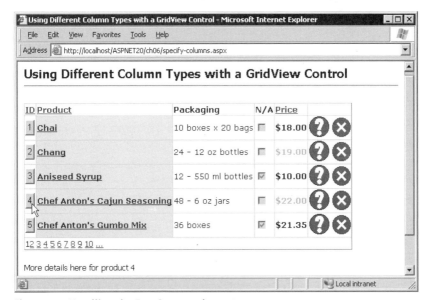

Figure 4.5. Handling the RowCommand event

The DetailsView Control

The GridView control we examined in the previous section is designed to display data as a table, with each row containing one data row (one record). However, sometimes it's useful to be able to display data one row at a time, especially when there is a large number of columns or when you want to be able to edit the values of each column without using the rather cramped in-line editing mode of the GridView.

To provide a one-row-per-page feature for displaying and editing data, ASP.NET 2.0 includes the new DetailsView control. It can be used stand-alone with paging controls that allow the user to scroll through the rows or combined with a GridView control to provide a master-detail display. In fact, you have already seen DetailsView-like rendering in action in the previous section of this chapter. When serving a page containing a Grid View to a small-screen or mobile device, ASP.NET automatically uses DetailsView-like rendering to create the details page containing all the columns from the current row.

Using a Stand-Alone DetailsView Control

The declaration and attribute set for the DetailsView control is similar to that of the GridView. When used on its own, however, you will need to either enable the paging feature in order to display the paging controls or add your own custom paging feature so that users can navigate through the rows.

Listing 4.21 shows a declaration of a DetailsView control that turns on the paging features and specifies that the mode should be NextPrev FirstLast so that the usual four links are displayed (the default mode is Numeric, where a numbered link is displayed for each row). The declaration also specifies the relative URLs of the images to display for the paging controls and the text to use as the alt attribute of each one.

LISTING 4.21. Declaring a DetailsView Control

```
<asp:DetailsView id="details1" DataSourceID="dvs1" runat="server"
  DataKeyNames="ShipperID" AllowPaging="True"
  PagerSettings-Mode="NextPrevFirstLast"
  PagerSettings-FirstPageImageUrl="f.gif"
  PagerSettings-FirstPageText="First Row"
  PagerSettings-PrevPageImageUrl="p.gif"
  PagerSettings-PrevPageText="Previous Row"
  PagerSettings-NextPageImageUrl="n.gif"
  PagerSettings-NextPageText="Next Row"
  PagerSettings-LastPageImageUrl="l.gif"
  PagerSettings-LastPageText="Last Row" />

<asp:SqlDataSource id="dvs1" runat="server"
```

```
ConnectionString="server=localhost;database=Northwind;uid=x;pwd=x"
SelectCommand="SELECT ShipperID,CompanyName,Phone FROM Shippers">
</asp:SqlDataSource>
```

After the `DetailsView` control comes the declaration of the data source control. You can see that this is identical to the way it is used with a `Grid View` control. The result is shown in the compound screenshot in Figure 4.6, with the paging controls and the alternate text captions visible.

The `DetailsView` control accepts the same styling attributes as the `GridView` control, so you can improve the appearance from the default shown here. You can also turn off automatic generation of the fields (by setting the `AutoGenerateRows` attribute to `False`) and then specify the fields you want to display as well as their appearance and behavior. The `DetailsView` control uses a `<RowFields>` section in place of the `<Column Fields>` section of the `GridView` control, but the same types of fields are used within it as in the `GridView`. You can declare your own sequence of `BoundField`, `ButtonField`, `CheckBoxField`, `HyperLinkField`, `Template Field`, and `CommandField` controls within the `<RowFields>` section.

Creating a Master-Detail Page with GridView and DetailsView Controls

For rowsets that have a large number of columns, the one-row-per-page approach provided by the `DetailsView` control is useful. However, it does make it harder to navigate through and generally scan the data by eye. For that, the table layout provided by the `GridView` control is better. The ideal is to combine the two so that a few selected columns are displayed in the `GridView`, and the user can select a row to see it displayed with all the fields visible in the `DetailsView`.

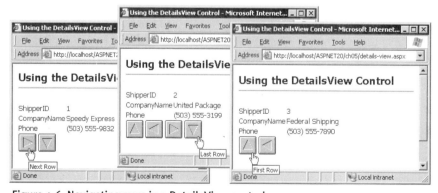

Figure 4.6. Navigating rows in a DetailsView control

The two controls provide features that link them together declaratively, without requiring any code to be written. Listing 4.22 shows how this works. In this example, the `GridView` is bound to a data source control named `dgs1`, and the `DataKeyNames` attribute specifies that the `ShipperID` column in the rowset exposed by that data source control is the primary key for each row. The `AutoGenerateSelectButton` attribute is set to `True` to display a Select link in each row, and the first row is selected when the page first loads. This is necessary because the `DetailsView` must have a current row to display.

LISTING 4.22. Master-Detail Pages: The GridView and SqlDataSource Controls

```
<asp:GridView id="grid1" DataSourceID="dgs1" runat="server"
    DataKeyNames="ShipperID" SelectedIndex="0"
    AutoGenerateSelectButton="True" />

<asp:SqlDataSource id="dgs1" runat="server"
  ConnectionString="server=localhost;database=Northwind;uid=x;pwd=x"
  SelectCommand="SELECT ShipperID,CompanyName,Phone FROM Shippers" />
. . .
```

Linking a GridView and DetailsView Control

The `DetailsView` control is declared next (see Listing 4.23). It is bound to the second data source control on the page, named `dvs1`, and again has the primary key column identified by the `DataKeyNames` attribute. The data source control has the same `SelectCommand` as the previous one, though it doesn't have to—if you display a different selection of columns in the two controls, you can select just the columns you need.

The link between the two data source controls, which ensures that the row selected in the `GridView` is displayed in the `DetailsView` control, is the addition of a filter to the second data source control. The `Filter Expression` declares a parameter `@ShipperID`, and the `FilterParameters` section of the control contains a `ControlParameter` that is bound to the `SelectedValue` property of the `GridView` control. As the user selects rows in the `GridView` control, the `SelectedValue` is automatically set to the ID of that row and thus filters the data source control that powers the `DetailsView` control on that ID value.

LISTING 4.23. Master-Detail Pages: The DetailsView and Filtered SqlDataSource Controls

```
. . .
<asp:DetailsView id="details1" DataSourceID="dvs1" runat="server"
    DataKeyNames="ShipperID" />
```

```
<asp:SqlDataSource id="dvs1" runat="server"
  ConnectionString="server=localhost;database=Northwind;uid=x;pwd=x"
  SelectCommand="SELECT ShipperID,CompanyName,Phone FROM Shippers"
  FilterExpression="ShipperID=@ShipperID">

  <FilterParameters>
    <asp:ControlParameter Name="ShipperID" ControlID="grid1"
                          PropertyName="SelectedValue" />
  </FilterParameters>

</asp:SqlDataSource>
```

The result can be seen in Figure 4.7. A Select link appears in each row of the `GridView` control, and clicking one displays that row in the `Details View` control below it.

Inserting and Editing Rows with a DetailsView Control

A task that is regularly required when working with data rows, and which is quite complex to achieve in ASP.NET 1.0, is inserting a new row into the source data table. In ASP.NET 2.0, with a `GridView` control, this can be achieved by using a `DetailsView` control instance declared separately on the page. The technique is very similar to that just seen for creating a master-detail page. First, a `GridView` control is declared and then the associated data source control that supplies the rows (see Listing 4.24).

Figure 4.7. Selecting a row in a master-detail page

LISTING 4.24. Inserting and Editing Rows: The GridView and SqlDataSource Controls for Lookups

```
<asp:GridView id="grid1" DataSourceID="dgs1" runat="server"
  DataKeyNames="ShipperID" SelectedIndex="0"
  AutoGenerateSelectButton="True" />

<asp:SqlDataSource id="dgs1" runat="server"
  ConnectionString="server=localhost;database=Northwind;uid=x;pwd=x"
  SelectCommand="SELECT ShipperID,CompanyName,Phone FROM Shippers" />
...
```

Enabling Editing in a DetailsView Control

To enable row edits, row deletes, and/or row inserts in a DetailsView control, you just add the relevant attributes to the control declaration. The first four highlighted attributes in Listing 4.25 turn on display of the Insert, Edit, Delete, and Cancel links, respectively (the Update link always appears when editing is enabled). For the automatic no-code updates to work, you also have to provide the relevant SQL statements or stored procedures. The highlighted attributes for the data source control in Listing 4.25 show the UPDATE, DELETE, and INSERT statements that will push changes to the rows back into the database.

LISTING 4.25. Inserting and Editing Rows: The DetailsView and SqlDataSource Controls for Edits

```
...
<asp:DetailsView id="details1" DataSourceID="dvs1" runat="server"
    DataKeyNames="ShipperID"
    AutoGenerateInsertButton="True" AutoGenerateEditButton="True"
    AutoGenerateDeleteButton="True" AutoGenerateCancelButton="True"
    OnItemDeleting="CheckDelete" OnItemUpdated="UpdateGrid"
    OnItemInserted="UpdateGrid" OnItemDeleted="UpdateGrid" />

<asp:SqlDataSource id="dvs1" runat="server"
  ConnectionString="server=localhost;database=Northwind;uid=x;pwd=x"
  SelectCommand="SELECT ShipperID,CompanyName,Phone FROM Shippers"
  UpdateCommand="UPDATE Shippers SET CompanyName=@CompanyName,
              Phone=@Phone WHERE ShipperID=@ShipperID"
  DeleteCommand="DELETE FROM Shippers WHERE ShipperID=@ShipperID"
  InsertCommand="INSERT INTO Shippers (CompanyName, Phone)
              VALUES (@CompanyName, @Phone)"
  FilterExpression="ShipperID=@ShipperID" >

  <FilterParameters>
    <asp:ControlParameter Name="ShipperID" ControlID="grid1"
                        PropertyName="SelectedValue" />
  </FilterParameters>
```

```
</asp:SqlDataSource>

<asp:Label id="lblError" EnableviewState="False" runat="server" />
```

The screenshot in Figure 4.8 shows two views of the process of editing a row. The `DetailsView` displays the Edit, Delete, and New links. Clicking the Edit link switches the `DetailsView` into edit mode, and the values of the non-key fields can be edited.

It's also possible to insert a row by clicking the New link, entering the values, and then clicking the Insert link (see Figure 4.9). Notice that the primary key is displayed as a text box so that the user can enter an appropriate value.

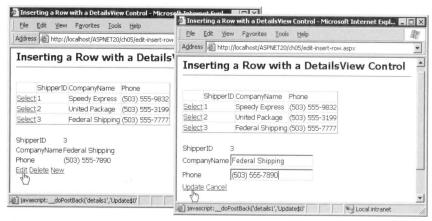

Figure 4.8. Editing a row with a DetailsView control

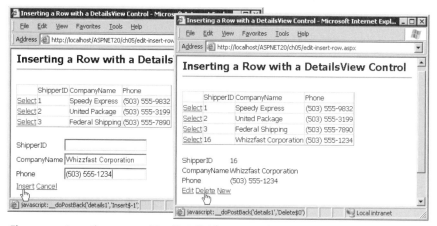

Figure 4.9. Inserting a row with a DetailsView control

In our case, however, the primary key column within the database table is auto-generated (an IDENTITY column). You don't need to enter a value, and the INSERT statement declared for the InsertCommand property of the data source control does not attempt to apply any value that you might enter anyway. You could create the fields for the DetailsView control manually, by setting the AutoGenerateRows attribute to False and using a BoundField with the InsertVisible property set to False, or by using a TemplateField, so that the value is not editable.

Handling DetailsView Control Events

There are a couple of other issues to look at as well. Although the Grid View and DetailsView controls are linked so that the DetailsView displays the row currently selected in the GridView, changes to the rows during editing (within the DetailsView) are not automatically displayed in the GridView control.

However, like the GridView, the DetailsView control exposes events that occur as rows are being manipulated. By handling these events you can link the controls together so that each reflects any changes made in the other. The declaration of the DetailsView control shown in Listing 4.25 and repeated in Listing 4.26 for convenience includes four attributes that specify event handlers that will be executed in response to the Item Deleting, ItemUpdated, ItemInserted, and ItemDeleted events.

LISTING 4.26. The Event Attribute Declarations for the DetailsView Control

```
<asp:DetailsView id="details1" DataSourceID="dvs1" runat="server"
    DataKeyNames="ShipperID"
    AutoGenerateInsertButton="True" AutoGenerateEditButton="True"
    AutoGenerateDeleteButton="True" AutoGenerateCancelButton="True"
    OnItemDeleting="CheckDelete" OnItemUpdated="UpdateGrid"
    OnItemInserted="UpdateGrid" OnItemDeleted="UpdateGrid" />
```

Preventing the Original Rows from Being Deleted

The ItemDeleting event occurs just before a row is deleted in the Details View control, and the page handles this to prevent attempts to delete the existing rows in the table (as shown earlier for the GridView control). Other than the fact that this event handler takes a DetailsViewDelete EventArgs instance as the second argument, rather than the GridView DeleteEventArgs instance used in the earlier example, the code is identical (see Listing 4.27).

LISTING 4.27. The Event Handler for the ItemDeleting Event

```
<script runat="server">
Sub CheckDelete(oSender As Object, _
                oArgs As DetailsViewDeleteEventArgs)
  Dim iKey As Integer = oArgs.Keys(0)
  If iKey < 4 Then
    oArgs.Cancel = True
    lblError.Text = "Cannot delete the original rows from the table"
  End If
End Sub
</script>
```

Updating the GridView Display with New or Changed Row Values

The other three event attribute declarations specify that the event handler named `UpdateGrid` will be executed after a row has been updated, inserted, or deleted. All the code has to do in this case is call the `DataBind` method of the `GridView` control so that it shows the changes to the rows made in the `DetailsView` control (see Listing 4.28). However, when a row is deleted, the currently selected row in the `GridView` is null, and this will cause an error when it tries to redisplay this row in the `DetailsView` control. To prevent this, the `SelectedIndex` property of the `GridView` is set to 0 (the first row, which cannot be deleted).

LISTING 4.28. Displaying the Changed Data

```
Sub UpdateGrid(oSender As Object, oArgs As DetailsViewStatusEventArgs)
  grid1.DataBind()
  grid1.SelectedIndex = 0
End Sub
```

Another situation where event handling might be useful is to highlight the current row in the `GridView` control when the user navigates through the rows using the `DetailsView` pager controls. The `GridView` would need to have a different style defined for the selected row (using the `SelectedItemTemplate`). Code that handles the `DataItemIndexChanged` event for the `DetailsView` would just set the `SelectedIndex` property of the `GridView` to the appropriate row index. This automatically displays the new row in the appropriate way.

The DetailsView Control Interface

As noted earlier, and as you'll have seen from the examples above, the `DetailsView` control interface is similar to that of the `GridView`. This isn't surprising because they both do effectively the same thing—display rows of data. The main difference is that the `GridView` displays the rows horizontally as a table, with the fields in columns, while the `DetailsView` displays each row as a separate single page with the fields laid out vertically. However, for completeness, the following sections list the members of the `DetailsView` that are not found in the `GridView`.

Properties Specific to the DetailsView Control

The `DetailsView` control does not support sorting and thus has none of the properties associated with this feature that apply to the `GridView` control. And the different ways that the rows are displayed mean that there is no concept of a selected row in a `DetailsView`, so there is no `AutoGenerateSelectButton` or selected row style properties. Properties that are available for the `DetailsView` control, and not for the `GridView` control, include those listed in Table 4.13.

TABLE 4.13. The Properties of the DetailsView Control

Property	Description
AutoGenerateInsertButton	Sets or returns a `Boolean` value that indicates whether the control will automatically generate a **New** button for each row.
AutoGenerateRows	Sets or returns a `Boolean` value that indicates whether the control will automatically generate fields for each column in the output based on the structure of the data rows.
DataItemIndex	Sets or returns an `Integer` value that is the zero-based index of the `DataItem` (row) currently displayed.
HeaderText	Sets or returns a `String` that is the text to be displayed immediately above the fields in the output generated by the control.
DefaultMode	Sets or returns a value from the `DetailsViewMode` enumeration that specifies how the fields are displayed when the page loads and after **Cancel, Update, Delete**, or **New** is pressed. Valid values are `ReadOnly` (the default), `Edit`, and `Insert`.
DataItem	Returns an `Object` reference to the `DataItem` object currently displayed by the control.
DataItemCount	Returns an `Integer` value that is the total number of rows in the underlying data source bound to the control.

TABLE 4.13. The Properties of the DetailsView Control (continued)

Property	Description
DataKey	Returns a DataKey instance containing the keys and values corresponding to the key names specified by the DataKeyNames attribute.
RowFields	Returns a DataControlFieldCollection instance that is a collection of all the DataControl Field objects that generate the output for the control.
CurrentMode	Returns a value from the DetailsViewMode enumeration that indicates the current mode of the DetailsView.

Events Specific to the DetailsView Control

The DetailsView control has the same DataBinding and DataBound events as the GridView, but the remaining events are specific to the DetailsView control (see Table 4.14).

TABLE 4.14. The Events of the DetailsView Control

Event	Description
DataItemIndexChanging	Raised before the DetailsView control changes from one row to the next. Passes a DetailsView ItemEventArgs instance to the event handler, which exposes the following properties: • Cancel: A Boolean property that can be set to True to prevent the control from changing to the new row. • NewDataItemIndex: The zero-based Integer index of the row that will be displayed next.
DataItemIndexChanged	Raised after the DetailsView control changes from one row to the next. Passes a standard EventArgs instance to the event handler.
ItemCommand	Raised when any control in the DetailsView causes a postback. Passes a DetailsViewCommandEvent Args instance to the event handler, which exposes the following properties: • CommandArgument: The value of the Command Argument property of the button that raised the event. • CommandName: The CommandName property of the control that caused the postback as a String. • CommandSource: An Object reference to the control that caused the postback.

continues

TABLE 4.14. The Events of the DetailsView Control (continued)

Event	Description
`ItemCreated`	Raised when a new row is created in the `DetailsView` control. Passes a standard `EventArgs` instance to the event handler.
`ItemDeleting`	Raised before the data source control bound to the `DetailsView` deletes a row. Passes a `DetailsViewDeleteEventArgs` instance to the event handler, which exposes the following properties: • `Cancel`: A `Boolean` property that can be set to `True` to cancel the delete operation. • `Keys`: An `IOrderedDictionary` instance containing the primary key values for the row. • `RowIndex`: An `Integer` value indicating the index of the row within the data source rowset. • `Values`: An `IOrderedDictionary` instance containing the values currently in the row. These values will not be passed to the `DataSource` control unless you move them into the `Keys IOrderedDictionary`.
`ItemDeleted`	Raised after the data source control bound to the `DetailsView` deletes a row. Passes a `DetailsViewStatusEventArgs` instance to the event handler, which exposes the `AffectedRows` property indicating the number of rows affected by the delete operation.
`ItemInserting`	Raised before the data source control bound to the `DetailsView` inserts a new row. Passes a `DetailsViewInsertEventArgs` instance to the event handler, which exposes the following properties: • `Cancel`: A `Boolean` property that can be set to `True` to cancel the insert operation. • `CommandArgument`: The value of the `CommandArgument` property of the control that raised the event. • `Values`: An `IOrderedDictionary` instance containing the values for the new row.
`ItemInserted`	Raised after the data source control bound to the `DetailsView` inserts a new row. Passes a `DetailsViewStatusEventArgs` instance to the event handler, which exposes the `AffectedRows` property indicating the number of rows affected by the insert operation.
`ItemUpdating`	Raised before the data source control bound to the `DetailsView` updates a row. Passes a `DetailsViewUpdateEventArgs` instance to the event handler, which exposes the following properties: • `Cancel`: A `Boolean` property that can be set to `True` to cancel the update operation. • `CommandArgument`: The value of the `CommandArgument` property of the button that raised the event. • `Keys`: An `IOrderedDictionary` instance containing the primary key values for the row.

TABLE 4.14. The Events of the DetailsView Control (continued)

Event	Description
	• `NewValues`: An `IOrderedDictionary` instance containing the values that will be placed into the row. • `OldValues`: An `IOrderedDictionary` instance containing the values currently in the row. These values will not be passed to the `DataSource` control unless you move them into the `NewValues` `IOrderedDictionary`.
`ItemUpdated`	Raised after the data source control bound to the `DetailsView` has updated a row. Passes a `DetailsView StatusEventArgs` instance to the event handler, which exposes the `AffectedRows` property indicating the number of rows affected by the update operation.
`ModeChanging`	Raised before the `DetailsView` changes from one mode to another (`ReadOnly`, `Edit`, or `Insert`). Passes a `DetailsViewModeEventArgs` instance to the event handler, which exposes the following properties: • `Cancel`: A `Boolean` property that can be set to `True` to prevent the control changing to the new mode. • `CancellingEdit`: A `Boolean` value that is `True` if the mode change was caused by the user clicking the **Cancel** button while in edit mode. • `NewMode`: The new mode as a value from the `DetailsViewMode` enumeration. The value can be changed to display a different mode.
`ModeChanged`	Raised after the `DetailsView` has changed from one mode to another (`ReadOnly`, `Edit`, or `Insert`). Passes a standard `EventArgs` instance to the event handler.

The New and Simplified Data Binding Syntax

You may have noticed that the code we used in the examples earlier in this chapter takes advantage of a simplified syntax for the data binding expressions. ASP.NET 2.0 fully supports the previous (version 1.0) syntax but adds a couple of new features as well. There is the simplified syntax for binding to nonhierarchical (rows and columns) data, plus new techniques that allow binding to hierarchical data such as XML documents.

The ASP.NET 1.0 Syntax for Data Binding

In ASP.NET 1.0, there are two ways to bind to data in a control that supports data binding. One choice is to use the early-bound approach that references the container directly:

```
<%# Container.DataItem("expression") %>
```

The *expression* is usually a column name from the rowset, though it can be the name of a property or field exposed by the object bound to the control.

The alternative, which is useful if you want to format the value, is the late-bound approach using the `Eval` method of the `DataBinder` responsible for carrying out the data binding:

```
<%# DataBinder.Eval(Container.DataItem,
        "expression"[, "format"]) %>
```

In this case, the optional *format* string can be used to output markup and literal content, with the value inserted into the string at the point where a {0} placeholder is located. The placeholder can also include a standard format string character to format the value at the same time, for example:

```
<%# DataBinder.Eval(Container.DataItem, _
        "TotalPrice", "Total Price: {0:C}") %>
```

You can see one of the issues that come into play here. The statement is verbose, and yet the majority is exactly the same in every occurrence. Moreover, because the content is executable code (the `Eval` method), line continuation characters are required in Visual Basic. Yet this is the only way to exert any real control over the format and content of the output.

Simplified ASP.NET 2.0 Syntax for Nonhierarchical Data Binding

In version 2.0, the most obvious simplification is that `DataBinder` is now the default context for data binding expressions, so the `Eval` method can be used like this:

```
<%# Eval("expression"[, "format"]) %>
```

The preceding example then becomes just:

```
<%# Eval("TotalPrice", "Total Price: {0:C}") %>
```

And, if no formatting of the value is required, you can use:

```
<%# Eval("TotalPrice") %>
```

Simplified ASP.NET 2.0 Syntax for Hierarchical (XML) Data Binding

ASP.NET 2.0 introduces new data source controls that can expose hierarchical data from XML documents. When a control is bound to such a data source control, the data is exposed to the control as a hierarchical structure that cannot be bound using the existing data binding syntax.

Instead, a development on the existing techniques is used, based on a new `XPathBinder` object exposed by the list control when bound to XML data. The `XPathBinder` exposes two methods named `Eval` and `Select`. Both take an instance of an object that exposes the `IXPathNavigable` interface (such as the container for a data source control bound to an XML document). The second parameter is an XPath expression that selects one or more nodes from the source data.

The Eval (XPath) Method

The `Eval` method returns a single value from the current "row" (a single element value) and can optionally format it using the same approach as described for nonhierarchical data in the previous section:

```
<%# XPathBinder.Eval(Container.DataItem,
            "expression"[, "format"]) %>
```

However, the simplified syntax is the obvious choice here, using an override of the `Eval` method named `XPath`:

```
<%# XPath("expression"[, "format"]) %>
```

The *expression* is an XPath that returns a single node (element or attribute) from the fragment or XML document to which the control is bound. The *format* is the same you use with the `Eval` method for nonhierarchical (rowset) data.

The Select (XPathSelect) Method

With hierarchical data, each node can be a collection of other nodes. For example, in an XML document, each `<employee>` element in a list of employees is likely to be the parent of several other nodes (see Listing 4.29).

LISTING 4.29. A Sample XML File for Data Binding

```
<employee-list>
  <employee id="1">
    <name>Mike</name>
    <department>Sales</department>
    <phone>3867</phone>
  </employee>
  <employee id="2">
    <name>Nikita</name>
    <department>Marketing</department>
    <phone>1442</phone>
  </employee>
  <employee id="3">
    ... etc ...
  </employee>
<employee-list>
```

In this case, a control bound to the data can use the XPath approach to select a specific employee name:

```
<%# XPath("employee[@id='2']/name") %>
```

However, a useful feature would be to bind a nested list control to each employee element so that it can display the details of each employee. In this case, the data binding statement must return a collection of nodes. The `Select` method of the `XPathBinder` does just this:

```
<%# XPathBinder.Select(Container.DataItem,
        "expression") %>
```

Again, there is a simplified approach that uses an override of the `Select` method called `XPathSelect`. (There is no format parameter because the method returns a collection and not a single value.)

```
<%# XPathSelect("expression") %>
```

As an example, the following statement will return all the child elements of the `<employee>` element that has the `id` value of 2:

```
<%# XPathSelect("employee[@id='2']") %>
```

Simplified Data Binding Syntax Options

In summary, you have five obvious choices for data binding expressions:

A: `<%# Container.DataItem("[column|property|field]") %>`
B: `<%# DataBinder.Eval("[column|property|field]"[, "format"]) %>`
C: `<%# Eval("[column|property|field]"[, "format"]) %>`
D: `<%# XPath("xpath-expression"[, "format"]) %>`
E: `<%# XPathSelect("xpath-expression") %>`

Table 4.15 shows how and where they can be used.

Building Data-Bound Pages with Visual Studio .NET "Whidbey"

In this and the previous chapter, we've concentrated on the new controls that are part of ASP.NET 2.0 and make it easy to build data-bound pages

TABLE 4.15. Availability of Data Binding Options

	Nonhierarchical (Rowset) Data	Hierarchical (XML) Data	Returns a Single Value	Returns a Collection	Supports Formatting
A	✓	✗	✓	✗	✗
B	✓	✗	✓	✗	✓
C	✓	✗	✓	✗	✓
D	✗	✓	✓	✗	✓
E	✗	✓	✗	✓	✗

that can display and update data. We showed you how easy it is to declare the controls you need and how to add attributes to change the appearance or behavior of the controls. But the main focus has been to help you understand what the controls do and how they are used as part of the overall page design process.

However, it is even easier to build these kinds of pages using a suitable development tool or environment. We introduced Microsoft's Visual Studio .NET "Whidbey" tool in Chapter 2, and you saw how comprehensive it is. It is ideal for building data-bound pages—you can open a connection to a database in the Data Explorer window and then simply drag a table onto the design surface. This automatically creates the appropriate SqlDataSource and GridView controls and sets the relevant properties (see Figure 4.10).

The resulting page displays all the rows from that table, as shown in Figure 4.11 on the next page. You can then use the Common Tasks menus or the Properties window to configure the GridView and SqlDataSource controls, apply formatting, add sorting and paging, and so on.

Note that, by default, Visual Studio .NET "Whidbey" changes the ProviderName property of the SqlDataSource control from the default of System.Data.SqlClient to System.Data.OleDb in order to provide maximum compatibility with all types of relational databases.

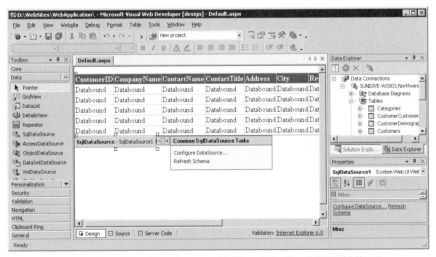

Figure 4.10. Creating a data-bound page with Visual Studio .NET "Whidbey"

CustomerID	CompanyName	ContactName	ContactTitle	Address	City	Region	PostalCode	Country	Ph
ALFKI	Alfreds Futterkiste	Maria Anders	Sales Representative	Obere Str. 57	Berlin		12209	Germany	030 007
ANATR	Ana Trujillo Emparedados y helados	Ana Trujillo	Owner	Avda. de la Constitución 2222	México D.F.		05021	Mexico	(5) 472
ANTON	Antonio Moreno Taquería	Antonio Moreno	Owner	Mataderos 2312	México D.F.		05023	Mexico	(5) 393
AROUT	Around the Horn	Thomas Hardy	Sales Representative	120 Hanover Sq.	London		WA1 1DP	UK	(17 778
BERGS	Berglunds snabbköp	Christina Berglund	Order Administrator	Berguvsvägen 8	Luleå		S-958 22	Sweden	092 65
BLAUS	Blauer See Delikatessen	Hanna Moos	Sales Representative	Forsterstr. 57	Mannheim		68306	Germany	062 084
BLONP	Blondesddsl père et fils	Frédérique Citeaux	Marketing Manager	24, place Kléber	Strasbourg		67000	France	88.
BOLID	Bólido Comidas preparadas	Martín Sommer	Owner	C/ Araquil, 67	Madrid		28023	Spain	(91 82
BONAP	Bon app'	Laurence	Owner	12, rue des	Marseille		13008	France	91

Figure 4.11. Viewing the results

SUMMARY

In this and the previous chapters we've looked at the topics new in ASP.NET 2.0 that are perhaps the most vital in business or commercial Web sites and Web applications—the presentation and manipulation of data stored in a database or other type of data store.

A whole new approach to extracting data from a data store and pushing updates back into a data store has been added in version 2.0. In 2002, Microsoft released a free development tool called ASP.NET Web Matrix, which pioneered the concept of data source controls and grid controls that require no code to be written when displaying data.

Building on that, ASP.NET 2.0 includes a whole raft of data source controls, with more on the way, allowing no-code data binding to be performed against almost any data source. And, even better, most of these data source controls also support updates, allowing changes to the data and the addition of new rows to be pushed back into the data store automatically.

In this chapter, we looked in depth at the new GridView and Details View controls. We also discussed the simplified syntax for data binding and the new XML binding syntax, as well as a quick overview of using Visual Studio .NET "Whidbey" to build data-bound pages.

You'll see more discussion of using data-bound controls in the next chapter, where—along with the use of the new master pages feature in ASP.NET—we'll look at other controls that are designed to work with data and how we can use them for page and site navigation purposes.

5

Master Pages and Navigation

T HE LOOK AND FEEL OF A SITE can be its savior or its downfall, and
there are plenty of books and Web sites that instruct in design and usability. This chapter discusses not site design but how ASP.NET 2.0 aids in
the design and consistency of sites. From the development perspective,
generating a site that is consistent isn't so hard, and there are plenty of
ways it can be achieved. However, these are all custom solutions, not part
of the underlying .NET Framework. ASP.NET 2.0 brings a solution that not
only improves ways of providing UI reuse but also aids in maintenance of
the site.

Likewise, providing navigation within a site can be achieved easily, but
you nearly always have to write code or buy a custom solution. ASP.NET
2.0 has a new framework that provides a simple and extensible solution for
providing navigation.

Master Pages in Detail

In Chapter 1 we had a brief look at the idea of master pages, showing how
they provide a template for all content pages. This provides a way to create a consistent look for a site, since the look is defined in the master page.
Let's refresh ourselves about how this works.

Figure 5.1 shows an example of two content pages using a master page.
The master page defines the page layout—that is, the shared UI and code
plus any default content. In this case it is the light shaded content at the

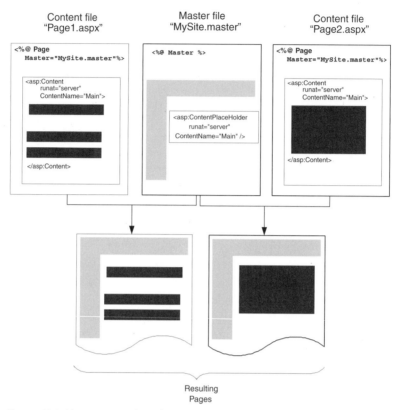

FIGURE 5.1. Master pages in action

top and left, representing menus and other navigation features. The master page defines content areas using the `ContentPlaceHolder` control, and it is into these areas that content pages place their content (shown as dark shaded areas in the figure). Pages that use a master page to define the layout can place content only in the areas defined by the `ContentPlace Holder`, thus enabling a consistent site design.

Creating Master Pages

In Visual Studio .NET "Whidbey," creating master pages is simply a matter of selecting Master Page from the Add New Item dialog. The newly created master page is just an ASP.NET page with a different file extension (`.master`), so it fits with your existing knowledge. You don't have to learn any new techniques, apart from the use of the `ContentPlaceHolder` control. Listing 5.1, for example, shows the contents of a master page newly added to a site.

FIGURE 5.2. The master page in design view

LISTING 5.1. A Simple Master Page

```
<%@ Master language="VB" %>

<script runat="server">

</script>

<html>
<head runat="server">
  <title>Untitled Page</title>
</head>

<body>
  <form runat="server">
    <asp:ContentPlaceHolder
        id="ContentPlaceHolder1" runat="server">
    </asp:ContentPlaceHolder>
  </form>
</body>
</html>
```

You can see that this looks similar to existing ASP.NET pages and contains simple HTML and ASP.NET controls. The main difference between this page and a standard ASP.NET page is the use of the Master directive and the file suffix .master. The critical point is the use of the Content PlaceHolder control, which dictates where content pages can insert content. The id attribute uniquely identifies the placeholder, allowing more than one placeholder to be in a master page. The master page can have code as well as content, allowing the master page to be dynamic.

Turning this empty master page into one that defines the look and feel of a site is simply a matter of adding controls to get the required look. Figure 5.2, for example, shows the addition of a table to define the page layout, with an area at the top where the logo and site description sit and a

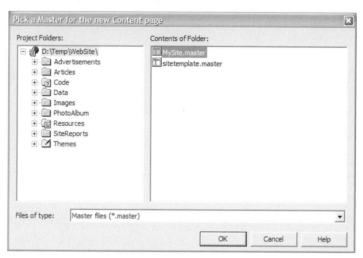

FIGURE 5.3. Picking a master page for a content page

region down the left for the menu. In the middle we have the Content PlaceHolder, which is the area we are leaving for content pages to fill in.

Using a Master Page

To create a page that uses the master page, you pick Content Page from the Add New Item dialog, at which point you get the opportunity to pick which master page you wish the content page to inherit from, as shown in Figure 5.3.

When first created, the content page contains a single line of code:

```
<%@ Page language="VB" master="~/mysite.master" %>
```

Figure 5.4 shows this content page in design view. Notice how the content defined in the master is grayed out and disabled—the only area allowed for editing is that defined by the Content control.

The confusing thing here is that this Content control doesn't seem to exist in the file—remember there was only a single line, the Page directive.

FIGURE 5.4. A content page with an attached master

This is because at design time the content of the master page is rendered, but our page defines no content, so an empty region is displayed so the Designer can prompt you where to add the Content control. This can be done either by selecting the Create Empty Content option from the Common Tasks menu or by simply dragging controls from the Toolbox into this region.

Listing 5.2 shows the source view for a content page with a couple of controls added.

LISTING 5.2. Using a Master Page (MyPage.aspx)

```
<%@ Page Language="VB" Master="MySite.master" %>

<asp:Content id="Content1" ContentPlaceHolderId="ContentPlaceHolder1"
    runat="server">
  <asp:Button id="Button1" runat="server" text="Button" />
  <asp:ListBox id="ListBox1" runat="server">
  </asp:ListBox"
</asp:Content>
```

The local content is within the Content control—content in a page that has a master page cannot be outside a Content control. This ensures that all content pages using a master have a consistent look. Since master pages can contain multiple content areas, the id of the ContentPlaceHolder control is used to link the Content control to the ContentPlaceHolder control in the master page. When the page is constructed, ASP.NET first adds all of the content from the master page. Then it loops through the ContentPlaceHolder controls and, for each, looks in the content page for a Content control where the ContentPlaceHolderId matches the id of the ContentPlaceHolder. This ensures that the correct content is placed in the correct holder.

Default Content

Along with layout and code that applies to all pages, the master page can also supply default content, which can be overridden by content pages or displayed if not overridden. This is achieved by simply inserting the content within the ContentPlaceHolder element. For example, our MySite.master page could have the following default content:

```
<asp:ContentPlaceHolder
    id="ContentPlaceHolder1" runat="server">

  <h2>Welcome</h2>
  Welcome to my site, where you'll find
  lots of interesting stuff.
</asp:ContentPlaceHolder>
```

FIGURE 5.5. A content page with no content other than default content

Creating a new content file based on this master would give us the following line of code:

```
<%@ Page Language="VB" master="~/MySite.master" %>
```

Since we haven't specified a Content control, all content is provided by the master page, as shown in Figure 5.5.

Nested Master Pages

Master pages aren't limited to a single master and content pages; the architecture allows for nested master pages, where a master page can have a master page. This is particularly useful for sites that require some overall branding and look but that also have subsites whose look must be consistent. For example, consider a corporation with group intranets—perhaps one for the sales department and one for research. The company wishes to have an overall look, including menus between the subsites, but allows the departments to design their parts of the site to fit their business needs. In this situation you could have three master pages—the top-level master defining the corporate site image, a submaster for the sales department, and a submaster for the research department. The sales and research submaster pages would define the corporate master as their master page. The inheritance rules of master pages mean that any pages using one of the submaster pages receives content from all master pages in the hierarchy (see Figure 5.6).

Notice that you can inherit from any level of the hierarchy—you aren't limited to using the bottom level. This allows you to provide generic content pages that apply to the whole site, as well as pages that apply to individual site areas. Let's take a look at the code that makes this possible, starting with the site master as shown in Listing 5.3.

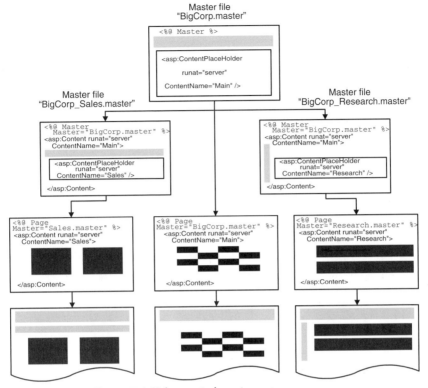

FIGURE 5.6. Using nested master pages

LISTING 5.3. The Site Master Page (BigCorp.master)

```
<%@ Master %>

<html>
<head>
  <link rel="stylesheet" type="text/css" href="MySite.css">
</head>

<body>
<form runat="server">
  <table width="100%" border="0">
    <tr>
      <td>
        <asp:Hyperlink ImageUrl="home.gif" runat="server"
            NavigateUrl="BigCorp_Default.aspx" />
      </td>
      <td>
        <h1>Big Corp Intranet</h1>
      </td>
      <td>
        <a href="BigCorp_SalesDefault.aspx">Sales</a>
```

continues

```
        </td>
        <td>
          <a href="BigCorp_ResearchDefault.aspx">Research</a>
        </td>
      </tr>
    </table>
    <asp:ContentPlaceHolder runat="server"
       id="MainContentRegion">
      Welcome to Big Corp. Please use the menus above
      to select the required department.
    </asp:ContentPlaceHolder>
</form>
</body>
</html>
```

This simple master page, containing some content and a placeholder, is shown in design view in Figure 5.7.

Now consider Listing 5.4, which shows a submaster page that inherits from the first master page.

LISTING 5.4. A Submaster Page (BigCorp_Sales.master)

```
<%@ Master Master="BigCorp.master"%>

<asp:Content ContentPlaceHolderId="MainContentRegion"
    runat="server">
<table border="0" width="100%">
  <tr>
    <td>
      <h2>Big Corp Sales</h2>
    </td>
  </tr>
  <tr>
    <td>
      <table border="0" width="100%">
        <tr>
          <td><a href="sales/page1.aspx" Menu 1</a></td>
          <td><a href="sales/page2.aspx" Menu 2</a></td>
          <td><a href="sales/page3.aspx" Menu 3</a></td>
          <td><a href="sales/page4.aspx" Menu 4</a></td>
```

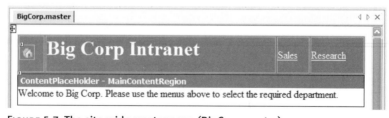

FIGURE 5.7. The site-wide master page (BigCorp.master)

```
        </tr>
      </table>
    </td>
  </tr>
  <tr>
    <td>
      <asp:ContentPlaceHolder runat="server"
          id="SalesContentRegion" />
    </td>
  </tr>
</table>
</asp:Content>
```

Because this page inherits from a master page, all content must be within a `Content` control, with a `ContentPlaceHolderId` matching that of the master `ContentPlaceHolder`. However, we can also include `Content PlaceHolder` controls in this master, allowing content pages to add content to our content. The design view for `BigCorp_Sales.master` is shown in Figure 5.8, where you can see that `Content1` is the content area defined by `BigCorp.master`, and `Content2` is the region defined for content pages to use.

Using the nested master page is the same as creating any other content page. For example, Listing 5.5 shows a content page using `BigCorp _Sales.master`.

LISTING 5.5. A Content Page Using a Nested Master Page

```
<%@ Page Master="BigCorp_Sales.master" %>

<script runat="server">
```

continues

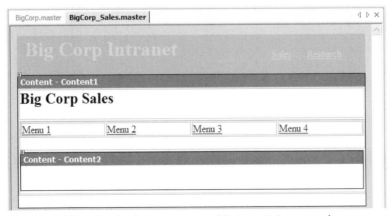

FIGURE 5.8. The nested sales master page (BigCorp_Sales.master)

```
Sub Page_Load(sender As Object, e As EventArgs)

End Sub

</script>

<asp:Content ContentPlaceHolderId="SalesContentRegion"
    runat="server">
  Welcome to the Big Corp Sales Intranet
</asp:Content>
```

Here the `ContentPlaceHolderId` matches the immediate parent, and since the parent inherits from another page, the ultimate result is a combination of both master pages and the child ASP.NET content page. So, if we have two child content pages, one for the sales division and one for the research division, we'll end up with a site as shown in Figure 5.9.

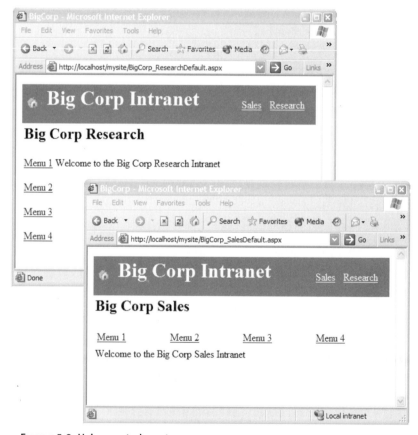

FIGURE 5.9. Using nested master pages

In Figure 5.9 you can see that although both departments have chosen a different style of menu (one vertical and one horizontal), the top of the page remains constant because it is defined in the top-level master.

Master Page Configuration

Attaching a master page directly to a page provides great flexibility but does have a downside. Not only must developers know the name of the master but they are also free to not use it, which could result in pages not fitting with the overall site design. To ensure that a master page cannot be omitted, master pages can be attached globally by modifying the Web configuration file, as shown in the following fragment:

```
<configuration>
  <system.web>

    <pages master="BigCorp.master" />

  </system.web>
</configuration>
```

A master page attached locally via the `Master` attribute, however, overrides any global master pages defined in `web.config`.

Device-Specific Master Pages

ASP.NET has a new architecture for detecting and rendering content to mobile devices, and this control architecture has also been implemented by the master page processing, enabling different master pages to be used for different devices. For example, it would be possible to supply different master pages for Internet Explorer and Mozilla. This is achieved by creating separate master pages and then in the page prefixing the `master` attribute with the name of the device, as shown below:

```
<%@ Page master="default.master"
        Mozilla:master="mozilla.master" %>
```

When this page is accessed by a Mozilla browser, `mozilla.master` is used. All other browsers use the default master page. The results can be seen in Figure 5.10, where the content simply differs for each browser. Where this comes into its own is in supporting multiple devices, such as small-screen devices, where your master page might need to be very different, perhaps to incorporate a different menu structure.

Mobile device support is covered in more detail in Chapter 10.

FIGURE 5.10. Device-specific master pages

Like the rest of the device-specific features, the list of devices can be found in the CONFIG directory under the .NET Framework installation directory. These are device capability files, detailing the exact features of each browser.

Event Ordering

Because events can be present in both the master and content pages, the event order follows that of User Controls. So, for events that are captured twice, such as the Page_Load event, the content page event is fired first.

Accessing the Master Page

Content pages that have a master have a property, Master, allowing access to the master page. The Master property returns an instance of Page (from System.Web.UI), and thus you can access all of the properties and methods in the same way as for other pages. For example, to access a control from the master page you can do one of two things. The first option is to expose the control through a public property on the master page (Listing 5.6) and access that property from the content page (Listing 5.7).

LISTING 5.6. Exposing Master Page Properties (MySite.master)

```
<%@ Master %>
<script runat="server">

Public ReadOnly Property Home() As Hyperlink
  Get
    Return homeUrl
  End Get
End Property

</script>

<form runat="server">

  <asp:Hyperlink id="homeUrl"
      NavigateUrl="default.aspx" />

</form>
```

LISTING 5.7. Accessing Exposed Master Page Properties (MyPage.aspx)

```
<%@ Page Master="MySite.master" %>
<script runat="server">

Sub Page_Load(sender As Object, e As EventArgs)

  Dim Url As String = Master.Home.NavigateUrl

End Sub

</script>
```

Listing 5.6 shows a master page with a control exposed as a `Public Property`, and Listing 5.7 shows a content page accessing that control through the exposed property.

The second approach is to access the controls late bound and use the `FindControl` method to find the controls, as shown in Listing 5.8.

LISTING 5.8. Accessing Master Page Contents Late Bound

```
<%@ Page Master="MySite.master" %>
<script runat="server">

Sub Page_Load(sender As Object, e As EventArgs)

  Dim Url As String = _
    CType(Master.FindControl("homeUrl"), _
        Hyperlink).NavigateUrl
```

continues

```
End Sub

</script>
```

While the first solution does require you to expose controls as properties, this is required only for controls that are needed external to the master page, and this approach does provide a more efficient solution than the late-bound approach.

Navigation

The importance of good navigation on a site cannot be underestimated. It doesn't matter how great your site looks or how well it was developed—if it's hard to navigate, users won't like using it. It's easy to see how seriously navigation is taken just by looking at the number of menu controls that have been written since ASP.NET 1.0 was released—there are now controls that use tree views, vertical expansion, horizontal layouts, flashy graphics, and so on.

Providing a good menu isn't the end of site navigation because it's important to ensure visitors know where they are within the site hierarchy. Too often we see sites with pages three or four levels deep within the menu structure, but when we navigate to those pages there's no indication of where we are. We are left wondering how to navigate back up the structure; at worst, we have to go back to the home page to navigate down again.

Site Maps

There are plenty of ways to implement navigation on a site, but none that are an intrinsic part of ASP.NET 1.x. With ASP.NET 2.0, there are controls and configuration files for providing a set way to define site structure and techniques for displaying the navigation information and extracting the current navigation path.

Like the rest of ASP.NET, the architecture for navigation has been broken down into logical parts, allowing customization. First, there is a configurable provider supplying the site map information, and then a set of controls that can take advantage of the data supplied by the provider. The provider not only exposes the site structure to other controls but also keeps track of the current navigation, allowing pages to identify where in the hierarchy they are. The entire structure and the current details can be exposed to users by binding controls to the provider. This pluggable architecture means that data defining the structure of a site can come from any data source—the site map provider is the link between the data and the navigation within a site.

Site Map Providers

A **site map provider** is a data provider that exposes the site structure by way of a set interface. Site maps are pluggable within the application configuration file, within the system.web section. The syntax for this section is shown in Listing 5.9.

LISTING 5.9. Site Map Configuration Syntax

```
<siteMap
    defaultProvider="string"
    enabled="[true|false]">
  <providers>
    <add
        name="string"
        description="string"
        provider-specific-configuration />
    <remove
        name="string" />
    <clear>
  </providers>
</siteMap>
```

The attributes for the siteMap element are shown in Table 5.1.
The attributes for the providers element are shown in Table 5.2.

TABLE 5.1. siteMap Configuration

Attribute	Description
defaultProvider	The name of the default provider. This should match one of the names supplied in the providers section.
enabled	A Boolean value indicating whether or not site maps are enabled.

TABLE 5.2. siteMap providers Configuration

Attribute	Description
name	The name of the site map provider.
description	A description of the provider.
type	A string containing the full .NET type of the provider.

TABLE 5.3. XmlSiteMapProvider-Specific Attribute

Attribute	Description
siteMapFile	The name of the XML file containing the site structure. The filename is configured as app.SiteMap.

With the Technology Preview of ASP.NET 2.0, the only provider is the XmlSiteMapProvider (in System.Web), allowing site navigation structure to be stored in an XML file. For a full description of the type attribute, see the machine.config file. The XmlSiteMapProvider has one provider-specific attribute, as shown in Table 5.3.

The pluggable architecture makes it extremely easy to add support for additional methods of site map storage. For example, you could write a FrontPage site map provider to read the site structure from the format used by Microsoft FrontPage, or perhaps one to build the structure from the file system, directly reading the names of the files and directories. To write your own site map provider you need to implement the ISiteMap-Provider interface. A discussion of this is outside the scope of the book, but details of the interface can be found in the documentation.

Site Map Configuration Files

The XmlSiteMapProvider defines a set schema for the app.SiteMap file, as shown in Listing 5.10.

LISTING 5.10. XmlSiteMapProvider Schema

```
<xs:schema xmlns:xs="http://www.w3.org/2001/XMLSchema"
           elementFormDefault="qualified">
  <xs:element name="siteMap">
    <xs:complexType>
      <xs:sequence>
        <xs:element ref="siteMapNode"
                    maxOccurs="unbounded"/>
      </xs:sequence>
    </xs:complexType>
  </xs:element>
  <xs:element name="siteMapNode">
    <xs:complexType>
      <xs:sequence>
        <xs:element ref="siteMapNode" minOccurs="0"
                    MaxOccurs="unbounded"/>
      </xs:sequence>
      <xs:attribute name="url" type="xs:string"/>
```

```
        <xs:attribute name="title" type="xs:string"/>
        <xs:attribute name="description" type="xs:string"/>
        <xs:attribute name="keywords" type="xs:string"/>
        <xs:attribute name="roles" type="xs:string"/>
        <xs:attribute name="SiteMapFile" type="xs:string"/>
        <xs:attribute name="Provider" type="xs:string"/>
      </xs:complexType>
    </xs:element>
</xs:schema>
```

This defines a structure consisting of a root `siteMap` element, with the site structure being contained by `siteMapNode` elements. There has to be one top-level `siteMapNode` element, and within that can be any number of `siteMapNode` elements of any depth. The attributes for the `siteMapNode` element are shown in Table 5.4.

The use of `SiteMapFile` allows the site map information to be split among different sources. This is especially useful when different divisions supply sections of a corporate site—each part of the site map can be authored independently and even stored in different providers.

Listing 5.11 shows a sample site map file. To create one within Visual Studio .NET "Whidbey," you simply create a new XML file and call it `app.SiteMap`—there isn't a template for this.

TABLE 5.4. siteMapNode Attributes

Attribute	Description
url	The URL to be used to navigate to the node. This must be unique within the entire site map file.
title	The title of the node.
description	A description of the node.
keywords	Keywords used to describe the node. Multiple keywords can be separated by semicolons (;) or commas (,).
roles	A list of roles allowed to view the node. Multiple roles can be separated by semicolons (;) or commas (,).
SiteMapFile	An external file containing additional `siteMap` nodes.
Provider	The name of the site map provider that will supply additional nodes specified in `SiteMapFile`.

LISTING 5.11. Sample app.SiteMap File

```
<siteMap>
  <siteMapNode title="Home"
               description="Home"
               url="SiteMaps.aspx?id=1">
    <siteMapNode title="Sales"
                 description="The Sales Site"
                 url="SiteMaps.aspx?id=2">
      <siteMapNode title="Customers"
                   url="SiteMaps.aspx?id=3"/>
      <siteMapNode title="Products"
                   url="SiteMaps.aspx?id=4/>
      <siteMapNode title="Region"
                   url="SiteMaps.aspx?id=5"/>
      <siteMapNode title="Futures"
                   url="SiteMaps.aspx?id=6"/>
    </siteMapNode>
    <siteMapNode title="Research"
                 description="The Research Site"
                 url="SiteMaps.aspx?id=7">
      <siteMapNode title="Widgets"
                   url="SiteMaps.aspx?id=8"/>
      <siteMapNode title="Doodads"
                   url="SiteMaps.aspx?id=9"/>
      <siteMapNode title="Thingies"
                   url="SiteMaps.aspx?id=10" />
    </siteMapNode>
  </siteMapNode>
</siteMap>
```

This provides the following structure for the site:

```
Home
  Sales
    Customers
    Products
    Region
    Futures
  Research
    Widgets
    Doodads
    Thingies
```

Using a Site Map File

Once the structure of your site is defined in the site map file, you then need a way to make use of it. For this you use a SiteMapDataSource control, which provides data access to the site map data, and then a control to display that data. From within Visual Studio .NET "Whidbey," you can just

FIGURE 5.11. A TreeView bound to a SiteMapDataSource

drag a `SiteMapDataSource` control onto the design surface—there's no need to set any properties because it defaults to using `app.SiteMap` as its data source. You can then drag a `TreeView` control onto the page and set its `DataSourceId` property to the `id` of the `SiteMapDataSource` control. Figure 5.11, for example, shows how our Big Corp site could be constructed using a single menu.

Other controls can be bound to site map data, but in the Technology Preview release, the `TreeView` provides the best option because of its hierarchical display. It's possible that a dedicated menu control will appear in future versions.

Site Maps in Depth

At its simplest, the use of site maps needs nothing more than has been discussed above, but there's actually more to them. Adding a `SiteMapData Source` control to a page provides all that's needed for site map handling, but there are properties that allow for more control over how the data is supplied from the `SiteMapDataSource` to controls. For example, the syntax of the `SiteMapDataSource` control is shown in Listing 5.12.

LISTING 5.12. SiteMapDataSource Syntax

```
<asp:SiteMapDataSource id="String" runat="server"
  FlatDepth="Integer"
  SiteMapProvider="String"
  SiteMapViewType="[Flat|Path|Tree]"
  StartingDepth="Integer"
  StartingNodeType="[Current|Parent|Root]"
  StartingNodeUrl="String"
/>
```

The attributes are shown in Table 5.5.

TABLE 5.5. SiteMapDataSource Attributes

Attribute	Description
FlatDepth	A number that defines how many nodes deep in the hierarchical structure are flattened. The default is -1, which indicates all nodes.
SiteMapProvider	The name of the provider supplying the site map data.
SiteMapViewType	One of the SiteMapViewType enumerations, whose values are: • Flat: Indicates that the data is presented without any structure. • Path: Indicates the data presented is a list of nodes between the root node and the current node. • Tree: Indicates the data is presented in the same hierarchical structure as the original data source. Binding nonhierarchical controls when using this mode shows only the top level of the hierarchy. This is the default value.
StartingDepth	Specifies the node depth at which to start representing data. The default is 0, which is the first node.
StartingNodeType	One of the SiteMapNodeType enumerations, whose values are: • Current: Indicates the node that represents the currently displayed page. • Parent: Indicates the parent node of the currently displayed page. • Root: Indicates the root node. This is the default value.
StartingNodeUrl	The URL of the node at which to start representing data.

The effects of some of these properties are not immediately apparent and depend on which control you bind to the data source and where you are in the navigation hierarchy. Probably the most useful control is the TreeView, which naturally displays hierarchical data, but the ListBox is also good for displaying site map data in a flat view. A good way to see the effects of these properties is to build a grid with three SiteMapDataSource controls, each set to a different SiteMapViewType. Then you can bind a TreeView and a ListBox to each type view of the site map, as shown in Listing 5.13.

LISTING 5.13. Sample Site Map Displays

```
<asp:SiteMapDataSource id="SiteDataFlat" runat="server"
    SiteMapViewType="Flat" />
<asp:SiteMapDataSource id="SiteDataPath" runat="server"
    SiteMapViewType="Path" />
<asp:SiteMapDataSource id="SiteDataTree" runat="server"
    SiteMapViewType="Tree" />

<table border="1" width="50%">
  <tr>
    <td>Flat</td>
    <td>Path</td>
    <td>Tree</td>
  </tr>
  <tr>
    <td>
      <asp:TreeView runat="server"
          DataSourceId="SiteDataFlat" />
    </td>
    <td>
      <asp:TreeView runat="server"
          DataSourceId="SiteDataPath" />
    </td>
    <td>
      <asp:TreeView runat="server"
          DataSourceId="SiteDataTree" />
    </td>
  </tr>
  <tr>
    <td>
      <asp:ListBox runat="server"
          DataSourceId="SiteDataFlat" />
    </td>
    <td>
      <asp:ListBox runat="server"
          DataSourceId="SiteDataPath" />
    </td>
    <td>
```

continues

```
    <asp:ListBox runat="server"
        DataSourceId="SiteDataTree" />
  </td>
 </tr>
</table>
```

The initial display is shown in Figure 5.12. By default the `TreeView` binds the `title` attribute of the site map to the `Text` property and the `url` attribute to the `NavigateUrl` property, giving you an instant menu control. For the `ListBox` the `title` attribute is bound to both the `DataTextField` and `DataValueField` properties.

You can see from this that when in `Tree` mode, the `TreeView` displays as you expect it to. However, the `Flat` view shows how all nodes (at whatever level) are shown. Nodes with children are expandable in the normal `TreeView` style. For the `Path` mode, nothing is shown because we haven't yet performed any navigation.

For the `ListBox` control, the `Tree` mode shows only the first node because it is a naturally flat control and can deal only with a single level of the hierarchy. However, in `Flat` mode you see all nodes because they have been flattened and therefore appear at the top level.

The results of navigating to the Sales Region page are shown in Figure 5.13.

Here you can see that the `Tree` and `Flat` views are essentially the same as their initial settings, and the `Path` view has now been filled. In the `Path` view column, note that the `TreeView` contains the same data as the `Tree` mode, but the `ListBox` shows only those nodes in the path between the root node and the selected node.

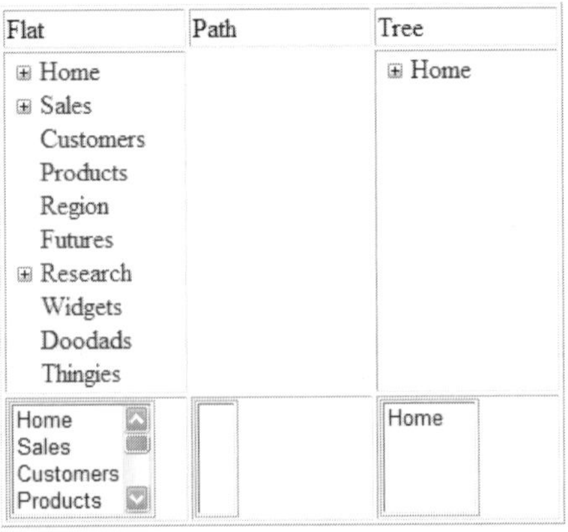

FIGURE 5.12. Initial site map display

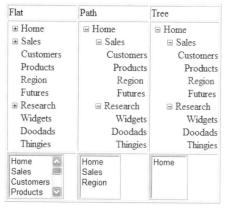

FIGURE 5.13. Navigating to a page

Flattening Nodes

Setting the `FlatDepth` property limits the depth of the nodes that are flattened. For example, on the left in Figure 5.14 you see a `FlatDepth` of `1`, so only one node is flattened. On the right a `FlatDepth` of `2` causes three nodes to be flattened—the top node, plus its two child nodes.

Setting the Starting Depth

The `StartingDepth` property indicates at which node level the data is displayed from, and it affects all three modes (`Flat`, `Path`, and `Tree`). For example, setting the `StartingDepth` to `1` (where no `FlatDepth` is set) is shown in Figure 5.15.

Here you can see that only nodes from level 1 down are shown and only those from our navigation point—remember, the `SiteMapDataSource` keeps track of where we are in the navigational structure.

FIGURE 5.14. Results of setting different FlatDepth properties

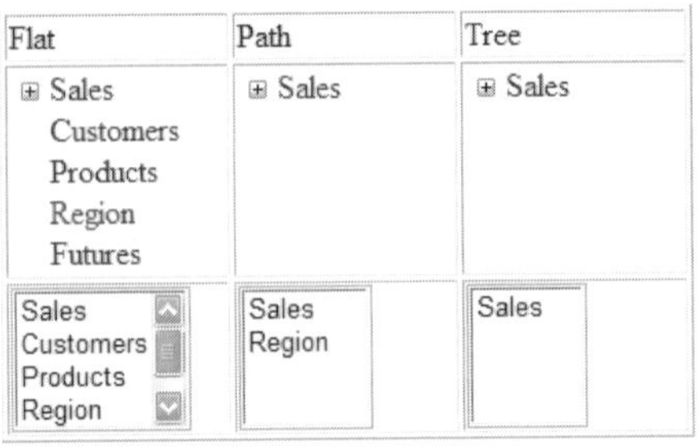

Flat	Path	Tree
⊞ Sales Customers Products Region Futures	⊞ Sales	⊞ Sales
Sales Customers Products Region	Sales Region	Sales

FIGURE 5.15. Results of setting the StartingDepth property to 1

Setting the Starting Node Type

The StartingNodeType property identifies what type of node to start displaying data from. For example, setting this property to Parent would give the results in Figure 5.16. We've navigated to the Region node, a node that is underneath Sales. In the ListBox, for the Flat view we see only the Parent of the current node, plus its children; for the Path view, we see only the current node and its parent; and for the Tree view, we see only the parent.

Setting the StartingNodeType to Current means that only the current node is displayed, as shown in Figure 5.17. Setting the CurrentNodeType to Root means that the current node becomes the root node as far as displaying the node hierarchy is concerned.

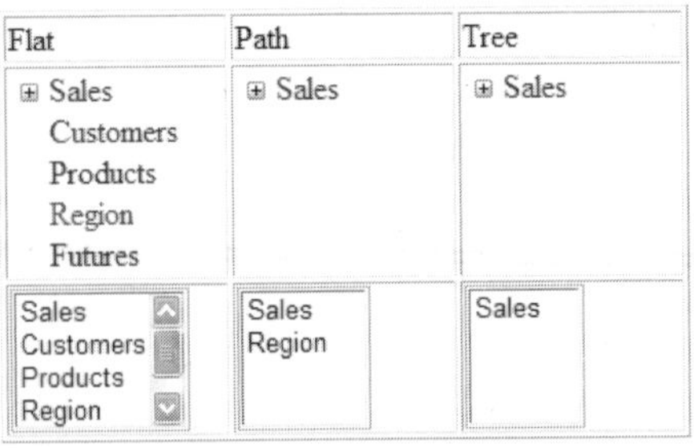

Flat	Path	Tree
⊞ Sales Customers Products Region Futures	⊞ Sales	⊞ Sales
Sales Customers Products Region	Sales Region	Sales

FIGURE 5.16. Results of setting the StartingNodeType property to Parent

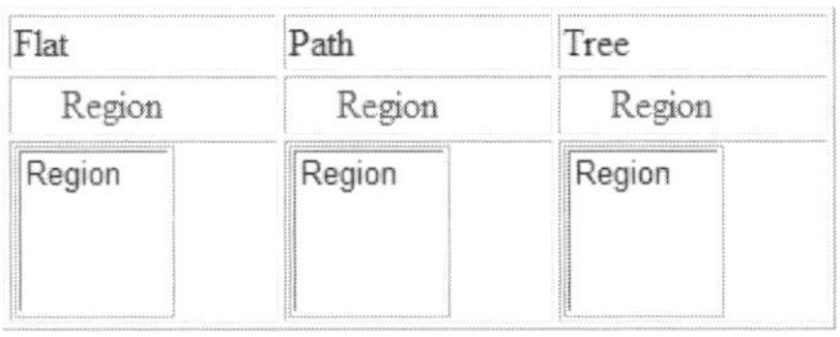

Flat	Path	Tree
Region	Region	Region
Region	Region	Region

FIGURE 5.17. Results of setting the StartingNodeType property to Current

Setting the Start Node URL

The `StartingNodeUrl` property allows us to set the starting point, given the URL of a page. Since URLs in the site map file must be unique, this allows us to navigate to a given node knowing only the URL, rather than its location in the hierarchy.

Showing a Navigation Path

When a site map provides the navigational architecture for a site, it's easy to add features that take advantage of this. With a hierarchy three deep or more, it has always been hard for users to remember where they are within that structure, so the idea of breadcrumbs came about, laying a trail of the path back to the root of the site.

With ASP.NET 2.0 this is simple: We have the `SiteMapPath` control, which automatically hooks into the site map architecture, so all you have to do is drop it on a page, as shown in Figure 5.18.

This figure shows the default implementation, just from adding the following line of code to our page:

```
<asp:SiteMapPath runat="server" />
```

To use the `SiteMapPath` control you don't need a `SiteMapDataSource` control because it works directly with the site map provider.

The current node is shown as simple text, and parent nodes are shown as hyperlinks, allowing quick navigation up the tree. The text for the tooltip is set to the `description` attribute from the site map file.

There are plenty of ways to customize this control to fit it to your site. The syntax is shown in Listing 5.14.

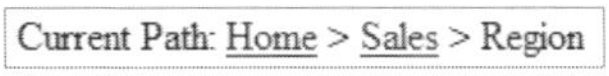

Current Path: Home > Sales > Region

FIGURE 5.18. The SiteMapPath control

LISTING 5.14. SiteMapPath Syntax

```
<SiteMapPath id="String" runat="server"
  CurrentNodeStyle="Style"
  CurrentNodeTemplate="Template"
  HoverNodeStyle="Style"
  NodeStyle="Style"
  NodeTemplate="Template"
  ParentLevelsDisplayed="Integer"
  PathDirection="[CurrentToRoot|RootToCurrent]"
  PathSeparator="String"
  PathSeparatorStyle="Style"
  PathSeparatorTemplate="Template"
  RenderCurrentNodeAsLink="Boolean"
  RootNodeStyle="Style"
  RootNodeTemplate="Template"
  ShowToolTips="Boolean"
  SiteMapProvider="String"
  />
```

These are just the unique properties for this control, described in Table 5.6. All other properties are inherited and are described in the documentation.

TABLE 5.6. SiteMapPath Properties

Property	Description
CurrentNodeStyle	Sets or returns the Style object that defines how the current node is displayed.
CurrentNodeTemplate	Sets a Template, allowing customization of how the current node is displayed.
NodeStyle	Sets or returns the Style to be used for nodes.
NodeTemplate	Sets a Template, allowing customization of how a node is displayed.
ParentLevelsDisplayed	Sets or returns the number of parent levels displayed. By default all parent levels are displayed.

TABLE 5.6. SiteMapPath Properties (continued)

Property	Description
PathDirection	Gets or sets the direction in which the nodes are displayed. This can be one of the `PathDirection` enumerations, whose values are: • `CurrentToRoot`: The current node is shown on the left, and child nodes are shown to the right. • `RootToCurrent`: The current node is shown on the left, and parent nodes are shown on the right. This is the default value. Setting the direction has no effect on the separator between nodes.
PathSeparator	Sets or returns a string to be used as a separator between nodes. This is replaced by the contents of the `PathSeparatorTemplate` if present. The default is >.
PathSeparatorStyle	Sets or returns the `Style` to be used for the `PathSeparator` string.
PathSeparatorTemplate	Sets a `Template`, allowing customization of the node separator.
RenderCurrentNodeAsLink	Sets or returns a `Boolean` that indicates whether or not the current node is rendered as a hyperlink. The default value is `False`.
RootNodeStyle	Sets or returns the `Style` to be used for the root node. Any `Style` values set here override those set in the `NodeStyle` property.
RootNodeTemplate	Sets a `Template`, allowing customization of the root node.
ShowToolTips	Sets or returns a `Boolean` indicating whether or not tooltips are shown on hyperlinks.
SiteMapProvider	Sets or returns a string indicating the site name of the provider supplying the site map data.

These properties give a great deal of flexibility in how the navigation path is shown. For example, consider the code shown in Listing 5.15.

LISTING 5.15. Setting the SiteMapPath Properties

```
<asp:SiteMapPath ID="SiteMapPath1" runat="server"
    NodeStyle-Font-Name="Franklin Gothic Medium"
    NodeStyle-Font-Underline="true"
    NodeStyle-Font-Bold="true"
    RootNodeStyle-Font-Name="Symbol"
    RootNodeStyle-Font-Bold="false"
    CurrentNodeStyle-Font-Name="Verdana"
    CurrentNodeStyle-Font-Size="10pt"
    CurrentNodeStyle-Font-Bold="true"
    CurrentNodeStyle-ForeColor="red"
    CurrentNodeStyle-Font-Underline="false">
  <PathSeparatorTemplate>
      <asp:Image runat="server" ImageUrl="arrow.gif"/>
  </PathSeparatorTemplate>
</asp:SiteMapPath>
```

This defines styles for the nodes and a separator that uses a custom image. The results are shown in Figure 5.19.

Notice that the root node is underlined even though it wasn't specified as part of the `RootNodeStyle`—the underlining was inherited from the `NodeStyle`.

SiteMapPath Events

The `SiteMapPath` is built dynamically from the data held by the underlying site map provider. As the tree of nodes is traversed, each item in the path, from the root node to the current node, is added to the `Controls` collection of the `SiteMapPath` control. Like other collection controls (such as the `DataList` or `DataGrid`), two events are fired when items are either created (`ItemCreated`) or bound (`ItemDataBound`) to the `SiteMapPath`. The signature for these events is the same:

```
Sub eventName(Sender As Object,
              E As SiteMapNodeItemEventArgs)
```

`SiteMapNodeItemEventArgs` has one property, `Item`, which returns an object of type `SiteMapNodeItem`, which in turn has three properties, as described in Table 5.7.

FIGURE 5.19. A customized SiteMapPath control

TABLE 5.7. SiteMapNodeItem Properties

Property	Description
ItemIndex	The zero-based index number of the item being added.
ItemType	The type of node being added, which can be one of the SiteMapNodeItemType enumerations: ● Current: Indicates the current node (page) within the navigation path. ● Parent: Indicates a parent of the current node. All nodes between the current node and the root node are parent nodes. ● PathSeparator: Indicates a separator between nodes. ● Root: Indicates the root node of the navigation path.
SiteMapNode	The SiteMapNode that represents the node being added to the SiteMapPath.

Intercepting the ItemCreated and ItemDataBound events gives you a chance to change the default behavior as the items are created. For example, Listing 5.16 shows how you could build up an HTML meta tag consisting of the Keywords from the site map details. If the SiteMapPath control were embedded into the master page, this meta tag would be automatically constructed for each page.

LISTING 5.16. SiteMapPath ItemCreated Event

```
<%@ Page %>

<head runat="server" id="PageHead" />

<script runat="server">

Sub ItemCreated(Sender As Object,
            E As SiteMapNodeItemEventArgs)

  If E.Item.ItemType = _
    SiteMapNodeItemType.Current Then

    Dim sb As New StringBuilder()
    Dim s As String

    For Each s In E.Item.SiteMapNode.Keywords
```

continues

```
      sb.Append(s)
      sb.Append(" ")
    Next

    Dim ctl As New HtmlGenericControl("meta")
    ctl.Attributes.Add("name", "keywords")
    ctl.Attributes.Add("content", sb.ToString())
    PageHead.Controls.Add(ctl)
  End If
End Sub

</script>

<form runat="server">
  <asp:SiteMapPath runat="server"
      onItemCreated="ItemCreated"/>
  </form>
```

The SiteMapNode Object

When the site map is constructed from the data provider, each of the items is built into a SiteMapNode object. These in turn are added to a SiteMapNodeCollection, which therefore represents all pages within a Web site. The SiteMapNode object provides links to nodes up, down, and next to it in the hierarchy and thus can be used to build a treelike structure. As shown in Listing 5.16, the ItemCreated event of the SiteMapPath object allows access to the SiteMapNode, which has the properties detailed in Table 5.8.

TABLE 5.8. SiteMapNode Properties

Property	Description
Attributes	Returns a collection of additional attributes applicable to the node. For the XmlSiteMapProvider, the list of attributes maps to existing properties, namely Title, Description, Url, Attributes, Roles, and Keywords.
ChildNodes	If applicable, returns a SiteMapNodeCollection containing child nodes of the current node.
Description	Returns the description of the current node.
HasChildNodes	Indicates whether or not the current node has any child nodes.

TABLE 5.8. SiteMapNode Properties (continued)

Property	Description
Keywords	Returns an IList containing keywords for the current node.
NextSibling	Returns the next node on the same level as the current node, or returns null (Nothing in Visual Basic) if there is no next node.
ParentNode	Returns the parent node of the current node, or returns null (Nothing in Visual Basic) if there is no parent node (i.e., the current node is the root node).
PreviousSibling	Returns the previous node on the same level as the current node, or returns null (Nothing in Visual Basic) if there is no previous node.
Roles	Returns an IList containing the roles applicable to the current node.
RootNode	Returns the root node.
Title	Returns the title of the current node.
Url	Returns the URL of the current node.

There are three methods for the SiteMapNode object, as described in Table 5.9.

TABLE 5.9. SiteMapNode Methods

Method	Description
GetAllNodes	Returns a SiteMapNodeCollection containing all child nodes of the current node.
GetDataSourceView	Returns a SiteMapDataSourceView, which is a view of the underlying site map data. This is useful for control developers who wish to interface to the site map architecture.
IsDescendantOf	Indicates whether or not the current node is a descendent of a supplied node.

Accessing the Site Map at Runtime

So far we've seen the site map be used by controls, but it can also be accessed directly because it is exposed through a static page property called SiteMap. For example, to access the current node within the site map, you can use the following code:

```
Dim currNode As SiteMapNode

currNode = SiteMap.CurrentNode
```

This means that even if you aren't using a SiteMapPath control, you can easily build links pointing back to the hierarchy, as shown in Listing 5.17.

LISTING 5.17. Using the SiteMap Property of the Page

```
<script runat="server">

Sub Page_Load(Sender As Object, E As EventArgs)

  ParentLink.NavigateUrl = SiteMap.CurrentNode.ParentNode.Url

End Sub

</script>

<form runat="server">

  <asp:HyperLink id="ParentLink" Text="Go Back" />

</form>
```

Table 5.10 details the properties of the SiteMap class.

TABLE 5.10. SiteMap Class Properties

Property	Description
CurrentNode	Returns a SiteMapNode object representing the current page.
Provider	Returns the site map provider.
Providers	Returns a collection (SiteMapProviderCollection) of all site map providers.
RootNode	Returns a SiteMapNode object representing the root node.

These properties give you access to the site map details and allow you to interface into it at the programmatic level, in case more flexibility is required than the standard server controls provide.

SUMMARY

In this chapter we've looked at two very important topics: how the look and feel of sites can be implemented in ASP.NET 2.0 and how navigation around those sites can be implemented.

We've seen how a great deal of time-consuming work has been removed by the introduction of master pages, allowing the site layout and default implementation to be easily centralized. Not only does this make it easier to develop individual pages, but since layout and code can be centrally contained, it also eases maintenance and reduces potential errors.

We've also seen how ASP.NET 2.0 supplies a comprehensive architecture for site navigation. The introduction of the `SiteMapDataSource` and the underlying flexibility of providers allow site structure to be easily defined and used within Web pages. By placing this navigation within a master page you also have the simplicity of having to define the navigation in only a single place.

Now it's time to move on to another important topic—security, and how to identify users and control what they can do once they reach your site.

6

Security

VERSION 1.1 OF ASP.NET provided many built-in security services for developers to take advantage of. A common favorite is Forms-based authentication.

Forms-based authentication allows Web developers to easily build applications that require authentication to access secured resources. However, rather than relying on Windows Authentication, Forms-based authentication allows us to author a simple ASP.NET login page. ASP.NET is then configured so that any unauthenticated requests are redirected to the login page (see Figure 6.1 on the next page).

The login page is a simple ASP.NET page used to collect and verify the user's credentials. It is the responsibility of the login page to determine whether the user credentials are valid; typically this information is stored in a database.

Listing 6.1 shows an example of a login page written in ASP.NET 1.1.

LISTING 6.1. Example Login Page

```
<%@ Page Language="VB" %>
<%@ import namespace="System.Data" %>
<%@ import namespace="System.Data.SqlClient" %>

<script runat="server">

  Public Sub Login_Click(ByVal sender As Object, ByVal e As EventArgs)
```

continues

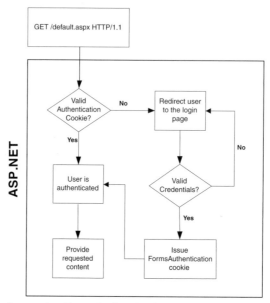

FIGURE 6.1. Forms Authentication

```
Dim userId As Integer
Dim reader As SqlDataReader
Dim connectionString = _
    ConfigurationSettings.ConnectionStrings("MyConnectionString")
Dim conn As New SqlConnection(connectionString)
Dim command As New SqlCommand("dbo.Authenticate", conn)

' Set the command type to stored procedure
command.CommandType = CommandType.StoredProcedure

' Set @Username and @Password
command.Parameters.Add("@Username", _
        SqlDbType.NVarChar, 256).Value = Username.Text
command.Parameters.Add("@Password", _
        SqlDbType.NVarChar, 256).Value = Password.Text

' Open the connection and execute the reader
conn.Open()
reader = command.ExecuteReader()

' Read the value we're looking for
reader.Read()

userId = Integer.Parse(reader("UserId"))

' Close connections
reader.Close()
conn.Close()
```

```
' Did we find a user?
If (userId > 0) Then
    FormsAuthentication.RedirectFromLoginPage(Username.Text, _
                                              False)
Else
    Status.Text = "Invalid Credentials: Please try again"

End If

End Sub

</script>

<html>
  <body style="FONT-FAMILY: Verdana">

  <H1>Enter your username/password</H1>

  <form id="Form1" runat="server">
    Username: <asp:textbox id="Username" runat="server" />
    <br>
    Password: <asp:textbox id="Password" runat="server" />
    <p>
    <asp:button id="Button1"
                text="Check if Member is Valid"
                onclick="Login_Click" runat="server"/>
  </form>

  <font color="red" size="6">
    <asp:label id="Status" runat="server"/>
  </font>

  </body>
</html>
```

In the above sample the login page raises the `Login_Click` event, connects to a database, calls a stored procedure to verify the submitted username and password, and then either uses the `FormsAuthentication` APIs to log the user in or tells the users that the credentials are invalid.

The ASP.NET `FormsAuthentication` class is used to encrypt the username and store it securely in an HTTP cookie. On subsequent requests this HTTP cookie, with its encrypted contents, is decrypted and the user automatically reauthenticated.

Forms Authentication is definitely a great feature, but what makes it even better is the reduction of the code the developer must write. Forms Authentication isn't something new introduced by ASP.NET. Rather, ASP.NET is simply providing an easier way to solve the problem; in the past, most developers would have needed to author this code plus infrastructure on their own.

One of the things you may have noticed about the ASP.NET team members: They are always looking for ways to make things easier. They want developers to solve problems without writing hundreds of lines of code. For ASP.NET 2.0 they're again tackling many security-related problems and providing new features to make things simpler.

In this chapter we're going to examine some of the security infrastructure and controls that have been added in ASP.NET 2.0. We'll start by looking at the new Membership feature. Membership solves the user credential storage problem, a problem most developers solved themselves in ASP.NET 1.0.

Membership

After Microsoft released ASP.NET 1.0 the team members immediately started looking for areas where they could simplify. One of the areas that came up was the management of user credentials, personalization, and user roles. All of these were problems that could be solved in ASP.NET 1.1, but they wanted to make it better . . . and easier!

The Membership feature of ASP.NET does just that—makes it better and easier. Membership provides secure credential storage with simple, easy-to-use APIs. Rather than requiring you to repeatedly develop infrastructure features for authenticating users, it is now part of the platform.

Forms Authentication and Membership complement one another. However, they can also act independently, that is, you don't have to use them together. The code sample in Listing 6.2 demonstrates how Membership is used with Forms Authentication.

LISTING 6.2. Using the Membership API

```
<script runat="server">

  Public Sub Login_Click(sender As Object, e As EventArgs e)

    ' Is the user valid?
    '
    If (Membership.ValidateUser (Username.Text, Password.Text)) Then

      FormsAuthentication.RedirectFromLoginPage (Username.Text, false)

    Else

      Status.Text = "Invalid Credentials: Please try again"

    End If
```

```
    End Sub

</script>

<html>
    <body style="FONT-FAMILY: Verdana">

    <H1>Enter your username/password</H1>

    <form id="Form1" runat="server">
      Username: <asp:textbox id="Username" runat="server" />
      <br>
      Password: <asp:textbox id="Password" runat="server" />
      <p>
      <asp:button id="Button1"
                  text="Check if Member is Valid"
                  onclick="Login_Click" runat="server"/>
    </form>

    <font color="red" size="6">
      <asp:label id="Status" runat="server"/>
    </font>

    </body>
</html>
```

As you can see, our custom code to validate the credentials is now re-placed with a single call to the static `Membership.ValidateUser()` method. The code is also much cleaner and more readable as a result—and much more concise!

The `Membership` class contains only static methods. You don't have to create an instance of the class to use its functionality; for example, you don't have to `new` the `Membership` class to use it. Behind the scenes the `Membership` class is forwarding the calls through a configured provider. The provider in turn knows which data source to contact and how to verify the credentials (see Figure 6.2).

Providers are a new "design pattern" introduced with ASP.NET 2.0. Providers are pluggable data abstraction layers used within ASP.NET. All ASP.NET 2.0 features that rely on data storage expose a provider layer. The provider layer allows you to take complete control over how and where data is stored.[1]

---

1. For more details on providers, see Chapter 7.

Membership Providers

The beauty of the provider model is the abstraction that it affords the developer. Rather than being pigeonholed into a particular data model, the provider pattern allows the developer to determine how and where the actual data storage takes place.

ASP.NET 2.0 will ship with several providers for Membership (not a complete list):

- Access
- SQL Server
- Active Directory[2]

You can also author your own provider and plug it in. The provider design pattern allows for one common API that developers can familiarize themselves with, such as Membership, but under the covers you still have

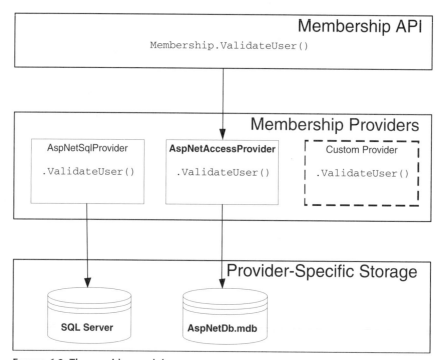

FIGURE 6.2. The provider model

_____

2. Not available with the alpha release of ASP.NET 2.0.

control over what exactly is happening. For example, if you have all of your customer information stored in an AS/400, you could write a provider for Membership. Users would call the familiar Membership APIs, but the work would actually be handled by the configured AS/400 provider.

The goal of Membership is to simplify managing and storing user credentials while still allowing you to control your data, but it does much more. Let's dig deeper.

Setting Up Membership

Setting up Membership is easy: It just works. By default all the providers that ship with ASP.NET 2.0 use a Microsoft Access provider and will use the default `AspNetDB.mdb` file created in the `\data\` directory of your application.[3]

If the `\data\` directory of your application does not exist, ASP.NET will attempt to create it. If ASP.NET is unable to create the `\data\` directory or the `AspNetDB.mdb` file due to security policy on the machine, an exception is thrown detailing what needs to be done.

Before we can begin using Membership for its most common task—validating user credentials—we need to have users to validate!

Creating a New User

The Membership API exposes two methods for creating new users:

```
CreateUser(username As String, password As String)

CreateUser(username As String, password As String,
           email As String)
```

These two APIs are somewhat self-explanatory. We call them to create a user with a username and password—optionally also providing the e-mail address. Both of these methods return a `MembershipUser` instance, which we'll look at later in this chapter.

Which of these two methods you use is determined by the Membership configuration settings. We can examine the settings in `machine.config` for the defaults (see Listing 6.3).[4]

---

3. Access is the configured default since it works without requiring the user to perform any further setup. SQL Server is the recommended provider for large applications.
4. You can also define these settings or change the defaults in the web.config file of your application.

TABLE 6.1. Configuration Elements for the Membership Provider

Attribute	Default Value	Description
connectionStringName[a]	AccessServices	Names the key within the `<connectionStrings />` configuration section where the connection string is stored.
enablePasswordRetrieval	False	Controls whether or not the password can be retrieved through the Membership APIs. When set to `False` (the default), the password cannot be retrieved from the database.
enablePasswordReset	True	Allows the password to be reset. For example, although the password may not be retrieved, the APIs will allow for a new random password to be created for the user.
requiresQuestionAndAnswer	False	Allows the use of a question and answer to retrieve the user's password. Only valid when the `passwordFormat` setting is not `Hashed` and `enablePasswordRetrieval` is `True`.
applicationName	/	Indicates the application to which the Membership data store belongs. Multiple applications can share the same Membership data store by specifying the same `applicationName` value.
requiresUniqueEmail	False	Requires that a given e-mail address can be used only once. This attribute can be used to prevent users from creating multiple accounts. Note that the uniqueness is constrained to the `applicationName` the user is created within.

a. All connection strings used by ASP.NET features are stored in the `<connectionStrings />` configuration section. As of this writing, this feature is not yet complete. Eventually data stored in `<connectionStrings />` will be encrypted.

TABLE 6.1. Configuration Elements for the Membership Provider (continued)

Attribute	Default Value	Description
passwordFormat	Hashed	Controls how the password is stored in the data store. Hashed is the most secure but does not allow password retrieval. Additional valid values include Encrypted and Clear.

LISTING 6.3. Membership Configuration

```
<configuration>
  <system.web>

    <membership defaultProvider="AspNetAccessProvider"
                userIsOnlineTimeWindow="15">
      <providers>

        <add
          name="AspNetAccessProvider"
          type="System.Web.Security.AccessMembershipProvider,
              System.Web,
              Version=1.1.3300.0,
              Culture=neutral, PublicKeyToken=b03f5f7f11d50a3a"
          connectionStringName="AccessServices"
          enablePasswordRetrieval="false"
          enablePasswordReset="true"
          requiresQuestionAndAnswer="false"
          appName="/"
          requiresUniqueEmail="false"
          passwordFormat="Hashed" />

      </providers>
    </membership>

  </system.web>
</configuration>
```

Table 6.1 shows an explanation of the various configuration settings.
Knowing what the defaults are, we can write a simple page for creating
new users (see Listing 6.4).

LISTING 6.4. Creating Users with the Membership API

```vb
<%@ Page Language="VB" %>

<script runat="server">

  Public Sub CreateUser_Click (sender As Object, e As EventArgs)

    Try

      ' Attempt to create the user
      Membership.CreateUser(Username.Text, Password.Text)

      Status.Text = "Created new user: " & Username.Text

    Catch ex As MembershipCreateUserException

      ' Display the status if an exception occurred
      Status.Text = ex.ToString()

    End Try


  End Sub

</script>
<html>
  <head>
  </head>

  <body style="FONT-FAMILY: Verdana">

    <H1>Create a new user</H1>

    <hr />

    <form runat="server">
    Desired username: <asp:TextBox id="Username" runat="server"/>
    <br>
    Password: <asp:TextBox id="Password" runat="server" />
    <p>
    <asp:button Text="Create Member"
                OnClick="CreateUser_Click" runat="server"/>
    </form>

    <font color="red" size="6">
    <asp:Label id="Status" runat="server" />
    </font>

  </body>
</html>
```

The code in Listing 6.4 calls the `Membership.CreateUser()` method, which accepts a username and a password.[5] If there is a problem creating the user, a `MembershipCreateUserException` is thrown. If there are no problems, the new user is created.

Once we've created some users, we can test the `Membership` `.ValidateUser()` method.

Validating User Credentials

As stated earlier, the primary purpose for Membership is to validate credentials. This is accomplished through the static `ValidateUser()` method:

```
ValidateUser(username As String,
             password As String) As Boolean
```

We can use this method, as seen earlier, along with Forms Authentication to validate user credentials. Here is a partial code example:

```
If (Membership.ValidateUser (Username.Text, Password.Text)) Then

  FormsAuthentication.RedirectFromLoginPage (Username.Text, False)

Else

  Status.Text = "Invalid Credentials: Please try again"

End If
```

Apart from `ValidateUser()`, most of the remaining Membership APIs are used for retrieving a user or users.

Retrieving a User

There are a few ways you can retrieve users that have already been created:

```
GetUser() As MembershipUser

GetUser(userIsOnline As Boolean) As MembershipUser

GetUser(username As String) As MembershipUser

GetUser(username As String,
        userIsOnline As Boolean) As MembershipUser
```

---

5. You may already wonder what we do with additional user data, such as first names. Membership is not used to store this type of data. Instead, the new Personalization feature is used to store user data—Membership is used only for storing user credentials used in authentication. Personalization is covered in Chapter 7.

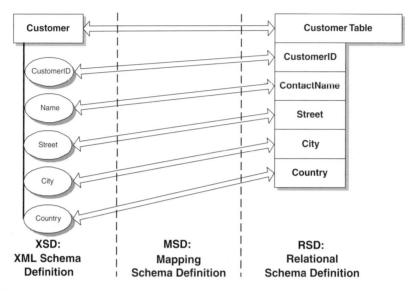

FIGURE 6.3. Getting a user

The first two methods that don't have a *username* parameter will attempt to return the currently logged on user. The parameter *userIsOnline*, when set to True, will update a timestamp in the data store indicating the date/time the user was last requested. This timestamp can then be used to calculate the total number of users on-line.[6] The remaining methods will perform similar operations but on a specified user.

Figure 6.3 shows an example of getting the MembershipUser class for the currently logged on user.

Listing 6.5 provides the code used for this page.

LISTING 6.5. Fetching the Logged on User

```
<%@ Page Language="VB" %>

<script runat="server">

  Public Sub Page_Load()
```

---

6. This functionality is similar to that used on the ASP.NET Forums (http://www.asp.net /Forums/). All users have a timestamp that can be updated. The number of users online is calculated by finding all users whose timestamps fall within a calculated window of time. This time window is configured in the <membership> configuration setting userIsOnlineTimeWindow.

```
    Dim user As MembershipUser

    ' Get the currently logged on user and
    ' update the user's on-line timestamp
    user = Membership.GetUser(True)

    UserName.Text = user.Username

  End Sub

</script>

<html>

  <body style="FONT-FAMILY: Verdana">

  <H1>Get User</H1>

  <hr />

  <form runat="server">
    The currently logged on user is:
    <asp:literal id="UserName" runat="server" />
  </form>

  </body>
</html>
```

If we want to find a user but don't have the username (e.g., the user forgot his or her username), we can use the GetUserNameByEmail() method:

```
GetUserNameByEmail(email As String) As String
```

Once we have the username, we can then look up the user with one of the GetUser() methods listed earlier.

We can additionally get multiple users with the following method:

```
Membership.GetAllUsers() As MembershipUserCollection
```

IMPORTANT

At the time of this writing, another Membership method, GetUsers(), is not yet implemented. The GetUsers() method will be designed to allow for multiple users to be returned by using specific criteria, including page ranges. Thus if there are millions of users in the data store, only the requested range will be returned. The GetAllUsers() method will likely be removed.

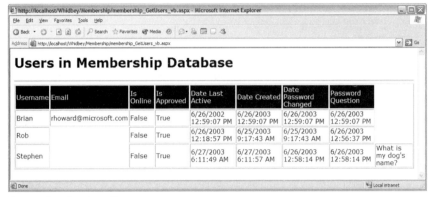

FIGURE 6.4. Getting all users

`Membership.GetAllUsers()` simply returns a `MembershipUser` `Collection`, which we can use to enumerate users or bind to a server control, such as a `Repeater` or `DataGrid` (see Figure 6.4).

Listing 6.6 shows the code.

LISTING 6.6. Displaying All Users

```vb
<%@ Page Language="VB" %>

<script runat="server">

  Public Sub Page_Load()

    Users.DataSource = Membership.GetAllUsers()
    Users.DataBind()

  End Sub

</script>

<html>
  <head>
  </head>

  <body style="FONT-FAMILY: Verdana">

    <H1>Users in Membership Database</H1>

    <hr />

    <asp:repeater id="Users" runat="server">
      <headertemplate>
        <table border="1">
          <tr>
            <td bgcolor="black" style="color:white">
```

```
                Username
            </td>

            <td bgcolor="black" style="color:white">
                Email
            </td>

            <td bgcolor="black" style="color:white">
                Is Online
            </td>

            <td bgcolor="black" style="color:white">
                Is Approved
            </td>

            <td bgcolor="black" style="color:white">
                Date Last Active
            </td>

            <td bgcolor="black" style="color:white">
                Date Created
            </td>

            <td bgcolor="black" style="color:white">
                Date Password Changed
            </td>

            <td bgcolor="black" style="color:white">
                Password Question
            </td>
        </tr>
</headertemplate>

<itemtemplate>
    <tr>
        <td>
            <%# Eval("Username") %>
        </td>

        <td>
            <%# Eval("Email") %>
        </td>

        <td>
            <%# Eval("IsOnline") %>
        </td>

        <td>
            <%# Eval("IsApproved") %>
        </td>

        <td>
            <%# Eval("LastLoginDate") %>
```

continues

```
      </td>

      <td>
        <%# Eval("LastActivityDate") %>
      </td>

      <td>
        <%# Eval("CreationDate") %>
      </td>

      <td>
        <%# Eval("LastPasswordChangedDate") %>
      </td>

      <td>
        <%# Eval("PasswordQuestion") %>
      </td>
    </tr>
  </itemtemplate>

  <footertemplate>
    </table>
  </footertemplate>
</asp:repeater>


</body>
</html>
```

Now that we've looked at how to create users and retrieve named users, let's look at the MembershipUser class, which allows us to set and retrieve extended properties for each user.

The MembershipUser Class

The MembershipUser class represents a user stored in the Membership system. It provides the following methods for performing user-specific operations, such as retrieving or resetting a user's password.

```
GetPassword() As String

GetPassword(answer As String) As String

ChangePassword(oldPassword As String,
               newPassword As String) As Boolean

ChangePasswordQuestionAndAnswer(password As String,
                                question As String,
                                answer As String) As Boolean

ResetPassword() As String

ResetPassword(answer As String) As String
```

Note that if a question and answer are being used, the overloaded GetPassword(*answer* As String) requires the case-insensitive question answer.

The ChangePassword() method allows changes to the user's password, and the ChangePasswordQuestionAndAnswer() method allows changes to the user's password question and answer. The code in Listing 6.7 allows the currently logged on user to change his or her password question and answer.[7]

LISTING 6.7. Changing a Password

```vb
<%@ Page Language="VB" %>

<script runat="server">

  Public Sub Page_Load()

    If Not Page.IsPostBack Then
      DisplayCurrentQuestion()
    End If

  End Sub

  Public Sub SetQandA_Click(sender As Object, e As EventArgs)

    Dim u As MembershipUser = Membership.GetUser()

    u.ChangePasswordQuestionAndAnswer(CurrentPassword.Text, _
                                      Question.Text, _
                                      Answer.Text)

    Membership.UpdateUser(u)

    DisplayCurrentQuestion()
  End Sub

  Public Sub DisplayCurrentQuestion()

    Status.Text = Membership.GetUser().PasswordQuestion

  End Sub

</script>
```

continues

---

7. When the <membership /> configuration's requiresQuestionAndAnswer is set to true, the GetPassword(*answer* As String) and ResetPassword(*answer* As String) must be used to either retrieve or reset the user's password. (The *answer* value is the answer to the user's question.)

```
<html>
  <body style="FONT-FAMILY: Verdana">

  <H1>Set Question Answer</H1>

  <hr />

  <form id="Form1" runat="server">
    Current Password: <asp:textbox id="CurrentPassword"
                                   runat="server" />
    <p></p>
    Question: <asp:textbox id="Question" runat="server" />
    <p></p>
    Answer:  <asp:textbox id="Answer" runat="server" />
    <p></p>
    <asp:button id="Button1" text="Set Question/Answer"
               onclick="SetQandA_Click" runat="server"/>
  </form>

  <font size="6"> Your new password question is:
  <asp:label id="Status" runat="server"/>
  </font>

</html>
```

The ResetPassword() methods are similar to the GetPassword() methods. However, rather than retrieving the user's password, they reset and then return a random password for the user.

Keep in mind that the ability to retrieve, change, or reset the user's password is determined by the settings within the configuration.

In addition to password management, the MembershipUser class has some useful properties that provide us some details about how and when the user last logged in, last changed passwords, and so on (see Table 6.2).

Updating a User's Properties

When changes are made to the user, for example, updating the user's e-mail address, we need to use the Membership.UpdateUser(user As Membership User) method to save the values.[8] For example, in Listing 6.7 above, the SetQandA_Click event (repeated for convenience below) shows an example of Membership.UpdateUser():

```
Public Sub SetQandA_Click(sender As Object, e As EventArgs)
```

---

8. The goal of this design is to allow multiple values to be changed without requiring multiple round-trips to the data store. By using the UpdateUser() method, all updates are batched together.

TABLE 6.2. MembershipUser Properties

Property	Description
LastLoginDate	Sets or returns a timestamp for the last time ValidateUser() was called for the current MembershipUser.
CreationDate	Sets or returns a timestamp value set when the user was first created.
LastActivityDate	Sets or returns a timestamp value set when the user authenticates or is retrieved using the overloaded GetUser() method that accepts a userIsOnline parameter.
LastPasswordChangedDate	Sets or returns a timestamp value set when the user last changed his or her password.
Email	Sets or returns the e-mail address, if set, of the user.
IsApproved	Sets or returns a value that indicates whether or not the user is approved. Users whose IsApproved property is set to false cannot log in, even when the specified credentials are valid.
PasswordQuestion	Returns the question used in question/answer retrieval.
Provider	Returns an instance (of type IMembershipProvider) of the current provider used to manipulate the data store.
Username	Returns the username of the current user.

```
Dim u As MembershipUser = Membership.GetUser()

u.ChangePasswordQuestionAndAnswer(CurrentPassword.Text,
                                  Question.Text,
                                  Answer.Text)

Membership.UpdateUser(u)

DisplayCurrentQuestion()
End Sub
```

So far we've learned how to create and update users, but what about removing users from the Membership system?

Deleting a User

Deleting a user from Membership is easy. Membership supports a single method for removing users:

```
DeleteUser(username As String) As Boolean
```

We simply need to name the user we wish to delete. If the operation is successful, the method returns True. If the delete operation fails, for example, if the user doesn't exist, False is returned.

Listing 6.8 shows a code example that allows us to specify a user to be removed from the Membership system.

LISTING 6.8. Deleting a User

```
<%@ Page Language="VB" %>

<script runat="server">

  Public Sub DeleteUser_Click(sender As Object, e As EventArgs)

    If (Membership.DeleteUser(Username.Text)) Then
      Status.Text = Username.Text & " deleted"
    Else
      Status.Text = Username.Text & " not deleted"
    End If

  End Sub

</script>
<html>
  <head>
  </head>

  <body style="FONT-FAMILY: Verdana">

    <H1>Delete a user</H1>

    <hr />

    <form runat="server">
      Username to delete: <asp:TextBox id="Username"
                                        runat="server"/>
      <p>
      <asp:button Text="Delete User"
                  OnClick="DeleteUser_Click" runat="server"/>
    </form>

    <font color="red" size="6">
```

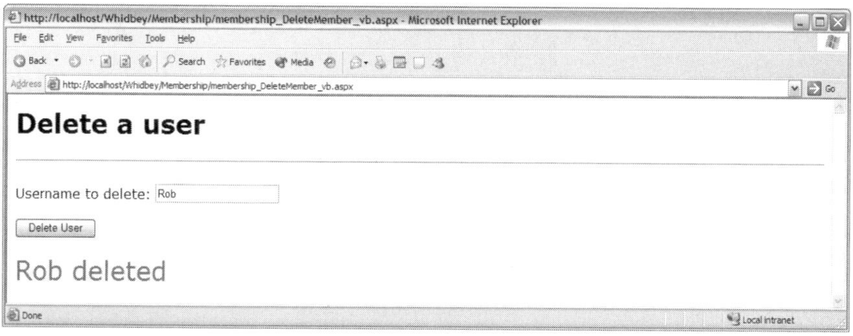

FIGURE 6.5. Deleting a user

```
      <asp:label id="Status" runat="server" />
      </font>

   </body>
</html>
```

Figure 6.5 shows how this page looks.

While the Membership APIs definitely simplify day-to-day tasks, there is also an alternative to using programmatic APIs: security server controls. In many cases we can use these server controls and never have to write code that uses the Membership APIs!

Security Server Controls

The new Membership infrastructure feature of ASP.NET simplifies the management and storage of user credentials. Using APIs, such as `Membership.ValidateUser()`, for Forms Authentication definitely makes things easy. However, some techniques are made even easier through the use of several new security-related server controls. For example, you can author your own login page with zero lines of code by using the new login control.

The Login Control

Figure 6.6 shows a `control_login.aspx` page that authenticates the user's credentials against the default Membership provider and uses the new `<asp:Login runat="server"/>` control. As you can see in Figure 6.6, it looks nearly identical to the login page we built with the Membership APIs. Listing 6.9 shows the source to the `control_login.aspx` page.

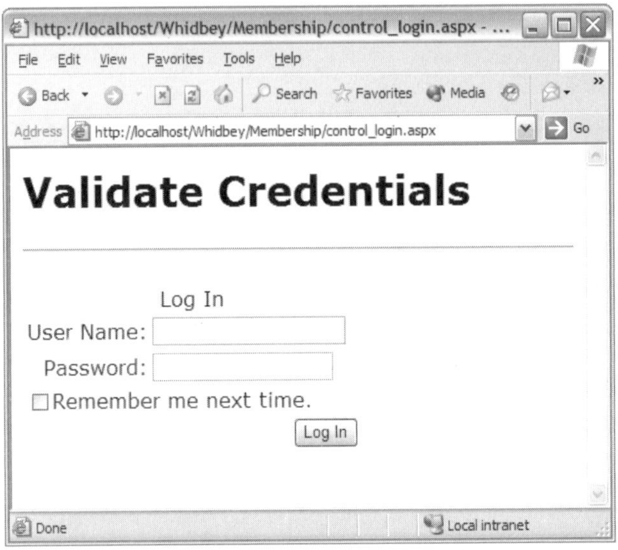

FIGURE 6.6. The login control

LISTING 6.9. Using the Login Control

```html
<html>

  <body style="FONT-FAMILY: Verdana">

    <H1>Validate Credentials</H1>
    <hr />
    <form id="Form1" runat="server">

      <asp:Login id="Login1" runat="server" />

    </form>

  </body>

</html>
```

When the username and password are entered, this control will automatically attempt to log in the user by calling `Membership.ValidateUser()`. If successful, the control will then call the necessary `FormsAuthentication.RedirectFromLoginPage` API to issue a cookie and redirect the user to the page he or she was attempting to access. In other words, all the code you would have needed to write in ASP.NET 1.1 is now neatly encapsulated in a single server control!

The `<asp:Login runat="server" />` control automatically hides itself if the user is logged in. This behavior is determined by the `AutoHide`

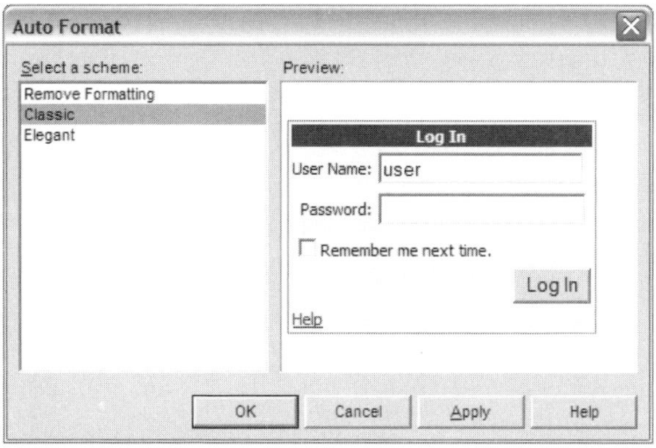

FIGURE 6.7. The Auto Format dialog

property, set to `True` by default. If the login control is used with Forms Authentication and hosted on the default login page (specified in the configuration for Forms Authentication) the control will not auto-hide itself.

We can further customize the login control's UI. To preview one UI option—we can't cover all of them in depth in this book—right-click on the login control within Visual Studio .NET "Whidbey" and select Auto Format. This will bring up the dialog box shown in Figure 6.7.

Once you've chosen an auto-format template, such as Classic, you can see the changes in the login control (see Listing 6.10).

LISTING 6.10. A Formatted Login Control

```
<asp:Login id="Login1"
           runat="server"
           font-names="Verdana"
           font-size="10pt"
           bordercolor="#999999"
           borderwidth="1px"
           borderstyle="Solid"
           backcolor="#FFFFCC">
  <TitleTextStyle Font-Bold="True"
                  ForeColor="#FFFFFF"
                  BackColor="#333399">
  </TitleTextStyle>
</asp:Login>
```

If you desire more control over the display of the control, right-click on the control, or from the Common Tasks dialog, select Convert to Template. You'll see no changes in the rendered UI of the control. However, you will see a notable difference in the declarative markup generated for the control. For brevity we are not including the updated markup.[9] What you will see is a series of templates that allow you to take 100% control over the UI rendering of the control. Note that it is important that the IDs of the controls within these templates remain because the control expects to find these IDs.

While the login control simplifies authoring the login page, several other controls help us display content to users based on their login status. Let's take a look at the login status control first.

The Login Status Control

The login status control, `<asp:LoginStatus runat="server" />`, is used to display whether the user is logged in or not. When the user is not logged in, the status displays a login link (see Figure 6.8). When the user is logged in, the status displays a logout link (see Figure 6.9).

Listing 6.11 shows the code required.

LISTING 6.11. The LoginStatus Control

```
<html>

  <body style="FONT-FAMILY: Verdana">

  <h1>Login Status</h1>

  <hr />
```

FIGURE 6.8. The login status control when the user is not logged in

---

9. One of the nice features in the Designer is a Reset feature. When you change your mind about using the template layout of the login control, you can simply select Reset from the Common Tasks menu.

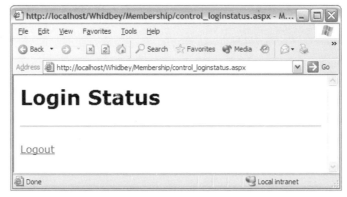

FIGURE 6.9. The login status control when the user is logged in

```
<form runat="server">
  <asp:LoginStatus id="LoginStatus1" runat="server" />
</form>

</body>

</html>
```

By default the text displayed for the link is "Login" when the user is not logged in and "Logout" when the user is logged in.[10] However, this text can easily be changed. To change the text, you simply need to change the LoginText or LogoutText properties of the control:

```
<asp:LoginStatus id="Loginstatus1" runat="server"
                 LoginText="Please log in"
                 LogoutText="Please log out" />
```

Other properties can also be set to control the behavior of this control. For example, you can use the LoginImageUrl and the LogoutImageUrl to use images rather than text for displaying the login status. Finally, there are two properties for controlling the behavior upon logout:

- LogoutAction: This property specifies the behavior when the logout button is clicked. Options include Refresh, Redirect, and RedirectToLoginPage.

---

10. Note the handy feature in Visual Studio .NET "Whidbey" in the Common Tasks dialog, Switch Logged In Status, which allows you to toggle the view of the control in the Designer.

- **LogoutPageUrl:** When the `LogoutAction` is set to `Redirect`, the `LogoutPageUrl` is the location to which the browser is redirected.

Whereas `<asp:LoginStatus runat="server" />` provides an easy way for the user to log in and log out, another server control, `<asp:LoginView runat="server"/>`, allows us to easily determine what content is shown to the user based on his or her login status.

The Login View Control

The `<asp:LoginView runat="server" />` server control is used to display different output depending on the login status of the user. Furthermore, the control can also be used to display different content based on the role(s) the user belongs to. Figure 6.10 shows an example of what the control might display for an anonymous user. The code that generates this page appears in Listing 6.12.

LISTING 6.12. Using the LoginView Control

```
<html>

  <body style="FONT-FAMILY: Verdana">

  <h1>Login View and Login Name Controls</h1>

  <hr />

  <form runat="server">

    <asp:LoginView id="Loginview1" runat="server">
      <anonymoustemplate>
        Unknown user please <asp:LoginStatus runat="server"
```

FIGURE 6.10. The login view for an anonymous user

```
                                   logintext="login" />
    </anonymoustemplate>

    <rolegroups>
      <asp:rolegroup roles="Admin">
        <contenttemplate>
          This is admin only content!
        </contenttemplate>
      </asp:rolegroup>
    </rolegroups>

    <loggedintemplate>
      You are logged in as: <asp:LoginName id="LoginName1"
                                           runat="server" />
    </loggedintemplate>
  </asp:LoginView>
 </form>

 </body>

</html>
```

In the code above you can see that two templates are defined for the
`<asp:LoginView runat="server" />` control:

- `<anonymoustemplate />` is used to control the displayed content
  when the user is not logged in.
- `<loggedintemplate />` is used to control the displayed content
  when the user is logged in.

In addition to the templates, there is also a special `<rolegroups />`
section that allows us to create different templates that are displayed if the
user is in a corresponding role or roles. If the user is logged in but no roles
apply, the `<loggedintemplate />` is used.[11]

You'll notice that we also made use of another control in Listing 6.12:
`<asp:LoginName runat="server" />`. This control simply displays the
name of the logged in user. If the user is not logged in, the control does not
render any output.

The last security-related server control is `<asp:PasswordRecovery
runat="server" />`, which is used to help users obtain their forgotten
passwords.

---

11. Template evaluation for `rolegroups` is done top to bottom. The first matched role
    group is used. If no match is found, the `<loggedintemplate />` is used.

The Password Recovery Control

The `<asp:PasswordRecovery runat="server" />` control works in conjunction with the Membership system to allow users to easily recover their passwords.[12]

The `<asp:PasswordRecovery runat="server" />` control relies on the `<smtpMail />` configuration options to be correctly set to a valid SMTP server—the control will mail the password to the user's e-mail address. By default, the `<smtpMail />` section will have the SMTP mail server set to `localhost` and the port set to `25` (the default SMTP port).

Similar to `<asp:Login runat="server" />`, this control supports auto-format and full template editing. Assuming we select an auto-format template, such as Classic, and use the default Membership settings, we should see the page shown in Figure 6.11.

Listing 6.13 presents the code that generates this page (auto-formatting removed).

LISTING 6.13. Using the PasswordRecovery Control

```
<html>
  <body style="FONT-FAMILY: Verdana">

    <H1>
      Password Recovery
```

Figure 6.11. Password recovery

---

12. For this server control to work, your Membership configuration must be set up to allow for password recovery.

```
    <hr />
    </H1>
    <form id="Form1" runat="server">
      <asp:PasswordRecovery runat="server">
        <maildefinition from="admin@mywebsite.com" />
      </asp:PasswordRecovery>
    </form>

  </body>

</html>
```

If we attempt to use the control with the default Membership settings—which do not allow password recovery—we will receive the following error:

"Your attempt to retrieve your password was not successful. Please try again."

To allow us to recover the password, we need to change some of the default membership settings. Below are the necessary changes to the <membership /> configuration settings to allow for password recovery:

- enablePasswordRetrieval="True"
- passwordFormat="Clear"

The enablePasswordRetrieval attribute must be set to True to allow for password retrieval, and the passwordFormat attribute must be set to either Clear or Encrypted.[13] Another alternative is that when enablePasswordReset is set to True, the new password can be e-mailed to the user.

In addition to configuring the <membership /> configuration settings, we must specify the <maildefinition /> element of the <asp:Password Recovery runat="server" /> control. The <maildefinition /> names the address from whom e-mails are sent.

Finally, we can also use the <asp:PasswordRecovery runat= "server" /> to retrieve the user's password using the question/answer support of Membership (see Figure 6.12).

---

13. The default passwordFormat value, Hashed, can be best thought of as one-way encryption; thus it is impossible to retrieve the original value once the value is hashed.

FIGURE 6.12. Password recovery with question and answer

The control still requires that we enter the username first, but before simply mailing the password it will first also request the answer to the user's question.

This behavior is forced by setting the <membership /> configuration setting requiresQuestionAndAnswer to true (the default is false).[14] Note that this configuration change is in addition to changing the enablePasswordRetrieval to True and setting the passwordFormat to a value other than Hashed.

Managing and storing user credentials are only one part of securely controlling access to resources within your site. In addition to validating who the user is, you need to determine whether the user is allowed to access the requested resource. The process of validating credentials is known as *authentication; authorization* is the process of determining whether the authenticated user is allowed to access a particular resource.

ASP.NET 1.x already provides authorization facilities, but just as we have done with Membership, there is more simplification to be done.

Role Manager

The ASP.NET Role Manager feature is designed to simplify managing roles and the users that belong to those roles. After authentication, when Role Manager is enabled, ASP.NET will automatically add the users to the role(s) he or she belongs to. When ASP.NET authorization occurs, the user

---

14. You will also need to ensure that the user set a question and answer when his or her account in the Membership system was created.

is either allowed or denied access to the requested resource based on his or her role(s).[15]

URL-based role authorization is a feature of ASP.NET 1.0. We can control what users are allowed to access by specifying access permissions within `configuration` (see Listing 6.14).

LISTING 6.14. Configuring Roles

```
<configuration>

  <system.web>
    <authorization>
      <deny users="?" />
    </authorization>
  </system.web>

  <location path="PremiumContent.aspx">
    <system.web>
      <authorization>
        <allow roles="Premium" />
        <deny users="*" />
      </authorization>
    </system.web>
  </location>

</configuration>
```

The above `web.config` file could be added to any application. It states that anonymous users are denied access to all resources. Furthermore, only users in the role Premium are allowed access to `PremiumContent.aspx`. All other users are denied access.

Before we can control access to resources through roles, we need to create some roles and then add users to them. Let's look at how we can do this with the new Role Manager feature.

Setting Up Role Manager

Similar to Membership, Role Manager relies on a provider to store data and thus allow us to create roles and associations between users and their roles.[16] Unlike Membership, Role Manager is not enabled by default. Therefore, before we can use the Role Manager API, we need to enable the feature.

---

15. Authorization always occurs after authentication, that is, first the user's credentials are validated, and if the credentials are valid, then the determination is made whether the user is allowed to access the requested resource.
16. This is identical to how Membership uses a provider. The difference is that a different set of providers exists for the Role Manager feature. Different providers are used to avoid making Role Manager providers dependent on Membership.

Similar to Membership configuration settings, Role Manager configuration settings are defined in `machine.config` and can be overridden or changed within an application's `web.config` file. Listing 6.15 shows a sample `web.config` for Role Manager.

LISTING 6.15. Configuring Role Manager

```
<configuration>
  <system.web>

    <roleManager enabled="true"
                 cacheRolesInCookie="true"
                 cookieName=".ASPXROLES"
                 cookieTimeout="30"
                 cookiePath="/"
                 cookieRequireSSL="false"
                 cookieSlidingExpiration="true"
                 cookieProtection="All"
                 defaultProvider="AspNetAccessProvider" >
      <providers>
        <add name="AspNetAccessProvider2"
             type="System.Web.Security.AccessRoleProvider, System.Web"
             connectionStringName="AccessFileName"
             applicationName="/"
        </providers>
      </roleManager>

  </system.web>
</configuration>
```

Table 6.3 shows an explanation of the various configuration settings.

TABLE 6.3. Role Manager Configuration Settings

Attribute	Default Value	Description
Enabled	false	Controls whether or not the Role Manager feature is enabled. By default it is disabled because enabling breaks backward compatibility with ASP.NET 1.0.[a]
cacheRolesInCookie	true	Allows for the roles to be cached within an HTTP cookie. When the roles are cached within a cookie, a lookup for the roles associated with the user does not have to be done through the provider.

a The class type returned by `User.Identity.Principal` is of type `RolesPrincipal` when Role Manager is enabled.

TABLE 6.3. Role Manager Configuration Settings (continued)

Attribute	Default Value	Description
cookieName	.ASPXROLES	Sets the name of the cookie used to store the roles when cookies are enabled.
cookieTimeout	30	Sets the period of time for which the cookie is valid. If cookieSliding-Expiration is true, the cookie timeout is reset on each request within the cookieTimeout window.
cookiePath	/	Sets the path within the application within which the cookie is valid.
cookieRequireSSL	false	Specifies whether or not the cookie must be sent over an SSL channel.
cookieSlidingExpiration	true	Sets the cookie timeout. When true, the cookie timeout is automatically reset each time a request is made within the cookieTimeout window, effectively allowing the cookie to stay valid until the user's session is complete.
cookieProtection	All	Controls how the data stored within the cookie is secured.
defaultProvider	AspNet Access Provider	Sets the default provider to be associated with the Role Manager APIs.

Now that we've seen how to configure the settings of Role Manager, let's create some roles.

Creating Roles

The Roles API supports a single method for creating roles:

```
CreateRole(rolename As String)
```

This API is used to create the friendly role name, such as Administrators, used to control access to resources. Listing 6.16 provides sample code for creating roles in an ASP.NET page.

LISTING 6.16. Creating and Viewing Roles

```
<script runat="server">

  Public Sub Page_Load (sender As Object, e As EventArgs)

    If Not Page.IsPostBack Then
      DataBind()
    End If

  End Sub


  Public Sub CreateRole_Click(sender As Object, e As EventArgs)

    Try

      ' Attempt to create the role
      Roles.CreateRole (Rolename.Text)

    Catch ex As Exception

      ' Failed to create the role
      Status.Text = ex.ToString()

    End Try

    DataBind()

  End Sub

  Public Overrides Sub DataBind()

    RoleList.DataSource = Roles.GetAllRoles()
    RoleList.DataBind()

  End Sub

</script>


<html>
  <body style="FONT-FAMILY: Verdana">

  <H1>Create Role</H1>
  Below is a list of the current roles:
  <asp:datagrid id="RoleList" runat="server" />

  <hr />

  <form runat="server">
```

```
    Rolename to create: <asp:TextBox id="Rolename" runat="server" />
    <asp:button Text="Create Role"
                OnClick="CreateRole_Click" runat="server"/>

</form>

<font color="red" size="6">
<asp:Label id="Status" runat="server"/>
</font>

</body>
</html>
```

The code sample above allows us to enter a role name, which is then created using the `Roles.CreateRole()` API. If the role already exists, an exception is thrown. Finally, all of the available roles are enumerated through a `DataGrid` using the `Roles.GetAllRoles()` API, discussed shortly.

Now that we can create roles, let's add some users to the roles.

Adding Users to Roles

Membership and Role Manager are not rigidly coupled. They are designed to work together, but you do not have to use one to use the other. Both use the authenticated username as the only shared piece of data. For example, it is possible to add a user to a role even if the user is not created through the Membership system.[17]

Adding users to roles is accomplished by using the following methods supported by the `Roles` API:

```
AddUserToRole(username As String, rolename As String)

AddUserToRoles(username As String, rolenames() As String)

AddUsersToRole(usernames() As String, rolename As String)

AddUsersToRoles(usernames() As String, rolenames() As String)
```

These various methods allow for adding users to roles in bulk or individually. Listing 6.17 demonstrates `Roles.AddUserToRole()`.

---

17. This flexible design allows for various providers to be used for data storage. For example, you could have an AS/400 Membership provider and an Access Role Manager provider.

LISTING 6.17. Adding Users to Roles

```vb
<%@ Page Language="VB" %>

<script runat="server">

  Public Sub Page_Load(ByVal sender As Object, ByVal e As EventArgs)

    DataBind()

  End Sub

  Public Sub AddUserToRole_Click(sender As Object, e As EventArgs)

    Roles.AddUserToRole(Username.Text, _
                        RoleList.SelectedItem.Value)

    DataBind()

  End Sub

  Public Overrides Sub DataBind()

    RoleList.DataSource = Roles.GetAllRoles()
    RoleList.DataBind()

  End Sub

</script>

<html>
  <body style="FONT-FAMILY: Verdana">

  <H1>Add User to role</H1>

  <form runat="server">
    User: <asp:TextBox id="Username" runat="server" />
    Role to add user to: <asp:DropDownList id="RoleList"
                                           runat="server" />
    <asp:button Text="Add User To Role"
                OnClick="AddUserToRole_Click" runat="server"/>
  </form>

  <font size="6" color="Red">
  <asp:Label id="StatusCheck" runat="server"/>
  </font>

  </body>

</html>
```

This code sample data binds the results of `Roles.GetAllRoles()` to a `DropDownList` control and then allows us to enter a user to add to a role.[18] The `Roles.AddUserToRole()` API is then used to add the user to the role.

When adding multiple users to roles or a user to multiple roles, the addition occurs within the context of a transaction. Either all updates succeed or all fail.

We can now use another `Roles` API to determine to what roles a particular user belongs.

Returning a User's Roles

To return a list of the roles to which a user belongs, we can simply use one of the following APIs:

```
GetRolesForUser() As String()

GetRolesForUser(username As String) As String()

GetUsersInRole(rolename As String) As String()
```

The `Roles.GetRolesForUser()` method will return a string array of all the roles that the current user is in. The overloaded version of this method that accepts a *username* parameter allows us to specify for which user we want a listing of roles. The last method, `Roles.GetUsersInRole()`, allows us to get a string array listing of usernames that belong to the specified role.

Listing 6.18 demonstrates the overloaded version of `Roles.GetRolesForUser()`.

LISTING 6.18. Finding the Roles for a User

```
<script runat="server">

  Public Sub GetRolesForUser_Click(sender As Object, e As EventArgs)

    RolesForUser.DataSource = Roles.GetRolesForUser(Username.Text)
    RolesForUser.DataBind()

  End Sub

</script>

<html>
  <body style="FONT-FAMILY: Verdana">
```

continues

18. You could also data bind to a list of the Members from the Membership system.

```
<H1>Roles user is in</H1>
<hr />

<form runat="server">
  Username: <asp:TextBox id="Username" runat="server" />
  <asp:button Text="Roles User Is In"
              OnClick="GetRolesForUser_Click" runat="server"/>
</form>

User is in roles:

<asp:DataGrid runat="server" id="RolesForUser" />

</body>
</html>
```

This code sample simply asks for the name of a user. When the page is posted back, the `Roles.GetRolesForUser()` API is called, passing in the name of the specified user. The results are then data-bound to a `DataGrid`.

Checking whether a User Is in a Role

Access to resources can be controlled by which roles the user belongs to. As was shown in the beginning of this section, it is possible to control access to URLs based on settings made in the configuration file. In addition to this declarative security access control, we can also perform programmatic checks for the role the user belongs to.

ASP.NET 1.1 allowed for programmatic checks for determining whether the user was in a role through `User.IsInRole(string username)`; the result of this method returned `True` or `False`. The `Roles` API supports a similar `Roles.IsUserInRole(rolename As String )` API:

```
IsUserInRole(rolename As String) As Boolean

IsUserInRole(username As String, rolename As String) As Boolean
```

Now that we've seen how to add users to roles and check whether users are in a particular role, let's look at how we can remove a user from a role.

Removing Users from Roles

Similar to the methods used for adding a user to roles, we have four different methods for removing users from roles:

```
RemoveUserFromRole(username As String, rolename As String)

RemoveUserFromRoles(username As String, rolenames() As String)
```

```
RemoveUsersFromRole(usernames() As String, rolename As String)

RemoveUsersFromRoles(usernames() As String, rolenames() As String)
```

Again, similar to adding users to roles, when the process of removing users from roles is transacted, either all succeed or all fail.

Deleting a Role

Roles can be deleted easily by using the Roles.DeleteRole(rolename As String) method. Listing 6.19 shows a sample ASP.NET page that demonstrates how to use this API.

LISTING 6.19. Deleting a Role

```vb
<%@ Page Language="VB" %>

<script runat="server">

  Public Sub Page_Load()

    If Not Page.IsPostBack Then
      DataBind()
    End If

  End Sub

  Public Sub DeleteRole_Click(sender As Object, e As EventArgs)

    Try
      Roles.DeleteRole(Rolename.Text)
    Catch ex As Exception
      StatusCheck.Text = "There was an error removing the role(s)"
    End Try

    DataBind()

  End Sub

  Public Overrides Sub DataBind()
    RoleList.DataSource = Roles.GetAllRoles()
    RoleList.DataBind()

  End Sub

</script>

<html>
  <body style="FONT-FAMILY: Verdana">
```

continues

```
<H1>Delete Role</H1>
Below is a list of the current roles:
<asp:datagrid id="RoleList" runat="server" />

<hr />

<form runat="server">
  Rolename to delete: <asp:TextBox id="Rolename" runat="server" />
  <asp:button Text="Delete Role" OnClick="DeleteRole_Click"
            runat="server"/>
</form>

<font color="red" size="6">
<asp:Label id="StatusCheck" runat="server"/>
</font>

</body>

</html>
```

The code above lists all the available roles by binding the result of Roles.GetAllRoles() to a DataGrid. It then allows for a specific role to be named and deleted using the Roles.DeleteRole() method.

Figure 6.13 is a screen capture of this page.

Role Manager uses a provider to write back to and read from a data store in which the roles and user-to-role mapping is done. Rather than reading/writing to this database on each request—since a list of the roles the user belongs to must be obtained—a cookie can optionally be used to cache roles, as described in the next subsection.

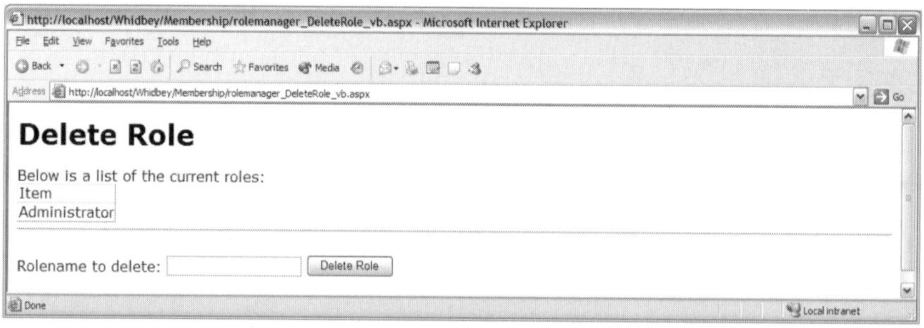

FIGURE 6.13. Deleting roles

Role Caching

Role caching is a feature of Role Manager that enables user-to-role mappings to be performed without requiring a lookup to the data store on each request[19] Instead of looking up the user-to-role mapping in the data store, the roles the user belongs to are stored, encrypted, within an HTTP cookie. If the user does not have the cookie, a request is made against the provider to retrieve the roles the user belongs to. The roles are then encrypted and stored within a cookie. On subsequent requests the cookie is decrypted and the roles obtained from the cookie.

Internally, in cases where there are more roles than can fit in the cookie, the cookie is marked as an incremental role cookie. That is, the cookie stores as many roles as possible but likely not all the roles. When role checking is performed, and the user is not in one of the roles being checked for, ASP.NET will call the `Roles` API and check whether the user belongs to that role. If not, access is denied. If the user is in the role and the role is not currently stored in the cookie, the last role stored within the cookie is removed and the requested role is added. Thereby, in cases where the user has more roles than can fit in the cookie, the cookie over time will contain a list of the most frequently accessed roles.

Cookieless Forms Authentication

ASP.NET 1.0 introduced the Forms Authentication feature to allow developers to easily author ASP.NET applications that rely on an authentication mechanism they could control. Forms Authentication exposed a set of APIs that developers can simply call to authenticate the user, such as:

```
FormsAuthentication.RedirectFromLoginPage(Username.Text, False)
```

Forms Authentication in ASP.NET 1.0 would the take the username, encrypt it, and store it within an HTTP cookie. The cookie would be presented on subsequent requests and the user automatically reauthenticated.

One of the common feature requests the ASP.NET team continually received was the ability for Forms Authentication to support cookieless authentication, that is, to not require an HTTP cookie. This is just what they've done in ASP.NET 2.0.

---

19. This is a similar implementation to what is done within all the ASP.NET Starter Kits.

Enabling Cookieless Forms Authentication

Cookieless Forms Authentication is enabled within the `machine.config` file or the `web.config` file of your application by setting the new `cookieless` attribute (see Listing 6.20).

LISTING 6.20. Configuring Cookieless Forms Authentication

```
<configuration>
  <system.web>
    <authentication mode="Forms">
      <forms name=".ASPXAUTH"
             loginUrl="login.aspx"
             protection="All"
             timeout="30"
             path="/"
             requireSSL="false"
             slidingExpiration="true"
             defaultUrl="default.aspx"
             cookieless="UseCookies" />
    </authentication>
  </system.web>
</configuration>
```

The `cookieless` attribute has four possible values:[20]

- `UseUri`: Forces the authentication ticket to be stored in the URL.
- `UseCookies`: Forces the authentication ticket to be stored in the cookie (same as ASP.NET 1.0 behavior).
- `AutoDetect`: Automatically detects whether the browser/device does or does not support cookies.
- `UseDeviceProfile`: Chooses to use cookies or not based on the device profile settings from `machine.config`.

If we set the `cookieless` value to `UseUri` within `web.config` and request and authenticate with Forms Authentication, we should see something similar to what Figure 6.14 shows within the URL of the requested page.

---

20. In case you forget the values, an incorrect value set for `cookieless` will cause an ASP.NET error page to be generated that lists the acceptable values.

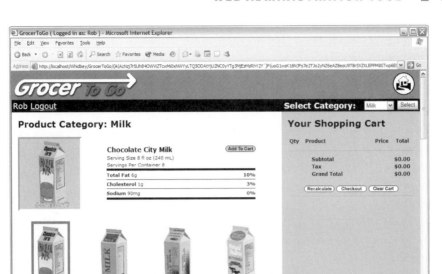

FIGURE 6.14. Cookieless Forms Authentication

Below is the requested URL—after authentication—in a more readable form:

```
http://localhost/Whidbey/GrocerToGo/(A(AcNzj7rSUh84OWViZTcwMioxNWYyLTQ5OD
AtYjU2NCoyYTg3MjEzMzRhY2Y`)F(uoG1wsK16NJFs7e2TJo2yNZ6eAZ8eoU9T8rSXZXLEP
PM8STwp6EONVtt4YCqEeb-9XDrrEpIHRpOOlKh8rO-9foAhP6AXWwL*obMbxYcfZc`))/d
efault.aspx
```

Web Administration Tool

Administration of ASP.NET applications has always been easy, although diving into the XML-based configuration file isn't the most user-friendly way to do it. For the 2.0 release of ASP.NET, there is the Web Administration Tool, which allows configuration of a Web application via an easy browser interface.

There are two main reasons why the Web Administration Tool is useful. First, it abstracts the XML configuration into an easy-to-use interface, and second, it provides administration features via a browser. This means that for remote sites (such as those provided by a hosting company), it's easy to administer an application without having to edit the configuration file (e.g., to add new security credentials) and then upload it.

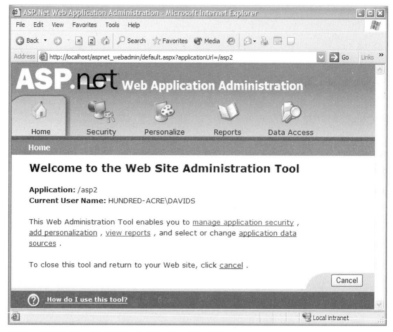

FIGURE 6.15. The Web Administration Tool Home page

The Web Administration tool is available for each directory configured as an application, by way of a simple URL:

http://website/WebAdmin.axd

This presents you with a home page and menu consisting of five main options.

The Home Page

The Home page, shown in Figure 6.15, details the current application and security details, as well as links to the other main sections.

The Security Page

The Security page, shown in Figure 6.16, offers two options for configuring security. The first is a wizard that takes you through the following steps:

1. **Select Access Method**, which defines whether the application is available from the Internet (in which case Forms Authentication is used) or from the LAN (in which case Windows Authentication is used)

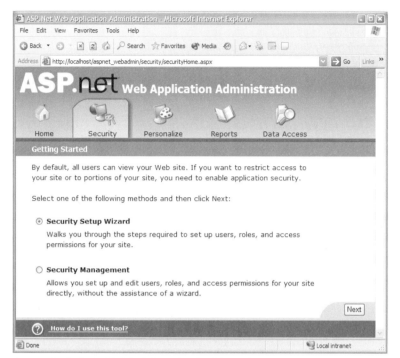

FIGURE 6.16. The Web Administration Tool Security page

2. **Specify Data Source**, where you can specify the database (Access or SQL Server) that will store the user credentials and what details are required (e.g., unique e-mail address, allow password retrieval, and so on)

3. **Define Roles**, where you can optionally specify Authorization roles

4. **Add New Users**, which allows addition of new users and allocation to roles

5. **Add New Access Rules**, which defines which files and folders users and roles have permissions for

6. **Complete**, to indicate that the security settings have been configured

The second option is for configuration of security that has already been enabled, as detailed in the following subsection.

Security Management

Once security is initially set up, or by selecting the second option titled Security Management on the main Security page, the Security page allows management of users, roles, and permissions without the use of the wizard. For

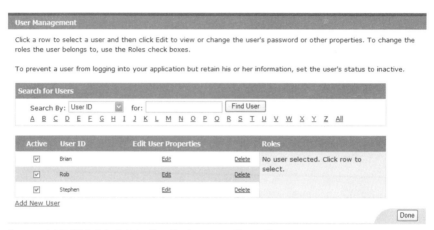

FIGURE 6.17. Web Administration Tool user configuration

example, consider the users added earlier in the chapter. If we select the Manage Users options, we see the User Management features shown in Figure 6.17.

Likewise, selecting Manage Roles allows you to customize roles and members, as shown in Figure 6.18.

Not all features of the user and role management are implemented in the preview release.

Other Pages

The Personalize, Reports, and Data Access pages are not currently implemented but will be available in a later release.

FIGURE 6.18. Web Administration Tool role configuration

SUMMARY

We've only sampled some of the new security capabilities in ASP.NET 2.0. The Membership and Role Manager features are specifically designed to solve problems we saw developers addressing over and over again. While both complement and can be used easily with Forms Authentication, they were also designed to work independently—independently of one another and independently of Forms Authentication. Furthermore, both support the provider design pattern. This design pattern allows you to take complete control over how and where the data used for these features is stored. The provider design pattern gives you the ultimate control and flexibility, since you can control the business logic, while developers can learn a simple, friendly, and easy-to-use API.

While writing code using Membership has become more concise, there are also now cases where no code is required. The new security server controls make many scenarios, such as login or password recovery, so much easier to implement. The other security-related server controls simply save you the time formerly required to write code to perform simple tasks such as checking who is logged in.

The cookieless support for Forms Authentication means you don't have to require the use of cookies for authenticating users—something many of you have been asking for.

Finally, the Web Administration Tool provides a simple way to administer site security without building custom tools.

Now it's time to extend the topic of users interacting with a site and look at how sites can be personalized.

7

Personalization and Themes

I N CHAPTER 6 WE DISCUSSED the new infrastructure feature of Membership. Membership is used to store user credentials and offers APIs for validating those credentials as well as managing users. A common question that often comes up when discussing Membership is how additional user details are stored; for example, your application may want to associate first and last names with the user or store a theme.

While Membership does store some user information, such as when the user last logged on, the logon username, and so on, it is not specifically designed to store additional user characteristics such as first and last names. Storing additional user data is the responsibility of the new Personalization feature.

Personalization is a persistent user storage system for storing any data related to the user of your application. Several good examples that we'll use to demonstrate Personalization in this chapter include the following:

- Common user characteristics such as first and last names
- User application properties such as a shopping cart
- Application-specific data, such as the personalization settings used by the ASP.NET Forums (http://www.asp.net/forums)
- UI properties, such as the look and feel of controls

The Personalization services feature of ASP.NET 2.0 was designed with several specific goals in mind. Understanding these goals will help you successfully use Personalization in your application.

1. *Strongly typed access*: Unlike features such as `Cache`, `Session`, or `Application`, which require a key to retrieve a value from a dictionary, Personalization uses strongly typed properties, meaning that properties are easier to discover and use. For example, you may replace `Session` code with Personalization for storing the user's first name, as shown below:

```
Dim firstName As String

' First name retrieved from Session
firstName = Session("FirstName")

' First name retrieved from Profile
firstname = Profile.FirstName
```

2. *On-demand look-up*: Unlike Session state, which looks up the values of `Session` on each request regardless of whether or not the data is used, Personalization retrieves data only when it is requested:

3. *Extensible data store*: Personalization implements the new provider model design pattern. This design pattern exists to allow you to abstract the Data Access Layer away from the Personalization APIs. For example, if you have data stored in an AS/400, you could use Personalization to access that data by authoring a provider to communicate to the AS/400. Later in this chapter we're going to look at a provider for the ASP.NET Forums to demonstrate how easy it is to author a provider. Providers can be configured as the default or set at runtime.

Below are the topics we're going to explore in this chapter:

- Storing and retrieving user personalization data
- Anonymous identification
- Anonymous personalization
- The provider model design pattern
- Authoring a customer Personalization provider
- Customizing the look of a site through themes

As we'll see, Personalization is a very powerful new feature of ASP.NET 2.0. It has been designed to integrate seamlessly with the new Membership services feature—but it can work independently as well.

Storing and Retrieving User Personalization Data

My first experience with a Personalization system was with the Site Server 3.0's Personalization and Membership feature. One of the frustrating aspects with Site Server's Personalization model, as well as all other commercially available Personalization systems, is that they are dictionary based. For example, were you to store or retrieve a value such as "John" as the first name of the user using ASP.NET's `Session` APIs:

```
' Store the user's first name value
Session("FirstName") = "John"

...

' Retrieve the user's first name
string firstName = Session("FirstName")
```

Using key/value pairs is a very common pattern. In fact, we see this type of data storage/retrieval used for `Application` state, `Session` state, `ViewState`, `Cache`, and so on. While this technique is both common and a very acceptable approach for storing data work, there are two problems.

1. *Key-based access*: The developer who writes the application must remember the key value `FirstName` used to retrieve the value from the dictionary. While this isn't problematic for simple values, for large applications and complex values this can be quite a lot to remember. It is common for these values to be defined as constant strings within the application.

2. *Not strongly typed*: In addition to remembering the key value of what was stored, the developer also must recall the data type the value was stored as. Values retrieved from the dictionary are returned as type `Object` for complex types, such as a business class `ShoppingCart`; a cast is required to coerce the `Object` back to the appropriate type.

Following is an example of non–strongly typed code that could be used to access a `ShoppingCart` class instance's `CartID` property from an instance of the `ShoppingCart` stored in `Session` state:

```
Dim cartID As Integer
Dim cart As ShoppingCart

' First get the Shopping Cart
cart = CType(Session("MyCart"), ShoppingCart)

' Next, get the cart id
cartID = cart.CartID
```

The key value `MyCart` is used to retrieve the object from `Session` state. We then cast the returned object to the appropriate type `ShoppingCart`.

Using the new ASP.NET 2.0 Personalization feature, this same code is written as:

```
Dim cartID As Integer

' Get the cart id
cartID = Profile.Cart.CartID
```

Rather than accessing the value with a key, `Cart` is a property of type `ShoppingCart` and the `cartID` property can be used directly. No casts and no keys to remember—and a nice side effect is that you get statement completion within your development environment too!

The ASP.NET 2.0 Personalization system can store any data type, from simple scalar values such as integers and strings to complex user data types such as shopping carts. The option of storing any data type gives you a great degree of flexibility in your applications.

You may be wondering how the `Cart` property became available on the `Profile` class. The `Profile` class is a special class dynamically compiled with your ASP.NET application. The addition of the `Profile` class is done automatically—without you needing to do anything.

Properties on the `Profile` class are added through the ASP.NET configuration system within a new `<personalization/>` section of the configuration file.

Configuring Personalization

Personalization properties are defined within the ASP.NET configuration system in the new `<personalization/>` section. Listing 7.1 is a sample `web.config` containing `<personalization/>` settings.

LISTING 7.1. Configuring Personalization

```
<configuration>
  <system.web>
```

```
  <personalization>

    <profile>
      <property name="FirstName" />

      <property name="TotalPosts"
                type="System.Int32"
                defaultValue="0" />

      <property name="LastPostDate"
                type="System.DateTime" />

      <property name="Cart"
                allowAnonymous="true"
                type="Market.ShoppingCart, market"
                serializeAs="Binary" />
    </profile>
  </personalization>

<system.web>
</configuration>
```

The <configuration/> section follows the same provider design pattern used by Membership, Role Manager, and other ASP.NET 2.0 features that require data storage services. We'll cover the provider model in detail later in this chapter.

Within the <personalization> element of the machine configuration file the defaultProvider is set to AspNetAccessProvider—the Access Personalization provider is therefore configured as the default. You can easily change the default by specifying a different provider from those available in the <providers/> element. We'll come back to the <providers/> section shortly.

The <profile/> section is where individual properties are specified. These properties are then made available automatically through the Profile class in the Page. In the configuration sample above we created four properties:

- FirstName: Property used to store the first name value.
- TotalPosts: Property of type Integer, with a default value of 0, used to store the total posts the user has made, for example, within the ASP.NET Forums application.
- LastPostDate: Property of type DateTime, used to store the last post date for a sample application such as the ASP.NET Forums.

- Cart: Property of type ShoppingCart. The property allows anonymous personalization, has a serialization type determined by the provider, and uses the ShoppingCartProvider to retrieve and store data.

Programmatically these properties are accessed as shown in Listing 7.2.

LISTING 7.2. Setting the Properties of a Profile

```
Dim totalPosts As Integer

' Set the user's first name
Profile.FirstName = "Rob"

' Access the user's total posts
totalPosts = Profile.TotalPosts

' DataBind to the user's cart and
' display items in his/her basket
DataGrid1.DataSource = Profile.Cart.Basket
DataGrid1.DataBind
```

If you want to take more control over how the data within the Profile object is organized, you can control the object model structure that is created in the Profile.

For example, if we wished to store personalization data from the ASP.NET Forums (http://www.asp.net/forums), we may wish for it to be organized logically together. This can be accomplished using a special <group/> element within <profile/> (see Listing 7.3).

LISTING 7.3. Configuring a Personalization Group

```
<profile>
  <property name="FirstName" />
  <property name="LastPostDate" type="System.DateTime" />

  <group name="Forums">
    <property name="TotalPosts" type="System.Int32"/>
    <property name="Location" />
    <property name="AllowAvatar" type="System.Boolean" />
    <property name="AvatarURL" />
  </group>

</profile>
```

Values within a group are accessed as follows:

```
Dim location As String

' Get the user's location
location = Profile.Forums.Location
```

As you can probably tell, the `<property/>` element is key to setting up Personalization properties. The `<group/>` element simply provides an easy way to logically organize these properties.

In the examples we've shown, we've seen several of the different attributes the `<property/>` element supports. Let's take a look at what all the different attributes are.

Configuring Personalization Properties

The `<property/>` element is what you use to add properties to the programmatic `Profile` API—when ASP.NET compiles your page, the default `Profile` class is replaced with a class instance that contains the properties you define. This all happens under the covers; all you need to know is how to specify the property.

The simplest use of `<property/>` is to declare a new Personalization property with only the `name` attribute defined:

```
<profile>
  <property name="FirstName" />
</profile>
```

This instructs the Personalization system to add a property named `FirstName` of type `String` with no default value, to not allow anonymous personalization, and to store/retrieve the value from the default Personalization provider.

When defining properties, the only required element is `name`; this is used to access the property from the programmatic `Profile` in the page. All other attributes, while important, are optional.

Table 7.1 on the next page lists all the `<property/>` elements.

Accessing Other Users' Personalization Data

The `Profile` API within your ASP.NET application will automatically be set to retrieve the personalization data for the authenticated user. However, if you wish to retrieve data for a different user, you can retrieve the user's profile using the `Profile.GetProfile(username)` API. You simply specify the username and you can access that user's personalization data.

TABLE 7.1. Personalization Property Attributes

Element	Description
name	Sets the name of the Personalization property. This is used as the key to access the data and also as the name of the property exposed on the programmatic `Profile` API. It is the only required attribute of the `<property/>` element.
readOnly	Specifies that the property is read-only and cannot have values set. This is useful for assigning values, such as `DisplayName`, that are not configurable but are specific to each user. If not specified, it defaults to `false`.
serializeAs	Determines how the data stored within Personalization properties, such as first name or shopping cart, is stored. Valid values include: • `String`: Attempt to convert the value to string. • `XML`: Serialize the data as XML. • `Binary`: Serialize the data as binary. • `ProviderSpecific`: Store the data as the provider determines. No serialization of the data occurs. It is the responsibility of the provider to determine how to store the data. The default is `String`.
provider	Names the provider used for setting and retrieving data for the property. If not specified, the default provider is used. We'll look at a sample later in the chapter demonstrating how you can author your own provider.
defaultValue	Allows for a default value to be specified. For example, a default theme could be specified if the user had not already selected one.
type	Specifies the type of the property. The default is `string`; however, this can be set to any data type.
allowAnonymous	When set to `true`, allows anonymous unauthenticated users to store data in the Personalization system. This also requires the anonymous identification feature to be enabled. If not specified, the default value is `false`. This attribute is discussed in more detail in the Anonymous Personalization section of this chapter.

Now that we've looked at how to set up the required configuration properties and how to access other users' personalization data, let's look at how to configure the databases required to store the personalization data.

Setting Up the Databases for Personalization

Two Personalization providers ship with ASP.NET 2.0:

1. Microsoft Access: Recommended for small Web sites or intranet applications.
2. Microsoft SQL Server: Recommended for large high-scale sites where performance and reliability are critical.

By default Personalization is set to use the Microsoft Access Personalization provider, defined in the class `AccessPersonalizationProvider`. This provider is found in the namespace `System.Web.Personalization` in the `System.Web.dll` assembly.

Personalization is instructed to use the `Access` provider through the configuration settings. The `defaultProvider` attribute on the `<personalization/>` element controls what the default provider is:

```
<personalization defaultProvider="AspNetAccessProvider">
```

The provider itself is then defined within the `<providers/>` section of `<personalization/>` (see Listing 7.4).

LISTING 7.4. Configuring the Access Personalization Provider

```
<add name="AspNetAccessProvider"
    type="System.Web.Personalization.
        AccessPersonalizationProvider,
        System.Web,
        Version=1.2.3400.0,
        Culture=neutral,
        PublicKeyToken=b03f5f7f11d50a3a"
    connectionStringName="AccessFileName"
    applicationName="/"
    description="Stores and retrieves personalization
        data from the local Microsoft Access
        database file" />
```

As mentioned, there is also a Personalization provider for Microsoft SQL Server (see Listing 7.5).

LISTING 7.5. Configuring the SQL Server Personalization Provider

```
<add name="AspNetSqlProvider"
    type="System.Web.Personalization.
        SqlPersonalizationProvider,
        System.Web,
        Version=1.2.3400.0, Culture=neutral,
        PublicKeyToken=b03f5f7f11d50a3a"
    connectionStringName="LocalSqlServer"
```

continues

TABLE 7.2. Personalization Providers' Supported Security Models

	SQL	Access
Windows Authentication	X	X
Small intranet (non-domain-based)	X	X
Internet (enterprise)	X	
Internet (personal/hobby)	X	X

```
applicationName="/"
description="Stores and retrieves personalization
            data from the local Microsoft
            SQL Server database" />
```

Table 7.2 gives you an idea of which provider to use depending on your application.

The ASP.NET team specifically recommends using SQL Server for enterprise-level Internet applications.

Let's take a look at both providers in more detail and see how we set them up.

Using the Access Personalization Provider and the \data\ Directory

The Microsoft Access database used by ASP.NET Personalization is the same Microsoft Access database used by other Access providers, such as Membership. To use Microsoft Access as your database, ASP.NET must have read/write permission on the actual Microsoft Access file.

If you create your project using the Visual Studio .NET "Whidbey" tool, the tool will attempt to grant the necessary permission for ASP.NET to have read/write access. In fact, what will happen is that a new directory, \data\, will be created within your application, and a copy of an existing template Access file containing all the necessary tables and procedures will be copied from:

\Program Files\Microsoft Visual Studio .NET Whidbey\vb\Webs\InternetWebSite\templ
ates\1033\InternetWebSite\data\AspNetDB.mdb

This file is created in your project as \data\AspNetDB.mdb.

If you receive a security error when attempting to use any of the features that utilize the Access provider, you will need to manually add the necessary permissions.

Granting Permissions to the Access Database. To grant ASP.NET permissions to the Microsoft Access database:

1. Open Windows Explorer and navigate to your Web application directory.
2. Create a \data\ directory if it does not already exist.
3. Right-click on the \data\ directory and select Properties.
4. Within the Properties dialog, select the Security tab (see Figure 7.1).
5. Click the Add button and add one of the following accounts:
   * If you are running Windows XP or Windows Server 2000, you need to add the user aspnet_wp.
   * If you are running Windows Server 2003, you need to add the group IIS_wpg.
6. Once the user or group is visible in the list of users and groups—as in Figure 7.1—select the user or group and check the Full Control Allow checkbox.

This grants permission to either the ASP.NET worker process or the IIS 6.0 worker process to have read/write permissions on the \data\ directory —allowing ASP.NET to modify the Access database.

Specifying Which Access Database to Use. You'll notice that the actual filename of the Access database to use for the Personalization provider is not named. Instead only the following reference exists:

FIGURE 7.1. Configuring permissions on the database

```
connectionStringName="AccessFileName"
```

All connection string information is now stored in the new connection string manager section of web.config. Data stored in the connection string manager section will eventually be encrypted (not implemented in the Technology Preview). If your web.config file were compromised, your connection strings would be safe.

Listing 7.6 shows the entry from machine.config for the new connection string manager feature.

LISTING 7.6. Configuring Connection Strings

```
<system.web>
  <connectionStrings>
    <add name="LocalSqlServer"
      connectionString="data source=127.0.0.1;
                        Integrated Security=SSPI" />
    <add name="AccessFileName"
      connectionString="~\DATA\ASPNetDB.mdb" />
  </connectionStrings>
</system.web>
```

All connection strings used by providers are stored within <connection Strings/>.

By default all Access providers will attempt to use the \Data\Asp NetDb.mdb file relative to the current application—specified by the tilde (~). You can easily change this to use an Access file from a different location. For example, you may want all your applications to share one Asp NetDB.mdb file. To do this, specify an absolute path, or each application's web.config could set its own value.

Using the SQL Server Personalization Provider

Microsoft Access is a great storage solution for small Web sites or intranet applications. However, as we stated earlier, Microsoft SQL Server is the recommended data storage location for enterprise-level Internet applications.

While providers that use Microsoft Access "just work," there is a bit of setup that needs to take place in order to use Microsoft SQL Server. There are several different options for configuring Microsoft SQL Server for ASP.NET services:

- The Web Administration Tool: As discussed in Chapter 6, you can use the Web Administration Tool to set up SQL Server databases for ASP.NET.

- The ASP.NET SQL Server Setup Wizard: This command-line and GUI tool can be used to set up a SQL Server for ASP.NET features.
- The .sql scripts: Use SQL Server tools to run the .sql files to configure features.

Let's look at how we can set up a SQL Server database for the ASP.NET Personalization feature using the ASP.NET SQL Server Setup Wizard.

ASP.NET SQL Server Setup Wizard. The ASP.NET SQL Server Setup Wizard is both a command-line and GUI-based utility. It is used to configure SQL Server to support the various application services (such as Membership, Personalization, and so on) used by ASP.NET.

The tool, `aspnet_regsql.exe`, can be found in `\Windows\Microsoft .NET\Framework\v1.2.30609\`. Note that the directory number corresponds to the version of .NET Framework installed. You will likely have a directory different than `\v1.2.30609\`.

The tool supports two modes: command line and GUI. The command-line mode gives you the most control over what is going to be set up, while the GUI tool simply installs or removes all features.

To run in command-line mode, first open a command shell, navigate to the directory where `aspnet_regsql.exe` tool is located, and type:

```
aspnet_regsql.exe /?
```

This will give you a listing of the command-line capabilities of this tool. In Figure 7.2 you can see some of the output in command-line mode. Instructions for using the tool as well as the various switches are also listed.

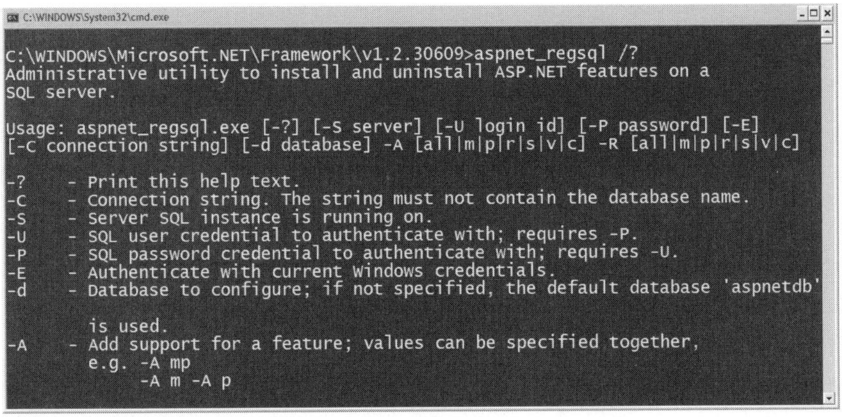

FIGURE 7.2. ASP.NET SQL Server configuration tool command line

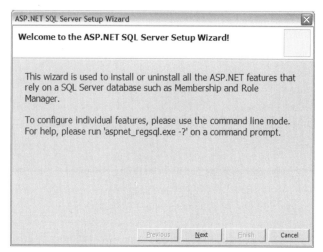

FIGURE 7.3. ASP.NET SQL Server configuration tool wizard

In future books we'll go into more detail on how all these command-line options work. For now we're going to focus on the GUI mode.

To run the `aspnet_regsql.exe` tool in GUI mode, type:

```
aspnet_regsql.exe
```

with no parameters or double-click on the file from Explorer. This will open the wizard and display the welcome screen (see Figure 7.3).

Click Next to select the setup options (see Figure 7.4). From this screen you have only two options.

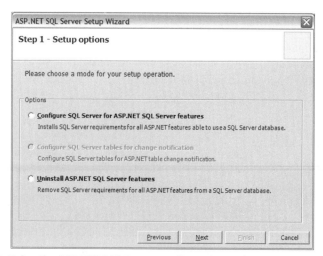

FIGURE 7.4. Using the ASP.NET SQL Server configuration tool, step 1

1. *Configure SQL Server*: Runs the necessary .sql scripts. These scripts exist within the same directory as the aspnet_regsql.exe tool. There are scripts for both installing and uninstalling the features.

2. *Uninstall SQL Server ASP.NET features*: Runs the uninstall scripts on the specified database.

(In the beta release you will be able to configure database cache invalidation —see Chapter 11—from the tool as well.) If you select to configure SQL Server, the tool will run all .sql scripts required for SQL Server support for all ASP.NET services.

The next screen (see Figure 7.5) will ask which SQL Server and database to execute these scripts on. You will need to select both the server and the database to install to. If a database does not exist, you can specify a new database by simply typing in the database name.

After clicking Next you will see a screen to confirm your selections, and installation will begin. Once complete, you will see a screen indicating success or failure, and you can then exit the wizard.

Finally, you will need to modify the <connectionStrings/> section of the configuration file to specify the username and password to access SQL Server. By default the connection string is set to use Windows Integrated Authentication.

Windows Integrated Authentication will attempt to log into SQL Server using the credentials of the process running ASP.NET (assuming impersonation is not enabled). This identity is either the aspnet_wp user for Windows Server 2000 or Windows XP or a user within the IIS_wpg group

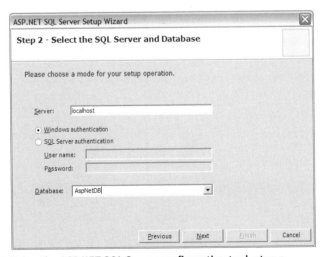

FIGURE 7.5. Using the ASP.NET SQL Server configuration tool, step 2

for Windows Server 2003. Alternatively you can specify a SQL username and password in the connection string.

Data Access Optimizations

When designing the Personalization system the ASP.NET team took great care to ensure the system is flexible for storing and accessing data but at the same time smart and performance-focused about how data is accessed.

Personalization vs. Session State

Many people may initially confuse Personalization and Session state. While similar in that both features store data for users, they are very distinct in how they operate on that data and how data is maintained.

Session state is for temporary user session data. When the user's session expires, the data stored in Session state is removed. Session state also is auto-populated on each request to the application. Whether you use it or not, you are likely paying the cost for Session state—this is even more costly when the Session state data is stored out-of-process.

Personalization is for long-lived data. Whereas with Session state the data is created and then, if the session is not active for a period of time, automatically removed, data created through Personalization—in theory—exists forever. For example, if you stored a ShoppingCart in Session state, the contents of the cart would be lost when the Session ended. However, with Personalization the contents of the cart could be persisted indefinitely.

The last and major difference between Personalization and Session state is the manner in which data is both retrieved and saved. Session state makes use of the two application events: Application_OnAcquire RequestState and Application_OnReleaseRequestState. When the request is starting, the OnAcquireRequestState event is raised, and the Session state module contacts the session store and retrieves all session data for the current user. It also then places a lock on this data in the Session store to prevent other threads from modifying the data. Lastly, once the request is complete the OnReleaseRequestState event is raised, the Session state data is updated—or left unchanged—and the lock is released.

If two requests, as in a frame-based Web application, both attempt to change a value in Session state, the lock would prevent one of the threads from accessing the data until the other request first fully completes. This locking and reading of Session state occurs on each request, no matter if Session state data is even used. This can be controlled through page- and application-level directives such as EnableSession, but nevertheless this approach can be inefficient.

Personalization, on the other hand, is designed to be very smart about how it accesses and saves data. Data stored in Personalization is not retrieved until it is requested. Unlike Session, which populates the Session dictionary each time, Personalization waits until the user requests a property. Then, when Personalization does need to retrieve data, it will retrieve the data for the requested property and all related properties within the same provider. For example, the configuration for Personalization shown in Listing 7.7 adds a new `AspNetForums` provider—which we'll create later in the chapter—and specifies that all properties in the Forums group use this provider.

LISTING 7.7. Configuring a New Personalization Provider

```
<configuration>
  <system.web>
    <personalization enabled="true"
                     defaultProvider="AspNetSqlProvider" >
      <providers>
        <add name="AspNetForums"
             type="AspNetForums.SqlDataProvider" />
      </providers>

      <profile>
        <property name="FirstName" />
        <property name="LastName" />
        <property name="ZipCode" />

        <group name="Forums">
          <property name="TotalPosts" type="System.Int32"
                    provider="AspNetForums"/>
          <property name="Location" provider="AspNetForums"/>
          <property name="AllowAvatar" type="System.Boolean" />
                    provider="AspNetForums"/>
          <property name="AvatarURL" provider="AspNetForums"/>
        </group>
      </profile>
    </personalization>
  </system.web>
</configuration>
```

When using Personalization and requesting the `FirstName` property, the values for `LastName` and `ZipCode` are also retrieved since they all come from the default provider:

```
Dim firstName As String

' Get the user's first name
firstName = Profile.FirstName
```

However, values for `TotalPosts`, `Location`, `AllowAvatar`, and `Avatar URL` are not retrieved. These properties belong to a different provider, and their values will not be retrieved until the value of one of those properties is requested. This means that you can easily partition your data into multiple providers and make intelligent decisions about when to retrieve what data, unlike Session, which would simply retrieve everything. As you'll see later in the chapter, creating providers was designed to be easy. In fact, the ASP.NET team fully expect you to create providers for your data.

Finally, when values are set using the `Profile` API, the data store is updated when the page completes execution.

Membership and Personalization

Personalization stores data by associating the data with the authenticated username as the key. While Membership provides services to authenticate the user and set the authentication username, Membership is not required to use Personalization. In fact, any authentication mechanism will work. As long as a value is set for `User.Identity.Name`, personalization data can be stored.

For anonymous users, that is, users accessing the application who might not necessarily be authenticated, the `User.Identity.Name` value will not be set. To store anonymous personalization data, you need to enable the new anonymous identification feature.

Anonymous Identification

Anonymous identification is another new feature in ASP.NET 2.0. The goal of the feature is to provide a unique identification to users that are not authenticated. The feature is not tied in any way to security but is rather a simple mechanism to assign a guaranteed unique ID to anonymous users. After authentication, the anonymous ID is removed from the request.

Anonymous identification is not enabled by default. To enable it you must either add an entry to your `web.config` file or modify `machine.config`. Below is a `web.config` that enables the anonymous identification feature:

```
<configuration>
  <system.web>
    <anonymousIdentification enabled="true" />
  </system.web>
</configuration>
```

Enabling the feature is simple. There are, however, several other attributes that can be set, as shown in Listing 7.8.

LISTING 7.8. Configuring Anonymous Identification

```
configuration>
  <system.web>
    <anonymousIdentification
        enabled="true"
        cookieName=".ASPXANONYMOUS"
        cookieTimeout="100000"
        cookiePath="/"
        cookieRequireSSL="false"
        cookieSlidingExpiration="true"
        cookieProtection="None"
        cookieless="UseCookies"
    />
  </system.web>
</configuration>
```

As you can see, there is a `Boolean`-enabled attribute used to enable the feature. When enabled, anonymous identification will use a cookie to store the anonymous ID. If you do not wish to use a cookie or do not know if the end user browser supports cookies, you can also set one of the following values for `cookieless`:

- `UseUri`: Store the anonymous ID within the address of the application. (This is similar to what is done in ASP.NET 1.0 with cookieless Session support.)
- `AutoDetect`: Automatically detect whether cookies are supported or not. When cookies are supported, use them. If not, store the anonymous ID in the URL.
- `UseDeviceProfile`: Use the configured profile for the device making the request.

However, `UseCookies` (shown in the listing above) is the recommended choice. This option is less intrusive, that is, the ID is not embedded in the URL, and nearly all users accept cookies. When using the `AutoDetect` option, keep in mind that ASP.NET will need to test the incoming request to see whether cookies are supported.

Once anonymous identification is enabled, unauthenticated requests are assigned an anonymous ID. This is different than the `Session` ID. The `Session` ID is a relatively small identifier and is guaranteed to be unique only for the duration of the session; the anonymous ID value is a GUID and is guaranteed to be globally unique.

The anonymous ID is accessed through the new `Request.Anonymous Id` property. Although the anonymous ID is a GUID, the ASP.NET team decided to make the return value type `string`—more users are familiar with working with `string` than GUIDs.

Anonymous Identification Events

Two events are raised by anonymous identification.

1. `AnonymousIdentification_OnCreate`: Raised when the anonymous ID is created. The `EventArgs` of the event delegate must be of type `AnonymousIdentificationEventArgs`. `AnonymousIdentification EventArgs` exposes an `AnonymousId` property that can be set. If you desire to change the auto-generated anonymous ID, you must change the value within this event.

2. `AnonymousIdentification_OnRemove`: Raised when the request is authenticated but an anonymous ID is still present. This event allows you to perform any cleanup with the anonymous ID before it is removed. Once a request is authenticated, the anonymous ID is no longer available.

As we'll see shortly, the `AnonymousIdentification_OnRemove` event is important since we use it in conjunction with Personalization to allow for the migration of anonymous personalization data.

Anonymous Personalization

Anonymous personalization refers to any personalization that is performed for users that are not already authenticated. By default Personalization is configured to not allow anonymous personalization—this was done purposely for the following reasons.

1. Anonymous personalization data can easily fill a database, and you need to have a strategy in place for managing this data.
2. Personalization, by default, relies on the username value of the authenticated users to store/associate personalization data for a user.

To use anonymous personalization you must take two steps.

1. Enable anonymous identification, which is disabled by default.
2. Specify which Personalization properties can be set for anonymous users.

Specifying which Personalization properties can be used by anonymous users is done by adding the `allowAnonymous` element to your Personalization property. For example, Listing 7.9 shows how to allow anonymous users to use the `Cart` property.

LISTING 7.9. Configuring Anonymous Personalization

```
<configuration>
  <system.web>

    <anonymousIdentification enabled="true" />

    <personalization>

      <profile>
        <property name="FirstName" />
        <property name="LastName" />
        <property name="Cart"
                  allowAnonymous="true"
                  type="Market.ShoppingCart, market"
                  serializeAs="Binary" />
      </profile>
    </personalization>
  </system.web>
</configuration>
```

Anonymous users browsing the site can now add items to the shopping cart without being required to first authenticate—a behavior most sites want to support! Personalization data for the user is then automatically keyed off the value of the anonymous ID.

While anonymous personalization is desirable, at some point the user may either authenticate or create an account on the system. For example, in an e-commerce site you would want the user to create an account before checking out. Giving the user an account would allow you to capture more specific data about the user required for fulfilling their order, such as the shipping address.

As discussed earlier in the Anonymous Identification section, when an authenticated user signs in, the anonymous ID is removed. With anonymous personalization this would orphan any anonymous data. When switching from an anonymous user to an authenticated user, you will potentially need to migrate anonymous personalization data to the authenticated user's profile.

Migrating from Anonymous to Authenticated Users

The migration strategy from anonymous to authenticated is designed to allow the developer to make the decisions through code as to which data is migrated and which data is not migrated (as opposed to automatically migrating all data). This design allows you to make intelligent decisions. For example, if you have a shopping cart populated by an anonymous user who then authenticates, you may find that the authenticated user's profile also has items within the shopping cart. Ideally you would add the anonymous shopping cart items rather than replacing them.

Migration is accomplished through a special event raised by Personalization:

```
Personalization_OnMigrateAnonymous
```

This event is raised after the `AnonymousIdentification_OnRemove` event is raised. Any migration code needs to exist within the `Personalization _OnMigrateAnonymous` event. The event allows you to access the anonymous profile through the `PersonalizationMigrateEventArgs.AnonymousId` property, and by using this property you can retrieve the profile of the anonymous user as well as values (see Listing 7.10).

LISTING 7.10. Migrating Anonymous Users

```
<%@ Import Namespace="System.Security.Principal" %>

<script runat="server">

  Public Sub Personalization_OnMigrateAnonymous (sender As Object,
                             e As PersonalizationMigrateEventArgs)

    ' Migrate the shopping Cart
    Profile.Cart = Profile.GetProfile(e.AnonymousId).Cart

    End Sub

</script>
```

The anonymous migration strategy provides you with the most flexibility since you make all the decisions about what data is migrated and what data is no longer needed.

The Provider Design Pattern

The provider design pattern exists to allow you to extend features of ASP.NET by swapping out the standard ASP.NET providers with yours. A provider is both a Data Abstraction Layer and a Business Logic Layer class that you create and plug into ASP.NET. When features such as Personalization are used, instead of calling one of the ASP.NET providers to retrieve or store user data, your class can be called, and within that class you can make decisions on how to operate on and store that data. Developers continue using the familiar APIs supported by ASP.NET, but it's your code that is running.

The beauty of the provider design is that it allows developers to learn to program to a well-known API, while internally the API can behave differently (e.g., SQL versus Oracle data stores).

Providers are based on the common object-oriented principles of abstraction. A class implements an interface and applications can then depend on the interface instead of directly on the class. Internally the functionality can be completely different from class to class, but the object model is the same. For example, ASP.NET Personalization supports a name/value table for storing personalization data. If you wish to use your own data structure, as shown later in this chapter, you would author a provider.

The provider design pattern is comprised of the following:

- Configuration
- Implementation of the `IProvider` interface
- Implementation of the specific feature interface

Configuration

All ASP.NET features that implement the provider model require a `<configuration/>` section where providers are added. Additionally the feature requires a `defaultProvider` attribute to identify which provider is the default.

Listing 7.11 demonstrates how this is used in the `<personalization/>` section.

LISTING 7.11. Configuring a Default Personalization Provider

```
<configuration>
  <system.web>

    <personalization defaultProvider="AspNetAccessProvider">

      <providers>
        <add name="AspNetAccessProvider"
            type="System.Web.Personalization.
                AccessPersonalizationProvider,
                System.Web,
```

continues

```
                    Version=1.2.3400.0,
                    Culture=neutral,
                    PublicKeyToken=b03f5f7f11d50a3a"
             connectionStringName="AccessFileName"
             applicationName="/"
             description="Stores and retrieves personalization
                          data from the local Microsoft Access
                          database file" />
        <add name="AspNetSqlProvider"
             type="System.Web.Personalization.
                   SqlPersonalizationProvider,
                   System.Web,
                   Version=1.2.3400.0, Culture=neutral,
                   PublicKeyToken=b03f5f7f11d50a3a"
             connectionStringName="LocalSqlServer"
             applicationName="/"
             description="Stores and retrieves personalization
                          data from the local Microsoft
                          SQL Server database" />
      </providers>

  </personalization>

 <system.web>
</configuration>
```

Implementers of providers should have a `defaultProvider` attribute on the main `<configuration>` section. If a default provider is not specified, the first item in the collection is considered the default.

Managing Providers in Configuration

The `<providers/>` configuration section contains one or more `<add>`, `<remove>`, or `<clear>` elements. The following rules apply when processing these elements.

- It is not an error to declare an empty `<providers/>` element.
- Providers inherit items from parent configuration `<add>` statements.
- It is an error to redefine an item using `<add>` if the item already exists or is inherited.
- It is an error to remove a nonexistent item.
- It is not an error to add, remove, and then add the same item again.
- It is not an error to add, clear, and then add the same item again.
- `<clear>` removes all inherited items and items previously defined (e.g., an `<add>` declared before a `<clear>` is removed, but an `<add>` declared after a `<clear>` is not removed).

TABLE 7.3. Provider Attributes

Element	Description
`<add>`	Adds a data provider. Supports the following attributes: • `name`: The friendly name of the provider. • `type`: A class that implements the required provider interface. The value is a fully qualified reference to an assembly. • Other name/value pairs: Additional name/value pairs may be present, such as `connectionName` for the default ASP.NET SQL Personalization Provider implementation. All name/value pairs are the responsibility of the provider to understand.
`<remove>`	Removes a named data provider. Supports the following attribute: • `name`: The friendly name of the provider to remove.
`<clear />`	Removes all inherited providers

Table 7.3 lists the elements of `<provider/>`.

Implementation of the IProvider Interface

All providers are required to implement the `IProvider` interface (see Listing 7.12).

LISTING 7.12. The IProvider Interface

```
namespace System.Configuration.Providers {
  interface IProvider {

    // Methods
    void Initialize(string name, NameValueCollection config);

    // Properties
    string Name { get; }
  }
}
```

The `IProvider` interface is used by ASP.NET to enforce a standard way to initialize providers. The `Initialize()` method should set the name of the provider from the `name` attribute within the configuration file, and the `config NameValueCollection` is a collection of attributes and values specified in the `<add/>` of the provider. This collection would contain any

TABLE 7.4. Feature Interfaces

Feature	Interface
Membership	System.Web.Security.IMembershipProvider
RoleManager	System.Web.Security.IRoleProvider
Personalization	System.Configuration.Settings.ISettingsProvider
Page Personalization	System.Web.Personalization.IUrlPersonalizationProvider
Site Map	System.Web.ISiteMapProvider
Site Counters	System.Web.ISiteCountersProvider
Health Monitoring	System.Web.Management.IWebEventProvider

additional properties needed by the provider, such as a connection string for connecting to the database.

Implementation of the Specific Feature Interface

All ASP.NET features that support providers will also support specific feature interfaces. Table 7.4 lists features as well as their interfaces.

The provider class implements the feature interface as well as IProvider.

Writing a Personalization Provider

When the ASP.NET team set out to build the ASP.NET Personalization system, the most challenging aspect of the design was the data model. They wanted to allow for the maximum amount of flexibility and extensibility. They initially examined several approaches with schemas within the database to describe properties and their types but found that this created very deep tables that couldn't efficiently be used without an intimate knowledge of the schema. They were also concerned that this approach would not perform well. They ideally desired for the data model to use the columns for each type of data, for example, a FirstName column of type nvarchar(256). While this gave them the best performance, it was the most difficult to extend; extensibility would have consisted of adding columns and tables.

They decided on an approach that gave the end developer the most flexibility; hence the provider design pattern was created. The provider pattern allows you to store or use data in any shape and use the friendly, easy-to-use Personalization APIs. In fact, they want you to write providers. Most developers already have lots of user data. Rather than forcing you to use a new data model, the provider pattern allows the data to remain in whatever format you desire, but at the same time you can easily expose that data through the Personalization APIs.

All providers must implement IProvider as well as the specific feature interface. For Personalization this is System.Configuration.Settings .ISettingsProvider. Earlier in the chapter we discussed a Personalization provider for the ASP.NET Forums; Listing 7.13 shows a simple implementation of that Personalization provider.

LISTING 7.13. Sample Personalization Provider

```
Imports System
Imports System.Web
Imports System.Collections
Imports System.Collections.Specialized
Imports System.Configuration.Provider
Imports System.Configuration.Settings
Imports System.Web.Personalization
Imports System.Data
Imports System.Data.SqlClient


Namespace Forums

  Public Class ForumsPersonalizationProvider
        Implements IProvider, ISettingsProvider

    Public Sub Initialize(name As String, _
               config As NameValueCollection) _
          Implements IProvider.Initialize
      ' Used to set the name and any
      ' config data from configuration
    End Sub

    ' Returns property values
    Public Sub GetPropertyValues (userName As String, _
       Properties As SettingsPropertyCollection) _
          Implements ISettingsProvider.GetPropertyValues

      Dim connection As SqlConnection
      Dim command As SqlCommand

      connection = New SqlConnection("connection string")
      command = New SqlCommand("SELECT * FROM Users " _
       & "WHERE Username = '" _
       & userName & "'", connection)
      Dim reader As SqlDataReader
```

continues

```
        connection.Open()

      reader = command.ExecuteReader()


      While reader.Read()
        properties("Email").PropertyValue = reader("Email")
        properties("FakeEmail").PropertyValue = reader("FakeEmail")
        properties("Trusted").PropertyValue = reader("Trusted")
        properties("DateCreated").PropertyValue = reader("DateCreated")
        properties("TotalPosts").PropertyValue = reader("TotalPosts")
      End While

      connection.Close()
    End Sub

    Public Sub SavePropertyValues (userName As String, _
                   properties As SettingsPropertyCollection, _
                   isAuthenticated As Boolean) _
          Implements ISettingsProvider.SavePropertyValues
    End Sub

    Public Property ApplicationName() As String _
          Implements ISettingsProvider.ApplicationName
      Get
        return "/"
      End Get
      Set (ByVal Value As String)
      End Set
    End Property

    Public ReadOnly Property Name() As String _
          Implements IProvider.Name
      Get
        return "ForumsProvider"
      End Get
    End Property
  End Class
End Namespace
```

Once compiled, we can use this provider by specifying it in our web.config, as demonstrated in Listing 7.14.

LISTING 7.14. Adding the Custom Provider

```
<configuration>
  <system.web>
    <personalization>
      <providers>
        <add name="ForumsProvider"
             type="Forums.ForumsPersonalizationProvider,
```

```
                    ForumsPersonalizationProvider"
              applicationName="/" />
      </providers>
      <profile>
        <property name="FirstName"/>
        <property name="LastName" />
        <property name="Email" provider="ForumsProvider" />
        <property name="FakeEmail" provider="ForumsProvider" />
        <property name="Trusted" type="System.Boolean"
                  provider="ForumsProvider" />
        <property name="DateCreated" type="System.DateTime"
                  provider="ForumsProvider" />
        <property name="TotalPosts" type="System.Int32"
                  provider="ForumsProvider" />
      </profile>
    </personalization>
  </system.web>
</configuration>
```

Finally, we can then write pages that display the property values (see Listing 7.15).

LISTING 7.15. Using the Custom Provider

```
Your email address is: <% =Profile.Email %>
<P>
Your fake email address is: <% =Profile.FakeEmail %>
<P>
Your total posts are: <% =Profile.TotalPosts %>
<P>
Your account was created:
<% =Profile.DateCreated.ToString("MM/dd/yy mm:ss")%>
```

Providers allow you to fully plug in to the APIs exposed by ASP.NET. You can take full control over what happens when those APIs are used within your application.

Themes

Themes provide a way to customize the look and feel of your site, including graphics, CSS styles, properties, and so on. Not only does this provide a way for you, the developer, to provide a consistent style, but it also allows the users to select the style. While this may not be required in every Web site, using themes does allow for consistency among pages and controls, giving an easy way to change the look of the site even if this isn't a user requirement.

The great beauty of the way themes work is that there are very few changes required to an ASP.NET page for them to be used. This means that from the development perspective, the work involved is minimal. Once theme support is included in a site or page, the addition, change, or removal of themes is simple, since themes are stored external to the pages themselves. To understand themes you have to understand the terminology and how it is applied within ASP.NET.

Themes and Skins

The theme architecture defines two terms—**themes** and **skins**. A skin defines the visual style applied to a control, such as the stylesheet attributes, images, colors and so on. A theme is a collection of skins and applies to an ASP.NET page. Themes are stored under the Themes directory under the application root, with a directory for each theme. Within the directory for a theme there is a file for the theme itself (containing the skin details for each control), stylesheets, and any images required for controls (e.g., images for the TreeView control).

Each theme can have a default look, where no skin is specified, or there can be multiple skins within each theme. This allows you to have themes that are distinct from each other and have multiple looks. For example, you could have a theme called Pastel and within it skins called Pink and Blue.

A theme doesn't have to provide a skin for every server control. Any controls that have no skin within the theme file will use the default look supplied by the browser (or as overridden by a stylesheet). For consistency, however, it is better to provide a skin for each control you use. Setting the skin for a control where no skin exists for that control type will generate an error.

You can use skins to do more than provide just a single look for the entire site. Skins are uniquely identified by the SkinID property applied to the control in a skin file, allowing the same control to be duplicated in the skin file with different SkinID values. This allows, for example, the same type of control to be used on different pages but to have a different look on each page. Theming can also be disabled at both the page and control levels, so page developers aren't forced to use themes.

Global Themes

In addition to theme support on a local application level, the Framework supports global themes, which are available to all applications. These are initially installed in the {windows}\Microsoft.Net\Framework\{version}

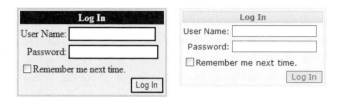

FIGURE 7.6. BasicBlue (left) and SmokeAndGlass (right) themes

`\ASP.NETClientFiles\Themes` directory and then copied to the Web root (`Inetpub\wwwroot\aspnet_client\{version}\Themes`). Local themes with the same name as a global theme replace the global theme in its entirety—no merging with or inheritance from the global theme takes place.

The Technology Preview release initially ships with two global themes, `BasicBlue` and `SmokeAndGlass`, but several more are planned for beta releases. As an example, login controls using these two global themes are shown in Figure 7.6.

Creating Themes

To create local themes, you simply create a directory called `Themes` under your application root, then create a directory for each theme. For example, consider Figure 7.7, where a theme called `Basic` has been created. The skin details for the theme are in the file called `Basic.skin`.

The name of the skin file doesn't have to match that of the theme, although for the default skin this makes sense. Any images relating to this theme can be placed either in the `Themes` directory itself or in a separate directory, as shown in Figure 7.7.

The contents of the skin file are simply control declarations. For example, the default skin for `Basic` has the following code:

```
<asp:Label runat="server"
    ForeColor="#FFFFFF" BackColor="#660000" />
```

This simply defines a single control, with white text on a red background. When the theme of a page is set to `Basic`, all `Label` controls will inherit this style. Since no other controls are defined in this skin they will use either the default HTML settings or those supplied by a stylesheet.

FIGURE 7.7. The directory and file for a simple theme

Creating Skins

An explicitly named skin is created by supplying a `SkinID` property on the controls in the skin file. For example:

```
<asp:Label runat="server" SkinID="Red"
    ForeColor="#FFFFFF" BackColor="#660000" />
```

Here the `SkinID` is set to `Red`. This wouldn't, therefore, be part of the default skin (which has no `SkinID`), and its look has to be explicitly set on a control within a page.

`SkinIDs` must be unique for each control, so you cannot have the same `SkinID` for the same control type with the same value. A compile error is generated if this occurs.

Creating Multiple Skins

Multiple skins can be supplied in one of two ways. The first method is to supply all of the skins within the same file. For example, to provide a default skin plus a red skin, the skin file could contain these lines:

```
<asp:Label runat="server"
    ForeColor="#000000" BackColor="#FFFFFF" />

<asp:Label runat="server" SkinID="Red"
    ForeColor="#FFFFFF" BackColor="#660000" />
```

Here you just add all of the controls and create duplicates for those that require multiple skins, setting the `SkinID` for each duplicate to a different name.

The second method is to split the skins into separate files. For example, consider the provision of a `Basic` theme, with default controls, and two skins—`Red` and `Blue`. We could use the structure shown in Figure 7.8.

In this example there is a skin file for each distinct skin. This method is easier to maintain because the skins are completely separate from each other, and it allows more skins to be created by simply copying an existing file and modifying it.

A theme directory can contain other resources, which can be accessed from skin files with relative paths. For example, Figure 7.8 shows an `Images`

FIGURE 7.8. Multiple skin files

directory, allowing skin files to include specific images. This is especially useful for the `TreeView` control; separate images can be used per theme. For example, consider the following fragment:

```
<%@ Page Theme="Basic" %>

<asp:TreeView SkinID="Basic"
    LeafNodeImage="images\MyTheme_Skin_LeafNode.gif" ...
```

In this example the `LeafNodeImage` property identifies the image to use for leaf nodes of the `TreeView`. Since this control is skinned, the images are taken from the `Images` directory under the theme.

Using Stylesheets in Themes

Skin files can also contain stylesheets, allowing a greater separation of styling features. A server-side stylesheet is used for this feature, as shown below:

```
<asp:StyleSheetInclude runat="server">
  <asp:StyleSheetItem href="Basic.css" />
</asp:StyleSheetInclude>
```

For this to work, the ASP.NET page must have a server-based `head` tag:

```
<head runat="server" />
```

This is required because the stylesheet is injected into the `head` tag at compile time.

Setting a Page Theme

To use a theme on a page, you simply set the `Theme` property of the page. This can be done either declaratively as an attribute of the `Page` directive:

```
<%@ Page Theme="Basic" %>
```

or within code:

```
Page.Theme = Request.QueryString("Theme")
Page.Theme = Profile.Theme
```

When setting the theme programmatically, it must be set within the new page-level `PreInit` event. For example:

```
Sub Page_PreInit(Sender As Object, E As EventArgs)

  Page.Theme = Profile.Theme

End Sub
```

This event must be used because the theme and skin details for controls need to be set before the controls are added to the page, and other events (such as Init, PreRender, Load, and so on) occur too late in the control creation chain.

Setting a Skin

Skins apply to controls, so the SkinID property of the controls must be set. Like the page theme, this can be set either declaratively:

```
<asp:Label SkinID="Red" Text="I'm Skinned" />
```

or programmatically:

```
Label.SkinID = "Red"
Label.SkinID = Profile.SkinID
```

The skin applies only to a single control and not child controls. Thus setting the SkinID for a Panel that contains other controls only sets the SkinID for the Panel. If you wish to ensure that all controls on a page have a SkinID applied, you can recurse the Controls collection. For example, Listing 7.16 shows how the page theme and skin could be set for all controls, based on the details set in the user Profile.

LISTING 7.16. Setting the Skin for All Controls

```
Sub Page_PreInit(Sender As object, E As EventArgs)

  Page.Theme = Profile.Theme
  SkinControls(Profile.SkinID, Page.Controls)

End Sub

Private Sub SkinControls(Skin As String, ctls As ControlCollection)

  Dim ctl As Control
  For Each ctl In ctls
    ctl.SkinID = Skin

    If ctl.HasControls Then
      SkinControls(Skin, ctl.Controls)
    End If
  Next

End Sub
```

One problem with this technique is that if a `SkinID` is not defined for a particular control type in use on the page, an exception is raised. For this reason it's better to explicitly set the skin for individual controls.

Controls dynamically added to a page will have the appropriate theme and skin applied by ASP.NET.

Allowing User Selection of Skins

If your site supports multiple themes and skins, allowing users to select their preferred look is a great feature. It's relatively easy to do dynamically if you stick to a strict convention, keeping individual skins in separate files so you can then simply search for skin files. For example, you could build a theme browser similar to that shown in Figure 7.9, where the themes are shown at the top and some sample controls are shown on the right. Selecting a theme file could then apply that theme.

The big problem with this approach is the event ordering. Remember that themes and skins are applied before controls are added to the page, and in this example we set the details in the `PreInit` event, which is executed before the postback event. This means that when you select the theme or skin, the server-side postback event occurs after the skin details have been set in `PreInit`. Selecting the same theme or skin again is a workaround as the selected value will already be set from the previous postback and so would be available at the `PreInit` stage. Another option is to have an Apply button that causes a postback, either to itself or to another page, thus giving you the second postback.

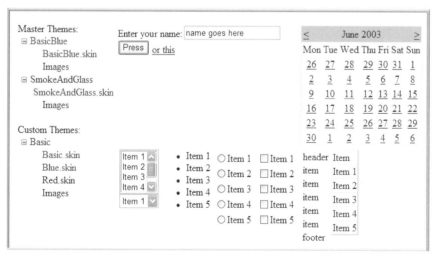

FIGURE 7.9. A theme browser

Using Personalization for Themes

Some of the code samples earlier showed the Profile being used to store the theme and skin names. Configuration of this simply requires the properties to be added to the <profile> section in web.config (see Listing 7.17).

LISTING 7.17. Configuring Personalization to Store Theme Details

```
<configuration>
  <system.web>

    <personalization>
      <profile>
        <property name="Theme" />
        <property name="SkinID" />
      </profile>
    </personalization>

  <system.web>
</configuration>
```

Now when storing the selected theme, perhaps from the theme browser shown earlier, you can simply store the user's selected theme in his or her profile when the user selects a particular theme from the appropriate link (see Listing 7.18).

LISTING 7.18. Storing the Theme in the Profile

```
<asp:LinkButton runat="server" Text="Basic Blue"
  onClick="SetTheme" CommandName="BasicBlue" />
<asp:LinkButton runat="server" Text="Smoke and Glass"
  onClick="SetThem" CommandName="SmokeAndGlass" />


<script runat="server">

Sub SetTheme(Sender As Object, E As CommandEventArgs)

  Profile.Theme = e.CommandName

End Sub

</script>
```

The theme details can then simply be ready from the Profile at any stage, especially during the Page_PreInit event where the theme can be set for the page.

Collections of Controls

Care has to be taken when skinning collections of controls because the themed collection replaces a collection applied in a page. For example, consider the following themed control within `MyTheme.skin` (see Listing 7.19).

LISTING 7.19. A Themed Collection Control

```
<asp:RadioButtonList runat="server">
  <asp:ListItem value="1">Option 1</asp:ListItem>
  <asp:ListItem value="2">Option 2</asp:ListItem>
  <asp:ListItem value="3">Option 3</asp:ListItem>
  <asp:ListItem value="4">Option 4</asp:ListItem>
</asp:RadioButtonList>
```

Now consider the page created by Listing 7.20.

LISTING 7.20. Using a Themed Collection Control

```
<%@ Page Theme="MyTheme" %>

<form runat="server">
  <asp:RadioButtonList id="list" runat="server">
    <asp:ListItem value="5">Option 5</asp:ListItem>
    <asp:ListItem value="6">Option 6</asp:ListItem>
    <asp:ListItem value="7">Option 7</asp:ListItem>
    <asp:ListItem value="8">Option 8</asp:ListItem>
  </asp:RadioButtonList>
</form>
```

The results of running this page are shown in Figure 7.10.

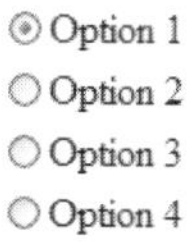

Notice that the collection from the theme is used instead of the collection from the page. This is because the controls on the page are replaced by their equivalents in the theme file.

◉ Option 1
○ Option 2
○ Option 3
○ Option 4

FIGURE 7.10. A themed collection

To get around this you can change the values in the `Page_Load` event, either by manually deleting the collection entries and adding them or by data binding, in which case the collection from the theme is replaced.

Disabling Themes

Theming can be explicitly disabled on controls by setting the `Enable Theming` property to `False`. When the controls are added to the page, any controls (and their children) with this property set to `False` will not have the theme applied (see Listing 7.21).

LISTING 7.21. Disabling Theming on Controls

```
<%@ Page Theme="BasicBlue" %>

<asp:Panel runat="server" EnableTheming="False">
  <asp:Label id="WelcomeMessage" runat="server" />
  <br />
  <asp:DataGrid id="News" runat="server" />
</asp:Panel>
```

In this case the `Panel`, the `Label`, and the `DataGrid` will not have the theme applied if the `EnableTheming` property has been set to `False`. This is particularly useful when including third-party controls, such as search controls, that must conform to a set look.

Adding Themes to a Site

In addition to setting themes at the page level, you can set them globally by modifying the application configuration file, as shown in Listing 7.22.

LISTING 7.22. Configuring a Site-Wide Theme

```
<configuration>
  <system.web>
    <pages theme="BasicBlue" />
  </system.web>
</configuration>
```

Like all page settings, this is overridden when set on individual pages.

Enabling Themes in Custom Controls

When building custom controls, theme support is automatically enabled if your control inherits from `System.Web.UI.Control` (either directly or indirectly). To disable theme support in your control, you can override the `EnableTheming` property, as shown in Listing 7.23.

LISTING 7.23. Disabling Theming in a Custom Control with Properties

```
Public Class MyControl
    Inherits System.Web.UI.Control

  Public Overrides Property EnableTheming() As Boolean
    Get
      Return False
    End Get
    Set(ByVal Value As Boolean)
      base.EnableTheming = Value
```

```
     End Set
   End Property
End Class
```

This property can also be set as an attribute on the entire class, to disable theme support for the control (see Listing 7.24).

LISTING 7.24. Disabling Theming in a Custom Control with Attributes

```
<EnableTheming(False)> _
Public Class MyControl
    Inherits System.Web.UI.Control

End Class
```

Individual properties can also have theme support disabled by use of an attribute (see Listing 7.25).

LISTING 7.25. Disabling Theming on a Property

```
Public Class MyControl
    Inherits System.Web.UI.Control

  Private _searchString As String

  <Themable(False)> _
  Public Property SearchString() As String
    Get
      Return _searchString
    End Get
    Set(ByVal Value As Boolean)
      _searchString = Value
    End Set
  End Property

End Class
```

SUMMARY

Personalization is a very powerful feature of ASP.NET 2.0. It gives you an easy, type-safe way to expose all sorts of user data. Personalization does require a database, but the ASP.NET team has tried hard to ensure that you can take full control over how this data is both operated on and stored. The provider model is the functionality that enables this, and we fully intend to publish more documentation on how providers are built.

ASP.NET ships with two providers: Microsoft SQL Server and Microsoft Access. Access is the default provider and when used, all personalization data is stored within an Access database located within the application. The ASP.NET team recommends using the Microsoft SQL Server provider for large enterprise applications.

In this chapter we built a simple provider for Personalization that allows ASP.NET Personalization to retrieve data from the ASP.NET Forums application. Building providers was designed to be simple, as demonstrated, and we fully expect you to write your own Personalization providers to control access to your data.

Finally, we looked at themes, one of the visual aspects of Personalization, which allow users to customize the look and feel of a site. Since this requires very few changes to existing pages and relies on some simple properties, it's ideal for storage as part of the Personalization Profile.

Now it's time to take Personalization to the next level by looking at the ASP.NET portal framework.

8

Web Parts and the Portal Framework

C USTOMIZATION IS A BIG TOPIC in application development. Users like to be able to change the layout, appearance, and behavior of their applications—fine-tuning them to better suit their business practices and working preferences. However, while this has become common in mainstream applications like the Microsoft Office programs and Windows itself, it has been rare to find Web sites that support this type of feature.

But all that changes in ASP.NET 2.0, as you've seen with the personalization features in earlier chapters. In this chapter, you'll see even more ways that users can customize their views of your Web applications and Web pages. We'll be looking at:

- The portal framework that is now a fundamental part of ASP.NET 2.0
- What Web Parts are and how you can use them in your pages
- Interacting with Web Parts using server-side code
- How the new version of Visual Studio will support these features

We start with a look at what Web Parts and the portal framework actually are and how they relate to building portal-style applications with ASP.NET 2.0 (and on different software platforms as well).

The ASP.NET 2.0 Portal Framework

In reality, the home page of any Web site or Web application is a "portal" to that site or application. In general, the home page carries things like news, information, and of course links to the other pages that make up the content of the site or application. However, the term "portal" has increasingly become associated with pages that offer a modularized view of information. This is one of the main aims of Microsoft SharePoint and other similar content management systems.

The ASP.NET 2.0 Web Parts technology is designed to make this kind of page and application easy to build, often without requiring the developer to write any code. The screenshot in Figure 8.1 shows a simple example of a portal page containing five Web Parts. They display different sets of information that would be useful for, say, a worker on the corporate intranet.

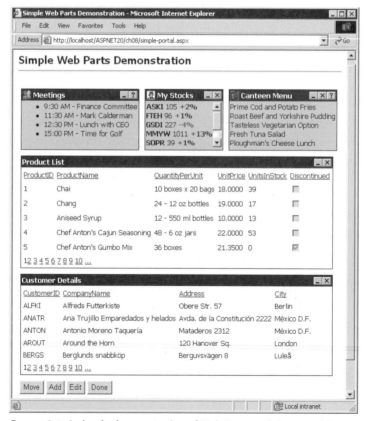

FIGURE 8.1. A simple demonstration of Web Parts and the portal framework

The Goals of the Portal Framework

Web Parts is not a brand-new technology, and in some ways it collects together existing development efforts in an attempt to provide a general solution. The goals for the technology are to:

- Provide a robust framework for Web pages and applications that support modular content and can be customized by end users
- Expose a programming model that is easy to understand and use and that requires no code to be written for the basic operations, while being capable of providing support for more complex scenarios as well
- Provide a rich user experience where this is supported by the client's software, plus safe fallback support for other clients
- Be easy to configure for individual users and groups of users, and to tie in with the underlying personalization features of ASP.NET 2.0
- Support the growth in Web Parts technology that is happening outside ASP.NET, for example, in SharePoint, Content Management Server, and Office 2003, by establishing a foundation of a single portal technology for use across all Microsoft applications
- Provide full support and integration for third-party Web Parts and assemblies to be used, expose backward compatibility as far as possible, and offer a migration path for other existing technologies
- Meet the performance demands of portal applications, which often experience bursts of high usage (such as when a group of users all start work at the same time)

Integration with SharePoint and Office Web Parts

One important aim of the new ASP.NET Web Parts technology is to allow it to be extended within SharePoint and other Microsoft applications, as well as to provide support for existing Web Parts. Web Parts have been around for a couple of years, in products like the Digital Dashboard and Content Management Server.

It's hoped that all of these Web Parts would be usable directly within the ASP.NET portal framework. The ongoing Web Parts development process aims to expose an interface that can be used by other Microsoft applications and other third-party tools and environments.

Customization and Personalization

The Web Parts technology used to create the page shown in Figure 8.1 also provides built-in capabilities for customizing the display. This can be just for the current session, or integrated with the ASP.NET personalization features so that the settings are persisted on a per-user basis and automatically retrieved when that user logs in again next time.

As an example of the customization features, the screenshot in Figure 8.2 shows how a rich client (Internet Explorer 6) allows the user to enter design mode and change the layout of the modules on the page by simply dragging them from one place to another.

Web Parts technology implements all the customization processes automatically and many other features as well. You can minimize or "roll up" a Web Part so that only the title bar is visible. And, as you'll see in the example page shown in this chapter, you can easily expose features that al-

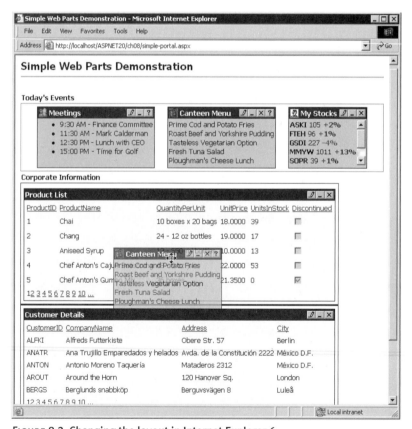

FIGURE 8.2. Changing the layout in Internet Explorer 6

low the user to edit the appearance and behavior of individual Web Parts, open dedicated Help windows for each one, close or hide individual Web Parts, and add new Web Parts to the page.

It all looks like a complex process, and it certainly does produce a page containing features that would take quite a considerable developer effort to achieve from scratch. Yet the example in Figure 8.2, which we'll discuss in more depth shortly, mainly contains only declarative content (ASP.NET server controls) and requires almost no server-side or client-side code to be written.

About the Web Parts Framework

The Web Parts technology is exposed through a series of ASP.NET server controls. In combination, they work together to generate the kind of output and feature set you saw in the previous screenshots. Underneath, the source for the page builds up a structured hierarchy of objects from the server control declarations. Figure 8.3 shows that structure.

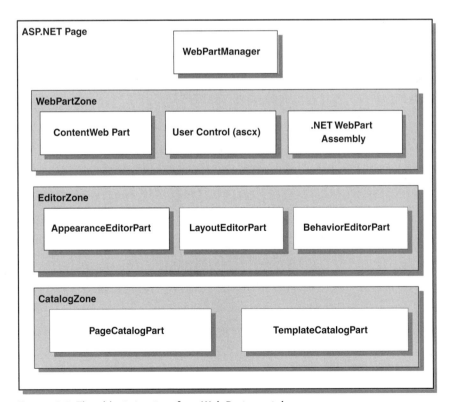

FIGURE 8.3. The object structure for a Web Parts portal page

Every page that uses Web Parts must contain a single instance of the `WebPartManager` control. This control is responsible for binding all the other controls together, reacting to events in the page, handling dynamic connections between Web Parts, and calling the methods on each Web Part to create the control tree for the page and generate the output. A `WebPartManager` requires only this simple declaration:

```
<asp:WebPartManager id="PartManager" runat="server" />
```

The remaining Web Parts features are declared within "zones" on the page (although other content for the page can, of course, be located outside the zones). Web Parts that appear when the page is first opened are declared or referenced within a `WebPartZone`.

Web Part Zones

It's possible to place a Web Part directly on an ASP.NET page, but in general you will place them within zones that are defined using a `WebPartZone` control. This is a templated control that contains all the Web Parts for the current zone and synchronizes the layout, appearance, and colors of these Web Parts. An ASP.NET page can contain more than one `WebPartZone`—the example in Figures 8.1 and 8.2 contains two zones. One shows today's events, and the other shows corporate information such as the product and customer lists.

A `WebPartZone` declaration follows the same principles as most other familiar templated controls. It accepts attributes that define the behavior of the zone and all of the Web Parts within the zone, elements that define the style of specific sections of the output, and a `ZoneTemplate` that contains the declaration of the Web Parts that will appear in this zone by default (see Listing 8.1).

LISTING 8.1. Outline of a WebPartZone Control Declaration

```
<asp:WebPartZone id="EventsZone" runat="server"
    Title="Today's Events"
    TitleStyle-Font-Bold="True"
    Orientation="Horizontal">
  <PartTitleStyle BackColor="Green" Font-Bold="True" />
  <PartStyle BackColor="Yellow" />
  <ZoneTemplate>
    ... Web Parts for this zone are declared here ...
  </ZoneTemplate>
</asp:WebPartZone>
```

Bear in mind that the layout of the Web Parts in the page may be different when the page is actually displayed. If this is a postback, and editing of the page layout is enabled, the user may have moved Web Parts from one zone to another. Likewise, if personalization is enabled for the page, Web Parts may appear in a different zone from that where they were originally located.

The following kinds of Web Parts can appear in a `WebPartZone`:

- In-line declarations defining the complete content and appearance of the Web Part, using a `ContentWebPart` control that can contain any HTML, content, and ASP.NET server controls
- Standard ASP.NET User Controls (referenced through a `Register` directive in the page), which can contain HTML, markup, dynamic content, or any other content that is available for use in a Web page
- Compiled .NET assemblies (referenced through a `Register` directive in the page), which generate the same kinds of content as a User Control or Web page

In the future, it's possible that support may also be extended to DLLs and components that do not run under the .NET Framework, to provide cross-application integration with Web Parts from other arenas.

Editor Zones

To allow the user to change the layout of the Web Parts, it's necessary only to shift the `WebPartManager` into design mode. This simply involves changing the `WebPartDisplayMode` property during a postback; the `WebPartManager` and the individual Web Part controls then update their output to reflect this mode.

In forthcoming beta releases and in the final version of ASP.NET 2.0, there will be dedicated server controls to achieve this mode switching. However, for the time being you can use any control to submit the page and then change the mode using server-side code. We demonstrate this approach in the example later in this chapter.

To enable the end user to edit the behavior and appearance of individual Web Parts, you must switch the `WebPartManager` into edit mode and provide an `EditorZone` containing instances of one or more of the different types of editor control (depending on which editing features you want to offer). The three editing controls most commonly used within an `EditorZone` are the `AppearanceEditorPart`, `LayoutEditorPart`, and `BehaviorEditor` `Part` controls, as seen in Listing 8.2.

LISTING 8.2. Declaring an EditorZone Control

```
<asp:EditorZone id="EditorZone" runat="server"
    TitleStyle-Font-Bold="True" BackColor="LightBlue"
    Style="padding:5px;margin-top:7px">
  <PartTitleStyle BackColor="Blue" ForeColor="White" />
  <ZoneTemplate>
    <asp:AppearanceEditorPart id="AppearanceEditorPart1"
                              runat="server" />
    <asp:LayoutEditorPart id="LayoutEditorPart1" runat="server" />
    <asp:BehaviorEditorPart id="BehaviorEditorPart1" runat="server" />
  </ZoneTemplate>
</asp:EditorZone>
```

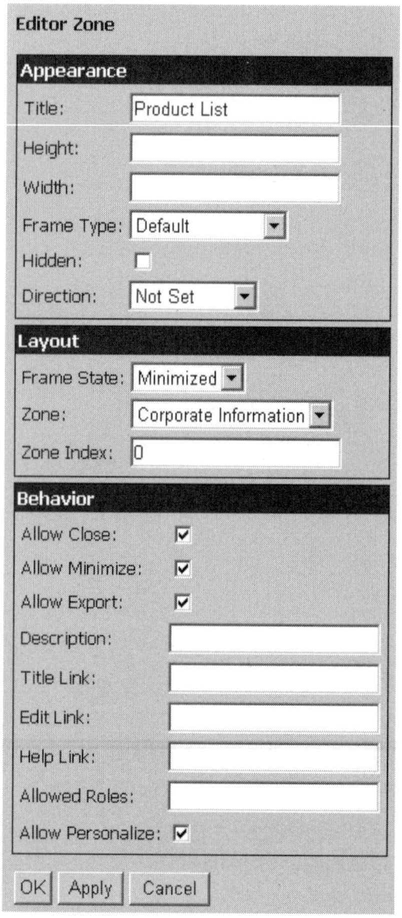

The screenshot in Figure 8.4 shows the output that these controls generate when the page is in edit mode and a single control is selected for editing. (At other times they do not appear in the output generated for the page.) You can, of course, provide just one or two of the different edit controls if you don't want users to be able to change all of the settings to which these controls provide access.

FIGURE 8.4. The EditorZone control in action

It is possible to expose custom properties from a Web Part, a topic we're not covering here. However, in this case, you can include a `PropertyGridEditorPart` in the `EditorZone` as well, allowing users to set the values of these custom properties when that Web Part is in edit mode.

Catalog Zones

By default, users can close a Web Part on the page by clicking the Close button or link in the title bar. They can later add this Web Part back to the page or add any other Web Parts you have associated with the page. Adding a new or a closed Web Part to the page is achieved through controls declared within a `CatalogZone`. Like the other zone controls, the `CatalogZone` is a templated control. The lists of available Web Parts are generated with a `PageCatalogPart` and/or a `TemplateCatalogPart` control (see Listing 8.3).

LISTING 8.3. Declaring a CatalogZone Control

```
<asp:CatalogZone id="CatalogZone" runat="server"
    TitleStyle-Font-Bold="True" BackColor="LightGray"
    Style="padding:5px;margin-top:7px">
  <ZoneTemplate>
    <asp:PageCatalogPart id="PagePart" runat="server" />
    <asp:TemplateCatalogPart id="CatalogPart" runat="server"
        Title="Catalog">
      <WebPartsTemplate>
        ... Web Parts for this zone are declared here ...
      </WebPartsTemplate>
    </asp:TemplateCatalogPart>
  </ZoneTemplate>
</asp:CatalogZone>
```

The `PageCatalogPart` control generates a list of the Web Parts for the page that are currently closed (i.e., Web Parts that the user has removed from the page by using the Close button on the title bar of that Web Part). It also generates UI elements where the end user can specify which of these Web Parts should be shown again and which zone they should appear in. You can see this in the left-hand screenshot in Figure 8.5 on the next page.

At the top of the Catalog Zone dialog are links to the two types of Catalog Part in the page—the Page Catalog (the Web Parts that are currently closed) and the Catalog (other controls that were not included in the page originally

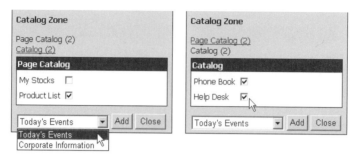

FIGURE 8.5. The two modes of the CatalogZone control

but are available to be added to the page). The right-hand screenshot in Figure 8.5 shows the display when the Catalog section is selected. These are the Web Parts defined within the WebPartsTemplate section of the CatalogZone control shown in Listing 8.3.

Like the EditorZone discussed previously, the CatalogZone is not visible in the page by default. It appears only when the WebPartDisplayMode property of the WebPartManager is changed—in this case to catalog mode.

So, by using the edit and catalog features, users can customize the page to suit their requirements, displaying just the Web Parts they want to see and laying them out in the page as they require.

A Simple Web Parts Example Page

The screenshots shown earlier are taken from a simple example page that demonstrates most of the features of the portal framework and Web Parts technologies. In this section, you'll see how this page is constructed and the way that the various attributes and control elements govern the behavior of the page.

The Page in Outline

Listing 8.4 shows the outline of the page with most of the attributes and all the explicit declarations of the individual Web Parts removed. The two User Controls that display the customer and product details are registered at the start of the page, and a WebPartManager control is added to the <body> section.

This is followed by a server-side <form> that contains the five zones used in the page:

- The `EventsZone` contains three `ContentWebPart` controls that explicitly define the output for the three Web Parts at the top of the page: Meetings, My Stocks, and Canteen Menu.

- The `CorpInfoZone` contains the two User Controls registered at the start of the page, which display the list of customers and the list of products.

- The `EditorZone` contains three of the editor controls: `Appearance EditorPart`, `LayoutEditorPart`, and `BehaviorEditorPart`.

- The `CatalogZone` contains a `PageCatalogPart` to display the Web Parts that are currently closed and a `TemplateCatalogPart` that defines two other controls that are available for use on the page.

- The `ControlsZone` contains the four buttons that switch the page between the four available modes: design (the Move button), catalog (the Add button), edit (the Edit button), and normal (the Done button).

LISTING 8.4. The Overall Outline of the Page

```
<%@ Register TagPrefix="ahh" TagName="Products"
             Src="products.ascx" %>
<%@ Register TagPrefix="ahh" TagName="Customers"
             Src="customers.ascx" %>

<html>
<head><title>Simple Web Parts Demonstration</title></head>
<body>

<asp:WebPartManager id="PartManager" runat="server" />

<form runat="server">

<asp:WebPartZone id="EventsZone" runat="server">
  <ZoneTemplate>
    <asp:ContentWebPart id="pMeetings" runat="server">
    ... explicit declaration of Web Part content here ...
    </asp:ContentWebPart>
    <asp:ContentWebPart id="pStocks" runat="server">
    ... explicit declaration of Web Part content here ...
    </asp:ContentWebPart>
    <asp:ContentWebPart id="pCanteen" runat="server">
    ... explicit declaration of Web Part content here ...
    </asp:ContentWebPart>
  </ZoneTemplate>
</asp:WebPartZone>
```

continues

```
<asp:WebPartZone id="CorpInfoZone" runat="server">
  <ZoneTemplate>
    <ahh:Products id="pProducts" runat="server"
                  Title="Product List" />
    <ahh:Customers id="pCustomers" runat="server"
                  Title="Customer Details" />
  </ZoneTemplate>
</asp:WebPartZone>


<asp:EditorZone id="EditorZone" runat="server">
  <ZoneTemplate>
    <asp:AppearanceEditorPart id="AppearanceEditorPart1"
                              runat="server" />
    <asp:LayoutEditorPart id="LayoutEditorPart1" runat="server" />
    <asp:BehaviorEditorPart id="BehaviorEditorPart1" runat="server" />
  </ZoneTemplate>
</asp:EditorZone>


<asp:CatalogZone id="CatalogZone" runat="server">
  <ZoneTemplate>
    <asp:PageCatalogPart id="PagePart" runat="server" />
    <asp:TemplateCatalogPart id="CatalogPart" runat="server"
                             Title="Catalog">
      <WebPartsTemplate>
        <asp:ContentWebPart id="pPhoneBook" runat="server">
          ... explicit declaration of Web Part content here ...
        </asp:ContentWebPart>
        <asp:ContentWebPart id="pHelpDesk" runat="server">
          ... explicit declaration of Web Part content here ...
        </asp:ContentWebPart>
      </WebPartsTemplate>
    </asp:TemplateCatalogPart>
  </ZoneTemplate>
</asp:CatalogZone>

<asp:WebPartZone id="ControlsZone" runat="server">
  <ZoneTemplate>
    <asp:ContentWebPart id="ControlsPart" runat="server">
    ... explicit declaration of Web Part content here ...
    </asp:ContentWebPart>
  </ZoneTemplate>
</asp:WebPartZone>

</form>

</body>
</html>
```

The default appearance of the page when first loaded is shown again in
Figure 8.6 so that you can see the relationship between the control declarations and the output they generate.

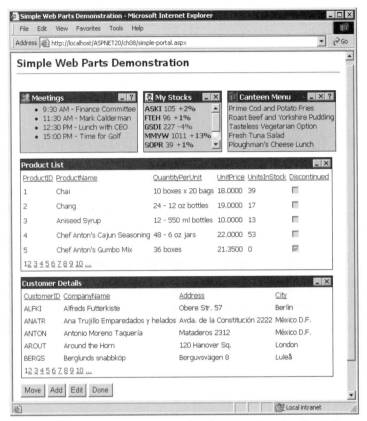

FIGURE 8.6. The example page, showing the view when first loaded

The Events Zone Declaration

Zones contain one or more Web Parts and also control the layout and appearance of these Web Parts. The Events zone at the top of the page contains three Web Part controls, arranged horizontally by setting the `Orientation` attribute. The zone attributes also define the text to display for the zone when in edit mode, the separation between individual Web Parts, whether an icon appears in the title bars, the type of links to use, and the relevant images for the Minimize, Help, Restore, Edit, and Close buttons (by default they appear as hyperlinks).

Zone attributes also define the appearance of the Web Part when it is being edited. You'll see the effects of this later. Within the main `WebPartZone` element are "style" elements that define individual features of the appearance of the contained Web Parts. In this example (see Listing 8.5) the declaration specifies a Windows-style appearance for the title bar of all contained Web Parts and a light green background.

LISTING 8.5. Declaring the Events WebPartZone

```
<asp:WebPartZone id="EventsZone" runat="server"
    Title="Today's Events"
    TitleStyle-Font-Bold="True"
    Orientation="Horizontal"
    WebPartPadding="5"
    ShowIconInPartTitle="True"
    VerbButtonType="Image"
    WebPartHelpVerb-ImageUrl="images/help.gif"
    WebPartMinimizeVerb-ImageUrl="images/minimize.gif"
    WebPartRestoreVerb-ImageUrl="images/restore.gif"
    WebPartCloseVerb-ImageUrl="images/close.gif"
    WebPartEditVerb-ImageUrl="images/edit.gif"
    EditWebPartStyle-BackColor="Red"
    EditWebPartStyle-ForeColor="White">
  <PartTitleStyle BackColor="Blue" ForeColor="White" Font-Bold="True" />
  <PartStyle BackColor="LightGreen" />
  . . .
```

The Individual Web Part Declarations

The rest of the content of the `WebPartZone` element shown in Listing 8.5 is a `ZoneTemplate` that contains the declarations of the Web Parts it will display by default (see Listing 8.6). Each Web Part is declared within a `ContentWebPart` control in this example, though you can mix any of the types of Web Parts listed earlier.

Notice that there are some specific attribute settings that vary the appearance and behavior of the Web Parts in this zone from each other. The first Web Part, Meetings, cannot be closed because it contains the `Allow Close="False"` attribute. It also specifies the image that will appear at the left of the title bar and the URL of the page that will be displayed when the user clicks the Help (question mark) button in the title bar for this Web Part. Simply setting this attribute causes the Help button or link to be displayed in the title bar. (You can see in Figure 8.6 that the My Stocks Web Part does not display this button.)

LISTING 8.6. Declaring the Events ZoneTemplate and Content

```
  . . .
  <ZoneTemplate>
    <asp:ContentWebPart id="pMeetings" runat="server"
        AllowClose="False" Title="Meetings"
        SmallIconImageUrl="images/titleicon3.gif"
        HelpUrl="meetings-help.htm">
      <ContentTemplate>
```

```
        <ul>
        <li>9:30 AM - Finance Committee</li>
        <li>11:30 AM - Mark Calderman</li>
        <li>12:30 PM - Lunch with CEO</li>
        <li>15:00 PM - Time for Golf</li>
        </ul>
      </ContentTemplate>
    </asp:ContentWebPart>
    <asp:ContentWebPart id="pStocks" runat="server"
        Title="My Stocks" Height="80"
        SmallIconImageUrl="images/titleicon2.gif"
        ScrollBars="Vertical">
      <ContentTemplate>
        <b>ASKI</b> 105 <font color="blue"><b>+2%</b></font><br />
        .... etc. ...
      </ContentTemplate>
    </asp:ContentWebPart>
    <asp:ContentWebPart id="pCanteen" runat="server"
        Title="Canteen Menu"
        SmallIconImageUrl="images/titleicon1.gif"
        HelpUrl="canteen-help.htm">
      <ContentTemplate>
        Prime Cod and Potato Fries<br />
        .... etc. ...
      </ContentTemplate>
    </asp:ContentWebPart>
  </ZoneTemplate>
</asp:WebPartZone>
```

The second `ContentWebPart` declaration specifies the My Stocks section and has the height fixed and a vertical scroll bar added. The same technique can be used to apply horizontal scrolling instead (or as well). This is useful to maintain a neat layout of the controls irrespective of the content of each one. Notice that while the first Web Part does not have a Close button, the second and third ones do because they do not contain the `Allow Close="False"` attribute.

Also notice that these three Web Parts have fixed declarative content, using ordinary HTML. However, they can contain any static or dynamic content that you might use when creating output in a Web page. For example, you could use a `Repeater` control and build the text lists dynamically at runtime through data binding—or perhaps even display tempting pictures of the canteen menu items!

The Help buttons shown for the Meetings and Canteen Menu Web Parts open a small browser window (modal in Internet Explorer 4 and higher) that displays custom help for that Web Part. The `HelpUrl` attribute in the declaration of the Web Part defines the URL that will open. In the example

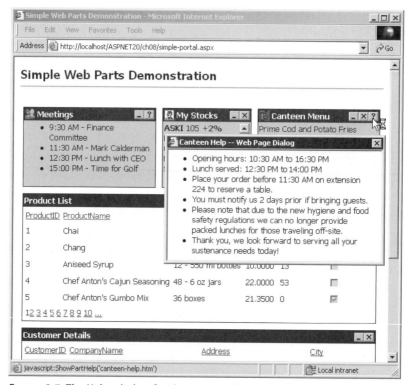

FIGURE 8.7. The Help window for the Canteen Menu Web Part

here, it is simply an HTML page that contains some details about the company canteen (see Figure 8.7).

The Corporate Information Zone Declaration

The second zone on the page contains the lists of products and customers. Notice that these are fully interactive—you can sort the rows by clicking the column headings and page through the rows using the links at the bottom of each list. In this zone there are no icons at the left of the title bars, and the orientation is set to `Vertical` this time, but otherwise the attributes in the `WebPartZone` element are similar to the previous zone (see Listing 8.7).

LISTING 8.7. Declaring the Corporate Information WebPartZone

```
<asp:WebPartZone id="CorpInfoZone" runat="server"
    Title="Corporate Information"
    TitleStyle-Font-Bold="True"
```

```
            Orientation="Vertical"
            WebPartPadding="5"
            VerbButtonType="Image"
            WebPartHelpVerb-ImageUrl="images/help.gif"
            WebPartMinimizeVerb-ImageUrl="images/minimize.gif"
            WebPartRestoreVerb-ImageUrl="images/restore.gif"
            WebPartCloseVerb-ImageUrl="images/close.gif"
            WebPartEditVerb-ImageUrl="images/edit.gif"
            EditWebPartStyle-BackColor="Red"
            EditWebPartStyle-ForeColor="White">
    <PartTitleStyle BackColor="Blue" ForeColor="White"
                    Font-Bold="True"/>
    <PartStyle BackColor="LightYellow" />
    <ZoneTemplate>
      <ahh:Products id="pProducts" runat="server"
          Title="Product List" />
      <ahh:Customers id="pCustomers" runat="server"
          Title="Customer Details" />
    </ZoneTemplate>
</asp:WebPartZone>
```

However, this time the `ZoneTemplate` contains instances of the two User Controls that are declared in `Register` directives at the top of the page. And, even though they don't expose public properties for the `Title`, this can be set as an attribute of the control instance element (the same applies for all of the Web Part–specific attributes).

The Products and Customers User Controls

The two User Controls for the lists of products and customers are extremely simple, despite the rich content they generate. They use a data source control and a `GridView` control (as demonstrated in Chapters 3 and 4). Notice that there is no `<form>` element in the control—one is already included in the main page. Listing 8.8 shows the entire code for the Product List User Control.

LISTING 8.8. Declaring the Product List User Control

```
<%@ Control Language="VB" debug="True" %>

<asp:SqlDataSource id="ds1" runat="server"
  ConnectionString="server=localhost;database=Northwind;uid=x;pwd=x;"
  SelectCommand="SELECT ProductID, ProductName, QuantityPerUnit,
              UnitPrice, UnitsInStock, Discontinued FROM Products" />

<asp:GridView id="grid1" runat="server" DataSourceID="ds1"
     Border="0" CellPadding="3" SummaryViewColumn="ProductName"
     AllowSorting="True" AllowPaging="True" PageSize="5" />
```

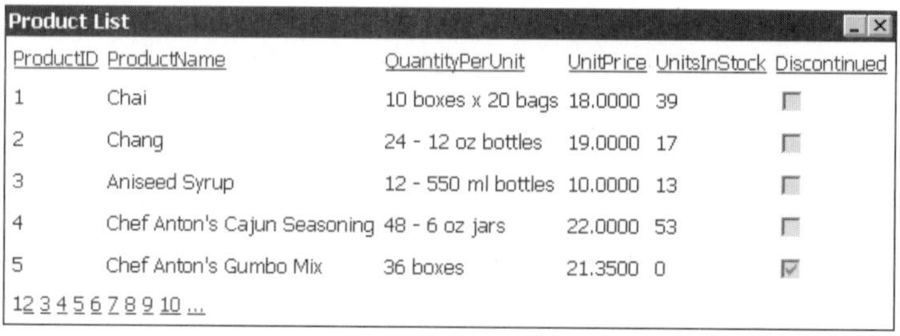

FIGURE 8.8. The output of the Product List User Control

The output of this simple declarative-only User Control (shown in Figure 8.8) provides the content that is exposed as a Web Part, and the list of customers is generated in exactly the same way but (of course) with a different SQL statement.

The EditorZone Declaration

Adding editing features to a page is extremely easy—the controls do all of the work for you pretty much automatically. However, bear in mind that there are effectively two ways that users can configure a page containing Web Parts. Simply switching the WebPartManager control into design mode causes the zone frames to be displayed, and users can drag controls from one place within a zone to another or drag them from one zone to another.

However, switching to edit mode causes the Edit button or link in the title bar of all the Web Parts to become visible as well, and when this is clicked that Web Part is displayed using the settings specified for the Edit WebPartStyle properties. However, this alone does not display the controls for editing the layout, behavior, or appearance of the selected Web Part. To display these controls, you must add an EditorZone to the page.

Listing 8.9 shows the declaration for the EditorZone, containing all three of the common editing controls. The attributes of the main Editor Zone element specify the appearance of the editing controls.

LISTING 8.9. Declaring the EditorZone Control

```
<asp:EditorZone id="EditorZone" runat="server"
    TitleStyle-Font-Bold="True"
    BackColor="LightBlue"
    Style="padding:5px;margin-top:7px">
  <PartTitleStyle BackColor="Blue" ForeColor="White"
               Font-Bold="True" />
```

```
<ZoneTemplate>
  <asp:AppearanceEditorPart id="AppearanceEditorPart1"
                            runat="server" />
  <asp:LayoutEditorPart id="LayoutEditorPart1" runat="server" />
  <asp:BehaviorEditorPart id="BehaviorEditorPart1" runat="server" />
</ZoneTemplate>
</asp:EditorZone>
```

In the screenshot in Figure 8.9 you can see the Edit button (we chose a pencil image) for the Product List Web Part, which is not itself in edit mode, while the Customer Details Web Part is being edited.

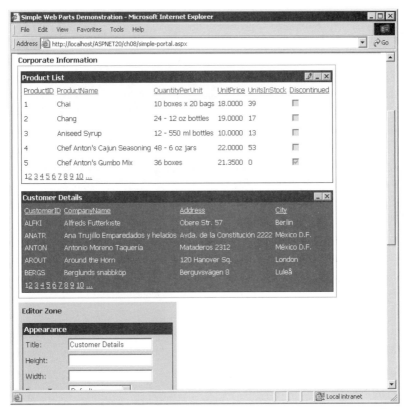

FIGURE 8.9. Edit mode, with highlighting that indicates the Web Part currently being edited

The Editor Controls

The three editing controls included in the declaration of the EditorZone can be seen in the next three screenshots. In the Appearance section (Figure 8.10), you can specify the text of the title bar of the Web Part and its size on the page. The Frame Type can be Default, Title and Border, Title Only, Border Only, or None. The Web Part can also be hidden within the page, and you can specify the layout direction (Left to Right, Right to Left, or Not Set).

For the Layout settings (Figure 8.11), you can specify the Frame State (Normal or Minimized), the zone that the Web Part will appear in, and the index (position) within that zone.

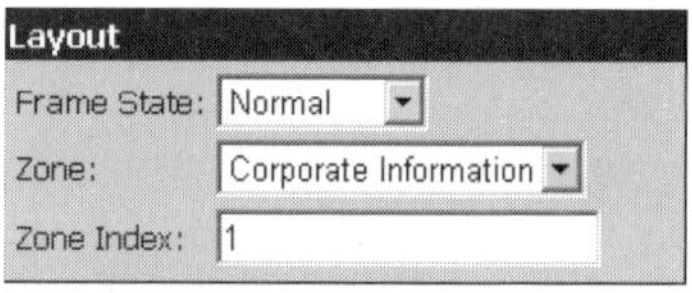

Finally, for the Behavior settings (Figure 8.12), you can specify whether the Web Part can be closed, minimized, or exported; the text for the alternate description of the Web Part; and URLs to open when a custom link in the title bar or the Edit or Help button is clicked. You can also specify a list of roles (as defined by the current personalization settings of the page and application) that can display the Web Part, as well as turn on or off personalization support for this Web Part.

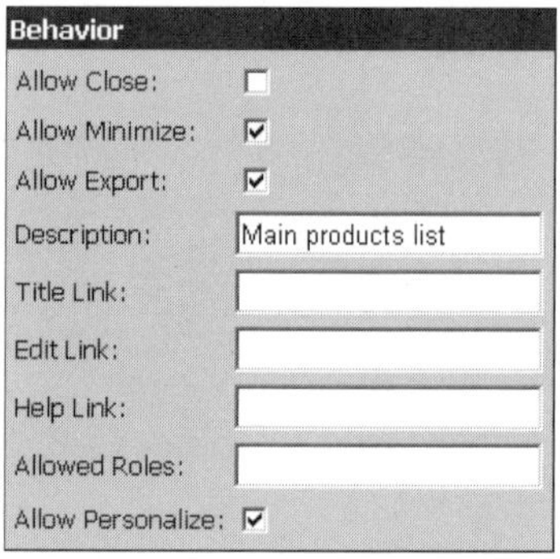

A Web Part developer can add custom properties to the Web Part and declare metadata defining other entries that will appear in the Behavior section.

The CatalogZone Declaration

The Catalog section of available Web Parts for the page is created using a `CatalogZone` control. By default this control is not displayed, but when the `WebPartManager` is switched into catalog mode the control displays its content. Listing 8.10 shows the `CatalogPart` control, with the attributes and the nested `PartTitleStyle` and `PartStyle` elements that specify its appearance within the page.

The `ZoneTemplate` contains the declarations of the two sections of the Catalog that will be shown. The `PageCatalogPart` displays any controls that are currently closed (but not hidden), while the `TemplateCatalog Part` defines two more controls that a user can add to the page.

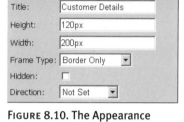

FIGURE 8.10. The Appearance section of the EditorZone control

FIGURE 8.11. The Layout section of the EditorZone control

FIGURE 8.12. The Behavior section of the EditorZone control

LISTING 8.10. Declaring the CatalogZone Control

```
<asp:CatalogZone id="CatalogZone" runat="server"
    BackColor="LightGray"
    BorderWidth="1"
    BorderColor="Black"
    TitleStyle-Font-Bold="True"
    Style="padding:5px;margin-top:7px">
  <PartTitleStyle BackColor="Blue" ForeColor="White"
                Font-Bold="True" />
  <PartStyle BackColor="White" />
  <ZoneTemplate>
    <asp:PageCatalogPart id="PagePart" runat="server" />
    <asp:TemplateCatalogPart id="CatalogPart" runat="server"
        Title="Catalog">
      <WebPartsTemplate>
        <asp:ContentWebPart id="pPhoneBook" runat="server"
            Title="Phone Book">
          <ContentTemplate>
            Cassandra Royce - 249<br />
            Joan Bone - 261<br />
            ... etc. ...
          </ContentTemplate>
        </asp:ContentWebPart>
        <asp:ContentWebPart id="pHelpDesk" runat="server"
            Title="Help Desk">
          <ContentTemplate>
            <asp:RadioButtonList id="bl1" runat="server">
              <asp:ListItem Text="Computer Fault" />
              <asp:ListItem Text="Software Fault" />
              ... etc. ...
            </asp:RadioButtonList>
            <asp:Button id="b1" runat="server" Text="Call" /><br />
          </ContentTemplate>
        </asp:ContentWebPart>
      </WebPartsTemplate>
    </asp:TemplateCatalogPart>
  </ZoneTemplate>
</asp:CatalogZone>
```

The screenshot in Figure 8.13 (repeated from earlier in the chapter for convenience) shows the two views of the Catalog section when the user has previously closed the My Stocks and Product List Web Parts but now wants to display the Product List again. The control automatically detects the closed controls, and the zones they can be placed in, by analyzing the page content.

The Controls Zone Declaration

The example page contains one more zone. This is a WebPartZone that contains the four buttons that switch the page and the WebPartManager

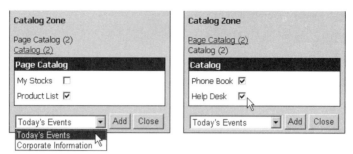

FIGURE 8.13. The two views of the CatalogZone control

from one mode to another. It seemed sensible to prevent users from moving, editing, or closing this zone, so it has attributes added that hide the edit link; prevent a frame from being displayed in normal, design, and edit modes; and prevent the layout from being changed (see Listing 8.11).

LISTING 8.11. Declaring the Controls Zone

```
<asp:WebPartZone id="ControlsZone" runat="server"
    Title=" "
    WebPartEditVerb-Visible="False"
    PartFrameType="None"
    AllowLayoutChange="False"
    BorderWidth="0"
    BorderStyle="None">
 ...
```

Displaying the Move, Add, Edit, and Done Buttons

The ZoneTemplate defines the content of this zone. In this case, it contains a single ContentWebPart that has attributes added to reinforce and complete the process of preventing the user from moving this Web Part to another zone or closing, minimizing, or hiding it.

Then, inside the ContentTemplate are declarations of four standard ASP.NET Button controls that initiate the switch from one mode to another. Each has its CommandName set to indicate the mode it should switch to. All have the OnClick attribute set to the same event handler named SwitchMode (see Listing 8.12).

LISTING 8.12. The ZoneTemplate for the Controls Zone

```
 ...
  <ZoneTemplate>
    <asp:ContentWebPart id="ControlsPart" runat="server"
```

```
            AllowZoneChange="False"
            AllowClose="False"
            AllowHide="False"
            AllowMinimize="False">
      <ContentTemplate>
        <asp:Button id="btnLayout" Text="Move" CommandName="Move"
                 OnClick="SwitchMode" runat="server" />
        <asp:Button id="btnAdd" Text="Add" CommandName="Catalog"
                 OnClick="SwitchMode" runat="server" />
        <asp:Button id="btnEdit" Text="Edit" CommandName="Edit"
                 OnClick="SwitchMode" runat="server" />
        <asp:Button id="btnCancel" Text="Done" CommandName="Done"
                 OnClick="SwitchMode" runat="server" />
      </ContentTemplate>    </asp:ContentWebPart>
   </ZoneTemplate>
</asp:WebPartZone>
```

You can see in the screenshot in Figure 8.14 (on the next page) that, even when the page is in edit mode, the section containing the buttons is

Putting the four "mode switching" buttons inside a `WebPartZone` actually has no real value, except that it allows us to illustrate how a zone can be declared with parts that cannot be moved, closed, edited, and so on. In general, however, you would probably put the buttons directly on the page. Remember that there will be special server controls to replace these standard buttons in forthcoming releases.

not available for editing and does not display the "drag" pointer that indicates it can be moved to another zone.

Changing the WebPartDisplayMode

The final section of the source for the example page is an event handler that runs when any of the four buttons in the Controls zone is clicked. Inside a server-side script section is the SwitchMode routine, which simply checks the value of the CommandName property of the control that raised the event and then calls the SetDisplayMode method of the WebPartManager with the appropriate value from the WebPartDisplayMode enumeration (see Listing 8.13).

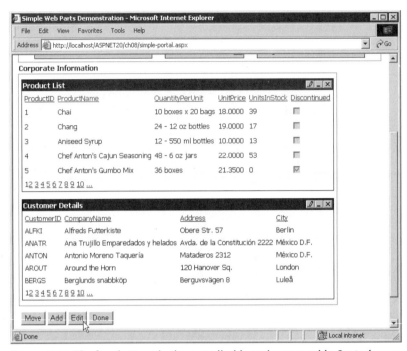

FIGURE 8.14. The four buttons in the noneditable and nonmovable Controls zone

LISTING 8.13. Switching the Display Mode of the WebPartManager

```
<script runat="server">

Sub SwitchMode(oSender As Object, oArgs As EventArgs)
  Select Case oSender.CommandName
    Case "Move"
      PartManager.SetDisplayMode(WebPartDisplayMode.Design)
    Case "Catalog"
      PartManager.SetDisplayMode(WebPartDisplayMode.Catalog)
    Case "Edit"
      PartManager.SetDisplayMode(WebPartDisplayMode.Edit)
    Case "Done"
      PartManager.SetDisplayMode(WebPartDisplayMode.Normal)
  End Select
End Sub

</script>
```

Of course, the controls used to create this page expose their interfaces to code running in the page. So, while this example used hardly any code (only the routine to switch modes), you can write code that interacts with the zone and Web Part controls and reacts to events in the page. We look briefly at this topic in the next section.

Working with Web Parts in Code

The controls used to generate portal pages are all ASP.NET server controls and become part of the control tree for the page when it is compiled and executed. So they can be accessed and manipulated using server-side code, and in some cases client-side code as well.

The three main classes described here are the `WebPartManager`, `Web PartZone`, and `WebPart`. Other classes are used to implement things like event handlers and the verbs that define the actions for each of the buttons on the title bar of a Web Part.

The WebPartManager Class

The `WebPartManager` is responsible for managing all the zones and Web Parts on the page. It exposes an interface that allows you to change the display mode, access and specify the behavior of zones and Web Parts, and react to events that occur within the page. The `WebPartManager` class is located in the `System.Web.UI.WebControls` namespace (as are the majority of classes used with Web Parts), and it is descended directly from `Control`.

The WebPartManager Constructor

There is a single constructor for the `WebPartManager`, which returns a new instance ready to add to the `Controls` collection of the `Page` (see Table 8.1).

The Properties of the WebPartManager Class

The `WebPartManager` class exposes all the interface members of the `Control` class. In addition, there are several properties that are specific to working with Web Parts. The ones you'll generally use are shown in Table 8.2 on the next page.

TABLE 8.1. The Constructor for the WebPartManager Class

Constructor	Description
WebPartManager()	Creates a new instance of the WebPartManager class with the default values for all its properties.

TABLE 8.2. The Properties of the WebPartManager Class

Property	Description
DisplayMode	Returns a value from the WebPartDisplayMode enumeration that indicates the display mode for the page. The display mode is set using the SetDisplayMode method.
Zones	Returns a reference to a WebPartZoneCollection that contains all the zones in the page.
WebParts	Returns a reference to a WebPartCollection that contains all the Web Parts for the page.
WebPartToEdit	Returns a reference to the WebPart instance that is currently being edited, or null if none are selected for editing.
EnablePersonalization	Sets or returns a Boolean value that indicates whether the properties of the zones and Web Parts can be set through the ASP.NET personalization system. The default is True.
PersonalizationType	Sets or returns a value from the ControlPersonalizationType enumeration that indicates the type of personalization to use. Valid values are AllPersonalizableProperties, Default, and None. See Chapter 7 for details of the ASP.NET 2.0 personalization features.
ConnectionPointManager	Returns a reference to a ConnectionPointManager instance for this page. This maintains details of all the connections between the Web Parts in the page.
Connections	Returns a reference to a ConnectionCollection instance that contains details of each connection between the Web Parts on the page.

The Methods of the WebPartManager Class

The WebPartManager class allows you to mirror the client-side user actions of adding, moving, and closing Web Parts by calling the methods directly. There are also methods to manage connection and one to change the display mode (see Table 8.3).

The Events of the WebPartManager Class

The WebPartManager class exposes six events that are specific to Web Parts and can be used to interact with the various actions taken by users, in

TABLE 8.3. The Methods of the WebPartManager Class

Method	Description
SetDisplayMode(mode)	Sets the display mode of the page using a value from the WebPartDisplayMode enumeration. Valid vales are Normal, Design, Catalog, and Edit. No return value.
GetWebPartsForZone(zone)	Takes a reference to a WebPartZone and returns a WebPartCollection that contains references to all of the Web Parts in the specified zone.
AddWebPart(part, zone, index)	Adds a Web Part to a zone given a reference to the WebPart to add, a reference to the WebPartZone to add it to, and an Integer that is the zero-based index of the position of the new Web Part within the target zone. No return value.
MoveWebPart(part, zone, index)	Moves a Web Part to another zone, or to another location within the same zone. Takes a reference to the WebPart to move, a reference to the WebPartZone to move it to, and an Integer that is the zero-based index of the new position of the Web Part within the target zone. No return value.
DeleteWebPart(part)	Removes the specified WebPart instance from the page. No return value.
BeginWebPartEditing(part)	Takes a reference to a WebPart instance, places it into Edit mode, and updates the WebPartToEdit property. No return value.
EndWebPartEditing()	Takes a reference to a WebPart instance, returns it from Edit mode to Normal mode, and sets the WebPartToEdit property to null. No return value.
CreateConnection(provider, consumer)	Creates a connection between the two specified ConnectionPoint instances. Returns a reference to the new Connection instance.
DeleteConnection(connection)	Deletes the specified Connection instance. No return value.

some cases allowing you to prevent actions they take from being carried out (see Table 8.4 on the next page).

TABLE 8.4. The Events of the WebPartManager Class

Event	Description
DisplayModeChanging	Raised immediately before the current mode of the page changes. Passes an instance of a WebPartDisplayModeCancelEventArgs to the event handler, which has the following properties: • Cancel: A Boolean value that can be set to True to prevent changes to the display mode. • NewDisplayMode: A value from the WebPartDisplayMode enumeration that indicates the new display mode and can be changed to specify a different display mode.
DisplayModeChanged	Raised after the current mode of the page has changed. Passes an instance of a WebPartDisplayModeEventArgs to the event handler, which has the following property: • OldDisplayMode: A value from the WebPartDisplayMode enumeration that indicates the previous display mode.
WebPartAdded	Raised after a Web Part has been added to the page. Passes an instance of a WebPartEventArgs to the event handler, which has the following property: • WebPart: A reference to the Web Part that was added.
WebPartDeleted	Raised after a Web Part is closed or removed from the page. Passes an instance of a WebPartEventArgs to the event handler, which has the following property: • WebPart: A reference to the Web Part that was closed or removed.
WebPartEditModeChanging	Raised immediately before an individual Web Part is placed into edit mode by clicking its Edit link or button. Passes an instance of a WebPartEditCancelEventArgs to the event handler, which has the following properties: • Cancel: A Boolean value that can be set to True to prevent the Web Part from entering edit mode. • WebPart: A reference to the Web Part that will change to edit mode.

TABLE 8.4. The Events of the WebPartManager Class (continued)

Event	Description
WebPartEditModeChanged	Raised after an individual Web Part returns from edit mode. Passes an instance of a WebPartEditEventArgs to the event handler, which has the following property: • WebPart: A reference to the Web Part that is in edit mode.

The WebPartZone Class

The WebPartZone class represents a zone within the page and is a member of the Zones collection of the current WebPartManager. It is descended from WebPartZoneBase, which in turn descends from Zone, which is itself descended from WebControl. So WebPartZone exposes all the members of these base classes as well as some that it adds itself. The tables in this subsection summarize all the interface members that are relevant to working with Web Parts.

The WebPartZone Constructor

There is a single constructor for the WebPartZone class, creating a new WebPartZone that can be added to the Zones collection of the WebPartManager (see Table 8.5).

The Behavior Properties of the WebPartZone Class

The WebPartZone has many properties, and to make it easier to see those that are relevant to this chapter, they are divided into three sections: behavior properties, appearance properties, and style properties. Table 8.6 on the next page summarizes the behavior properties.

TABLE 8.5. The Constructor for the WebPartZone Class

Constructor	Description
WebPartZone()	Creates a new instance of a WebPartZone with the default values for all its properties.

TABLE 8.6. The Behavior Properties of the WebPartZone Class

Property	Description
AllowLayoutChange	Sets or returns a `Boolean` value that indicates whether the Web Parts in this zone can be moved to another zone or to another position within this zone. The default is `True`.
DragMode	Sets or returns a value from the `DragMode` enumeration that indicates the appearance of the Web Parts in this zone when they are dragged to a new position in design or edit mode. Valid values are `Normal` (the default), `Image` (as defined by the `DragImageUrl` property), and `WebPartTitle` (just the title bar).
DragHighlightColor	Sets or returns a `Color` instance that specifies the color of the "target block" that will receive the Web Part. This "block" appears when a Web Part is dragged to another position, indicating the actual location it will take if dropped at that point.
DragImageUrl	Sets or returns a `String` that is the URL of an image to use when dragging a Web Part to a new position in design or edit mode. The `DragMode` property must be set to `DragMode.Image`.
Orientation	Sets or returns a value from the `Orientation` enumeration that indicates how the Web Parts in this zone will be laid out. Valid values are `Horizontal` and `Vertical`.
WebPartCloseVerb	Returns a reference to a `WebPartVerb` instance that describes the command verb that will be used to create the Close link or button for the Web Parts in this zone. Read-only. The `WebPartVerb` class is described in Table 8.7.
WebPartEditVerb	Returns a reference to a `WebPartVerb` instance that describes the command verb that will be used to create the Edit link or button for the Web Parts in this zone. Read-only.
WebPartHelpVerb	Returns a reference to a `WebPartVerb` instance that describes the command verb that will be used to create the Help link or button for the Web Parts in this zone. Read-only.
WebPartMinimizeVerb	Returns a reference to a `WebPartVerb` instance that describes the command verb that will be used to create the Minimize link or button for the Web Parts in this zone. Read-only.

TABLE 8.6. The Behavior Properties of the WebPartZone Class (continued)

Property	Description
WebPartRestoreVerb	Returns a reference to a `WebPartVerb` instance that describes the command verb that will be used to create the Restore link or button for the Web Parts in this zone. Read-only.
VerbButtonType	Sets or returns a value from the `ButtonType` enumeration that indicates how the command verbs for the Web Parts in this zone will appear in their title bars. Valid values are `Link` (the default), `Button`, and `Image`.
ZoneTemplate	Sets or returns a reference to an `ITemplate` class that represents the `ZoneTemplate` section of the declaration of this zone.
Enabled	Sets or returns a `Boolean` value that indicates whether all of the Web Parts within this zone are enabled. The default is `True`.

The WebPartVerb Class. The `WebPart`*xxx*`Verb` properties shown in Table 8.6 contain a reference to a `WebPartVerb` class, which defines the appearance and behavior of the command links or buttons in the title bar of each Web Part. Table 8.7 shows the properties of the `WebPartVerb` class.

TABLE 8.7. The Properties of the WebPartVerb Class

Property	Description
Text	Sets or returns a `String` value that is the name of the command verb, such as Edit.
Description	Sets or returns a `String` that is displayed as a tooltip or long description of the command, such as **Closes the Web Part.**
ImageUrl	Sets or returns a `String` that is the URL of the image to display for this command in the title bar of the Web Part when command links are shown as images.
Visible	Sets or returns a `Boolean` value that indicates whether this command link is displayed.
Enabled	Sets or returns a `Boolean` value that indicates whether the command is available.

continues

TABLE 8.7. The Properties of the WebPartVerb Class (continued)

Property	Description
Checked	Sets or returns a `Boolean` value that indicates whether a "tick" should appear in a menu containing this verb.
ServerClickHandler	Returns a reference to the `WebPartEventHandler` that will be executed when the command is carried out. Read-only.
ClientClickHandler	Returns a `String` value that is the name of the client-side function, or the client-side script code, that runs when the user executes the command. Read-only.

The Appearance Properties of the WebPartZone Class

Many of the properties of a `WebPartZone` are the same as those you use with any other ASP.NET server control. For example, you can set and retrieve the values for the `BackColor`, `ForeColor`, `BorderColor`, `BorderWidth`, and `BorderStyle`; specify the URL of an image for the background of the zone as the `BackImageUrl` property; and specify CSS styles directly in the `CssClass` property. Table 8.8 summarizes other properties that specify the appearance of Web Parts and are more directly applicable to this technology.

TABLE 8.8. The Appearance Properties of the WebPartZone Class

Property	Description
Title	Sets or returns a `String` that is the text to display at the top of the zone when the page is in catalog, design, or edit mode.
EmptyZoneText	A `String` that is the text to display within the zone when it contains no Web Parts.
ShowIconInPartTitle	Sets or returns a `Boolean` value that indicates whether the image specified in the `SmallIconImageUrl` property of the Web Parts in this zone will be displayed at the left end of the title bars.
TitleHorizontalAlign	Sets or returns a value from the `HorizontalAlign` enumeration that indicates the alignment of the text within the zone when the page is in catalog, design, or edit mode. Valid values are `Left`, `Right`, `Center`, `Justify`, and `NotSet`.

TABLE 8.8. The Appearance Properties of the WebPartZone Class (continued)

Property	Description
Font	A reference to a `FontInfo` class that specifies the font type and style for the text displayed by the `Title` property.
Width	Sets or returns the width of the zone as a `Unit` value.
Height	Sets or returns the height of the zone as a `Unit` value.
WebPartPadding	Sets or returns an `Integer` that is the number of pixels of space between Web Parts within this zone.
EnablePersonalization	Sets or returns a `Boolean` value that indicates whether the properties of the Web Parts in this zone can be set through the ASP.NET personalization system. The default is `True`.
PersonalizationType	Sets or returns a value from the `ControlPersonalizationType` enumeration that indicates the type of personalization to use. Valid values are `AllPersonalizableProperties`, `Default`, and `None`. See Chapter 7 for details of the ASP.NET 2.0 personalization features.
ToolTip	Sets or returns a `String` that is displayed as a pop-up tooltip for the zone.
Visible	Sets or returns a `Boolean` value that indicates whether the zone and its content will be visible. The default is `True`. When `False`, the zone and its constituent controls still appear in the control tree of the page.
PartFrameType	Sets or returns a value from the `PartFrameType` enumeration that specifies the type of frame to display around the constituent Web Parts of this zone, unless they override the value individually. Valid values are `TitleAndBorder`, `TitleOnly`, `BorderOnly`, `None`, and `Default`.
PartTitleFormatString	Sets or returns a `String` that indicates how the `Title` and `Caption` property values of each Web Part are combined in the title bar. The default is `{0}-{1}`, indicating that they are separated by a hyphen.

continues

TABLE 8.8. The Appearance Properties of the WebPartZone Class (continued)

Property	Description
PartTitleHorizontalAlign	Sets or returns a value from the HorizontalAlign enumeration that indicates how the title text of the constituent Web Parts is aligned. Valid values are Left, Right, Center, Justify, and NotSet.

The Style Properties of the WebPartZone Class

The final set of properties for the WebPartZone class that affect the Web Parts in a zone are those that use a standard ASP.NET Style class to specify the appearance of specific sections of each Web Part. The applicable properties are shown in Table 8.9.

TABLE 8.9. The Style Properties of the WebPartZone Class

Property	Description
TitleStyle	A reference to a Style instance that specifies the style and appearance of the text that appears at the top of the zone when the page is in catalog, design, or edit mode.
PartStyle	A reference to a Style instance that specifies the style and appearance of all the Web Parts in this zone unless overridden at Web Part level.
PartContentStyle	A reference to a Style instance that specifies the style and appearance of the content within all the Web Parts in this zone unless overridden at Web Part level.
PartTitleStyle	A reference to a Style instance that specifies the style and appearance of the title bar for all the Web Parts in this zone unless overridden at Web Part level.
PartVerbStyle	A reference to a Style instance that specifies the style and appearance of the links in the title bar for all the Web Parts in this zone unless overridden at Web Part level.
FooterStyle	A reference to a Style instance that specifies the style and appearance of any footer sections in the Web Parts in this zone unless overridden at Web Part level.
EditWebPartStyle	A reference to a Style instance that specifies the style and appearance of the Web Part in this zone that is currently being edited unless overridden at Web Part level.

TABLE 8.9. The Style Properties of the WebPartZone Class (continued)

Property	Description
EmptyZoneTextStyle	A reference to a Style instance that specifies the style and appearance of the text that appears within the zone when it contains no Web Parts.

The Events of the WebPartZone Class

The WebPartZone class exposes a single event that is directly relevant to Web Parts (see Table 8.10).

TABLE 8.10. The Event of the WebPartZone Class

Event	Description
CreateVerbs	Raised when the zone creates the links for the title bars of each Web Part. Passes an instance of a WebPartVerbsEventArgs to the event handler, which exposes a WebPartVerbCollection instance that contains all the verbs for the Web Part.

The WebPart Class

The WebPart class represents an individual Web Part on the page and is a member of the WebParts collection of the WebPartZone that contains this Web Part. The WebPart class is descended from Part, which itself descends from Panel (all of these reside in the System.Web.UI.WebControls namespace).

Many of the properties of the WebPart class are inherited from Panel, as this is effectively how a Web Part is represented in the markup that is generated and sent to the client. However, a number of properties are specific to Web Parts, and for clarity these have again been divided into sections: behavior properties and appearance properties.

The Behavior Properties of the WebPart Class

The WebPart class exposes several properties that specify what actions a user can take with this Web Part, plus a set of properties that define the content of various sections of the Web Part (in particular the items that will appear in the title bar). There are also properties that indicate the location of the Web Part within the page and allow it to be moved (see Table 8.11).

TABLE 8.11. The Behavior Properties of the WebPart Class

Property	Description
AllowMinimize	Sets or returns a `Boolean` value that indicates whether the Web Part can be minimized or "rolled up" so that only the title bar is displayed. The default is `True`.
AllowClose	Sets or returns a `Boolean` value that indicates whether the Web Part can be closed (i.e., removed from a zone). The default is `True`.
AllowHide	Sets or returns a `Boolean` value that indicates whether the Web Part can be hidden using the controls in an `EditZone`, so that it still remains in the zone but is not visible. The default is `True`.
AllowZoneChange	Sets or returns a `Boolean` value that indicates whether the Web Part can be moved to another zone when the page is in design or edit mode. The default is `True`.
AllowPersonalize	Sets or returns a `Boolean` value that indicates whether the properties of the Web Part can be set through the ASP.NET personalization system. The default is `True`.
AllowExport	Sets or returns a `Boolean` value that indicates whether the properties of the Web Part can be exported. The default is `True`.
AllowPaginate	Sets or returns a `Boolean` value that indicates whether the content of the Web Part can be paginated using a `Pager` control. See Chapter 10 for details of the paging mechanism in ASP.NET 2.0.
ConnectionPoints	Returns a reference to a `ConnectionPointCollection` that contains the connection points for this Web Part. Each `ConnectionPoint` instance in the collection defines how the Web Part connects to another Web Part and whether it is a provider or consumer. Read-only.
TitleUrl	Sets or returns a `String` that is the URL of a page containing more information about the Web Part. When set, a link appears in the title bar of the Web Part.
HelpMode	Sets or returns a value from the `WebPartHelpMode` enumeration that indicates how the Help window will be displayed. Valid values are `Modal` (the default—help content is displayed in a modal window if the client supports this feature or in a separate pop-up window if not), `Modeless` (help content is displayed in a separate pop-up window), and `Navigate` (the current browser instance navigates directly to the help page).

TABLE 8.11. The Behavior Properties of the WebPart Class (continued)

Property	Description
HelpUrl	Sets or returns a `String` that is the URL of the help page to display for this Web Part when the Help icon or link on the title bar is clicked.
EditUrl	Sets or returns a `String` that is the URL of a page that can be used to edit any custom properties of this Web Part. Allows control-specific editing actions to be defined instead of using the default editing process provided by an `EditZone`.
IsShared	Returns a `Boolean` value that indicates whether this Web Part is shared between multiple users or is available only to the current user.
Roles	Sets or returns a `String` array that is the list of roles to which the Web Part is available. The roles are defined by the ASP.NET personalization configuration. When not specified (`null`), any user can load the Web Part. A comma-delimited list of roles can be specified for the `Roles` attribute when declaring a Web Part.
Verbs	Returns a reference to a `WebPartVerbCollection` that contains the verbs or commands that the user can execute for this Web Part, such as Minimize, Edit, Close, and Help.
Zone	Returns a reference to the zone containing this Web Part as a `WebPartZone` instance. Read-only.
ZoneID	Sets or returns a `String` that is the `ID` of the zone containing this Web Part. Setting this property moves the Web Part to the specified zone.
ZoneIndex	Sets or returns an `Integer` value that is the zero-based index of the Web Part within the current zone. Setting this property moves the Web Part to the specified position within the zone.

The Appearance Properties of the WebPart Class

The `WebPart` class exposes many of the same appearance properties as the `WebPartZone` class, for example, `Style`, `CssClass`, `BorderWidth`, `BackColor`, `TitleStyle`, `Height`, `Width`, `Enabled`, `EnablePersonalization`, and so on. There are also several other appearance properties relevant only to Web Parts (see Table 8.12).

TABLE 8.12. The Appearance Properties of the WebPart Class

Property	Description
Title	Sets or returns a `String` value that is the text to display in a catalog, as a tooltip, and in the title bar of the Web Part.
Caption	Sets or returns a `String` that is added to the end of the title bar text. Intended to be a dynamic value that is used to display instance-specific details for Web Parts that are used more than once on a page, for example, a document name.
SmallIconImageUrl	Sets or returns a `String` that is the URL of the image to display at the left end of the title bar for the Web Part.
LargeIconImageUrl	Sets or returns a `String` that is the URL of the image to display when representing the Web Part, for example, in a gallery of available Web Parts.
FrameType	Sets or returns a value from the `PartFrameType` enumeration that specifies the type of frame to display around the Web Part. Valid values are `TitleAndBorder`, `TitleOnly`, `BorderOnly`, `None`, and `Default`.
FrameState	Sets or returns a value from the `PartFrameState` enumeration that specifies the way the Web Part will be displayed. Valid values are `Normal` (the default) and `Minimized`.
Direction	Sets or returns a value from the `ContentDirection` enumeration that specifies the text layout direction for the Web Part content. Valid values are `LeftToRight` (the default), `RightToLeft`, and `NotSet`.
ScrollBars	Sets or returns a value from the `ScrollBars` enumeration that indicates whether the Web Part will display scroll bars when the size of the content exceeds the available space (the `Height` and/or `Width` properties must be set to force this to occur). Valid values are `Auto` (the default), `Both`, `Horizontal`, `Vertical`, and `None`.
Wrap	Sets or returns a `Boolean` value that indicates whether the text and markup content of the Web Part will wrap when the line length exceeds the width of the Web Part. The default is `True`.
Hidden	Sets or returns a `Boolean` value that indicates whether the user has hidden the Web Part using the options in the `EditZone`. When hidden it remains within the current zone but is not displayed. The default is `False`.

TABLE 8.12. The Appearance Properties of the WebPart Class (continued)

Property	Description
Visible	Sets or returns a `Boolean` value that indicates whether the Web Part is displayed. It remains as part of the control tree when not displayed. The default is `True`.
MissingAssembly	Sets or returns a `String` that is the text to display in the Web Part content area if the user attempts to add a Web Part that is implemented as an assembly and that assembly cannot be found.

Web Parts and Visual Studio

While the overall structure of a portal framework page is not that difficult to grasp, the multiple nested layers of style elements and zone templates, and the Web Parts themselves declared within content templates, do make it quite taxing to create pages from scratch. However, as you'd expect, the new version of Visual Studio makes it all much easier.

Figure 8.15 on the next page shows some of the example page you saw earlier loaded into an early version of Visual Studio. You can see that the `WebPartManager` allows you to switch the page mode on demand so that you see how the page will look in each mode. It also contains all the relevant controls in the Toolbox on the left, allowing you to drag them onto a page as required and simply set the properties in the lower right-hand section of the window.

SUMMARY

Building portal-style pages that contain multiple items of information and yet are neat, attractive, and—more important—customizable has been a complex task in the past. In ASP.NET 2.0, the new portal framework, which integrates Web Parts of different types into a single development model, makes it extremely easy to build these kinds of pages.

As we demonstrated in this chapter, by simply declaring a mix of several different types of `Zone` server controls plus a single `WebPartManager` instance on the page, you can create complex interactive layouts that require almost no server-side code. This includes enabling features for changing the layout of the page sections using drag and drop; changing

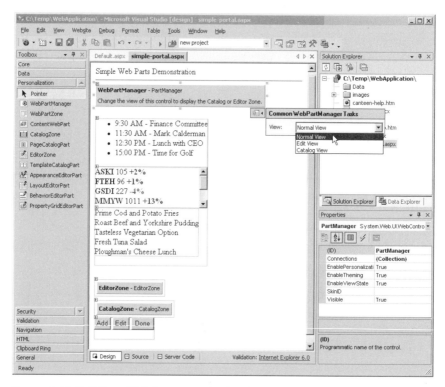

FIGURE 8.15. Building a Web Parts page in Visual Studio

the behavior and appearance of individual Web Parts; rolling up, closing, and/or hiding individual controls; and even being able to add new Web Parts to the page.

Then, if you want to expand the capabilities of the page, you can write code that reacts to events in the page and interacts with the various controls that implement the zones and Web Parts. While we didn't cover this topic in any detail, you can find lists of properties and methods in the SDK provided with ASP.NET or on-line.

Other features that we have not covered here in depth, mainly due to lack of space, include the following:

- The ability to connect Web Parts together so that changes in one are reflected in another. For example, selecting an order row in one Web Part could automatically update the connected Web Part so that it displays details of that order.

- The ability to export and import Web Parts (as XML documents), allowing them to be moved from one page to another and one application to another.
- The ability to expose custom properties from a Web Part, which can then be configured in a `PropertyGridEditorPart` control declared within the `EditorZone`.

In the next chapter, we'll move on to look at how ASP.NET has evolved in version 2.0 to allow you to more easily accomplish some of the tasks that users found difficult in version 1.x. This includes things like cross-page posting and group validation.

9

Pages, Posting, and Validation

ONE OF THE GREATEST IMPROVEMENTS of ASP.NET over ASP is the postback architecture, allowing client-side events to be linked to server code. Not only does it provide a richer programming model, but it also leads to more structured (and therefore more maintainable) code. This architecture is used whenever a control posts back to a page, and there are times when this needs controlling to a fine degree.

In this chapter we are going to look at several topics revolving around ASP.NET pages and the page architecture, in particular:

- How cross-page posting has been improved and simplified
- How validation has been improved by way of groups, allowing only controls within selected groups to participate in validation
- How to use the `Wizard` control to provide multistep pages
- How to map pages to other pages with URL mapping
- What improvements have been made to client-side scripting support
- What new attributes for pages have been added
- How new events fit within the existing life cycle of control and page creation

Cross-Page Posting

The postback architecture of ASP.NET is undoubtedly good, but it can be confusing to many traditional ASP programmers. The problem people have is not with automatically posting back to the same page but with not being able to specify another page to post to. There are reasons both for (security) and against (big pages) posting to another page and many people used Server.Transfer to move between pages. Content from the posting form was accessible only by ensuring the posting page was strongly typed or by storing it before posting (such as in the Items collection of the page). The biggest problem with Server.Transfer is that the original URL still shows in the browser.

ASP.NET 2.0 has made cross-page posting easier by allowing button controls to indicate the form they are posting to. This actually sets the action attribute on the form, but specifying this attribute manually will not work because it continues to be ignored. Security issues regarding the ViewState are not relevant; the post will instruct the receiving page to ignore it. The previous page can be accessed with the new page property PreviousPage.

Posting to Another Page

Let's consider two pages—Page1 (Page1.aspx) needs to post to Page2 (Page2.aspx). Page1 could look like the code shown in Listing 9.1.

LISTING 9.1. Posting to Another Page

```
<form runat="server">

  This is the first page
  <p />
  Please select a country:
  <asp:DropDownList id="Country" runat="server">
    <asp:ListItem text="USA" value="0" />
    <asp:ListItem text="Canada" value="1" />
    <asp:ListItem text="UK" value="2" />
  </asp:DropDownList>


  <p />
  <asp:Button id="Button1"
    Text="This button just posts back to itself"
    onClick="btn_click" runat="server" />
  <br />
  <asp:Button id="Button2"
    Text="This button posts to another page"
    PostTargetUrl="Page2.aspx" runat="server" />

</form>
```

The important section is that containing `Button2`, where you see the `PostTargetUrl` attribute, which is set to the page being posted to. When the button is clicked, instead of posting back to the same page, the postback is redirected to the requested page, which can then access controls from Page1. However, controls on a page are protected, so they either have to be exposed on the previous page as a `Public Property` or accessed via `FindControl`. For example, we could add the following to Page1 to expose the list of countries:

```
Public ReadOnly Property SelectedCountry() As DropDownList
  Get
    Return Country
  End Get
End Property
```

The exposed control doesn't have to be `ReadOnly`, but it works well for this example.

Accessing the Previous Page

Once the postback has been completed, you are now in the second page, and with the addition of the `PreviousPage` property, `Page2.aspx` now has the capability to access content from `Page1.aspx`. However, by default, `PreviousPage` is not strongly typed and will therefore be of type `Page`. To strongly type the page, use the `PreviousPage` directive:

```
<%@ PreviousPage VirtualPath="page_name.aspx" %>
```

or

```
<%@ PreviousPage TypeName="type" %>
```

Only one of the attributes can be used at a time.

Now the exposed controls can be accessed easily. For example, consider Page2 (see Listing 9.2).

LISTING 9.2. Using a Strongly Typed Page

```
<%@ Page Language="VB" %>
<%@ PreviousPage VirtualPath="Page1.aspx" %>

<script runat="server">

  Public Sub Page_Load()

    PrevMessage.Text = "On the previous page you selected: " & _
```

continues

```
        PreviousPage.SelectedCountry.SelectedItem.Text

    End Sub

</script>

<form runat="server">

  This is the second page
  <p />

  <asp:Label id="PrevMessage" runat="server" />

</form>
```

Here you can see that the `PreviousPage` directive indicates that `Page1.aspx` is the previous page—this ensures that the `PreviousPage` property will be strongly typed. From `Page1.aspx` the `DropDownList` is exposed via the `SelectedCountry` property.

You can have only one `PreviousPage` directive on a page, although this doesn't prevent multiple pages from cross-posting to a single page. However, setting the `PreviousPage` directive will mean that all pages will be strongly typed as the same type. Under these circumstances it's best to not use the `PreviousPage` directive and instead access late-bound controls.

Transferring to Another Page in Code

Transferring execution to another page can also be achieved with `Server .Transfer`, and with ASP.NET 2.0 this has another overloaded method:

`Server.Transfer(IHttpHandler, preserveForm)`

The parameters are:

- *IHttpHandler* indicates an object that implements the `IHttpHandler` interface (such as the `Page` object) and thus the `PreviousPage` property.
- *preserveForm* is a `Boolean` value indicating whether or not the form contents (i.e., `ViewState`) should be preserved across the transfer.

Detecting Cross-Page Posting

The question that naturally arises out of the preceding code is what happens if Page2 is accessed directly, without having been posted to from `Page1.aspx`, or perhaps if it posts back to itself. As well as the `PreviousPage` property, there is an `IsCrossPagePostBack` property, which indicates whether or not a page is participating in a cross-page postback. This property is `True` only for Page1 during its second instantiation, when accessed via the `PreviousPage` property of Page2. The following lists show what properties are set under what circumstances.

Page1 Posting Back to Itself

`Page1.IsPostBack`	`True`
`Page1.PreviousPage`	`null` (`Nothing` in Visual Basic .NET)
`Page1.IsCrossPagePostBack`	`False`

Page1 Cross-Posting to Page2

`Page2.PreviousPage`	Reference to Page1
`Page1.IsCrossPagePostBack`	`True`
`Page1.IsPostBack`	`True`
`Page2.IsPostBack`	`False`
`Page2.IsCrossPagePostBack`	`False`

Page1 Transfers to Page2 with `Server.Transfer`

`Page2.PreviousPage`	Reference to Page1
`Page1.IsCrossPagePostBack`	`False`
`Page1.IsPostBack`	`False`
`Page2.IsPostBack`	`False`
`Page2.IsCrossPagePostBack`	`False`

Here you can see that the existing ASP.NET 1.0 behavior isn't changed. When a page posts back to itself, the `IsPostBack` property is `True`, and the new properties are `False`. When posting to another page, however, the new properties are set. The use of these properties allows you to detect at what stage in a postback you are.

The Page Life Cycle

It is important to understand the life cycle of the pages when posting across pages. The following list indicates what happens when Page1 posts to Page2, and in what order:

1. Page1 cross-posts to Page2 via a button with its `PostTargetUrl` property set.
2. `ViewState` from Page1 is stored by Page2 but ignored.
3. The `PreviousPage` property is accessed in Page2.

4. Page1 is instantiated and the stored ViewState from Page1 is applied.

5. Page1 executes up to the OnLoadComplete event. For more details on which events will be fired, see Table 9.9 later in the chapter.

Understanding this life cycle ensures that you realize the implications of using cross-page posting. For example, posting from a page with a large amount of ViewState means the ViewState is stored and then reposted when the PreviousPage is accessed.

Validation

One issue that was identified with the ASP.NET validation controls in version 1.x was that they all belonged to the same "group" within a page. For example, take a page that contains a login and password text box for existing users, plus a set of controls where new users can register their details instead. In Internet Explorer, the page cannot be submitted because the client-side validation checks will fail on the controls that have no values. In other browsers the page can be submitted, but the Page.IsValid property will return False.

One way around this is to arrange to disable the validators on the sets of controls for which users are not entering values, but this depends on knowing which sets of controls they will use. The other alternative is to disable all the validators, then enable the appropriate ones and call their Validate method in code when the page is submitted.

The ValidationGroup Property

In ASP.NET 2.0, the problem goes away courtesy of the new Validation Group property exposed by the BaseValidator control from which all the validation controls inherit. You assign the same String value to this property for all the validators that are in the same group, and different values for different groups. This is particularly useful for those scenarios where multiple forms are required or on pages that use the Wizard and MultiView controls.

The three controls you can use to submit a form (the Button, Link Button, and ImageButton controls) also expose the ValidationGroup property, and you set this to the same value as the validators in the group that the button corresponds to. For example, in Figure 9.1, the page contains a Login and a Register section.

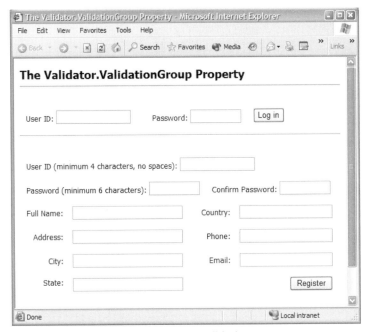

FIGURE 9.1. An ASP.NET page with two validation groups

All the validation controls in the Login section at the top carry the attribute `ValidationGroup="LoginGroup"`, as does the `Button` control labeled Log in. All the validation controls in the lower Register section carry the attribute `ValidationGroup="RegisterGroup"`, as does the `Button` control labeled Register.

When the page is submitted, an event handler defined in the `OnClick` attribute of the `Button` controls is executed. For example, the Log in button has the `OnClick="DoLogin"` attribute so the event handler named `DoLogin` runs. In it we check whether the user's values are valid by examining the `IsValid` property of the current `Page`:

```
If Page.IsValid Then
    ... code to run when valid values have been provided ...
Else
    ... code to run when the values provided are not valid ...
End If
```

In ASP.NET 2.0, the `IsValid` property now automatically takes into account the value of the `ValidationGroup` property, using the value set for this property on the button that caused the postback. So, if the user clicks the Log in button, which carries the attribute `ValidationGroup="LoginGroup"`,

TABLE 9.1. Page Validation Methods

Method	Description
Page.GetValidators("*group_name*")	Returns a collection of validation controls that have the specified value for their ValidationGroup property.
Page.Validate("*group_name*")	Performs validation for only the validation controls that have the specified value for their ValidationGroup property. Returns True if all these contain valid values, or returns False otherwise.

only the validation controls with the same value for their ValidationGroup property are checked. Validators and buttons with no ValidationGroup property set are regarded as being in the default group, so ASP.NET 1.x pages will continue to work as before under ASP.NET 2.0.

To go with the new ValidationGroup property are a couple of new or changed methods for the Page class (see Table 9.1). These allow you to interact with the validation controls in code at runtime.

The SetFocusOnError Property

Another new feature of the validation controls is the ability to make the page more user-friendly by automatically setting the input focus to the first control that contains an invalid value. All the validation controls now expose the SetFocusOnError property, which you can set to True (in code or by adding an attribute when you declare the control) to turn on this feature. The default if not specified is False.

Wizards

Modern applications increasingly use "wizards" to help users configure systems, provide information, or achieve some complex task that requires a number of selections to be made. Developers have found ways to build wizards in their Web applications, but ASP.NET 2.0 makes it easier than ever by providing a new Wizard control.

The aims of the Wizard control are listed below.

- Make it easy for developers to build wizards, and have the control automatically look after all the requirements other than the actual UI of each step. In other words, the Wizard control looks after things like maintaining values between postbacks, handling navigation, and so on.

- Provide both linear (step 1, step 2, step 3, and the reverse) and nonlinear (from any step to any step) navigation. This allows a user to change his or her mind about the values in one step without having to go back through every step. It also allows navigation paths to be changed at runtime in response to selections made by the user.
- Provide opportunities to build the UI using styles, templates, and themes. Some parts of the UI that are auto-generated (such as the Previous, Next, and Finish buttons) can instead be overridden using templates in the same way as is possible in controls like the DataGrid.
- Provide support for User Controls, allowing reuse of certain UI and code sections throughout an application.
- Ensure that you don't have to create a page per step and create complex code to pass data or controls between those pages.

The Wizard control uses postbacks to the same page and does not support cross-page posting. The advantage is that all the controls, whether visible in the current step or not, are still part of the control tree of the page, have their values maintained through the ViewState, and are available to code in the page.

From all this you will gather that the Wizard control is quite complex and exposes a great many properties and methods, plus some useful events. In this book we only have room for a description of the more useful basic properties; however, this will be enough for you to get started using the control. You can get a good idea of what the Wizard control provides by simply dragging one onto a page in Visual Studio .NET "Whidbey" (see Figure 9.2).

FIGURE 9.2. The Wizard control design view

The Basic Structure of a Wizard

The following code shows the declaration of a very basic wizard. The Wizard control shown takes an attribute, sideBarEnabled, that determines whether or not the navigation links between steps are shown at the side of the page. Within the Wizard control element declaration is a WizardSteps element, and this in turn contains one or more WizardStep elements. Each Wizard

Step element defines one step, or one "screen" that will appear in the Wizard (see Listing 9.3).

LISTING 9.3. Using the Wizard Control

```
<asp:Wizard id="Wizard1" runat="server"
    sideBarEnabled="True" >
  <WizardSteps>
    <asp:WizardStep id="WizardStep1" Title="Step 1">
      Step 1 Content
    </asp:WizardStep>
    <asp:WizardStep id="WizardStep2" Title="Step 2">
      Step 2 Content
    </asp:WizardStep>
  </WizardSteps>
</asp:Wizard>
```

Notice that there are no navigation instructions and no declarations of buttons or links. However, this code produces a fully functional (if not very useful) wizard, as shown in Figure 9.3.

Each step is shown as a link in the left-hand side, and the appropriate Next, Previous, and Finish buttons appear in the right-hand side for each step.

Specifying the Wizard Step Types

Each step (i.e., each WizardStep control) is automatically assigned a value from the WizardStepType enumeration for its StepType property. By default

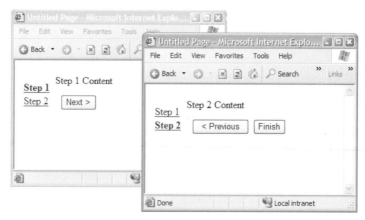

FIGURE 9.3. The Wizard control in action

the value is `Auto`, and the order of the steps is determined by the order they are declared within the `Wizard` control.

However, you can assign specific values to the `StepType` property to change the default behavior. The first step should be `StepType="Start"` (which has only a Next button) and the last should be `StepType="Finish"` (which has Previous and Finish buttons). The intervening steps should be `StepType="Step"` (which has Previous and Next buttons). One exception is if you want a final "confirmation" page that contains no navigation features to appear as the last step. In this case, assign one of the steps the value `StepType="Complete"`, as shown below:

```
<asp:WizardStep id="Done" StepType="Complete">
  Congratulations! The process is complete and your
  new software will now work faultlessly forever.
</asp:WizardStep>
```

Using Styles and Templates in a Wizard

While the basic `Wizard` control output is extremely plain and functional, it's possible to improve the appearance using styles or themes, or you can even replace the UI by defining templates. The three style properties of the `Wizard` control are `NavigationButtonStyle`, `SideBarButtonStyle`, and `TitleStyle`. Meanwhile, the templates you can define are listed below.

- `HeaderTemplate` specifies the UI content, controls, and styles for the section at the top of each step, which is the same for every step.

- `SideBarTemplate` specifies the UI content, controls, and styles for the left-hand list of steps.

- `StartNavigationTemplate` specifies the UI content, controls, and styles for the bottom section of the first step (the one with `StepType="Start"` or the first step in the declaration of the control).

- `StepNavigationTemplate` specifies the UI content, controls, and styles for the bottom section of the intermediate steps (the ones with `StepType="Step"` or the steps other than the first and last ones in the declaration of the control).

- `FinishNavigationTemplate` specifies the UI content, controls, and styles for the bottom section of the final step (the one with `StepType="Finish"` or the last step in the declaration of the control).

Listing 9.4 shows in outline how these templates are used.

LISTING 9.4. Customizing the Wizard Control

```
<asp:Wizard id="Wizard1" runat="server">

  <HeaderTemplate>
    ... content for header goes here ...
  </HeaderTemplate>

  <SideBarTemplate>
    <asp:ImageButton OnClick="Wizard_Step" runat="server" />
  </SideBarTemplate>

  <StartNavigationTemplate>
    <asp:ImageButton OnClick="Wizard_Next" runat="server" />
  </StartNavigationTemplate>

  <StepNavigationTemplate>
    <asp:ImageButton OnClick="Wizard_Previous" runat="server" />
    <asp:ImageButton OnClick="Wizard_Next" runat="server" />
  </StepNavigationTemplate>

  <FinishNavigationTemplate>
    <asp:ImageButton OnClick="Wizard_Previous" runat="server" />
    <asp:ImageButton OnClick="Wizard_Finish" runat="server" />
  </FinishNavigationTemplate>

  <WizardSteps>
    <asp:WizardStep id="Step1">
      ... visual content and controls go here ...
    </asp:WizardStep>
    ... more WizardStep declarations go here ...
  </WizardSteps >

</asp:Wizard>
```

To change the text displayed on the buttons, set the `NextStepButton Text`, `PreviousStepButtonText`, and `FinishStepButtonText` properties to the text you want to display. You can even replace the Next, Previous, and Finish buttons with `LinkButton` controls (hyperlinks) by setting the `UseLinkButton` property of the `Wizard` to `True`:

```
<asp:Wizard id="Wizard1" runat="server"
    NextStepButtonText="Forward" PreviousStepButtonText="Back"
    FinishStepButtonText="Done" UseLinkButtons="True">
```

Navigation Methods and Events in a Wizard

The `Wizard` control also exposes properties, methods, and events that you can use to change the default navigation path through the steps or react to

TABLE 9.2. Wizard Control Events

Event	Description
ActiveViewChanged	Raised when the user moves from one step to another.
NextButtonClick	Raised when the user clicks the Next button or link.
SideBarButtonClick	Raised when the user clicks one of the buttons or links on the sidebar.
PreviousButtonClick	Raised when the user clicks the Previous button or link.
FinishButtonClick	Raised when the user clicks the Finish button or link.

events as the user interacts with the control. The events are shown in Table 9.2.

This allows you to intercept the postback event for the navigation. For example, to have an event procedure run when the Finish step is reached, you would declare the Wizard this way:

```
<asp:Wizard id="Wizard1" runat="server"
    onFinishButtonClick="Wizard_Finish">
```

The event procedure would then be declared as shown below:

```
Sub Wizard_Finish(Sender As Object, E As WizardNavigationEventArgs)

    ' code here to carry out the actions selected in the Wizard
    ' all values in all controls in all steps are available

End Sub
```

WizardNavigationEventArgs has the properties shown in Table 9.3.

TABLE 9.3. Properties of WizardNavigationEventArgs

Property	Description
Cancel	Determines whether to cancel the event. If set to True in the event procedure, the event is canceled.
CurrentStepIndex	Sets the index number of the current step.
NextStepIndex	Sets the index number of the next step.

Note there is no concept of a previous step as you are either moving forward or backward by way of the Next and Previous buttons. The `NextStep Index` therefore indicates the index number irrespective of direction. Thus for consecutively numbered steps, moving backward from Step 2 to Step 1 would leave `NextStepIndex` as 1.

And, at any stage, you can access the individual steps and the content of each one through the `WizardSteps` property:

```
Dim steps As WizardStepCollection
steps = MyWizard.WizardSteps
```

Other useful properties, methods, and events exposed by the `Wizard` control are the following:

- `ActiveStep`, which returns the currently displayed step in the Wizard as a `WizardStep` object
- `ActiveStepIndex`, which returns the `Integer` index of the currently displayed step within the `WizardSteps` collection or specifies the index of the step that will be displayed
- `MoveTo(WizardStep)`, which moves to the selected `WizardStep`
- `GetHistory()`, which returns an `ArrayList` of `WizardStep` items containing the steps the user has taken

URL Mapping

With the increasing complexity of many sites, it's important to provide not only easy-to-use menu controls but also easy-to-remember URLs. For example, consider the ASP.NET community site at http://www.asp.net/, as shown in Figure 9.4, which has a number of different tabs.

FIGURE 9.4. The ASP.NET community site menu

Although there are a number of tabs, all navigation goes through the `default.aspx` page, passing in the tab number as part of the query string.

The hard-coding of these query string parameters means that should tabs be added, deleted, or reordered, bookmarked pages will potentially break.

To solve this problem, mapping URLs is now easy with a new section in the application configuration file, specifying the target URL and the actual URL. The syntax of the configuration section is shown below:

```
<urlMappings enabled="[true|false]">
  <add
    url="String"
    mappedUrl="String" />
</urlMappings>
```

The properties are detailed in Table 9.4.
For example, we could have the following code:

```
<urlMappings enabled="true">

  <add url="~/Home.aspx"
    mappedUrl="~/default.aspx?tab=0" />
  <add url="~/Forums/default.aspx"
    mappedUrl="~/default.aspx?tab=1" />

</urlMappings>
```

With the configuration shown above, any requests for `Forums/default.aspx` will result in `default.aspx` being called with the `tab` parameter set to `1`, but `Forums/default.aspx` will still be displayed in the browser search bar.

TABLE 9.4. urlMappings Properties

Property	Description
enabled	Indicates whether or not the urlMappings service is enabled. The default is true.
url	Sets the displayed URL. This must be a relative URL starting with ~/.
mappedUrl	Sets the actual URL. This must be a relative URL starting with ~/.

It should be noted that although a directory name alone can be included for the `url` attribute, no mapping will take place. This is because this is an ASP.NET service, and without a specified ASP.NET page, the URL mapping is not executed. For example, consider the following mapping:

```
<add url="~/Forums/"
  mappedUrl="~/default.aspx?tab=1" />
```

Although this is legal, ASP.NET never sees this request because it is for a directory; IIS sees there is no directory present and so issues a 404 error. Creating the directory doesn't work either because you'll then receive a Directory Listing Denied error or a directory listing if browsing is allowed. You can, however, create directories and empty ASP.NET pages purely to facilitate the mapping.

Client-Side Script Features

Although ASP.NET is a server-side programming environment, there are times when client-side script is required. This is especially true when dealing with smart browsers, such as Internet Explorer, where programming client-side can enhance the user experience. To improve this interaction ASP.NET 2.0 introduces several new features, including the ability to set the focus of a control, the concept of a default button, and some advanced client-to-server processing.

Form Focus

To set the client-side focus, there are two new methods and an attribute on the form. Each control has a `Focus` method:

```
btn1.SetFocus()
```

The `Page` has a `SetFocus` method:

```
Page.SetFocus(btn1)
```

Finally, the form has an additional attribute (`DefaultButton`) to set the default button:

```
<form runat="server" DefaultButton="btn2">
```

These can be used as shown in Listing 9.5.

LISTING 9.5. Using the Focus and SetFocus Methods

```
<script runat="server">

  Sub btn1_click(sender As Object, E As EventArgs)
    btn3.Focus()
  End Sub

  Sub btn2_click(sender As Object, E As EventArgs)
    ...
  End Sub

  Sub btn3_click(sender As Object, E As EventArgs)
    Page.SetFocus(btn1)
  End Sub

</script>
<form runat="server" DefaultButton="btn2">
  <asp:Button id="btn1" Text="Button 1"
      onClick="btn1_click" runat="server" />
  <asp:Button id="btn2" Text="Button 2"
      onClick="btn2_click" runat="server" />
  <asp:Button id="btn3" Text="Button 3"
      onClick="btn3_click" runat="server" />
</form>
```

The default focus is applied only when no other focus methods are used.

Client Click Events

For server controls, the OnClick event refers to a server event. To hook a client-side event procedure into the click of a server button requires adding an attribute. To make this easier, ASP.NET 2.0 has the OnClientClick method:

```
<asp:Button runat="server" OnClientClick="ClientScript" />
```

The onClientClick event is supported by the Button, ImageButton, and LinkButton controls.

Registering Script Blocks

Programmatically adding client-side script to a page is achieved with RegisterClientScriptBlock and RegisterStartupScript, which both take a key and the script. This causes problems because it's not possible to use the same key for both a start-up script and another script block. To preserve compatibility, these methods still work, but a new ClientScriptManager, accessible from the `ClientScript` property of the page, provides enhanced features. For example:

```
Sub Page_Load(Sender As Object, E As EventArgs)

  Dim Script As String = "alert('Morning everyone');"

  Page.ClientScript.RegisterClientScriptBlock(Me.GetType(), _
                            "FormValidation", Script)

End Sub
```

An additional parameter has also been added to allow the insertion of the `<script>` tags. For example:

```
Page.ClientScript.RegisterClientScriptBlock(Me.GetType(), _
                          "FormValidation", Script, True)
```

Script Includes

In version 1.x of ASP.NET, to include a reference to an included script you had to do the following:

```
Sub Page_Load(Sender As Object, E As EventArgs)

  Dim URL As String = Page.ResolveUrl("~/Scripts/MyScript.js")
  Dim Script As String = "<script language='javascript'" & _
                    " src='" & URL & "'></script>"

  Page.ClientScript.RegisterClientScriptBlock(Me.GetType(), _
                            "FormValidation", Script)

End Sub
```

With version 2.0 there is now a `RegisterClientScriptInclude` method to make this easier. For example:

```
Sub Page_Load(Sender As Object, E As EventArgs)

  Dim URL As String = "Scripts/MyScript.js"

  Page.ClientScript.RegisterClientScriptInclude(Me.GetType(), _
                            "FormValidation", URL)

End Sub
```

This will generate the following:

```
<script language="javascript" src="Scripts/MyScript.js"></script>
```

Client Callbacks

Client callbacks allow client-side script to call server-side events asynchronously, without causing a postback. This opens up a whole avenue for creating responsive interfaces, where data can be fetched or commands can run in the background.

ASP.NET 2.0 introduces the `CallBackManager`, which acts as an intermediary between client code and server code. It is responsible for accepting requests from the client, firing the appropriate server event, and then passing the results back to the client, as shown in Figure 9.5.

Several things are required for this process to work.

- The `CallBackManager` code must know the name of the client-side method that instantiates the callback. This is accomplished by using the `GetCallbackEventReference` method of the `Page`,

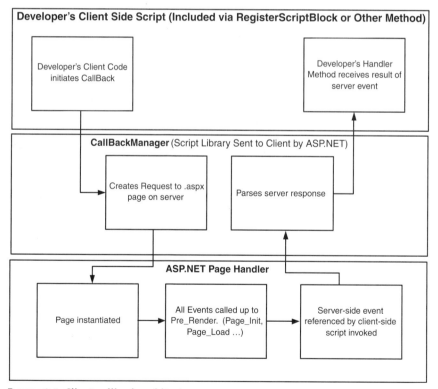

FIGURE 9.5. Client callback architecture

which returns a string containing the client script required to initiate the callback.

- A client-side method must be created to handle the data returned by the `CallBackManager`.
- The browser must support XmlHTTP because it is this that provides the client functionality to send requests to the server. To check for this, the BrowserCaps object has two new capabilities—SupportsXmlHTTP and SupportsCallBacks. In version 2.0 these will reflect the same capabilities, but having them separate allows for the callback implementation to be changed so that it is independent of XmlHTTP.

We'll look at the individual implementation details first, then look at a simple example.

Implementing the Callback Event Handler

If a page or control wishes to receive callback events, it must implement the `ICallbackEventHandler` interface. For a control developer this is simply a matter of adding the `Implements` keyword to the class definition:

```
Public Class MyControl
  Inherits WebControl
  Implements ICallbackEventHandler

End Class
```

For a Web page the `Implements` directive is used:

```
<%@ Page Language="VB" %>
<%@ Implements Interface="System.Web.UI.ICallbackEventHandler" %>
```

Implementing the interface is simple because it has only one method, which is the method that will be called from the client. Its signature is:

```
Function RaiseCallbackEvent(eventArgument As String) As String
```

The single argument will contain data from the client, and the return value is returned back to the client. For example:

```
Function MyCallbackEvent(eventArgument As String) As String _
    Implements ICallbackEventHandler.RaiseCallbackEvent

  Return "The server saw " & eventArgument

End Function
```

Client-Side Script

On the client, there needs to be a minimum of two scripts—one to call the server, and one to act as the callback from the server. The latter of these must match the following signature:

```
<script>

  function MyCallback(result, context) { }

</script>
```

The return value from the server `RaiseCallbackEvent` will be passed into the above function in the `result` parameter, and `context` is passed from the `context` parameter of `GetCallbackEventReference`, which is described in the next subsection.

There can also be a third script, of the same signature as the `MyCallback` script, which is run if an error occurs during the callback procedure.

Generating the Client Callback Code

For the client script to call back to the server, the client needs to know the control implementing the `ICallbackEventHandler` interface. For this the `GetCallbackEventReference` method is used (in much the same way that `GetPostbackEventReference` is used for controls responding to postbacks). The `GetCallbackEventReference` method is overloaded, having the signatures shown in Listing 9.6.

LISTING 9.6. GetCallbackEventReference Syntax

```
Public Function GetCallbackEventReference(
              control As Control,
              argument As String,
              clientCallback As String,
              context As String) As String

Public Function GetCallbackEventReference(
              control As Control,
              argument As String,
              clientCallback As String,
              context As String,
              clientErrorCallback As String) As String

Public Function GetCallbackEventReference(
              target As String,
              argument As String,
              clientCallback As String,
              context As String,
              clientErrorCallback As String) As String
```

TABLE 9.5. Parameters for GetCallbackEventReference

Parameter	Description
control	The control that implements RaiseCallbackEvent
argument	A value to be sent to the RaiseCallbackEvent via the eventArgument parameter.
clientCallback	The name of the client-side event handler that will receive the results of the server event if successful.
context	A value that will be passed back to the client-side event handler via the context parameter.
clientErrorCallback	The name of the client-side event handler that will receive the results of the server event if an error occurs.
target	The ID of the control to which the callback should be sent if the default control is not required.

Parameters for these signatures are shown in Table 9.5.

Listing 9.7 shows how to get the reference and register it as a script block.

LISTING 9.7. Generating the Client Callback

```
Dim refscr As String = _
  Page.GetCallbackEventReference(Me, "arg", "MyCallBackHandler", _
                                "ctx", "null")

Dim scr As String = _
  "function CallTheServerCallBack(arg, ctx) {" _
  & refscr & "; }"

Page.ClientScript.RegisterClientScriptBlock(Me.GetType(), _
  "CallTheServerCallBack", scr, True)
```

The first line constructs the actual line of client script that will generate the callback. For example, if this is run from the Page_Load event of an ASP.NET page, it will generate:

```
__doCallback('__Page',arg,MyCallBackHandler,ctx,null)
```

These parameters are:

- `__Page`, which is the current page
- `arg`, which is the string to be passed into the server `RaiseCallbackEvent`
- `MyCallBackHandler`, which is the name of a client script to receive the callback from the server
- `ctx`, which is the string to be passed directly through to the `MyCallBackHandler` in the context parameter
- `null`, indicating that no error callback function is required

This `__doCallback` function needs to be hooked into a client-side event to trigger the callback. This can be either directly triggered (such as from the `onClick` event of a button) or wrapped in another function, which is what the following line does:

```
Dim scr As String = _
  "function CallTheServerCallBack(arg, ctx) {" _
  & refscr & "; }"
```

This simply turns the callback routine into:

```
function CallTheServerCallBack(arg, ctx)
{
  __doCallback('__Page',arg,MyCallBackHandler,ctx,null)
}
```

The final part of the required action is to register this block of client script:

```
Page.ClientScript.RegisterClientScriptBlock(Me.GetType(), _
  "CallTheServerCallBack", scr, True)
```

At this stage you now have a client script function that will perform the callback. The server implementation of `RaiseCallbackEvent` will process the argument and return its data back to `MyCallBackHandler`. Figure 9.6 on the next page shows a new copy of the client callback architecture diagram to make things clearer.

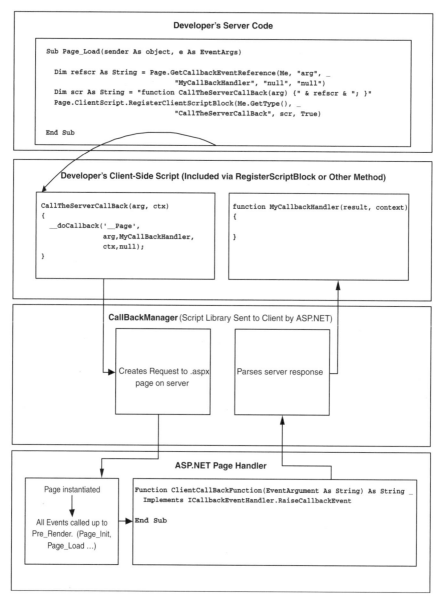

FIGURE 9.6. Client callback architecture with code

Client Callbacks in Action

Since the code for this is confusing without a good example, let's look at the entire code for a page called `ClientSideCallback.aspx` (see Figure 9.7).

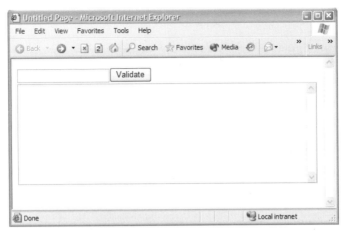

FIGURE 9.7. ClientSideCallback.aspx

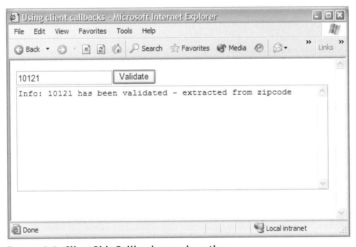

FIGURE 9.8. ClientSideCallback.aspx in action

Entering a value into the top text box and pressing the button performs a client callback—in this case simulating the validation of a zip code. The results are displayed in the lower text area (see Figure 9.8).

The code for this is shown in Listing 9.8.

LISTING 9.8. Using Client Callbacks

```
<%@ page language="VB" %>
<%@ implements interface="System.Web.UI.ICallbackEventHandler" %>

<script runat="server">

  Function ClientCallBackFunction(EventArgument As string) As String _
         Implements ICallbackEventHandler.RaiseCallbackEvent
```

```
        Return EventArgument & " has been validated"

    End Function

    Sub Page_Load(sender As object, e As EventArgs)

        Dim refscr As String = Page.GetCallbackEventReference(Me, "arg", _
                          "MyCallBackHandler", "ctx", "null")
        Dim scr As String = "function CallTheServerCallBack(arg, ctx){ " _
                          & refscr & "; }"
        Page.ClientScript.RegisterClientScriptBlock(Me.GetType(), _
                          "CallTheServerCallBack", scr, True)

    End Sub

</script>

<html>
<head runat="server">
    <title>Untitled Page</title>
</head>
<body>
  <form runat="server">
    <script language="javascript">
      function CallTheServer()
      {
        var zc = document.forms[0].elements['zipcode'];
        CallTheServerCallBack(zc.value, zc.id);
      }
      function MyCallBackHandler(result, context)
      {
        l = document.forms[0].elements['resultlabel'];
        l.value = "Info: " + result + ' - extracted from ' + context;
      }
    </script>
    <input type="text" id="zipcode" name="zipcode"></input>
    <button id="myBtn" onclick="CallTheServer()">Validate</button>
    <br />
    <textarea id="resultlabel" name="resultlabel"
          rows="10" cols="60"></textarea>
  </form>
</body>
</html>
```

The Page_Load event is exactly as we've discussed in earlier sections—it simply constructs the CallTheServerBack function, which wraps the __doCallback function.

The server ClientCallBackFunction event simply returns a string—in a real application this perhaps would perform some sort of data lookup.

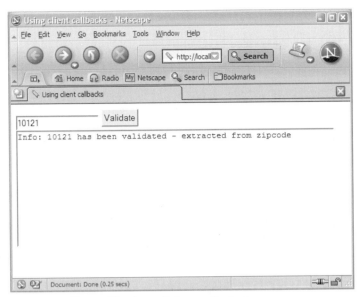

FIGURE 9.9. Client callbacks on Netscape Navigator

On the client side there is a button with an `onClick` event procedure, which takes the `value` from the top text box (`zipcode`) and the `id` and calls the server callback routine with those values. Giving the `CallTheServer CallBack` function two parameters allows for a flexible approach, where the value and context can be passed in. You could also do this for the callback functions if required.

Finally, the `MyCallBackHandler` function just accepts the `result` and `context` from the callback handler and displays them in the text area.

You can see that although there are several steps in this code, it's actually quite simple. This example uses an ASP.NET page, but it's just as easy to put the implementation into a custom server control. Although this technique relies on `XmlHTTP`, it is cross-browser friendly and works on Netscape Navigator (see Figure 9.9).

Uses for Client Callbacks

Client callbacks are perfect for those situations where you want to provide quick access to server functionality—this approach avoids the rendering phase for a page or control. This could be used for validation, preloading of data, or even timed execution of server code to simulate a push scenario.

Another perfect situation for the use of client callbacks is to solve a problem discussed earlier in the book, in Chapter 7's Allowing User Selection of

Skins subsection. There we discussed the problem of a theme browser that would allow users to select a theme to see how it looks. The problem was that the server event procedure that resulted from the selection of the theme fires too late for the theme to be applied—remember that themes have to be applied in the `PreInit` event. With this new technique, selection of the theme can now perform a client callback that sets the theme, for example:

```
Function MyCallBackEvent(EventArgument As String) As String _
    Implements ICallbackEventHander.RaiseCallbackEvent

  Profile.Theme = EventArgument

End Function
```

The client callback function can then simply invoke a standard postback:

```
<script language="javascript">

  function MyCallBackHandler(result,context)
  {
    __doPostBack('btnUpdate',,)
  }

</script>
```

The real postback will then run the `PreInit` event, at which stage the theme can be read from the `Profile`. Now a single selection can change the theme of a page.

Changes to Page Directives

To cater to some of the new features in ASP.NET 2.0, there are new page-level directives and attributes that apply to a variety of files. These new directives are listed below:

- `Image`, which applies to dynamic image files of type `.ASIX` (see Chapter 12)
- `Master`, used to identify a master page
- `PreviousPage`, used to identify the previous page in a cross-page posting scenario

Detailed explanation of master pages appears in Chapter 5, although the attributes are outlined here.

The Page Directive

The `Page` directive has several new attributes, as shown in Table 9.6.

The Master Directive

The `Master` directive can have the following attributes:

- `AutoEventWireup`
- `CompilerOptions`
- `CodeBehind`
- `Description`
- `EnablePersonalization`
- `Inherits`
- `LinePragmas`
- `Src`
- `TargetSchema`
- `ClassName`
- `CompileWith`
- `Debug`
- `EnableViewState`
- `Explicit`
- `Language`
- `Master`
- `Strict`

All of these are similar to those for the `Page` directive, having either the functionality described in Table 9.6 for new attributes or the same functionality as in version 1.x of ASP.NET.

TABLE 9.6. New Attributes for the Page Directive

Attribute	Description
`CompileWith`	A `String` indicating the path (relative or absolute) to the code-separation file. A `Namespace` is required for the code-beside file, and the `ClassName` attribute must also be specified.
`EnablePersonalization`	A `Boolean` indicating whether Personalization is enabled for the page.
`LinePragmas`	A `Boolean` indicating whether line pragmas are added to the compiled assembly.
`Master`	A `String` indicating the path (relative or absolute) to the master page.
`PersonalizationProvider`	The name of a Personalization provider, as detailed in the configuration file.
`TargetSchema`	This attribute is currently ignored and is intended for future releases.
`Theme`	The name of a theme.

The Control Directive

The `Control` directive has the following new attributes:

- `CompileWith`
- `EnablePersonalization`
- `LinePragmas`
- `Master`
- `TargetSchema`

The attributes have the functionality described in Table 9.6.

The PreviousPage Directive

The `PreviousPage` directive is covered in more detail in the Cross-Page Posting section earlier in this chapter. This directive has two attributes, as shown in Table 9.7. Only one of these can be used at a time—that is, you cannot specify both the `TypeName` and the `VirtualPath`.

TABLE 9.7. Attributes for the PreviousPage Directive

Attribute	Description
`TypeName`	The strong type of the previous page. If this is not set, it defaults to type `Page`.
`VirtualPath`	The relative path of the ASP.NET page from which the request originated.

The Image Directive

The `Image` directive, used in `.ASIX` pages as part of the image generation service, has two attributes, as shown in Table 9.8.

TABLE 9.8. Attributes for the Image Directive

Attribute	Description
`Language`	The language used within code in the page.
`Class`	The class name of the new image class.

The Page and Control Life Cycle

There are several new events for an ASP.NET page:

- `LoadComplete`, which occurs when the page has finished handling postback data
- `PreInit`, which occurs before the `Init` event for controls on the page
- `PreLoad`, which occurs before the `PreLoad` event for controls on the page
- `PreRenderComplete`, which occurs after the `PreRender` event for all controls on the page

The life cycle of events is shown in Table 9.9. This table covers both public and private events so that the interaction between page and control events can be seen. `Page` corresponds to a page event, and `Ctl` corresponds to a control event. New events are shown in bold. The phase and subphase are logical and do not exist as physical events or phases—they are purely to show the stage in the life cycle. The Adapter Handling column indicates which phases involve the device adapter. (Device adapters are covered in Chapter 10.)

TABLE 9.9. The Page and Control Life Cycle

Phase	Subphase	Adapter Handling	Event/ Method	Notes
Start	Detect postback	Yes	`Page.DeterminePostbackMode`	If there is no `ViewState` or the `posteventSourceID` is empty, an initial request is assumed.
Initiali-zation			**`Page.PreInit`**	The place to load Personalization and theme details.
			`Page.ApplyControlTheme`	
			`Page.ApplyPersonalization`	
		Yes	`Page.Init` `Ctl.Init`	

continues

TABLE 9.9. The Page and Control Life Cycle (continued)

Phase	Subphase	Adapter Handling	Event/ Method	Notes
	Begin tracking ViewState		Ctl.TrackViewState	
			Page.InitComplete	
Load State	Load Control State		Ctl.LoadControlState	For controls that require private state.
	Load ViewState	Yes	Ctl.LoadViewStateRecursive Ctl.LoadViewState	Occurs for each control in the collection.
	Process post data	Yes	Page.ProcessPostData Ctl.LoadPostData	For controls that implement IPost BackDataHandler. First attempt for the RaisePostback event handler.
Load			**Page.PreLoad**	
		Yes	Ctl.LoadRecursive Ctl.Load	Occurs for each control in the collection.
	Process postback	Yes	Page.ProcessPostData Ctl.LoadPostData	For controls that implement IPost BackDataHandler. Second attempt for RaiseChanged events and Post BackEvent.
			RaiseCallbackEvent	If the page or control has a callback event handler.
	Post back events		RaiseChangedEvents RaisePostBackevent	
			Page.LoadComplete	
Pre- Render	Create child controls		Ctl.EnsureChildControls	
		Yes	Ctl.CreateChildControls	
			Page.PreRenderComplete Page.SavePersonalizationData	
Save State	Save Control State		Ctl.SaveControlState	

TABLE 9.9. The Page and Control Life Cycle (continued)

Phase	Subphase	Adapter Handling	Event/ Method	Notes
	Save ViewState		`Ctl.SaveViewStateRecursive`	Occurs for each control in the collection.
		Yes	`Ctl.SaveViewState`	
Render			`Page.CreateMarkupTextWriter` `Ctl.RenderControl` `Ctl.Render` `Ctl.RenderChildren`	
Unload			`Page.UnLoadRecursive` `Ctl.UnLoadRecursive` `Ctl.Unload`	Occurs for each control in the collection.
		Yes	`Page.UnLoad`	
	Dispose		`Ctl.Dispose`	

SUMMARY

In this chapter we've looked at several topics that deal with ASP.NET pages. We first looked at cross-page posting and how some new properties have made it easy to use the standard postback architecture to post to another page and then from that other page to easily access the details of the previous page.

We then looked at improvements to validation, showing how the introduction of validation groups has enabled validation to be limited to selections of controls. This is particularly useful when dealing with wizards, which provide a simple way to create multistep pages. Since all of the controls exist on the same page there's no problem about having to store the values from the previous step, and the validation groups allow each step to be validated as a whole but separately from the other steps.

We then looked at URL mapping, showing how virtual URLs can be mapped to real pages while preserving the original URL. This allows for easier site navigation without the work of constructing complex site hierarchies.

We then moved to the client-side features, first looking at simple improvements such as setting the default button and the focus of controls. This took us into improvements for registering client-side script blocks and then into the client callback architecture, which brings a powerful way to run server code without involving a postback.

We finished with the new and changed page directives and the page event life cycle, showing where the new events fit into the event order.

Now it's time to take a look at pages of a different kind and how to cater to mobile devices.

10

Mobile Device Support

I N VERSION 1.0 OF THE .NET FRAMEWORK, the core controls from the WebControls and HtmlControls namespaces were "hard-coded" to create HTML output. This makes sense because most ASP.NET pages are aimed at standard Web browsers that recognize only HTML (albeit different versions, such as HTML 3.2 or HTML 4.0).

However, the growth in the use of mobile devices that don't recognize HTML, such as cellular phones that connect to the network through the Wireless Access Protocol (WAP), means that Microsoft has had to consider how ASP.NET can support such devices. The result for version 1.0 of the Framework was the Microsoft Mobile Internet Toolkit (MMIT), which was released as a separate install that added the classes required to the Framework class library.

In version 1.1 of the Framework, the MMIT controls became the ASP.NET Mobile Controls and were integrated into the class library rather than being a separate install, but this still doesn't solve the real underlying issues. In particular, what is the best way to make it easier for developers to create pages that work on different types of client devices without having to learn new programming techniques and new APIs as well as figure out the complex matrix of capabilities of the multitude of device types in use today?

In this chapter, we'll look at support for mobile devices and different types of markup requirements by examining the following:

- The issues of programming for different types of client devices
- The unified control and adapter architecture in ASP.NET 2.0
- The controls and attributes specific to mobile devices
- Some of the available mobile browser emulators

We'll start with a look at the whole issue of supporting different types of client browsers.

Programming for Different Types of Devices

The main issue with trying to write pages that target multiple devices lies in knowing exactly what each device expects to receive. For example, most mobile phones expect the content to be Wireless Markup Language (WML), of which there are several versions in current use. The devices connect to the Internet through a telecom provider's WAP gateway, which takes the output from a Web site and compiles it into a special format to deliver over what is currently a very narrow bandwidth connection to the device. Then it does the converse with the page requests and any posted content from the client, converting that back into standard HTTP format to send to the server.

However, there are several versions of this gateway software in use with different telecom providers, and each version may treat the content slightly differently during the compilation and decompilation processes. Add to this the huge number of different phones and devices currently available (which support different versions or different implementations of WML or other languages such as cHTML) and it soon becomes a real challenge to decide what output to send to each client.

The Microsoft Mobile Internet Toolkit

The MMIT went a long way toward solving these issues by including support for a large number of popular devices. You use the special controls that are part of the MMIT to build a page, and these controls interact with the page framework to detect the device type (and in some cases the gateway) and generate content that will produce the correct output in the current device. At the last count, over 200 device combinations were documented.

To understand what has changed in version 2.0 of the .NET Framework with respect to mobile devices, it's useful to see how the MMIT was designed. One way to change the output generated by a control is to hard-code within it the equivalent of one (or more) huge `case` statements.

However, this is prone to errors and difficult to implement successfully, and it makes updating the control as new devices appear extremely cumbersome.

Device Adapters

Instead, the MMIT uses **device adapters** to generate the output. A set of device adapters (one for each markup language) is available, and all the controls can use these device adapters to generate output suitable for a particular device. The device adapter overrides some of the events in the life cycle of the control, in particular the `Render` event.

This allows the device adapter to generate the appropriate output when the page recursively calls the `Render` method of each control and its child controls. It means that the control doesn't have to worry about the output format, while the device adapter doesn't have to know what the control actually does.

Device adapters may also have to override other events to ensure that the device is properly supported. For example, they may have to carry out specific actions for the load or save events for the viewstate of the page. (Many mobile devices require special handling of the viewstate because limitations in the total size of the posted values prevent it from being stored in a hidden control within the page.) They may also have to handle special situations for a postback, including issues where redirection to another page is handled differently in mobile devices.

And now Microsoft has moved all the ASP.NET server controls to a new unified control and adapter architecture. This was part of the original intentions for ASP.NET, but it was not fully developed in time to be implemented in version 1.0.

The Unified Control and Adapter Architecture

Effectively, the new page framework in version 2.0 works like the special `MobilePage` class that is used in the MMIT for version 1.x. It does so using a **page adapter** that exposes a full range of information about the capabilities of the current client. This information includes things like the device type and version, the kind of markup language it expects to receive, and more detailed data such as the screen size, support for scripts, cookies and frames, and much more.

Then, each control that will produce output tailored for the device uses a **control adapter** that generates the appropriate markup output to suit the current device. This process is often referred to as **adaptive rendering**.

Externally, to the developer, very little changes other than the addition of a few extra properties on the controls and a change of the control name prefix for the mobile controls from `mobile` to `asp`. This unified architecture therefore provides several advantages.

- There is no longer any need to make an initial design time decision as to whether the page should support mobile devices (though other factors such as the physical size of the page must still be considered).

- The developer does not have to learn the API of different sets of controls for standard and mobile pages nor install a separate toolkit.

- Existing MMIT (version 1.x) applications will run on ASP.NET version 2.0 without any reconfiguration or code changes because of the continued use of the ASP.NET Mobile Control classes instead of the new adaptive controls (i.e., they use the `mobile` namespace prefix rather than the `asp` namespace prefix).

- It makes it much easier to create development tools that can use and display the output of the controls for the various devices that are supported.

- The developer will generally have to write less code than in version 1.x with the MMIT controls because most of the new rich ("high-functionality") controls will work in pages targeted at mobile devices.

However, there is one issue to watch out for. Adaptive rendering requires that the ASP.NET controls are located on a server-side form (a `<form>` element with the `runat="server"` attribute) when accessed by a WML-enabled device. A `Hyperlink`, for example, generates an error if not placed on a form, while a `Label` is ignored and not displayed in the page. Standard HTML browsers require a server-side form only if controls participate in a postback.

As an example of how adaptive rendering works, take a look at the ASP.NET code in Listing 10.1, which displays some text and uses a `Calendar` control to provide a date selection feature.

LISTING 10.1. Using an ASP.NET 2.0 Calendar Control

```
<%@ Page Language="VB" %>
<html>
<head>
  <style>
    .Normal {font-family:Arial; font-size:xsmall}
  </style>
</head>
<body>
  <form runat="server">
    <p class="Normal">
    Select a date:<br />
    <asp:Calendar id="MyCal" cssClass="MyStyle" runat="server" />
    </p>
  </form>
</body>
</html>
```

You can see that it uses only "ordinary" HTML, including the `<html>` and `<body>` elements, a style definition, and two ASP.NET server controls. There is the `Calendar` control itself plus a `<form>` control that the `Calendar` requires to perform postbacks when a date is selected or the month is changed. Both of these server controls are standard ASP.NET 2.0 controls.

When viewed in an ordinary HTML browser, the page generates standard HTML (see Listing 10.2). We've removed some of the sections that are not pertinent to our discussion for clarity.

LISTING 10.2. The Output from the Calendar Control in Internet Explorer

```
<html>
<head>
  <style>
    .Normal {font-family:Arial; font-size:xsmall}
  </style>
</head>
<body>
  <form name="_ctl0" method="post" action="test2.aspx" id="_ctl0">
    ...
    <p class="Normal">
    Select a date:<br />
    <table id="MyCal" class="MyStyle" cellspacing="0" cellpadding="2"
    border="0" style="border-width:1px;border-style:solid;border-
    collapse:collapse;">
    <tr><td colspan="7" style="background-color:Silver;">
    <table class="MyStyle" cellspacing="0" border="0"
    style="width:100%;border-collapse:collapse;">
    <tr><td style="width:15%;">
    <a href="javascript:__doPostBack('MyCal','V1155')"
```

continues

FIGURE 10.1. The Calendar control viewed in Internet Explorer

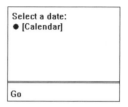

FIGURE 10.2. The Calendar control viewed in a mobile device

```
      style="color:Black">&lt;</a></td><td align="Center"
      style="width:70%;">April 2003</td><td align="Right"
      style="width:15%;">
      <a href="javascript:__doPostBack('MyCal','V1216')"
      style="color:Black">&gt;</a></td>
      ...
    </table>
    </p>
  </form>
</body>
</html>
```

Figure 10.1 shows that this gives the kind of output you would expect in Internet Explorer.

However, if you open the same page in a mobile device, WML output is generated. You'll see output like that shown in Figure 10.2 (depending on which emulator you are using). Selecting the [Calendar] link causes the control to provide a multistep menu for selecting the date you need.

The point to note is that while the original page was written as though we expected the client to accept HTML (e.g., we enclosed the page content in an `<html>` element and used the standard ASP.NET `Form` and `Calendar` server controls rather than those from the MMIT), the output has been converted automatically into the correct WML syntax for our mobile phone client. Listing 10.3 shows the actual WML sent to an emulator client.

LISTING 10.3. The Output from the Calendar Control in a Mobile Device Emulator

```xml
<?xml version='1.0'?>
<!DOCTYPE wml PUBLIC '-//WAPFORUM//DTD WML 1.1//EN'
                'http://www.wapforum.org/DTD /wml_1.1.xml'>
<wml>
<head>
  <meta http-equiv="Cache-Control" content="max-age=0" forua="true"/>
</head>
<card>
  <onevent type="onenterforward">
    <refresh>
      <setvar name="mcsvt" value="" />
      <setvar name="mcsva" value="" />
    </refresh>
  </onevent>
  <onevent type="onenterbackward">
    <refresh>
      <setvar name="mcsvt" value="" />
      <setvar name="mcsva" value="" />
    </refresh>
  </onevent>
  <p>
  Select a date:<br/>
  <anchor title="Go">
    Calendar
    <go href="/test/test2.aspx?__ufps=309633" method="post">
    <postfield name="__EVENTTARGET" value="MyCal" />
    <postfield name="__EVENTARGUMENT" value="1" />
    </go>
  </anchor>
  </p>
</card>
</wml>
```

It's clear that the controls, including the `Page` itself, have recognized the device and—through adaptive rendering—have generated the correct output to create the equivalent functionality in the mobile device. There is the correct `DOCTYPE` to identify the document type, and the `<html>` and `<body>` elements have been replaced by the appropriate `<wml>` and `<card>` elements. And the great thing is that it all happened automatically. There are no references to the MMIT in the source code for the page, no controls from the MMIT `mobile` namespace, and no code to tailor the output to suit this type of client.

This hugely powerful built-in feature of the page and control framework in ASP.NET 2.0 makes it a lot easier to create pages that work in different types of devices without having to explicitly design for this. For example, if you were using the MMIT in ASP.NET version 1.x, you would have to specifically avoid using any HTML-specific elements that cause a syntax error in a WML device and use the specific MMIT controls instead of the ASP.NET core controls.

Browser Definitions

One of the issues discovered with the MMIT was that it added extremely large sections of browser definitions to the `machine.config` file. This could make working with `machine.config` cumbersome and also made simple updates to the definitions more complex than it really should be. In version 2.0, all browser definitions (including definitions for specific WAP gateways) have been moved to separate files that have the `.browser` file extension. They are stored in the `$windir\Microsoft.NET\Framework\` `[version]\Config\Browsers\` folder of the machine. These browser definition files follow the general format shown in Listing 10.4.

LISTING 10.4. The General Format of a Browser Definition File

```
<browsers>
  <browser id="device-name" parentID="family-type-to-inherit-from">
    <identification>
      <!-- Specifies how to identify this browser -->
    </identification>
    <capture>
      <!-- Specifies additional header values to capture -->
    </capture>
    <capabilities>
      <!-- Specifies capabilities values to set -->
    </capabilities>
    <controlAdapters>
      <!-- Specifies control adapters to use for this browser -->
    </controlAdapters>
    <sampleHeaders>
      <!-- Specifies sample headers for this browser -->
    </sampleHeaders>
  </browser>
</browsers>
```

All these files are compiled into a single compact representation when the Framework is installed. If a definition is updated, recompilation must be manually initiated by running the `aspnet_regbrowsers.exe` utility. This utility is installed along with the Framework. To use it, you just specify the location of the folder containing the browser definition files:

```
aspnet_regbrowsers.exe browsers-folder
```

An interesting possibility arising from this is that automated updates to browser definitions will be much easier to implement and might even become part of the Framework process in time.

> Any browser definitions within a `<browserCaps>` element in a `web.config` file are still recognized and are merged into the final set of definitions used by the Framework. However, any definitions in `machine.config` are ignored.

The BrowserCapabilities Class

Although the plumbing and implementation of the device detection system is different from version 1.0, its use is familiar in version 2.0. The current `Request` (`HttpRequest`) class exposes an instance of the `Http BrowserCapabilities` class through its `Browser` property. This means that you can still write code that interrogates the browser capabilities properties, just as in version 1.0:

```
Dim sPlatform As String = Request.Browser("Platform")
```

Page Design and Device Support

Under the unified control and adapter architecture, all the ASP.NET standard server controls will change their behavior and the markup they generate depending on the type of device accessing the page. So does this mean that you can now build pages and even complete Web sites or applications that will work on any device? The answer is "yes," but—to a greater extent—you probably won't want to.

The reason has to do with the design of the page and how well it matches the devices it will be viewed on. Although the new 2.5G and 3G cellular phones are appearing, with increased bandwidth and screen size, the fundamental issues are related more to the actual rendered page versus available screen size, as well as the input devices available on the client.

For example, a common design for pages aimed at the traditional Web browser is multiple columns, separate navigation bars at the top or left, and a multitude of small text links or clickable images. This kind of page generally depends on the use of a mouse to navigate.

On the latest cellular phones there is generally no mouse, though there may be some kind of navigation pad. However, the majority of mobile phone devices use only simple text, perhaps up to 20 characters per line over six lines, and may not even be able to display images.

So, while a `Label`, `Hyperlink`, or `Textbox` control can modify its behavior to suit the device and the markup language required, there is no real possibility of designing the layout of the entire page so that it "works" (in the usability sense) on all devices. And this is not the aim of the unified control and adapter architecture. Instead, it does allow you to build pages using the same techniques, tools, and programming model, but you will generally have to implement different versions of your Web applications to suit the different major categories of devices you want to support (probably one version for ordinary Web browsers and one version for mobile devices).

Device Filters

Even though the controls automatically tailor their output to suit the current device, it's useful to be able to adjust the output in specific ways to suit your own requirements. In version 2.0 of ASP.NET, this is accomplished by filtering on specific devices or on classes of devices. All you have to do is prefix a property or attribute within a control declaration with the device class or name.

For example, if there is a browser definition with `id="Nokia"` (which matches any Nokia device), you can change the text and display style of a `Label` control for devices of this type simply by adding the device-specific attributes (see Listing 10.5).

LISTING 10.5. Using Device-Specific Attributes to Change Behavior

```
<asp:Label id="MyLabel" runat="server"
        Text="Welcome to our site"
        Nokia:Text="Time to upgrade your Nokia phone!"
        cssClass="StandardStyleClass"
        Nokia:cssClass="SpecialNokiaStyleClass" />
```

Device-Specific Templates

It's also possible to use the same approach to change the output from bound controls. A good example is where you want to display data in an HTML table. However, most mobile devices do not support tables, so the output has to be formatted in a different way for these devices. And, due to the limited screen area, you often need to provide more compact output, perhaps by omitting some of the columns.

The code in Listing 10.6 shows this concept in action, with browser definitions for the general device categories `HtmlBrowsers` and `Wml Browsers`. The `HeaderTemplate`, `ItemTemplate`, and `FooterTemplate` for the `Repeater` control contain different output, depending on which of these categories the current device falls into.

LISTING 10.6. Using Device-Specific Templates to Change Behavior

```
<asp:Repeater runat="server" ...>

  <HtmlBrowsers:HeaderTemplate>
    <table>
      <tr><td>UserName</td><td>Address</td><td>Phone</td></tr>
  </HtmlBrowsers:HeaderTemplate>

  <HtmlBrowsers:ItemTemplate>
    <tr>
      <td><%# Container.DataItem("UserName") %></td>
      <td><%# Container.DataItem("Address") %></td>
      <td><%# Container.DataItem("Phone") %></td>
    </tr>
  </HtmlBrowsers:ItemTemplate>

  <WmlBrowsers:ItemTemplate>
    <asp:Panel runat="server">
      <%# Container.DataItem("UserName") %>
      <%# Container.DataItem("Phone") %>
    </asp:Panel>
  </WmlBrowsers:ItemTemplate>

  <HtmlBrowsers:FooterTemplate>
    </table>
  </HtmlBrowsers:FooterTemplate>

</asp:Repeater>
```

An alternative approach is to set the values of control properties dynamically at runtime. For example, to change the text displayed in a `Label` control if the current device matches the filter `WmlBrowsers`, you can simply use code like that shown in Listing 10.7.

LISTING 10.7. Changing the Output Dynamically at Runtime

```
MyLabel.Text = "Welcome to our site"
If Request.Browser.IsType("WmlBrowsers") Then
  MyLabel.Text = "Call us now on your mobile phone!"
End If
```

When multiple browser definitions or device filters match the current client, the one that specifies the device with the most precision is chosen, though the settings specified in definitions from which this one inherits are also available if not overridden. For example, an Ericsson T86 phone will expose all the properties defined for a browser definition named `Ericsson T86` plus any that are not overridden here from a general definition aimed at all Ericsson devices, as well as any that are exposed from the `WmlBrowsers` definition.

Controls and Attributes Specific to Mobile Devices

As you've just seen, most of the ASP.NET server controls within version 2.0 of the .NET Framework can modify their output to suit different types of devices. So the techniques for using the controls that you saw in earlier chapters are identical when building pages targeted at mobile devices. However, several controls are specific to mobile devices—in particular devices that have built-in phone capabilities. These controls consist of:

- The `Pager` control, which works as part of the underlying page architecture to divide pages into separate sections for small-screen and mobile devices
- The `PhoneLink` control, which can be used in phone-enabled devices to initiate a phone call to a specified number
- The `SoftKeyLabel` attribute, which is added to most of the controls to allow the developer to provide better soft-key support for mobile devices such as cellular phones

> The `MultiView` and `View` controls were also originally designed to provide better small-screen device support, though they are often used in pages targeted at other types of browsers as well.

We'll look at each of these controls and attributes next to see what they do and how they are used. Also remember that a couple of the standard ASP.NET 2.0 controls from the `WebControls` namespace are specifically designed to better support mobile and WML-based devices such as cellular phones, in addition to the other new features they offer aimed at traditional client devices.

- The new `DynamicImage` control will automatically convert images into the correct `.wbmp` format for cellular phones.
- The new `Table` control can provide two different modes for viewing the content: summary view and details view.

We describe these two controls in detail in Chapter 12.

The System.Web.UI.WebControls.Pager Control

Although the `Pager` control can be used in pages that target any type of browser or other client device, it is generally most useful for small-screen devices. These devices, particularly mobile phones, have extremely limited memory capacity and a slow bandwidth connection, so it is good practice to minimize the amount of content sent to the device for each "screen" (or page) displayed.

One way to minimize the content when there is a lot of information to display is to separate it into individual pages and provide Next and Previous buttons so that the user can navigate from one page to the next. However, this often involves considerable extra coding. In ASP.NET 2.0, the new `Pager` control can handle all the issues of creating the appearance of separate pages from a single source page.

The `Pager` control is placed within an ASP.NET page and its `Control ToPaginate` property set to the `id` of a container control on the page (which must have the `runat="server"` attribute). A common approach is to use the `Pager` control to paginate the contents of a `<form>`. In Listing 10.8, the `<form>` contains eight `<div>` controls and one `<p>` control. Each of these `<div>` and `<p>` controls contains one or more child controls.

LISTING 10.8. Using a Pager Control with a <form>

```
...
<form id="MyForm" runat="server">

  <div runat="server">
  <asp:Label Text="Name:" runat="server" />
  <asp:Textbox id="txtName" runat="server" />
  </div>
  <div runat="server">
  <asp:Label Text="Phone:" runat="server" />
  <asp:Textbox id="txtPhone" runat="server" />
  </div>
  <div runat="server">
  <asp:Label Text="Email:" runat="server" />
  <asp:Textbox id="txtEmail" runat="server" />
  </div>
```

```
<div runat="server">
<asp:Label Text="Address:" runat="server" />
<asp:Textbox id="txtAddress" runat="server" />
</div>
<div runat="server">
<asp:Label Text="City:" runat="server" />
<asp:Textbox id="txtCity" runat="server" />
</div>
<div runat="server">
<asp:Label Text="State:" runat="server" />
<asp:Textbox id="txtState" runat="server" />
</div>
<div runat="server">
<asp:Label Text="Zip:" runat="server" />
<asp:Textbox id="txtZip" runat="server" />
</div>
<div runat="server">
<asp:Button Text="Submit" runat="server" />
</div>
<p>
<asp:Pager id="MyPager" ControlToPaginate="MyForm"
           ItemsPerPage="6" runat="server" />
</p>

</form>
...
```

After the Submit button comes the declaration of the Pager control. The ControlToPaginate attribute specifies the <form> as the container control whose content (the controls that are direct children of the container being paginated) will be divided into separate pages. The number of controls that will appear on each page is controlled by the ItemsPerPage property, here set to 6 using the ItemsPerPage attribute.

That's all you need to do to provide pagination of the output. In a browser and in a mobile device, the output now consists of three separate screens, with the Next and Prev buttons displayed automatically at the appropriate times. Figure 10.3 shows the results in Internet Explorer, and Figure 10.4 shows the same page viewed in a mobile device emulator.

We see three screens because ItemsPerPage applies to the maximum number of pageable controls that are to be paged irrespective of whether they are top-level controls. The <div> control is not a pageable control, whereas the Label, Textbox, and Button are. Therefore we see three Label controls and three Textbox controls for screens one and two, and a Label, Textbox, and Button for screen three. The <div> control ensures that controls within it aren't split between pages; thus changing ItemsPerPage to 5 would show not five controls on the first page but only four.

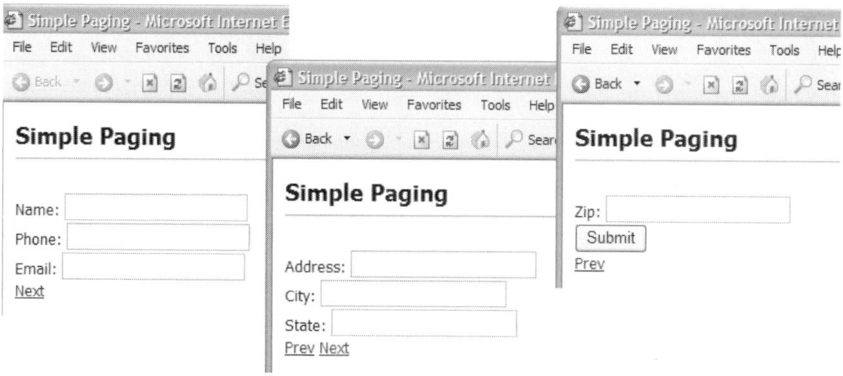

FIGURE 10.3. The Pager control viewed in Internet Explorer

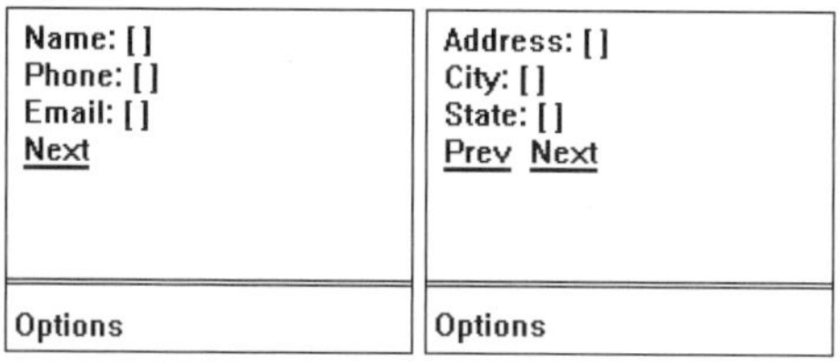

FIGURE 10.4. The Pager control viewed in a mobile device emulator

You can also put more than one `Pager` control on a page if you wish. This might be useful if you want the Next and Prev links to appear at the top and bottom of the list—you just insert them into the page at the points you want their output to appear. Note that you must set their `ItemsPerPage` attributes to the same value.

Displaying Page Numbers

The `Pager` control exposes properties named `CurrentPage` and `PageCount` so you can easily indicate to users where they are in the set of pages by displaying these values (see Listing 10.9).

LISTING 10.9. Displaying the Page Number and Page Count with the Pager Control

```
. . .
<p>
<asp:Pager id="MyPager" ControlToPaginate="MyForm"
           ItemsPerPage="6" runat="server" />
</p>
<p>
Page <% = MyPager.CurrentPage + 1 %>
  of <% = MyPager.PageCount %>
</p>
</form>
```

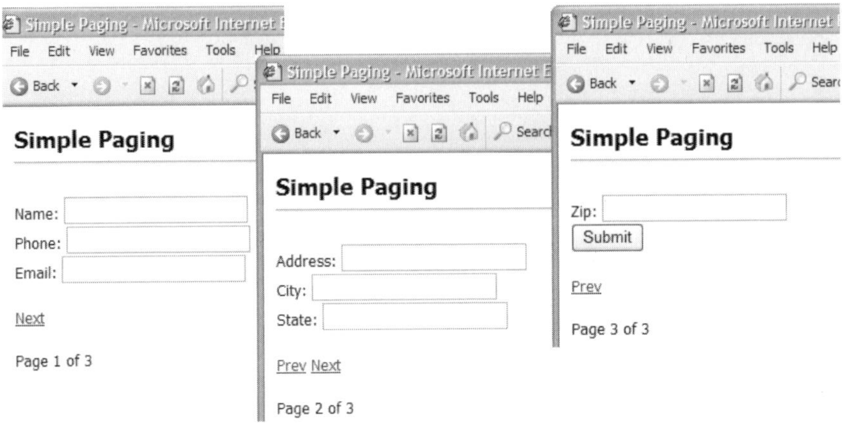

FIGURE 10.5. Displaying the page number and page count

The `PageCount` property is read-only, but you can set the `CurrentPage` property in code to force a specific page to be displayed. However, notice that the pages are numbered from 0—we add 1 to the value of the `CurrentPage` property in the code in Listing 10.9 so that it displays the page numbers as 1, 2, and 3 (which tends to be more intuitive for users). The screenshot in Figure 10.5 shows the values of `CurrentPage` and `PageCount` when we add to the page the highlighted code shown previously.

Alternatively, you can force the `Pager` control to display a list of all the available page numbers as hyperlinks so that users can jump directly to any one of them. All that's required is to add the `Mode` attribute with the value `NumericPages`:

```
<asp:Pager id="MyPager" ControlToPaginate="MyForm"
        Mode="NumericPages" ItemsPerPage="6" runat="server" />
```

Figure 10.6 shows how this looks in Internet Explorer, and the result is much the same in a mobile device. As you can see from the screenshot, the page numbers now show the "proper" values, indexed from 1.

To control how many page numbers are displayed in this mode, change the `Page-ButtonCount` property from its default of `10`. The usual format of three dots after the last page number shown (or before the first one) signifies that there are more pages available:

FIGURE 10.6. Displaying the page numbers as hyperlinks

<u>0</u> <u>1</u> <u>2</u> <u>3</u> 4 <u>5</u> <u>6</u> ...   or   ... <u>7</u> <u>8</u> <u>9</u> <u>10</u> <u>11</u> <u>12</u>

You can also set the Mode property to PagerMode.NumericPages at runtime, or you can set it to PagerMode.NextPrev to display the default Next and Prev buttons. And you can change the text displayed in NextPrev mode by setting the NextPageText and PrevPageText properties to different String values or by adding the NextPageText and PrevPageText attributes to the control declaration (see Listing 10.10).

LISTING 10.10. Changing the Default Properties of the Pager Control

```
<asp:Pager id="MyPager" ControlToPaginate="MyForm"
           ItemsPerPage="6" runat="server"
           NextPageText="More"
           PrevPageText="Back" />
```

Page Weightings

So far, all the examples we've shown set a specific value for the ItemsPer Page property of the Pager control. This is fine if each item takes up roughly the same amount of vertical space on the page. However, if they don't, the lengths of the pages will vary even when each one contains the same number of items.

To get around this, the Pager control can use **weightings** to determine where the page breaks should occur. Page weightings are automatically used if you don't specify a value for the ItemsPerPage attribute when declaring the Pager control and don't set the ItemsPerPage property at runtime.

If the controls used within the container control implement the I PaginationInfo or IItemPaginationInfo interfaces, they can be assigned specific weights for their ItemWeight property. Otherwise, the Pager control uses the number of contained controls for each top-level item to work out the weightings. (The default is 100, but this can be changed by setting the DefaultItemWeight property of the Pager control.) Then, taking into account the value of the container control's Available Weight property, the Pager control can calculate where to place the page breaks.

Keeping Child Controls Together

The IPaginationInfo interface exposes a property named Paginate Children. When this is set to True (the default varies depending on the control type), the pagination process will break up the pages between the child controls of the same top-level item. When set to `False`, all child controls are kept together for each top-level item in the container control that is being paginated. The `Panel` control is probably the most suitable server control to act as the parent container in this case. For plain HTML controls, the `<div>` control, as shown previously, also keeps child controls together.

Pager Control Events

Like most server controls, the `Pager` control raises a series of events that can be handled by code in your page. The `Paginated` event occurs after the control has figured out what is located on the current page, so code here can discover the number of pages and the controls that are on this page before it is rendered—and even change the output by assigning new values to the control properties.

Custom Paging

The final topic we consider here for the `Pager` control is the way you can abandon the built-in pagination features and instead create build routines and UIs to suit your own specific requirements. This requires more effort, but it does allow you to exert full control over the way it works.

The `Pager` control can be wired up to separate controls that will activate the Next and Back operations. Any control that exposes the `Command Name` property (e.g., `Button`, `LinkButton`, or `ImageButton`) is an ideal candidate:

```
<asp:Button runat="server" CommandName="Prev" Text="Previous" />
...
<asp:Button runat="server" CommandName="Next" Text="Next" />
```

Simply set the `CommandName` attribute to the same value as the `NextPageCommandName` and `PrevPageCommandName` properties of the `Pager` control, and they will automatically cause the postback that moves to the next or previous page. The default values for the `NextPageCommandName` and `PrevPageCommandName` properties of the `Pager` control are `Next` and `Prev`, respectively, but you can change this if you need to wire the buttons up to different instances of the `Pager` control.

The PhoneLink Control

One useful technique in voice-enabled devices such as mobile phones is to provide a link that dials a specified number when activated. A `PhoneLink` control to achieve this is part of the MMIT, and an equivalent is now part of the core controls set in ASP.NET 2.0.

The `PhoneLink` control has a property named `PhoneNumber`, which specifies the number to be dialed when activated. It also supports the display and formatting properties that are standard for the controls that inherit from `WebControl`, plus the `SoftKeyLabel` attribute that we discuss in more detail later.

```
<asp:PhoneLink cssClass="Normal" id="Phone1" runat="server"
               PhoneNumber="123-456-7890" />
```

In a device that does not support voice calls, the control will usually just render the phone number in the page as text within an HTML anchor element:

```
<a id="Phone1" class="Normal">123-456-7890</a>
```

However, in a voice-enabled device, the output is a hyperlink that specifies the protocol `wtai:`, which initiates a voice call. Notice how the number in the `href` attribute below is prefixed with a special URL as well, which is used by the phone to make the connection, and the number has all non-numeric formatting characters removed:

```
<a href="wtai://wp/mc;1234567890">123-456-7890</a>
```

The result in a mobile device emulator is shown in Figure 10.7.

FIGURE 10.7. The PhoneLink control in a mobile device emulator

The SoftKeyLabel Attribute

Some of the interactive controls in the ASP.NET 2.0 `WebControls` namespace (mainly link and button controls) have the `SoftKeyLabel` attribute. This can be set programmatically or declaratively through the `SoftKeyLabel` attribute. The value is a `String` displayed by many mobile devices that have softkey buttons (usually located just below the screen). It provides a useful hint to users about which button to press to activate or interact with the control.

As an example, the code in Listing 10.11 creates a page containing a `Hyperlink` and a `PhoneLink` control. Both of these controls carry a definition of the `SoftKeyLabel` attribute.

LISTING 10.11. Using the SoftKeyLabel Attribute

```
<%@ Page Language="VB" %>
<html>
<head>
  <style>
    .Heading {font-family:Arial; font-size:xsmall; font-weight:bold}
    .Normal {font-family:Arial; font-size:xsmall}
  </style>
</head>
<body>
  <form runat="server">

    <asp:Hyperlink cssClass="Normal" id="Link1" runat="server"
      Text="Next Page" NavigateUrl="nextpage.aspx"
      SoftKeyLabel="Next" />

    <br />

    <asp:PhoneLink cssClass="Normal" id="Call1" runat="server"
      PhoneNumber="123-456-7890" SoftKeyLabel="Dial" />

  </form>
</body>
</html>
```

When viewed in a cellular phone, the value of the `SoftKeyLabel` is displayed above the soft-key button as each control receives the focus, making it easy to see what each one does (see Figure 10.8).

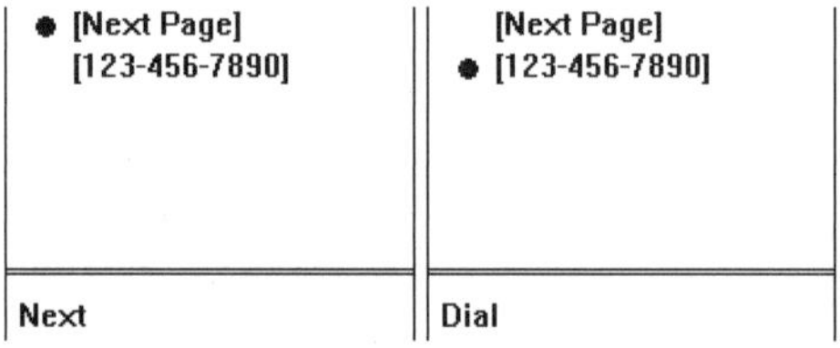

```
┌─────────────────────┬─────────────────────┐
│ ● [Next Page]       │   [Next Page]       │
│   [123-456-7890]    │ ● [123-456-7890]    │
│                     │                     │
│                     │                     │
│                     │                     │
├─────────────────────┼─────────────────────┤
│ Next                │ Dial                │
└─────────────────────┴─────────────────────┘
```

FIGURE 10.8. The results of setting the SoftKeyLabel attribute

Mobile Browser Emulators

If you don't have a mobile device to test your pages, you can use one of several emulators to simulate a mobile phone, including the following:

- Deck-It WML Previewer from PyWeb, available at
  http://www.PyWeb.com/
- WAP 2.0 Phone Simulator from OpenWave, available at
  http://developer.openwave.com/
- R380 WAP Emulator from Symbian, available at
  http://www.symbian.com/
- Nokia Mobile Browser from Nokia, available at
  http://secure.forum.nokia.com/
- SmartPhone Emulator from Yospace, available at
  http://www.yospace.com/

Using one of these emulators allows you to easily test how well your pages work on a WML-enabled device.

Mobile devices do, of course, include PDAs and phones based on Windows Pocket PC. Although these devices feature a version of Internet Explorer, you still face the problems of a small screen size, so your pages may need to be adjusted and tested accordingly. Find out more about Microsoft Mobile Support at http://www.microsoft.com/windowsmobile/.

SUMMARY

In this chapter we've looked at the ways that ASP.NET 2.0 provides improved support over version 1.x for mobile and small-screen devices such as cellular phones and PDAs. You can see that building pages to suit these types of devices is much easier and more intuitive than in earlier versions of ASP.NET and, in fact, in any other Web programming environment.

We saw how the Framework now automatically detects the client device type and through adaptive rendering changes the output to suit that client. You no longer have to decide what types of clients you want to support or write special code to suit each type of device.

We looked at the three controls and attributes that are generally specific to mobile devices, including the `Pager` control, which makes it easy to break a page into separate screens; the `PhoneLink` control, which can initiate a voice connection; and the `SoftKeyLabel` attribute, which can improve the user experience.

In the next chapter, we'll change tack completely to look at another important aspect of ASP.NET 2.0, namely, how the caching features have been vastly improved in this new version.

11.

CACHING

O NE OF THE MOST FREQUENTLY requested features for the ASP.NET Cache is the ability to invalidate cached items from the database. This capability, along with some changes to the underlying plumbing of the ASP.NET Cache, has been added in ASP.NET 2.0. However, the Technology Preview release does not contain all the planned additions to the caching features of ASP.NET. Microsoft still intends to add some additional capabilities, but they won't be available until the beta release.

The caching features in ASP.NET are specifically designed to increase throughput and decrease load on the server by keeping frequently accessed content in memory versus constantly running code. There are two primary uses of the Cache.

1. *Output caching* involves storing the response generated by an ASP.NET page, User Control, or Web Service in memory and using the in-memory response on subsequent requests rather than executing code. This is extremely fast since the server simply needs to copy the response from memory. A good example of this technique is a report. The contents used to render the report are generated once and stored in the output cache. Then the cached versions are used for subsequent requests.

2. *The Cache API* is a programmatic, dictionary-based API for accessing and storing frequently used data. Unlike output caching, which

caches the contents of the response, the `Cache` API is used within running code to cache frequently accessed data. For example, a `DataSet` used in 50% of the pages within an application could be cached so that each page that requires the data doesn't have to re-calculate the data on each request.

Behind the scenes, pages marked for output caching are stored and re-trieved through the `Cache` API. The `Cache` itself is simply a hashtable with enhanced capabilities.

- *Least recently used (LRU)*: When ASP.NET needs more memory, the `Cache` will automatically evict items by using an LRU algorithm to remove items that are accessed infrequently.
- *Cache dependencies*: Items added to the `Cache` can be made dependent on external conditions whereby they are removed. For example, ASP.NET 1.0 supported three dependencies: `Time`, `File`, and `Key`. Items could be expired at a point in time (by using the `Time` dependency), when a file changed (by using the `File` dependency), and when another item in the `Cache` changed (by using a `Key` dependency). This functionality is encapsulated in the `CacheDependency` class found in the `System.Web.Caching` namespace.

While the `Cache` and its dependency features allowed complex applications to be built, the ASP.NET team soon realized that most cached data came from a database and there was not a dependency that allowed for invalidation when data in the database changed. Database change dependency is now possible in the ASP.NET 2.0 `Cache`.

Listing 11.1 demonstrates how this is used in a page—using the new `sqldependency` attribute of the `<%@ OutputCache %>` directive.

LISTING 11.1. SQL Server–Based Cache Dependency

```
<%@ Page Language="VB" %>
<%@ Import Namespace="System.Data" %>
<%@ Import Namespace="System.Data.SqlClient" %>
<%@ OutputCache duration="5555"
                varybyparam="none"
                sqldependency="Northwind:Products"  %>

<h1>Last update: <%=DateTime.Now.ToString("r")%></h1>
<hr>
<form runat="server">
    <asp:gridview id="GridView1"
```

```
                    datasourceid="SqlDataSource1"
                    runat="server" />

    <asp:sqldatasource id="SqlDataSource1"
                    runat="server"
                    providername="System.Data.OleDb"
                    selectcommand="SELECT * FROM dbo.[Products]"
                    connectionstring="provider=sqloledb;
                                      database=northwind;
                                      uid=sa;pwd=00password" />
    </form>
```

Database cache invalidation allows for the removal of an item from the Cache when data stored in the database changes.

ASP.NET 2.0 adds support for database cache invalidation for Microsoft SQL Server 7, Microsoft SQL Server 2000, and the next version of Microsoft SQL Server (code-named "Yukon").

Although support for these three databases is built into ASP.NET, there are some significant differences.

- *Microsoft SQL Server 7 and Microsoft SQL Server 2000*: For these database products, only table-level changes are supported. For example, if you cached data from the Products table in the Northwind database and the table was updated, all cached data dependent on that table would be evicted from the Cache.
- *Microsoft SQL Server "Yukon"*: "Yukon" has implicit support for invalidation built directly into the database. Data can be invalidated from the Cache when the specific results of a request, such as a stored procedure, change.

The level of granularity between the databases is very relative. For example, if you output cache a page for each product in the Products table, you would output cache 77 pages. If you were using SQL Server 7 or SQL Server 2000, each of the 77 pages would be invalidated if the Products table were updated. However, with "Yukon" you can be more selective about how items are invalidated; you can invalidate only output-cached pages that changed (e.g., the page displaying information for the product with ID 35).

We are not going to focus on the "Yukon" caching capabilities in this chapter but will instead examine how we enable database cache invalidation from Microsoft SQL Server 7 and 2000. In order to use database cache invalidation on these databases, we first need to enable it.

Enabling Database Cache Invalidation

In the Technology Preview release of ASP.NET 2.0, the command-line tool `aspnet_regsql.exe` is used to configure databases for SQL cache invalidation. In the beta release, this tool will likely no longer exist and will be replaced with `aspnet_regsqlcache.exe`, a combination command-line and GUI tool. Additionally, in the beta release you will also be able to use the new Web Administration Tool (see Chapter 6) to configure SQL Server cache invalidation. Note that this tool is only required to enable Microsoft SQL Server 7 and Microsoft SQL Server 2000 databases. Microsoft SQL Server "Yukon" has implicit support for database change notification.

> **IMPORTANT**
>
> You can also use the `SqlCacheDependencyAdmin` class in the `System.Web.Caching` namespace to enable the database and tables for Microsoft SQL Server 7 and 2000 databases. This functionality is not examined in this book.

To use `aspnet_regsqlcache.exe`, first open a command prompt window and navigate to the installation directory of the .NET Framework:

```
\Windows\Microsoft.NET\Framework\v1.2.30609\
```

Note that your version-specific directory (`\v1.2.30609\`) will differ. Use the highest number available.

Next, type `aspnet_regsqlcache`, as shown in Figure 11.1.

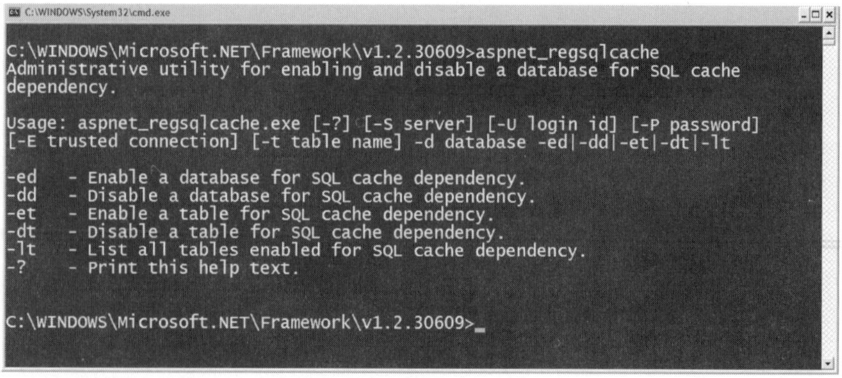

```
C:\WINDOWS\Microsoft.NET\Framework\v1.2.30609>aspnet_regsqlcache
Administrative utility for enabling and disable a database for SQL cache
dependency.

Usage: aspnet_regsqlcache.exe [-?] [-S server] [-U login id] [-P password]
[-E trusted connection] [-t table name] -d database -ed|-dd|-et|-dt|-lt

-ed   - Enable a database for SQL cache dependency.
-dd   - Disable a database for SQL cache dependency.
-et   - Enable a table for SQL cache dependency.
-dt   - Disable a table for SQL cache dependency.
-lt   - List all tables enabled for SQL cache dependency.
-?    - Print this help text.

C:\WINDOWS\Microsoft.NET\Framework\v1.2.30609>_
```

FIGURE 11.1. Use of aspnet_regsqlcache.exe

Table 11.1. Options for aspnet_regsqlcache.exe

Flag	Description
-?	Displays a help listing of the various flags supported by the tool.
-S	Names the SQL Server to connect to. This can be either the computer name or the IP address.
-U	Names the user to connect as when using SQL Server Authentication (e.g., the SQL Server administrator account, sa).
-P	Used in conjunction with the -U flag to specify the user's password.
-E	Connects to the SQL Server when using Windows Authentication and the current user has administrator capabilities on the database. The -U and -P flags are not needed when using -E.
-t	Specifies the table to apply necessary changes for SQL Server cache invalidation to.
-d	Specifies the database to apply changes for SQL Server cache invalidation to.
-ed	Enables a database for SQL cache dependency.
-dd	Disables a database for SQL cache dependency.
-et	Enables a table for SQL cache dependency.
-dt	Disables a table for SQL cache dependency.
-lt	Lists all tables enabled for SQL cache dependency.

The command-line tool options should be familiar if you have used command-line SQL tools such as osqlw.exe. Table 11.1 describes the various options in more detail. Note that the tool is case-sensitive.

The following subsections contain some sample sessions using aspnet_regsqlcache.exe.

Enabling a Database for SQL Cache Invalidation

Before a database table can participate in SQL cache invalidation, both the database and table must be enabled. To enable a database on the same machine:

```
aspnet_regsqlcache.exe -U [user] -P [password] -d [database] -ed
```

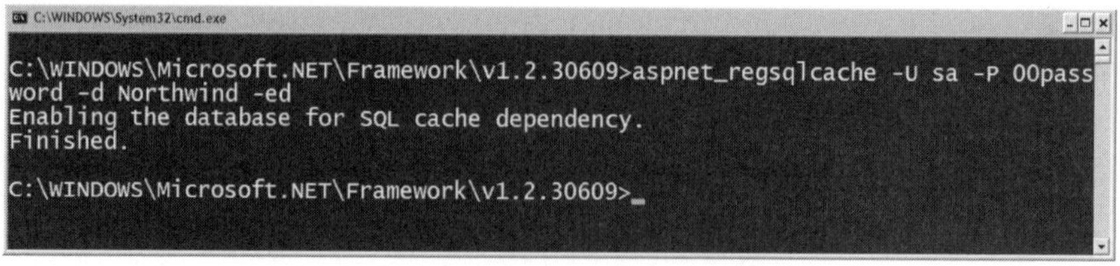

FIGURE 11.2. Enabling a database for SQL cache invalidation

TABLE 11.2. Columns of AspNet_SqlCacheTablesForChangeNotification

Column	Description
tableName	Stores the name of all tables in the current database capable of participating in change notifications.
notificationCreated	Sets the timestamp indicating when the table was enabled for notifications.
changeId	Sets the numeric change ID incremented when a table is changed.

In Figure 11.2 we assume that SQL Server is running on the same machine and we specify a user sa with the password 00password on the Northwind database. This creates a new table named AspNet_SqlCacheTables ForChangeNotification.

This new table contains the columns shown in Table 11.2.

Now that the database is enabled for change notifications, we need to enlist tables that we wish to watch for changes.

Enabling a Table for SQL Cache Invalidation

After we enable the database for change notifications, we need to enlist selected tables for change notifications. For example, if we desire to enable the Customers, Employees, and Products tables in the Northwind database, we execute aspnet_regsqlcache.exe with the following parameters:

```
aspnet_regsqlcache.exe -U [user] -P [password]
                       -d [database] -t [table] -et
```

In Figure 11.3 we enable the Products table in the Northwind database. This creates a trigger Products_AspNet_SqlCacheNotification_Trigger on the Products table and also adds an entry into the AspNet_SqlCache Tables-ForChangeNotification table for the Products table. Whenever data within the

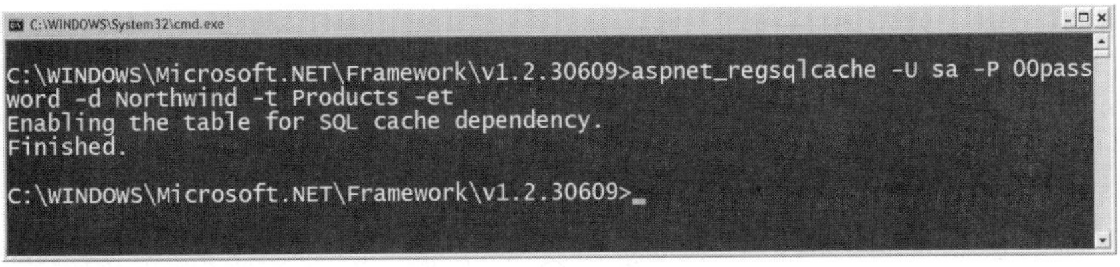

FIGURE 11.3. Enabling a table for SQL cache invalidation

Products table is updated, inserted, or deleted, the trigger causes the changeId value stored in the AspNet_SqlCacheTablesForChangeNotification table to be incremented.

We'll see how this all works in conjunction with ASP.NET shortly. Let's first look at how we list all the tables participating in change notifications for a database.

Listing Tables Enabled for SQL Cache Invalidation

To list tables for a particular database that are enabled for change notifications, use this code:

```
aspnet_regsqlcache.exe -U [user] -P [password] -d [database] -lt
```

In Figure 11.4 we use the -lt flag to retrieve a listing of all the tables in the Northwind database enabled for SQL cache invalidation.

Now that we've enabled the Northwind database and several tables to participate in SQL Server cache invalidation, let's see how we can use this in our ASP.NET application.

Invalidating the ASP.NET Cache

ASP.NET uses polling to retrieve change notifications for Microsoft SQL Server 7 and 2000. This polling occurs on a background thread apart from the threads used to service requests—a request will never be slowed down due to a polling operation. When there are no changes being monitored,

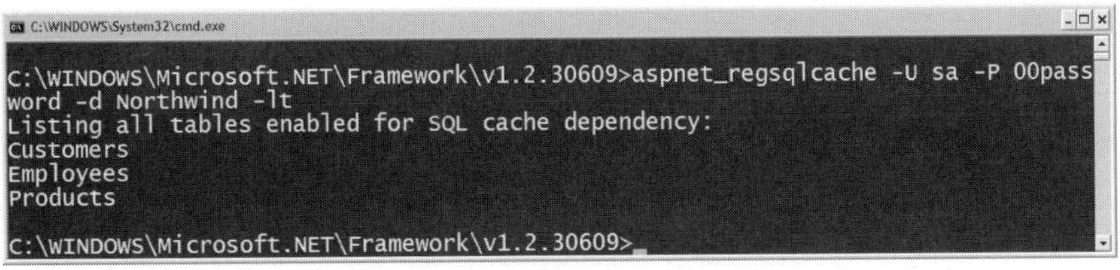

FIGURE 11.4. Listing tables enabled for SQL cache invalidation

the polling is stopped automatically; when a new `SqlCacheDependency` is created, the polling begins again.

Configuration

The poll simply asks SQL for all of the records in the AspNet_SqlCacheTables-ForChangeNotification table. The number of records in this table will not exceed the number of tables in the database. This is a fast operation since there are no joins or other complex SQL operations and the table is very small. The poll time can be configured for each application, but it defaults to once every 5 seconds.

Before we can create a `SqlCacheDependency`, we need to add some entries in the `web.config` file of our application (see Listing 11.2).

LISTING 11.2. SQL Server Cache Dependency Configuration

```
<configuration>
  <connectionStrings>
    <add name="Northwind"
         connectionString="server=localhost;
                           database=Northwind;
                           uid=sa;pwd=00password" />
  </connectionStrings>

  <system.web>
    <cache>
      <sqlCacheDependency enabled="true">
        <add name="Northwind"
             connectionString="Northwind"
             pollTime="500" />
    </cache>
  </system.web>
</configuration>
```

The above configuration file adds an entry for the Northwind database in the `<connectionStrings/>` configuration section. Although not implemented for the Technology Preview release, this configuration section will eventually support encryption to securely store connection string information. The `<cache>` section is a new entry for the `<system.web>` configuration section group. In the Technology Preview release, `<cache>` only supports configuration options for SQL Server change notifications though the `<sql CacheDependency />` section.

The `<sqlCacheDependency />` section contains the elements and attributes shown in Table 11.3.

Now that SQL cache invalidation is configured, we can begin using it in our ASP.NET application.

TABLE 11.3. The <sqlCacheDependency /> Configuration Section

Element	Description
sqlCacheDependency	Contains entries for individual connection strings that can be used for dependencies. This is the root element and allows for two attributes: • enabled: Controls whether or not the feature is enabled or disabled. • pollTime: If specified, sets a default pollTime for all entries added.
add	Adds a named entry for databases that support SQL change notification. The element allows for three attributes: • name: A string name used to identify the SQL database on the page. • connectionString: A reference to the <connectionStrings /> configuration section as to what connection string to use to connect to the database. • pollTime: The time interval between polls made to the database using the connection string to ask for changes.
remove	Removes an inherited entry. For example, if the Northwind entry has already been defined, the <remove/> element could be used to first remove it in a subapplication and then <add/> could be used to redefine it using a different connection string or pollTime. It supports a single attribute: • name: The string name used to identify the entry to remove.

Invalidating Output-Cached Pages

There are two ways you can use SQL Server invalidation within pages: through directives or through the page output-cache APIs. The easiest way is to use the new sqldependency attribute of the <%@ OutputCache %> directive.

The sqldependency attribute accepts two types of values:

1. [name: table]: This value sets the cache entry and table name, where name represents the name of the entry from <sqlCache Dependency /> within the web.config file and table is the name of the table enabled for change notification.

2. CommandNotification: Used only by SQL Server "Yukon," this value instructs the ASP.NET page to make any and all SqlCommand instances needed to notify ASP.NET of changes.

The Syntax for SQL Server 7 and 2000

To use sqldependency for SQL Server 7 or 2000, here's the syntax:

```
<%@ OutputCache duration="9999"
                varybyparam="none"
                sqldependency="Northwind:Products" %>
```

You can also specify multiple dependencies by separating items with a semicolon. For example, if you also want the page dependent on the Pubs Authors table, use this syntax:

```
<%@ OutputCache duration="9999"
                varybyparam="none"
                sqldependency="Northwind:Products;Pubs:Authors" %>
```

The Syntax for SQL Server "Yukon"

To use sqldependency for SQL Server "Yukon," here's the syntax:

```
<%@ OutputCache duration="9999"
                varybyparam="none"
                sqldependency="CommandNotification" %>
```

> **IMPORTANT**
> At the time of this writing, the sqldependency feature works only on Microsoft 2003 Server. Support for Windows Server 2000 will be added in the next Windows Server 2000 Service Pack. The decision about whether to add support for Windows XP Professional has not yet been made.

When the page is created, the page uses the value of the sqldependency attribute as parameters for the constructor of SqlCacheDependency. (We'll look at the SqlCacheDependency class shortly.)

Using Response.Cache API

An alternative to using the <%@ OutputCache %> directive is to use the Response.Cache API and create the SqlCacheDependency ourselves (see Listing 11.3).

LISTING 11.3. Using the Cache API for SQL Server Dependency

```vb
<%@ Page Language="VB" %>
<%@ Import Namespace="System.Data" %>
<%@ Import Namespace="System.Data.SqlClient" %>

<script runat="server">

  Public Sub Page_Load(ByVal sender As Object, ByVal e As EventArgs)

    ' Create the SqlCacheDependency
    '
    Dim dp As New SqlCacheDependency("Northwind", "Products")

    ' Set up page output caching
    '
    Response.Cache.SetExpires(DateTime.Now.AddSeconds(60))
    Response.Cache.SetCacheability(HttpCacheability.Public)
    Response.Cache.SetValidUntilExpires(True)

    ' Make this page dependent on the SqlCacheDependency
    '
    Response.AddCacheDependency(dp)

    Dim connection As New SqlConnection( _
        "server=.; database=Northwind;uid=sa;pwd=00password")
    Dim command As New SqlCommand("SELECT * FROM Products", _
                                  connection)

    connection.Open()

    DataGrid1.DataSource = command.ExecuteReader()
    DataGrid1.DataBind()

    connection.Close()

  End Sub

</script>
<h1>Last update: <%=DateTime.Now.ToString("r")%></h1>
<hr>
<asp:DataGrid runat="server" id="DataGrid1" />
```

Immediately when `SqlCacheDependency` is created, polling begins.

How It Works

On the first poll, the list of notification-enabled tables is returned from the database. This list of tables is used to construct a cache entry for each table returned. Any dependencies requested through `SqlCacheDependency` are then made on this hidden cache entry. Thus, multiple `SqlCacheDependency` instances can be made for the same table, all dependent on one entry in the cache. When the table cache entry changes, it invalidates all dependent cache items.

Below is an example session (which assumes that the Northwind database and Products table are already configured for change notifications).

1. The user creates the page `default.aspx` and instructs the page to output to the cache and be dependent on the Northwind database's Products table.
2. The page is requested.
   a. `SqlCacheDependency` is created and polling begins.
   b. An entry in the cache is created for the Products table (e.g., `Products_Table`) by ASP.NET. This entry stores the `changeId` value returned from the database.
   c. The output-cached page is made dependent on the `Products_Table` cache entry.
3. The page is output cached and subsequent requests draw the page from the cache.
4. A sales manager updates the Products table for a new Web site special sale.
   a. The Northwind Products table changes and the `changeId` for this table is updated in the AspNet_SqlCacheTablesForChangeNotification table.
   b. The next poll by ASP.NET gets the new `changeId` value for the Products table.
   c. The `Products_Table` cache key is updated with the new `changeId` value, causing all dependent cache keys to be invalidated, including the `default.aspx` page.
5. The next request to the ASP.NET application causes the page to reexecute (because it is no longer in the output cache) and get added again.

Let's look at `SqlCacheDependency` in more detail.

The SqlCacheDependency Class

`SqlCacheDependency` is a new class in ASP.NET 2.0. It is found in the `System.Web.Caching` namespace and is used to create cache dependencies on Microsoft SQL Server 7, 2000, and "Yukon" databases.

The class inherits from `CacheDependency`, which has been unsealed for ASP.NET 2.0. Interaction with `SqlCacheDependency` can be achieved only through the two public constructors:

```
SqlCacheDependency (databaseEntry As String, tableName As String)

SqlCacheDependency (sqlCmd As SqlCommand)
```

Creating SQL Server 7 and 2000 Dependencies

The following constructor is used to create database dependencies on Microsoft SQL Server 7 and 2000 databases:

```
SqlCacheDependency (databaseEntry As String, tableName As String)
```

It requires that the `web.config` `<sqlCacheDependency />` section is defined; the *databaseEntry* parameter matches the *name* value added in `<sqlCacheDependency />`. The *tableName* parameter is used to name a table in the database to monitor for changes. The named table must be enabled for change notifications. If the table name contains special characters or spaces, use brackets, as shown below:

```
Dim dp As New SqlCacheDependency("MyDatabase", "[Some Table]")
```

Creating SQL Server "Yukon" Dependencies

The following constructor can be used to create dependencies only for SQL Server "Yukon":

```
SqlCacheDependency (sqlCmd As SqlCommand)
```

Although not discussed in this book, a dependency created on a "Yukon" database requires only the `SqlCommand` used when accessing the database (see Listing 11.4).

LISTING 11.4. Creating a SqlCacheDependency on a "Yukon" Database

```
<%@ Page Language="VB" %>
<%@ Import Namespace="System.Data" %>
<%@ Import Namespace="System.Data.SqlClient" %>

<script runat="server">
```

continues

```vbnet
Public Sub Page_Load(ByVal sender As Object, ByVal e As EventArgs)

    Dim connection As New SqlConnection( _
        "server=.;database=Northwind;uid=sa;pwd=00password")
    Dim command As New SqlCommand("SELECT * FROM Products", _
                                    connection)

    ' Create the SqlCacheDependency on a "Yukon" database
    '
    Dim dp As New SqlCacheDependency(command)

    ' Set up page output caching
    '
    Response.Cache.SetExpires(DateTime.Now.AddSeconds(60))
    Response.Cache.SetCacheability(HttpCacheability.Public)
    Response.Cache.SetValidUntilExpires(True)

    ' Make this page dependent on the SqlCacheDependency
    '
    Response.AddCacheDependency(dp)

    connection.Open()

    DataGrid1.DataSource = command.ExecuteReader()
    DataGrid1.DataBind()

    connection.Close()

End Sub
</script>
<h1>Last update: <%=DateTime.Now.ToString("r")%></h1>
<hr>
<asp:DataGrid runat="server" id="DataGrid1" />
```

As mentioned above, SqlCacheDependency inherits from Cache Dependency, which was a sealed class in ASP.NET 1.0. In ASP.NET 2.0 Microsoft has unsealed CacheDependency, added a default public constructor, and changed some of the internal plumbing of the class so that you can inherit from it and create your own cache dependencies.

Let's take a look at the changes to the CacheDependency class.

The CacheDependency Class

Version 1.0 of ASP.NET introduced the ASP.NET Cache, an application-specific hashtable used to store frequently accessed data. The structure and API of the Cache is very similar to two other structures, Application and Session, insofar as they all support similar APIs. Application is most similar to the Cache because it is global to the application, whereas Session is memory set aside for each user.

The biggest differentiator between Application and Cache is the Cache's support of Cache dependencies. Cache dependencies allow developers to build solutions that can automatically remove cached items from the Cache on the occurrence of certain events. The support events are listed below.

- Time: After a specific duration of time, the item is removed from the Cache. This feature is most evident in the page output caching features of ASP.NET.
- File: If a file or files change, the item is removed from the Cache.
- Key: If another Cache key changes, the item is removed from the Cache.

The above functionality is encapsulated in the CacheDependency class found in the System.Web.Caching namespace.

While these three dependency features address a great number of the needs for most developers, people are constantly requesting the ability to add more. For example, the dependency feature most requested is database dependency—which Microsoft added to ASP.NET 2.0. Another common request is to generalize the CacheDependency class so that anyone can implement a CacheDependency (e.g., a cache dependency that relies on values returned from an XML Web Service).

Microsoft has unsealed the CacheDependency class and has done other work to make it possible for you to extend CacheDependency; in fact, this is just what was done for SqlCacheDependency!

SUMMARY

Although the ASP.NET team hasn't completed all of the feature work for the ASP.NET Cache (at the time of this writing there is yet another coding milestone currently in progress), the features that are available address two of the main requests most customers had: support for database change notifications and the ability to inherit from CacheDependency. The remaining work items will include new APIs for managing partial page caching as well as new configuration for managing the Cache at the application level.

Database cache invalidations are different for Microsoft SQL Server 7 and 2000 versus Microsoft SQL Server "Yukon." Microsoft SQL Server 7 and 2000 support only table-level change notifications. Microsoft SQL Server "Yukon" supports more granular notifications (e.g., the results of a stored procedure).

There are three ways to enable a Microsoft SQL Server 7 or 2000 database for change notifications: the `aspnet_regsqlcache.exe` tool, the `Sql CacheDependencyAdmin` class, or the Web Administration Tool (see Chapter 6). In this chapter we looked at the `aspnet_regsqlcache.exe` tool and learned how to enable the database and tables, as well as return a listing of all tables within a database enabled for change notifications.

Enabling caching in your ASP.NET application is easy. You can either use the new `sqldependency` attribute of the `<%@ OutputCache %>` directive or create an instance of `SqlCacheDependency` directly. Either option will ensure that the page is dependent on the named database and table.

Finally, we learned about the changes to the `CacheDependency` class and how it is now designed so that you can inherit from it and create your own cache dependencies.

In the next chapter, we will look at the ASP.NET server controls, examining the new and changed features.

12

Control Enhancements

T HROUGHOUT THIS BOOK you've seen many examples of the great new
features of ASP.NET 2.0, including some of the new server controls. In
this chapter we are going to focus on server controls, looking at new controls as well as enhancements to existing controls. Some controls, such as
the new data controls, have been covered elsewhere so we won't repeat
that coverage.

We're also going to look at services that support the controls, such as
the Image Generation Service and the Site Counters Service. The former of
these can be accessed directly as well as through a server control, and the
latter is exposed as an API as well as through properties on server controls.

Summary of the New Controls in ASP.NET 2.0

As well as the switch to a unified control architecture, there are other
changes to the range of controls provided with version 2.0 of ASP.NET.
There are changes to many of the existing controls, which we'll examine
later in this chapter, plus a whole range of new controls. We don't have
room in this book to fully detail every control, and it's possible that the interfaces may change as ASP.NET moves from the current Technology Preview to a release version. However, we will discuss and demonstrate the
important features of each control—starting with a summary of all the new
controls.

This section summarizes all the controls that are either completely new or substantially updated. We've divided them into six groups:

- **Standard form- and page-based controls**, such as the bullet list and HTML table controls
- **Rich controls**, such as the `DynamicImage` control and the `Wizard` control
- **Login and authentication controls**, used in conjunction with the ASP.NET authentication and access control features
- **Site navigation controls** and **counters**, such as the tree view and site map controls
- **Data controls** designed to display **relational data, XML data**, and data held in other formats
- **Mobile device controls**, such as the phone call and pagination controls

Standard Form- and Page-Based Controls

Several new controls are "standard" elements for use in a Web page, including some that generate elements for use in a `<form>` section.

- The `BulletedList` control creates either a `<ul>` or `<ol>` bullet list. It exposes properties that allow developers to specify the bullet type and the start number for numeric lists. It inherits from `ListControl`, so its use is familiar—including the ability to populate it using server-side data binding.
- The `FileUpload` control generates an `<input type="file">` element, allowing users to upload files to the server. On postback, it exposes properties that can be used to access the uploaded file stream.
- The `HiddenField` control generates an `<input type="hidden">` element and exposes its value on postback.
- The new `Table` control has a built-in "details view" mode that automatically kicks in when a page containing a table is viewed on a small-screen device such as a cellular phone. There are also new controls to create header rows and footer rows.

We look at these controls in more detail later in this chapter. For the Technology Preview release of ASP.NET this won't be the final story because more controls will be added during the beta phase—but these haven't been written, so we can't cover them yet!

Rich Controls

ASP.NET 1.x contained several rich controls, and these proved to be a big hit with developers. We define a rich control as one that generates multiple different elements, and often client-side code as well, so as to create whole sections of UI or to provide features not supported by ordinary single HTML (or other) elements. A good example is the `Calendar` control, which generates a whole month of clickable dates and has navigation built in to scroll to other months.

In ASP.NET 2.0, there are a few new rich controls included in the Technology Preview of the Framework, and several others are planned for beta releases and the final release. The controls that are implemented now are listed below.

- The `DynamicImage` control automatically translates an image into the correct format for different devices and can stream the bytes for an image from an external source via a `Byte` array.
- The `MultiView` and `View` controls provide the same kind of features as seen in the Internet Explorer Web Controls pack that is available for ASP.NET 1.x. The new controls allow developers to create different blocks of UI and insert the appropriate one into the page at runtime.
- The `Wizard` control, which makes it easier to build multipage wizards that have the same look and feel as those encountered in non-Web applications.

The `Wizard` control was covered in Chapter 9. The other controls listed above will be covered later in this chapter.

Login and Authentication Controls

ASP.NET introduced built-in authentication and access control features as part of the Framework. In ASP.NET 2.0, the way that you interact with the classes exposed by the Framework when creating secured pages or folders is much simpler. Instead of writing code, you can use the new login controls.

- The `Login` control presents the user with the customary Username and Password text boxes.
- The `LoginName` control displays the name of the currently authenticated user.

- The LoginStatus control displays the authentication status for the current user, such as Log In when not authenticated or Log Out when authenticated.
- The LoginView control provides two templates in which the UI for a section of the page is declared. The appropriate template content is displayed, depending on the authentication status of the current user.
- The PasswordRecovery control displays a three-step wizard that guides a user through the process of providing the details required to have a forgotten password sent to him or her.

The login controls were covered in detail in Chapter 6.

Navigation Controls and Counters

One area where there is no real support for developers in ASP.NET 1.x is when building effective navigation systems for a Web site or application. In ASP.NET 2.0, several new controls make it easier to build menus and other types of site navigation UI, as well as adding support for recording the number of times that users click on specific links or visit specific pages. The new or updated controls are listed below.

- The AdRotator control now exposes properties, methods, and events that allow developers to record impressions and click-throughs, display pop-up ads, and provide better interactivity.
- The ImageMap control makes it easier to define client-side image maps and react to events that they raise.
- The SiteMapPath control displays the hierarchical path through the site's menu system to the current page and supports navigation between pages.
- The navigation controls, such as Button, HyperLink, and so on, can be used to record page impressions and user actions.
- The TreeView control generates a collapsible tree view in the browser.

The SiteMapPath and TreeView controls were covered in detail in Chapter 5. The other controls listed above will be covered later in this chapter.

Data Controls

One of the major changes in the way pages that use separate sources of data are created in ASP.NET 2.0 is the provision of **data source controls**.

This concept was originally pioneered in Web Matrix, which contained a simple data source control that makes server-side data binding much easier to achieve.

Web Matrix also included a new type of grid control, designed to make it easier to display the data exposed by a data source control. There are several data source controls included in the Technology Preview version of ASP.NET 2.0, with more on the way for the final release version, plus a great new "grid" control. The controls provided with the Technology Preview version are listed below.

- The `SqlDataSource` control, `AccessDataSource` control, `DbDataSource` control, `OdbcDataSource` control, and `OleDbDataSource` control provide access to various relational databases.
- The `ObjectDataSource` control provides access to strongly typed data layers, as well as object stores such as those exposed by the new version of SQL Server (code-named "Yukon").
- The `XmlDataSource` control uses XML documents and exposes the content as a set of data rows.
- The `GridView` control can display data in a range of ways, including a new built-in details view mode.

The data controls were covered in detail in Chapters 3 and 4.

Mobile Device Controls

Support for different types of client devices is now integrated into the `Page` framework and all the controls from the `System.Web.UI.WebControls` namespace. However, some new controls are primarily aimed at particular types of devices, such as cellular phones.

- The `Pager` control works as part of the underlying page architecture to divide pages into separate sections for small-screen and mobile devices.
- The `PhoneLink` control can be used in phone-enabled devices to initiate a phone call to a specified number.

The mobile device controls were covered in Chapter 10. You'll see that some features of the controls we describe in this chapter are also particularly useful when the client is a small-screen device such as a cellular phone.

The New Form- and Page-Based Controls in ASP.NET 2.0

In this section we examine the new controls that have been added to ASP.NET 2.0 predominantly to implement single elements such as those used for the individual parts of the UI in a Web page.

The BulletedList Control

The `BulletedList` control provides an easy route to creating `<ol>` and `<ul>` lists in a page. Because it inherits from `ListControl`, the contents of the list can be created by using child `ListItem` controls or through data binding. It also adds extra features; for example, you can display each item as a `HyperLink` or a `LinkButton` and then handle the `OnClick` event that the `BulletedList` control exposes to see which item was clicked.

The style of bullet used in the list is specified as the `BulletStyle` property, using values from the `BulletStyle` enumeration. They are pretty much self-explanatory and consist of: `Numbered`, `LowerAlpha`, `UpperAlpha`, `LowerRoman`, `UpperRoman`, `Disc`, `Circle`, `Square`, and `CustomImage`. The default, if not specified, is a decimal numbered list. It is also possible to specify the starting number for the list by setting the `FirstBulletNumber` property. Listing 12.1 shows the simplest form of a declaration of a `Bulleted List` control, followed by one that specifies a numeric list starting at 4.

LISTING 12.1. Using the BulletedList Control

```
<asp:BulletedList id="List1" runat="server">
  <asp:ListItem runat="server">test1</asp:ListItem>
  <asp:ListItem runat="server">test2</asp:ListItem>
  <asp:ListItem runat="server">test3</asp:ListItem>
</asp:BulletedList>

<asp:BulletedList id="List2" BulletSyle="Numbered"
    FirstBulletNumber="4" DisplayMode="Text"
    runat="server">
  <asp:ListItem runat="server">test1</asp:ListItem>
  <asp:ListItem runat="server">test2</asp:ListItem>
  <asp:ListItem runat="server">test3</asp:ListItem>
</asp:BulletedList>
```

The second `BulletedList` control shown in Listing 12.1 also specifies the `DisplayMode` property (attribute), which is a value from the `Bulleted ListDisplayMode` enumeration. The default if not specified is `Text`. The other two options for this property are `HyperLink`, which turns each item in the list into a hyperlink, and `LinkButton`, which renders each item with an attached JavaScript URL that runs client-side code to submit the form (it works just like a standard LinkButton).

Listing 12.2 shows these two options in use. The first sets the bullet style to a square and specifies that the list items should be displayed as hyperlinks. The Value property of the ListItem control is used as the href attribute of the hyperlink. If the Value property is not declared (as in the third item), the Text property is used instead.

LISTING 12.2. A BulletedList Using Hyperlinks

```
<asp:BulletedList id="List3" DisplayMode="HyperLink"
    BulletSyle="Square" runat="server">
  <asp:ListItem Text="test1" runat="server"
              Value="http://www.mypage.aspx" />
  <asp:ListItem Text="test2" runat="server"
              Value="http://otherpage.aspx" />
  <asp:ListItem Text="test3" runat="server" />
</asp:BulletedList>

<asp:BulletedList id="List4" DisplayMode="LinkButton"
    BulletSyle="CustomImage" BulletImageUrl="bullet.gif"
    runat="server">
  <asp:ListItem Text="test1" runat="server" />
  <asp:ListItem Text="test2" runat="server" />
  <asp:ListItem Text="test3" runat="server" />
</asp:BulletedList>
```

The declaration of the fourth BulletedList control in our series of examples (i.e., the second control in Listing 12.2) shows the use of the value CustomImage for the BulletStyle property, with the URL of the image provided in the BulletImageURL property. We've also specified Link Button for the DisplayMode property, so each item will be rendered in the page as a link button (a hyperlink that uses a JavaScript URL to submit the form containing the control).

Data Binding to a BulletedList Control

The BulletedList class exposes the same properties, methods, and events as the ListControl and DataBoundControl classes from which it inherits, so we can use standard data binding techniques, just like we would with a DropDownList or ListBox control. First we declare the BulletedList with no content:

```
<asp:BulletedList id="List2" BulletSyle="Numbered"
    FirstBulletNumber="4" DisplayMode="Text"
    runat="server" />
```

Then we assign a suitable data source to the `DataSource` property of the control at runtime. In Listing 12.3, we use a simple routine that creates a `String` array and assign the array to the `BulletedList` during the `Page_Load` event.

LISTING 12.3. A Data-Bound BulletedList Control

```
Sub Page_Load()
  If Not Page.IsPostback Then
    List2.DataSource = GetListArray()
    Page.DataBind()
  End If
End Sub

Function GetListArray() As String()
  Dim aList(2) As String
  Dim iLoop As Integer
  For iLoop = 1 To 3
    aList(iLoop - 1) = "bound item " & iLoop.ToString()
  Next
  Return aList
End Function
```

Figure 12.1 shows the four instances of the `BulletedList` control we've described so far, with the second one having the literal content replaced by data binding as demonstrated in Listing 12.3. You can see in the first "column" of the figure that the first `BulletedList` control displays a "normal" `<ul>` list, and the second displays a numeric `<ol>` ordered list starting at 4 and containing our data-bound values. The third instance, at

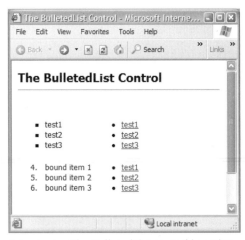

FIGURE 12.1. The BulletedList control in action

the top of the second "column," displays hyperlinks, and the fourth uses link buttons (though these two do, of course, look just the same in the page).

Detecting Which Item Was Clicked in a BulletedList Control

One reason for using `LinkButton` controls in the list is to cause a postback so that you can handle the user's selection (using `Hyperlink` controls means that the user will navigate directly to the page specified in the list). The `OnClick` attribute specifies the event handler that will be executed on a postback.

This event handler accepts a `BulletedListEventArgs` object, which has the single property `Index` containing the index of the item that was clicked. The code shown in Listing 12.4 just displays that index in a `Label` control on the page.

LISTING 12.4. Specifying an OnClick Event Handler

```
<asp:BulletedList id="List4" DisplayMode="LinkButton"
    BulletStyle="CustomImage" BulletImageUrl="bullet.gif"
    OnClick="ShowItem" runat="server">
  <asp:ListItem Text="test1" runat="server" />
  <asp:ListItem Text="test2" runat="server" />
  <asp:ListItem Text="test3" runat="server" />
</asp:BulletedList>

<asp:Label id="lblResult" runat="server" />

<script runat="server">
Sub ShowItem(Sender As Object, E As BulletedListEventArgs)
  lblResult.Text = "Selected item index is: " & E.Index
End Sub
</script>
```

The FileUpload Control

Uploading files to the server in ASP.NET 1.x is accomplished by using the `HtmlInputFile` control from the `HtmlControls` namespace, as `<input type="file" runat="server">`. In ASP.NET 2.0, there is a new `File Upload` control that considerably simplifies the work required to upload files. It exposes properties that provide a reference to the uploaded (or "posted" file) and details about the file.

The `FileUpload` control must be placed on a server-side form, though there is no need to specify the `enctype` attribute for the form, as you previously had to do with the `HtmlInputFile` control. When ASP.NET 2.0 detects that a form contains a `FileUpload` control, it automatically adds the attribute `enctype="multipart/form-data"` to the form. Listing 12.5 shows how easy it is to declare the control, together with the `Alternate Text` that will be displayed if the current client's browser doesn't support file uploads.

LISTING 12.5. Using the FileUpload Control

```
<form runat="server">
<asp:FileUpload id="MyFile" runat="server"
    AlternateText="Sorry, cannot upload files" /><p/>
<asp:Button id="btnUpload" Text="Go" runat="server"
         OnClick="GetFile" /><p />
<asp:Label id="lblResult" runat="server" />
</form>
```

We've included a `Button` control to start the upload and a `Label` control that will display the results of the process. The `Button` control generates an HTML submit button, and this will cause the file that the user chooses in the `FileUpload` control to be posted to the server. However, the `OnClick` attribute of the button will also cause the event handler named `GetFile` to run when the postback occurs. The code in this event handler is responsible for collecting the file from the request and storing it on disk (see Listing 12.6).

LISTING 12.6. Processing the Uploaded File

```
Sub GetFile(Sender As Object, E As EventArgs)

  ' first see if a file was posted to the server
  If MyFile.HasFile Then
    Try

      ' display just the filename
      lblResult.Text = "Uploading '" & _
                  MyFile.FileName & "'...<br />"

      ' save to disk with specified path
      ' and existing filename
      MyFile.SaveAs("D:\Temp\" & MyFile.FileName)

      ' display results
      ' - FileName of PostedFile contains the full
      ' - path entered into the
      ' - FileUpload control textbox by the user
      lblResult.Text &= "Received '" _
          & MyFile.PostedFile.FileName _
          & "Type: " _
          & MyFile.PostedFile.ContentType _
```

```
            & "Length: " _
            & MyFile.PostedFile.ContentLength.ToString() _
            & " bytes"
      Catch
        lblResult.Text &= "Cannot save uploaded file"
      End Try
    Else
      lblResult.Text &= "No file received"
    End If

End Sub
```

Figure 12.2 shows the results. You can see from the preceding code that the file was uploaded and stored in `D:\Temp` on the server. Note that a full path for the saved file must be used, otherwise an exception occurs.

> The maximum size of a file that can be uploaded is governed by the `maxRequestLength` value in the `<httpRuntime>` section of `machine.config`. The default is 4096K. You can change it in `machine.config` to a larger or smaller value, or you can do the same in the `web.config` file for your application.

The HiddenField Control

Hidden-type `<input>` elements are useful for storing values in a Web page, especially where you don't want to rely on using ASP.NET sessions.

FIGURE 12.2. The FileUpload control in action

In ASP.NET 1.x, the only way to generate a hidden control is by using the `HtmlInputHidden` control from the `HtmlControls` namespace, as `<input type="hidden" runat="server">`. In ASP.NET 2.0, the new `HiddenField` control can be used instead.

One nice feature of this control is the ability to detect changes to the value after a postback. This is useful if the page uses hidden controls to submit values to the server because the `OnValueChanged` event of the `HiddenField` control is raised on the server after a postback only when the value currently in the control is different from that when the page was sent to the client.

Listings 12.7 through 12.9 demonstrate this. The server-side form contains a `HiddenField` control, together with two buttons. The first is a simple HTML button that only runs a client-side script function named `ChangeValue`. The other is an ASP.NET `Button` control that submits the form to the server. Finally, there is a `Label` control to display the results.

LISTING 12.7. Declaring the HiddenField Control

```
<form runat="server">
  <asp:HiddenField id="MyField" Value="some value"
      OnValueChanged="ShowValue" runat="server" /><p/>
  <input type="button" Value="Change value"
      onclick="ChangeValue()">
  <asp:Button Text="Submit" runat="server" /><p />
  <asp:Label id="lblResult"
      Text="Field contains: 'some value'" runat="server" />
</form>
```

The client-side script function is listed next (see Listing 12.8). All it does is change the value in the first control on the first `<form>` of the page to include the current date and time, then display a confirmation message.

LISTING 12.8. Accessing the HiddenField Content in Client Script

```
<script language="JavaScript">
// NB: this is client-side script
function ChangeValue() {
  var ctrl = document.forms[0].elements['MyField'];
  ctrl.value = 'Whoops, I changed it on ' + Date() + '!';
  alert('OK, I changed it');
}
</script>
```

The server-side code that runs when the Submit button is clicked is even simpler (see Listing 12.9). It just displays the value of the `HiddenField` control in the `Label` control on the page. `Value` is the only property exposed by the `HiddenField` control in the Technology Preview version of ASP.NET 2.0.

LISTING 12.9. Accessing the HiddenField Content in Server Script

```
Sub ShowValue(oSender As Object, oArgs As EventArgs)
  lblResult.Text = "New value is '" & MyField.Value & "'"
End Sub
```

Figure 12.3 shows the result. Clicking the Change value button updates the `HiddenField`, and then the Submit button posts the form containing the control to the server. If the value has been changed, the `ValueChanged` event is raised and the new value is displayed.

The Table Control

ASP.NET 2.0 automatically adapts the output it generates to suit different types of clients, as we saw in Chapter 10. One specific issue is with devices that have only limited screen real estate available—cellular phones are a prime example. If you want to display a table but the page may be delivered to a small-screen device, it's likely that device will not be able to display the information in any meaningful way.

The ideal approach for a small-screen device is to break up the table into individual rows and display these separately. But for the user to be

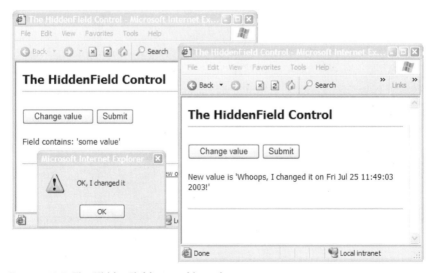

FIGURE 12.3. The HiddenField control in action

able to grasp the whole picture, he or she needs to see how many rows there are and look at each one individually or choose one from the table. Conversely, in a normal Web browser, the user generally wants to see the whole table.

Three Views of the Content

To meet these requirements, the Table control automatically provides three views of the data in a table. For normal Web browsers, it outputs a standard HTML table. By taking advantage of the new header and footer rows features, you can generate a table that contains `<th>` elements as well as the usual `<td>` elements (see Figure 12.4).

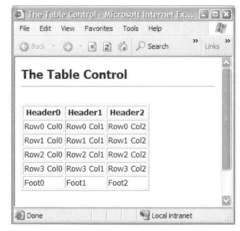

FIGURE 12.4. The Table control from a Windows browser

However, the same page viewed in a cellular phone contains a table with the same number of rows but only one column. This view is called **summary view**, and the column shown is the **summary column**. Notice that each row (except for the header and footer) is a link that can be followed (see Figure 12.5).

Activating the link for any of the rows switches the page to **details view**. In this view, all the columns for the selected row are displayed (see Figure 12.6). At the bottom of the page are links that allow the user to go back to summary view or move to the next or previous row. So the user can easily browse the table, and the developer didn't have to do anything to make all this happen!

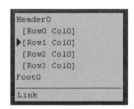

FIGURE 12.5. The Table control from a phone browser

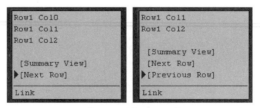

FIGURE 12.6. Paging a Table control

The Code to Build the Table

The page you've been looking at contains four rows of three columns, with each cell containing the row and column number so that you can see what's happening. The `Table` control itself is declared in the page, but with no rows defined. (Note that it has to be located on a server-side form.)

```
<form runat="server">
<asp:Table id="MyTable" GridLines="Both" runat="server" />
</form>
```

The page also contains a subroutine named `CreateTable` that dynamically builds the rows for the table and adds them to the `Table` control (see Listing 12.10). The technique is the same as that used with the ASP.NET 1.x `Table` control, but here we're taking advantage of the new `TableHeaderRow` and `TableFooterRow` controls to create the header and footer rows.

LISTING 12.10. Creating a Table Control Dynamically

```
Sub CreateTable()
  Dim Rows As Integer = 4
  Dim Cols As Integer = 3
  Dim RowCount, ColCount As Integer
  Dim Row As TableRow
  Dim Cell As TableCell

  ' header row
  Row = New TableHeaderRow()
  For ColCount = 0 To Cols - 1
    Cell = New TableHeaderCell()
    Cell.Controls.Add( _
          New LiteralControl("Header" & ColCount))
    Row.Cells.Add(Cell)
  Next
  MyTable.Rows.Add(Row)

  ' data rows
  For RowCount = 0 To Rows - 1
    Row = New TableRow()
    For ColCount = 0 To Cols - 1
      Cell = New TableCell()
      Cell.Controls.Add( _
            New LiteralControl("Row" _
            & RowCount & " Col" & ColCount))
      oRow.Cells.Add(Cell)
    Next
    MyTable.Rows.Add(Row)
  Next
```

```
' footer row
Row = New TableFooterRow()
For ColCount = 0 To Cols - 1
  Cell = New TableCell()
  Cell.Controls.Add( _
        New LiteralControl("Foot" & ColCount))
  oRow.Cells.Add(Cell)
Next
MyTable.Rows.Add(Row)
End Sub
```

Then, in the `Page_Load` event, we can call this routine when the page loads each time:

```
Sub Page_Load()
  CreateTable()
End Sub
```

This is all that's required. Of course, we could simply declare each row of the table using the usual <tr>, <th>, and <td> elements, without building it at runtime using code. However, in that case, the header and footer rows will be treated as "ordinary rows" and will be selectable in summary view.

Programmatically Selecting the View Mode and Row

When the `Table` control is serving content to a small-screen device, the view mode can be selected by using the `ViewMode` property (the options from the `TableViewMode` enumeration are `Details` and `Summary`) or by adding the `ViewMode` attribute to the declaration of the `Table` control (see Listing 12.11). And when the table is in `details` mode, the current row (the row actually being displayed) can be specified by using the `Current Row` property. Of course, you probably want to do this only when the page is first loaded, and not on a postback, or the user will not be able to browse from row to row and switch from one mode to the other.

LISTING 12.11. Setting the ViewMode of a Table Control

```
Sub Page_Load()
  CreateTable()
  If Not Page.IsPostback Then
    MyTable.ViewMode = TableViewMode.Details
    MyTable.CurrentRow = 1
  End If
End Sub
```

By default, the column displayed in summary view mode is the one at index `0` (the first column). However, you can change this by specifying the index of any other column in the table for the `SummaryViewColumnIndex` property or by adding the attribute `SummaryViewColumnIndex="index"` to the declaration of the `Table` control. And if the table has more than one header row, you can specify which one is used in details view mode with the `DetailsHeaderRowIndex` property.

You can also change the text displayed for the links below the row details in details view mode by setting the `DetailNextRowText`, `DetailPrev RowText`, and `DetailSummaryRowText` properties or attributes to the `String` values you require. And there are "style" properties for each section of the table in both view modes as well.

Finally, it's also possible to specify extra information for the table as a whole in the `Summary` property and for each details view in the `Detail SummaryText` property for each cell. (Some specialist user agents and aural page readers will use these values when they cannot display the table.)

The DynamicImage Control

We've just seen how the `Table` control in ASP.NET 2.0 automatically adapts its output to better suit the limited screen space available on some devices, in particular cellular phones. However, another issue arises with these kinds of devices in that many don't recognize the common image types used in HTML, such as the `.gif`, `.png`, and `.jpg` formats. To get around this problem, you can use a new control named `DynamicImage`.

The `DynamicImage` control uses the Image Generation Service, accessed via a special `.axd` HTTP handler, to dynamically generate a suitable stream of bytes for the image, rather than the more usual technique of specifying a file on the server as the `src` attribute of an `<img>` element. By providing the correct MIME type when it responds to the request for the image stream, the `DynamicImage` control ensures that the client can display the image just as it would an image file from disk.

The `DynamicImage` control can also accept as its image source an array of bytes that represents the image or a reference to an `ImageGenerator` service that "contains" an image that has been created using drawing commands. You can create classes that inherit from `ImageGenerator` and that create an image, then use these as the input to the `DynamicImage` control.

To demonstrate the basic uses of the `DynamicImage` control, the following code declares two instances of the control. The first (see Listing 12.12) simply uses a disk file named `car.gif`, specifying that it is an image file on disk in the `DynamicImageType` property (attribute). The second of the control instances specifies `ImageBytes` for the `DynamicImageType` property, so the control will expect to receive a reference to a `Byte` array containing the data for the image.

LISTING 12.12. Declaring the DynamicImage Control

```
<form runat="server">

<asp:DynamicImage DynamicImageType="ImageFile"
                  ImageFile="car.gif" runat="server" />

<asp:DynamicImage DynamicImageType="ImageBytes"
                  id="MyImage" runat="server" />

</form>
```

This image data is generated in code and then assigned to the `Image Bytes` property at runtime. Listing 12.13 shows the code we used.

LISTING 12.13. Streaming Content into the DynamicImage Control

```
Sub Page_Load()

  Dim Stream = New FileStream("c:\temp\car.gif", _
               FileMode.Open, _
               FileAccess.Read)
  Dim MyArray(oStream.Length - 1) As Byte
  Stream.Read(MyArray, 0, Stream.Length)
  Stream.Close
  MyImage.ImageBytes = MyArray

End Sub
```

You can see that we are simply opening the image file on disk and reading it into the array as a stream. Of course, you would probably store the image data in a database instead and stream it from there into an array. The final line of code in the `Page_Load` event handler shown in Listing 12.13 then assigns the array to the `ImageBytes` property of the `Dynamic Image` control. Figure 12.7 shows the output generated by these two `DynamicImage` controls.

The `DynamicImage` control can also be used to convert images between different types. For example, consider the following:

FIGURE 12.7. The DynamicImage control from a Windows browser

```
<asp:DynamicImage runat="server"
    imageType="Jpeg"
    imageFile="logo.gif" />
```

This converts `logo.gif` into a JPEG file.

Automatic Translation of Images for Other Devices

When a `DynamicImage` control is used in a page that is being served to a non-HTML device, such as a cellular phone, the Image Generation Service that is generating the image automatically converts the image into the correct representation for the device where possible. Opening a page that contains just the first instance of the `DynamicImage` control shown in Listing 12.12 results in the following output being sent to the client in response to the GET request for the image:

```
HTTP GET Request:
HTTP://LOCALHOST/aspnet20/ch03/CachedImageService.axd?data=07c
e61a2-b688-436a-9cb1-c94f91d582e4
---------------- DATA SIZE ----------------------
Uncompiled data from HTTP is 1373 bytes.
...found Content-Type: image/vnd.wap.wbmp.
Compiled WAP binary is 1458 bytes.
-------------------------------------------------
Measured image is 150 x 72
```

You can see that now it appears as a .wbmp file, with the content type image/vnd.wap.wbmp, and it looks like Figure 12.8.

The Image Generation Service

ASP.NET 2.0 introduces several new extensions for file types, such as themes, skins, and masters, and although these are part of the page architecture, they aren't ASP.NET pages themselves. The Image

FIGURE 12.8. The DynamicImage control from a phone browser

Generation Service, however, introduces a new type (.ASIX) to ease the dynamic creation of images. It was possible to create images dynamically in ASP.NET 1.x, but there was no standard way to do it—you invariably used an ASP.NET page or a Web Service, created the image, and then saved it to the output stream.

With ASP.NET 2.0 there is a base control, ImageGenerator, that provides much of this default behavior. All you need to do is inherit from this control and then perform the actual drawing. For example, Listing 12.14 shows how an .ASIX file could be used.

LISTING 12.14. Using the ImageGenerator Control

```vb
<%@ Image Class="Test" Language="VB" %>

Imports System

Public Class Test
  Inherits System.Web.UI.Image.ImageGenerator

    Protected Overrides Sub RenderImage(g As Graphics)

      g.FillRectangle(Brushes.Black, g.ClipBounds)

      Dim f As New Font("Ariel", 22)

      g.DrawString("Welcome", f, _
        Brushes.White, 0, 0)
      g.DrawString("to our site", f, _
        Brushes.White, 10, 30)

    End Sub
End Class
```

This simply draws a rectangle and then two lines of text, resulting in the image shown in Figure 12.9.

FIGURE 12.9. The ImageGenerator control in action

The beauty of this method of image creation is its simplicity—all you have to do is concentrate on creating the image itself, letting the Framework handle how it is to be rendered to the browser.

Image Generation Service Configuration

The Image Generation Service can be configured by modifying the image Generation section in web.config or machine.config. The syntax is shown below:

```
<system.web>
    <imageGeneration
        storageType="[Cache|Disk]"
        storageExpiration="[number]"
        storagePath="[string]" />
</system.web>
```

The attributes are detailed in Table 12.1.

TABLE 12.1. Image Generation Configuration Attributes

Attribute	Description
storageType	Determines where the images will be stored. The default is Cache.
storageExpiration	Sets the number of seconds until the image expires. The default is 300.
storagePath	Indicates the location for images if Disk storage is used. An empty string (the default) will cause an exception if storageType is Disk.

The MultiView and View Controls

If you installed and played with the Internet Explorer Web Controls pack in ASP.NET 1.x, you were probably impressed with the way you can easily create quite complex effects that are common in executable applications in a Web page. One of the many useful controls in the Internet Explorer Web Controls pack is the MultiView control. This control allows you to declare several "screens" or "views," which are each separate sections of the UI for a page, and then display any one of them in the page on demand.

However, while the Internet Explorer Web Controls version can take advantage of some clever client-side code to provide these features in Internet Explorer without requiring a postback, the MultiView control in ASP.NET 2.0 works only with a postback to the server every time you want to change the screen or view displayed.

To declare a MultiView control and its content, you use the ASP.NET MultiView as the container and then place within it one or more View controls. Listing 12.15 shows a simple MultiView declaration containing two View controls. Each View contains just a Label control and a Button control.

LISTING 12.15. Declaring the MultiView Control

```
<asp:MultiView id="MyMulti"
    ActiveViewIndex="0" runat="server">

  <asp:View id="View1">
    <asp:Label id="lblView1"
        Text="This is View 1" runat="server" /><p />
    <asp:Button id="btnView1" Text="Next"
        OnClick="ShowNext" runat="server" />
    </asp:View>

  <asp:View id="View2">
    <asp:Label id="lblView2" Text="This is View 2"
      runat="server" /><p />
    <asp:Button id="btnView2" Text="Previous"
      OnClick="ShowPrev" runat="server" />
  </asp:View>

</asp:MultiView><p />
```

The MultiView control chooses which View to display based on the value of the ActiveViewIndex property (indexed from 0). By default this property is set to -1 (no View is shown), so when the page loads for the first time we specify that the first of the View controls should be displayed by setting the `ActiveViewIndex` attribute to `0`. We could alternatively set it in code in a `Page_Load` event handler.

In the `View` controls, the two buttons named `ShowNext` (in the first view) and `ShowPrev` (in the second view) execute event handlers when clicked. We've also included a `Button` and a `Label` control on this page, but outside the `MultiView` control.

```
<asp:Button id="btnSetView2" Text="Go to View 2"
            OnClick="ShowView2" runat="server" /><p />
<asp:Label id="lblStatus" runat="server" />
```

This `Button` control executes an event handler named `ShowView2`, which switches the `MultiView` control to display the second view (indexed 1), and the `Label` control is used to display the current value of the `Active ViewIndex` property. The code to implement these three event handlers appears in Listing 12.16.

LISTING 12.16. Moving between the Views

```
Sub ShowNext(oSender As Object, oArgs As EventArgs)
  MyMulti.ActiveViewIndex += 1
  lblStatus.Text = "ActiveViewIndex = " _
          & MyMulti.ActiveViewIndex
End Sub

Sub ShowPrev(oSender As Object, oArgs As EventArgs)
  MyMulti.ActiveViewIndex -= 1
  lblStatus.Text = "ActiveViewIndex = " _
          & MyMulti.ActiveViewIndex
End Sub

Sub ShowView2(oSender As Object, oArgs As EventArgs)
  MyMulti.ActiveViewIndex = 1
  lblStatus.Text = "ActiveViewIndex = " _
          & MyMulti.ActiveViewIndex
End Sub
```

You can see that all these event handlers do is set the `ActiveViewIndex` property to the appropriate value and then display this value in the `Label` control. Figure 12.10 shows the results.

Navigating Using Query String Values

As well as setting the `ActiveViewIndex` property directly, you can have this automatically set from a query string value (see Listing 12.17).

FIGURE 12.10. The MultiView control in action

LISTING 12.17. Setting the ActiveViewIndex from a QueryString

```
<asp:MultiView id="MyMulti" runat="server"
    QueryStringParam="view">

  <asp:View id="View1">
    ...
  </asp:View>

  <asp:View id="View2">
    ...
  </asp:View>

</asp:MultiView>
```

Now the current view will be changed depending on the value of the View control's query string parameter. For example:

```
http://www.somesite.com/default.aspx?view=View1
```

Navigating Views Using Commands

Navigation can also be automatic from controls that support the Command Name and CommandArgument properties, such as the Button and Link Button controls. When these properties are set on controls within the MultiView, switching views will automatically take place depending on the property values.

For example, consider the code in Listing 12.18.

LISTING 12.18. Using Commands to Navigate through a MultiView Control

```
<asp:MultiView id="MyMulti" runat="server"

  <asp:View id="View1">
```

```
    <asp:Button Text="Next" runat="server"
        CommandName="NextView" />
    <asp:Button Text="Go to 2" runat="server"
        CommandName="SwitchViewByID"
        CommandArgument="View2" />
  </asp:View>

  <asp:View id="View2">
    <asp:Button Text="Prev" runat="server"
        CommandName="PrevView" />
    <asp:Button Text="Go to 1" runat="server"
        CommandName="SwitchViewByIndex"
        CommandArgument="0" />
  </asp:View>

</asp:MultiView>
```

When CommandName is NextView or PrevView, the active View is auto-matically switched when the button is clicked. If CommandName is Switch ViewByID, the CommandArgument should contain the ID of the View to switch to, which happens automatically when the button is clicked. With CommandName set to SwitchViewByIndex, the CommandArgument should be the index number (zero-based) of the View to switch to.

The CommandName values can be changed by changing the values de-fined by four static fields of the MultiView (see Table 12.2).

Table 12.2. MultiView CommandName Properties

Field	Description
NextViewCommandName	A string containing the name of the command that moves to the next View. The default value is NextView.
PrevViewCommandName	A string containing the name of the command that moves to the previous View. The default value is PrevView.
SwitchViewByIDCommandName	A string containing the name of the command that moves to the View whose ID is given in the CommandArgument property. The default value is SwitchViewByID.
SwitchViewByIndexCommandName	A string containing the name of the command that moves to the View whose index is given in the CommandArgument property. The default value is SwitchViewByIndex.

Obviously you can include a lot more views or screens in a `MultiView` than we've shown in the preceding samples, and the handy thing is that all the controls declared in all the views are available to your server-side code, even when not included in the output sent to the client. They all maintain their values using the viewstate of the page, so it's easy to build tabbed dialogs or wizard-style pages using this control. (However, if you really want to build wizards for your Web applications, the `Wizard` control makes it even easier.)

Other features implemented in the `MultiView` for the Technology Preview release (there are more coming up for the final release) extend the ways you can use the `MultiView`. The `View` controls declared within the `MultiView` are exposed through the `Views` property, which is a reference to a `ViewCollection`. Each member of the collection is a `View`, and the collection has the `Add(view As Control)` and `AddAt(index As Integer, view As Control)` methods so that you can change the views available at runtime. And there is also an `ActiveViewChanged` event for the `MultiView` control that can be handled by specifying an event handler for the `OnActiveViewChanged` property or attribute.

The ImageMap Control

The `ImageMap` control provides a server implementation of the HTML `MAP` element, allowing sections of images to be used as clickable hot spots. There are three hot spot types:

- `RectangleHotSpot`, to define the bounds of a rectangular portion of the image
- `CircleHotSpot`, to define the bounds of a circular portion of the image
- `PolygonHotSpot`, to define the bounds of an irregular portion of the image

The syntax for the `ImageMap` control is shown below:

```
<asp:ImageMap id="String" runat="server"
  HotSpotMode="[Navigate|Postback]"
  ImageUrl="String"
  />
```

The properties are described in Table 12.3.

Table 12.3. ImageMap Properties

Property/Attribute	Description
HotSpotMode	Sets or returns the mode in which hot spots work. This can be one of the HotSpotMode enumerations: • Navigation: Indicates that navigation takes place when the hot spot is clicked. In this mode the Value property of the hot spot should contain the Url of the target navigation. • Postback: Indicates that postback should take place when the hot spot is clicked. In this mode the contents of the hot spot's Value property are passed into the server-side event handler.
HotSpots	Returns a HotSpotCollection containing all defined hot spot regions.
ImageUrl	Sets or returns the Url to the image.
SiteCounterProvider	Indicates the site counter provider to use.

In addition to these properties, the ImageMap control implements the Site Counters Service and therefore supports the following properties:

- CountClicks
- CountGroup
- CounterName
- RowsPerDay
- TrackApplicationName
- TrackNavigateUrl
- TrackPageUrl

Specifying Hot Spots

On its own the ImageMap control isn't much use because you need to specify the areas within the image that will act as hot spots, as well as what happens when those regions are clicked. For example, consider the page shown in Figure 12.11, which has two rectangular hot spot regions and one circular region. The code to implement this appears in Listing 12.19.

FIGURE 12.11. Sample ImageMap Control

LISTING 12.19. Declaring the ImageMap Control

```
<asp:ImageMap id="YesNoMaybe" runat="server"
  ImageUrl="YesNoMaybe.jpg" onClick="ImageClicked">
  <asp:RectangleHotSpot
          Top="3" Left="3"
          Right="68" Bottom ="68"
          HotSpotMode="Postback"
          Value="Yes"
          AlternateText="Yes, I love ASP.NET" />

  <asp:RectangleHotSpot
          Top="3" Left="86"
          Right="149" Bottom ="68"
          HotSpotMode="Postback"
          Value="No"
          AlternateText="No, I don't love ASP.NET" />

  <asp:CircleHotSpot
          x="78" y="104"
          Radius="22"
          HotSpotMode="Navigate"
          Value="http://www.asp.net/"
          AlternateText="I don't know" />
</asp:ImageMap>
```

The `RectangleHotSpot` has four properties to define its region—`Top`, `Left`, `Right`, and `Bottom`—which contain pixel values. The `CircleHot Spot` has three properties—`x` and `y` to define the center point and `Radius` to define the circle radius. Both types of controls have an `AlternateText` property, for the tooltip text, as well as `HotSpotMode` and `Value` properties to define what action is to be taken when the image region is clicked. If the `HotSpotMode` is `Navigate`, the `Value` is used as the URL to navigate to; if it is `Postback`, the `Value` is passed into the event procedure defined by the `onClick` property of the `ImageMap`. The event procedure could look something like Listing 12.20.

LISTING 12.20. Implementing the onClick Event Handler

```
Sub ImageClicked(Sender As Object, E As ImageMapEventArgs)

  Select Case E.Value
  Case "Yes"
    ' take some action

  Case "No"
    ' take some action
  End Select

End Sub
```

Irregular Hot Spots

Irregular hot spots are enabled by a `PolygonHotSpot` control that defines a series of x- and y-coordinates that define the bounds of the image region. For example, consider a map of the United Kingdom, perhaps used to pick sales regions, as shown in Figure 12.12. To set hot spots for the regions, we would use code like Listing 12.21.

FIGURE 12.12. ImageMap of the United Kingdom

LISTING 12.21. Defining Irregular Hot Spots

```
<asp:ImageMap id="UKMap" runat="server"
    HotSpotMode="Postback"
    ImageUrl="UKMap.jpg" onClick="MapClicked">
  <asp:PolygonHotSpot
      Coordinates="205,17,328,38,346,99,200,160,270,132"
      Value="North Scotland"/>
  <asp:PolygonHotSpot
      Coordinates="209,166,225,224,339,200,335,112"
      Value="South Scotland"/>
  <asp:CircleHotSpot  x="411" y="452" radius="11"
      Value="London"/>
  ...
</asp:ImageMap>
```

There is no real limit to the number of coordinates you put in—more of them leads to a finer-grained and smoother polygon but is more time consuming to type. In reality you don't have to be 100% accurate to the area you are defining because users tend to click near the middle of a region anyway.

Changes to the Existing ASP.NET Controls

The unified control architecture implemented in ASP.NET 2.0 means that all the controls in the System.Web.UI.WebControls namespace have changed in order to take advantage of control adapters and the new architecture. The good news is that, to maintain backward compatibility with existing code (and to make it easier for developers to move to ASP.NET 2.0), almost all of the controls expose the same interfaces as before, so they are declared and programmed against in just the same way as in ASP.NET 1.x.

However, several of the controls have also changed in other minor ways, allowing them to integrate with new features in other controls (such as the new validation groups feature and page/site counters) or simply to fill in the "gaps" left when they were first implemented in version 1.0. The controls we'll be covering here are listed below.

- The Button, LinkButton, and ImageButton controls can now be used to raise client-side events as well as server-side events. They also integrate with site and page counters.
- The Hyperlink control now integrates with site and page counters.
- The Image control now has the facility to include the longdesc attribute, giving better accessibility to all users.

- The Label control can now be attached to another control so as to redirect client-side UI hot-key presses to that control.

- The ListItem control now allows individual items in the list to be enabled or disabled on demand.

- The Literal control now allows developers to specify how the content should be translated or encoded (in markup terms) before being sent to the client.

- The Panel control can display scroll bars if it is defined with a fixed size and the content is too large for the available space. It can also now display content from left to right or from right to left.

- The AdRotator control can now take data from non-XML data sources and includes support for the Site Counters Service

Changes to the Button, LinkButton, and ImageButton Controls

One issue discovered with the WebForms button-type controls in ASP.NET 1.x was how to arrange for the button to raise a client-side event as well as a server-side event. It's often useful to be able to run some client-side script when a button is clicked, before the page is submitted to the server. There is a workaround, of course, involving adding the OnClick attribute to the control at runtime using the Attributes collection. However, now you can simply set the OnClientClick property to the name of your client-side script function or specify it as the OnClientClick attribute when declaring your control:

```
<asp:Button Text="Click Me" OnClick="MyServerSideCode" runat="server"
            OnClientClick="MyClientSideFunction()"/>
```

The same approach works for the LinkButton and ImageButton controls.

The SoftKeyLabel Property

As we described in more detail in Chapter 10, several button-type controls now carry the SoftKeyLabel property. This includes the Button, Link Button, ImageButton, and PhoneLink controls. When the page is sent to a mobile device, the string specified for this property can (depending on the device) be displayed next to one of the "one-touch" buttons on the device. This property is usually implemented in devices such as cellular phones, where there is only limited input capability (basically a number keypad and a few soft-key buttons).

Support for Site and Page Counters

The three button-type controls are often used to process actions or navigate to other pages in situations where you want to track the movements of visitors. The site and page counters feature of ASP.NET is ideal for this, and the button-type controls (as well as the `Hyperlink` control) have properties you can use to integrate them with this feature. These are described in the Site and Page Counters section later in the chapter

Changes to the Hyperlink Control

The `Hyperlink` control now exposes a `SoftKeyLabel` property, as described earlier for the three button-type controls. It also supports integration with site and page counters, again as described earlier for the button-type controls. However, because a hyperlink element causes a client-side action to take place (through the `href` value set by the `NavigateUrl` property), there is an extra property for the `Hyperlink` control named `TrackNavigateUrl`, which is described in the Site and Page Counters section later in the chapter.

Changes to the Image Control

HTML 4.0 and higher specify an attribute named `longdesc` for the `<img>` element. This attribute is useful where the user might not be able to view the image for a variety of reasons (e.g., he or she may be using a text-only browser or one specially designed for blind or partly sighted users). The new `String` property named `DescriptionUrl` can be set to the URL of a page that contains a text or aural description of the image. Specialist browsers and user agents should provide the user with the opportunity to retrieve this page instead of the image file.

Changes to the Label Control

One useful capability of HTML 4.0 and higher, when building pages that use the various interactive form controls (such as lists, buttons, checkboxes, and text boxes), is to associate a text label with a control. In most modern browsers, including Internet Explorer, you can define a "hot key" for the control and then display this hot key in the associated label to make the form more like a traditional Windows executable application.

In ASP.NET 2.0, the `Label` control gains a new property named `AssociatedControlID`. You set it to a `String` value that is the `ID` of the interactive control you want to associate the `Label` control with and then set the `AccessKey` property for the label to the key you want to act as the hot key. You can also indicate this key to the user by underlining it in the `Label` text:

```
<asp:Label id="MyLabel" Text="<u>N</u>ame" runat="server"
        AccessKey="N" AssociatedControlID="MyTextBox" />
<asp:TextBox id="MyTextBox" runat="server" />
```

Now, when the hot-key combination *ALT + N* is pressed, the focus moves to the `Textbox` control automatically (see Figure 12.13). However, remember you cannot use keys that are already defined for the various UI features of the browser. For example, *ALT + T* cannot be used in Internet Explorer because it activates the Tools menu.

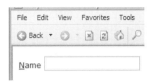

FIGURE 12.13. Using access keys

Changes to the ListItem Control

Ever since version 4.0 of Internet Explorer, it's been possible to disable controls in a page in that browser by setting their client-side `disabled` attribute, for example:

```
<input type="text" disabled="disabled" />
```

In ASP.NET, you achieve the same effect by setting the `Enabled` property to `False` on the server, either in code or by adding the `Enabled="False"` attribute to the control declaration. However, for list controls such as a `ListBox` or `DropDownList`, you can only enable or disable the complete control, not specific items within the list. Most browsers do not actually support this feature anyway, so to provide something like the same functionality ASP.NET 2.0 allows individual items in the list to be removed from the display but still exist server-side in the list.

In other words, if the `Items` collection of a list control contains five `ListItem` controls, but one has the `Enabled` property set to `False` (or carries the `Enabled="False"` attribute), this item will not be rendered in the list client-side. However, it is still accessible in server-side code as part of the `Items` collection.

Changes to the Literal Control

A common approach to inserting content into a page without using a control that generates its own markup (e.g., a `Label` that generates a `<span>` element in the page) is to use the `Literal` control. You simply set the `Text` property to any `String` value, and that string is inserted into the page at the point where the `Literal` control is located.

In ASP.NET 2.0, a new property named `Mode` has been added to the `Literal` control, which allows you to control how the `String` assigned to the `Text` property value is "processed" before being sent to the client. The reason for this is simple: The page needs to be able to tailor its output to suit different types of device. For example, an `<hr />` element in the `String` assigned to the `Literal` control will cause an error if sent to a device that expects to receive WML.

The `Mode` property can take one of the three values defined for the `LiteralMode` enumeration (see Table 12.4).

Changes to the Panel Control

One of the features that many developers have requested is a control that can be of fixed size and can display scroll bars when there is more content than will fit into an area of the specified size. In ASP.NET 2.0, the `Panel` control has been extended to provide these features. It has also been adapted to work better with pagination through a `Pager` control, allowing output to be broken up into separate "screens" for small-screen devices such as PDAs and cellular phones.

Figure 12.14 shows how the `Panel` control can now provide fixed-size scrollable regions in a page. The first and second panels have only a vertical scroll bar, while the third one has both horizontal and vertical scroll bars. The second panel also changes the layout direction, so the text is aligned to the right and the scroll bar appears on the left. (The control adds the HTML attribute `dir="RTL"` to the page element in the page to achieve

TABLE 12.4. The LiteralMode Enumeration Values

Value	Description
Transform	All markup not supported by the current client device is removed from the output generated by the control (e.g., `<hr />` is removed for WML devices). If there is content within an unsupported element (e.g., `<mytag>Some text</mytag>`), the tags are removed and the content is sent to the client. This is the default setting if not specified, meaning that backward compatibility is maximized for pages that don't specify a `LiteralMode` value and may be sent to a mobile device. If you use nonstandard markup in your pages, perhaps to interact with client-side code or special controls, you may have to change the `LiteralMode` property to `PassThrough` to ensure that it is delivered correctly.
PassThrough	The content of the `Text` property is sent to the client unchanged.
Encode	The content of the `Text` property is HTML-encoded before being sent to the client (e.g., `<img>` becomes `&lt;img&gt;`).

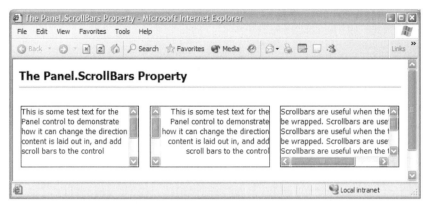

FIGURE 12.14. The Panel control with scroll bars

this.) Finally, the text in the third panel does not wrap like the other two because we set the `Wrap` property to `False` in the declaration of that `Panel` control.

The first `Panel` control is declared like this:

```
<asp:Panel id="MyPanel1" BorderStyle="Solid" BorderWidth="1"
    Width="200" Height="100" ScrollBars="Vertical" runat="server">
  <asp:Label runat="server">This is some test text...</asp:Label><p />
  <asp:Label runat="server">This is some test text...</asp:Label><p />
</asp:Panel>
```

You can see the `Width` and `Height` attributes, and the `ScrollBars` attribute is set to `Vertical`. This value comes from the `ScrollBars` enumeration, which contains the four expected values (`Vertical`, `Horizontal`, `Both`, and `None`) plus `Auto` to automatically add scroll bars as needed.

To force right-to-left layout in the `Panel` control, we just have to add the `Direction="RightToLeft"` attribute to the declaration. The default for `Direction` depends on the language and international settings of your machine. Right-to-left is, of course, the default for some languages.

The third `Panel` control simply carries the `ScrollBars="Vertical"` attribute. To prevent the text in the control from wrapping, we add the `Wrap="False"` attribute to the declaration and use `<br />` elements in the text to break it into separate lines.

```
<asp:Panel id="MyPanel3" BorderStyle="Solid" BorderWidth="1"
    Width="200" Height="100" runat="server"
    ScrollBars="Vertical" Wrap="False">
  <asp:Label runat="server">
    Scrollbars are useful when the text
```

```
        cannot<br />be wrapped. Scrollbars are useful<br />
        Scrollbars are useful when the text cannot<br />...
    </asp:Label>
</asp:Panel>
```

Pagination in a Panel Control

We discussed the pagination features in general terms and in more detail in Chapter 10, where we looked at the Pager control. However, to integrate with the Pager control, the Panel control gains two new properties, which we describe briefly here (see Table 12.5).

TABLE 12.5. New Properties of the Panel Control

Property	Description
AllowPaginate	A Boolean value that indicates whether the contents of the Panel control can be broken up across pages. When True, the Pager control can divide the content of the Panel control over more than one page or screen when displayed in a device that requires pagination. When False (the default), the content always appears together on the same page or screen.
MaximumWeight	An Integer value that defines the maximum weighting for the content of the Panel control in respect to the pagination algorithm used by the Pager control to decide where to divide the content.

Changes to the AdRotator Control

ASP.NET 1.0 shipped with an AdRotator control to randomly display banner advertisements, and in ASP.NET 2.0 it has been updated with support for:

- Displaying advertisements in pop-up or pop-under windows
- Binding advertisement data from non-XML data sources
- Using site counters that track impressions and click-throughs
- Sending advertisements to mobile devices
- Caching that allows display of a dynamic advertisement even if the page is cached

The syntax for the AdRotator control is shown in Listing 12.22.

LISTING 12.22. The AdRotator Control Syntax

```
<asp:AdRotator runat="server"
  AdType="[Banner|Popup|Popunder]"
```

```
AdvertisementFile="String"
AlternateTextField="String"
DataSource="String",
DataSourceId="String"
Font="String"
ImageUrlField="String"
KeywordFilter="String"
NavigateUrl="String"
PopFrequency="Integer"
PopPositionLeft="Integer"
PopPositionTop="Integer"
Target="String"
/>
```

Some of these are the same as the properties used in the existing version of the control. The new properties are shown in Table 12.6.

TABLE 12.6. New Properties of the AdRotator Control

Property/Attribute	Description
AdType	Indicates the type of advertisement, which can be one of the AdType enumerations: ● Banner: For a banner ad. This is the default value. ● Popup: For a pop-up ad. ● Popunder: For a pop-under ad.
AlternateTextField	Sets or returns the element name or database field from which the alternate text is returned. The default is AlternateText.
DataSource	Sets or returns the data source to bind the AdRotator against. DataSource and AdvertisementFile cannot be defined simultaneously.
DataSourceId	Sets or returns the data source control to bind the AdRotator against. DataSourceId and AdvertisementFile cannot be defined simultaneously.
ImageUrlField	Sets or returns the element name or database field from which the image URL is returned. The default is ImageUrl.
NavigateUrlField	Sets or returns the element name or database field from which the navigation URL is returned. The default is NavigateUrl.

TABLE 12.6. New Properties of the AdRotator Control (continued)

Property/Attribute	Description
PopFrequency	Sets or returns the frequency, as a percentage, with which to create pop-up or pop-under ads. This applies only when the AdType property is Popup or Popunder. The default is 100.
PopPositionLeft	Sets or returns the screen position that defines the left side of the ad. If not defined, the advertisement is centered horizontally on the screen. This applies only when the AdType property is Popup or Popunder.
PopPositionTop	Sets or returns the screen position that defines the top of the ad. If not defined, the advertisement is centered vertically on the screen. This applies only when the AdType property is Popup or Popunder.

In addition to these properties, the AdRotator control implements the Site Counters Service and therefore supports the following properties:

- CountClicks
- CountGroup
- CounterName
- CountViews
- RowsPerDay
- SiteCountersProvider
- TrackApplicationName
- TrackNavigateUrl
- TrackPageUrl

Pop-ups and Pop-unders

Support for pop-up advertisements is achieved by simply setting the AdType property. For example, a pop-up advertisement could be created like this:

```
<asp:AdRotator runat="server"
  AdvertisementFile="adverts.xml"
  AdType="Popup" />
```

No position is defined in this pop-up, so it will be centered on the screen.

Tracking Banners

The addition of site counter support allows easy tracking of ad data. For example, a simple banner advertisement could be:

```
<asp:AdRotator runat="server"
  AdvertisementFile="adverts.xml"
  CountClicks="True" CountViews="True"
  TrackNavigateUrl="True" />
```

Tracking details for these advertisements can be obtained either directly from the Site Counters table or via the Site Counters API, as shown in Figure 12.15. With this information it is easy to work out the hit percentages to see how effective ads are.

XML Advertisements File

There are a number of new elements supported in the XML advertisements file (see Table 12.7). Listing 12.23 shows an example of these in use.

Views:

Url	Total
http://www.softartisans.com/	20
http://www.awprofessional.com/	9
http://www.symbian.com/	8
http://p2p.wrox.com/	8
http://www.asptoday.com/	8
http://www.cyscape.com/	7
http://www.softwired-inc.com/	5

Clicks:

Url	Total
http://www.awprofessional.com/	3
http://www.softartisans.com/	3
http://www.softwired-inc.com/	2

FIGURE 12.15. Banner ad clicks and views

TABLE 12.7. XML Advertisements File New Elements

Element	Description
CounterGroup	The site counter group to use when tracking this ad.
CounterName	The site counter name to use when tracking this ad.
Height	The height of the ad. If not supplied, the Height of the AdRotator control is used.
Width	The width of the ad. If not supplied, the Width of the AdRotator control is used.

LISTING 12.23. Sample Advertisements File

```
<Advertisements>
  <Ad>
    <ImageUrl>ads/awpro.gif</ImageUrl>
    <NavigateUrl>http://www.awprofessional.com/</NavigateUrl>
    <AlternateText>Addison-Wesley</AlternateText>
    <Impressions>20</Impressions>
    <Keyword>Books</Keyword>
    <Height>40</Height>
    <Width>160</Width>
    <CounterGroup>Publishers</CounterGroup>
    <CounterName>Addison-Wesley</CounterName>
  </Ad>
  <Ad>
    ...
  </Ad>
</Advertisements>
```

Like previous versions, the advertisements file also supports custom fields, which are mapped to the `AdProperties` property of the `AdCreated` `EventArgs` for the `AdCreated` event.

Support for Mobile Devices

Support for mobile devices has been integrated into the `AdRotator` control as it supports the standard devices. Also, support has been added to the XML file, allowing device-specific elements. For example, consider an advertisement for a site that supports both standard browsers and WML browsers. The advertisement could look like this:

```
<Ad>
  <ImageUrl>ads/awpro.gif</ImageUrl>
  <NavigateUrl>http://www.awprofessional.com/</NavigateUrl>
  <WmlImageUrl>ads/awpro.gif</WmlImageUrl>
  <WmlNavigateUrl>http://wml.awpro.com/</WmlNavigateUrl>
  <AlternateText>Addison-Wesley</AlternateText>
  ...
```

This specifies a normal `ImageUrl` and `NavigateUrl` properties, as well as custom properties to a WML-specific image and navigation URL. Unlike standard custom properties, these can be mapped directly to device attributes by the `AdRotator` control. For example:

```
<asp:AdRotator runat="server"
  AdvertisementFile="adverts.xml"
  Wml:ImageUrl="WmlImageUrl"
  Wml:NavigateUrl="WmlNavigateUrl" />
```

This allows you to easily add support for custom devices without changing the infrastructure of your site.

Support for Data Binding

Data binding support has been added for both the existing data binding architecture and the new `DataSource` controls, as long as the underlying data matches the allowable schema. For example, Listing 12.24 shows binding the `AdRotator` to a `DataSet`, using the ASP.NET 1.x data binding syntax.

LISTING 12.24. Binding the AdRotator Control to a DataSet Control

```
<script runat="server">

Sub Page_Load(Sender As Object, E As EventArgs)

  Dim conn As New _
    SqlConnection(ConfigurationSettings.AppSettings("Ads"))
  Dim da As New SqlDataAdapter("select * from ads", conn)
  Dim ds As New DataSet()

  da.Fill(ds, "Ads")

  BannerAds.DataSource = ds
  BannerAds.DataBind()

End Sub

</script>

<form runat="server">

  <asp:AdRotator runat="server" id="BannerAds" />

</form>
```

This is also possible using the ASP.NET 2.0 data binding controls (see Listing 12.25).

LISTING 12.25. Binding the AdRotator Control to a SqlDataSource Control

```
<form runat="server">

  <asp:SqlDataSource id="AdData" runat="server"
    ConnectionString="..." />

  <asp:AdRotator runat="server" DataSourceId="AdData" />

</form>
```

Adding data binding to the `AdRotator` means that advertisement data can be supplied by any data provider.

Site and Page Counters

Counting page hits is a requirement for many large Web sites and hosting companies, and some excellent commercial packages provide a range of services to track and analyze data. However, there is often a need for a smaller, more localized set of services to track page hits or click-throughs.

This has been implemented in ASP.NET 2.0 with an easy-to-use Site Counters Service, which tracks clicks and hits in a configurable data provider (Access and SQL Server being the supplied providers). The Site Counters Service tracks a number of pieces of information, such as the current page, the target page, named counter groups and counters, and the application name. Each unique combination of these results, within a configurable time period, results in the creation of a new counter and a new row in the database. Subsequent instances cause the counter to be updated.

The database provides the columns shown in Table 12.8.

TABLE 12.8. Site Counters Database Columns

Column	Description
Id	A unique key, automatically generated.
Application	The name of the application, as configured in the IIS metabase.
PageUrl	The URL of the source page.
CounterGroup	The group to which the counter belongs.
CounterName	The name of the counter.
CounterEvent	The event that generated the counter. This will either be `Click` or `View`, to indicate tracking of a click-through or a page view.
NavigateUrl	The URL of the target page, if navigating.
StartTime	The time tracking started for this counter. This time is dependent on the number of rows per day and is the time the counter interval started, not the time the first page was tracked. For example, with a `RowsPerDay` value of `24`, the start time would always be on the hour.
EndTime	The time tracking ended for this counter.
Total	The total number of clicks/hits for this counter for this interval.

TABLE 12.9. Site Counters Database Schema

Column	Access Data Type	SQL Server Data Type
Id	AutoNumber	int (Identity)
Application	Memo	nvarchar(256)
PageUrl	Memo	nvarchar(512)
CounterGroup	Memo	nvarchar(256)
CounterName	Memo	nvarchar(256)
CounterEvent	Memo	nvarchar(256)
NavigateUrl	Memo	nvarchar(512)
StartTime	Date/Time	datetime
EndTime	Date/Time	datetime
Total	Number (Long Integer)	int

The schema for these is shown in Table 12.9. Data will be truncated if it exceeds the lengths specified by the schema.

Using Site Counters

The underlying implementation of site counters is an easy-to-use API that can be used directly or built into controls. The following list shows which controls have built-in support for the Site Counters Service:

- AdRotator
- HyperLink
- Button
- ImageButton
- LinkButton
- PhoneLink
- ImageMap

As these implement the service, they automatically have the option of exposing the properties shown in Table 12.10.

TABLE 12.10. Site Counter Properties Added to Controls

Property/Attribute	Description
CountClicks	Sets or returns a value that indicates whether or not the number of clicks is counted by site counters.
CountViews	Sets or returns a value that indicates whether or not the number of views is tracked (e.g., each time an ad is shown).
CounterGroup	Sets or returns the group name to which this counter belongs. If this is not specified, the default is the type of control being tracked.
CounterName	Sets or returns the name of the counter. If this is not specified, the default is the name of the control being tracked.
RowsPerDay	Sets or returns the maximum number of rows that will be stored in the logging database. The default value is 1, and the maximum value is 1440, indicating one row per minute.
SiteCountersProvider	Sets or returns the provider used to log site counter data. If not set, the default provider from the application configuration file will be used.
TrackApplicationName	Sets or returns a value that indicates whether or not the application name is tracked with the site counter details. The default value is True.
TrackNavigateUrl	Sets or returns a value that indicates whether or not the URL of the target page is tracked with the site counter details.
TrackPageUrl	Sets or returns a value that indicates whether or not the URL of the current page is tracked with the site counter details. The default value is True.

By default, tracking is disabled for these controls, but it's simple to enable. For example, at its simplest it's just a matter of setting the Count Clicks property to True:

```
<asp:Hyperlink runat="server" NavigateUrl="products.aspx"
    Text="Product List" CountClicks="True" />
```

Every time this link is clicked, the details will be tracked. To add more details to the tracking, you can set more of the properties to differentiate different links:

```
<asp:Hyperlink runat="server" NavigateUrl="products.aspx"
    Text="Product List" CountClicks="True"
    CounterGroup="Products" CounterName="Overview"/>

<asp:Hyperlink runat="server"
    NavigateUrl="products.aspx?ProductID=123"
    Text="Special Offer" CountClicks="True"
    CounterGroup="Products" CounterName="Special"/>
```

Here both links have the same `CounterGroup` but a different `Counter Name`, ensuring they are tracked as separate items. To track items with different URLs as though they are the same (e.g., all hits on `products.aspx` no matter what the query string or which page the URL is on), the same `CounterName` can be used. Any session information stored as part of the URL is stripped before being logged.

> When enabling counting on a control that navigates, the URL must be a virtual path. This means that you cannot turn on tracking for a control that has multiple navigation links (such as an `ImageMap`), some local and some remote. Remember that the Site Counters Service isn't designed to be an all-encompassing tracking system but a simple way to track local applications, so this implementation is deliberate.

Using the Site Counters API

Access to the site counter data is available through an API exposed via the `SiteCounters` property on the `Page`. There are only two properties— `Enabled`, to indicate whether the service is enabled, and a `SiteCounters ProviderCollection`, which is a collection of all available site counters. The methods of the API are detailed in Table 12.11.

The Web Administration Tool (covered in Chapter 6) will have details of the site counters (this is unavailable in the Technology Preview), but the `Get` methods allow you to provide your own interface if required. The `Write` method allows you to control the tracking of hits from within code.

TABLE 12.11. SiteCounter Methods

Method	Returns	Description
`Flush`		Flushes the tracking information for a given provider to the database, or all providers if no provider is specified.
`FlushAll`		Flushes the tracking information for all providers to the database.
`GetGroupRows`	`DataSet`	Returns the rows for a given `CounterGroup`.
`GetNameRows`	`DataSet`	Returns the rows for a given `CounterName`.
`GetNavigateUrlRows`	`DataSet`	Returns the rows for a given source page URL.
`GetRedirectUrl`	`String`	Returns the target URL given a selection of counter details.
`GetRows`	`DataSet`	Returns the rows for a selection of counter details.
`GetTotalCount`	`Integer`	Returns the total number of hits for a selection of counter details.
`GetTotalGroupCount`	`Integer`	Returns the total number of hits for a given `CounterGroup`.
`GetTotalNameCount`	`Integer`	Returns the total number of hits for a given `CounterName`.
`GetTotalNavigateUrlCount`	`Integer`	Returns the total number of hits for a given source page URL.
`Write`		Writes site counter details to the provider.

For example, although site counters do not allow absolute URLs, you could implement tracking of these manually, as shown in Listing 12.26.

LISTING 12.26. Manually Adding URLs to the Site Counters Service

```
<script runat="server">

Sub NavigateAway(Sender As Object, E As EventArgs)
```

```
SiteCounters.Write("Navigate", "Away", "Click", _
                   "http://www.asp.net/", True, True)
Response.Redirect("http://www.asp.net/")

End Sub

</script>

<form runat="server">

  <asp:LinkButton runat="Server" onClick="NavigateAway"
      Text="ASP.NET" />

</form>
```

The `Write` method is overloaded and has several forms. See the documentation for complete details.

Configuring Site and Page Counters

The default installation of ASP.NET 2.0 ships with two providers for page tracking—one for Microsoft Access and one for Microsoft SQL Server—and these are configured in the application configuration file. The syntax is shown in Listing 12.27.

LISTING 12.27. Site Counters Configuration

```
<siteCounters
  enabled="[true|false]"
  defaultProvider="String"
  handlerPath="String"
  handlerType="String"
  rowsPerDay="Integer"
  type="String">
    <providers>
      <add
        name="String"
        type="string"
        provider-specific-configuration />
      <remove
        name="string" />
      <clear/>
    </providers>

    <pageCounters
      enabled="[true|false]"
      defaultProvider="String]"
      rowsPerDay="[Integer]"
      trackApplicationName="[true|false]"
      trackPageUrl="[true|false]"
```

```
      counterGroup="[String]"
      counterName="[String]">


        <pagesToCount>


          <add path="String" />
          <remove path="String" />
          <clear/>
        </pagesToCount>
      </pageCounters>
  </siteCounters>
```

The configuration is broken down into two sections. The first defines the properties and providers for the Site Counters Service itself (see Table 12.12).

The `<providers>` element is where the actual site counter providers are added (see Table 12.13). The properties for the Access and SQL Server providers are the same.

The attributes of the `<pageCounters>` element map directly to the properties we have already discussed, although by default `page counters` are disabled.

TABLE 12.12. Site Counters Configuration Properties

Property/Attribute	Description
enabled	Indicates whether or not the service is enabled. The default value is `true`.
defaultProvider	Indicates the provider to use if no explicit provider is named. The default is the Access provider.
handlerPath	Indicates the URL used to handle click-throughs. The default is `~/counters.axd`, which is an `HttpHandler` that intercepts page clicks and tracks the data.
handlerType	Defines the full name of the class that handles the site counter data. The shortened default is `System.Web.Handlers.SiteCountersHandler`—full class details can be found in the configuration file.
rowsPerDay	Defines the granularity with which data is logged to the provider. The default value is `1`.
type	Indicates the full class name of the default provider.

TABLE 12.13. Site Counter Database Provider Properties

Property/Attribute	Description
name	The name of the provider.
type	The full class name of the provider.
connectionStringName	The name of the connection string, from the connectionStrings configuration elements, that defines the connection details for the tracking database. This property is Access and SQL Server specific.
description	A description of the provider.
commitInterval	The interval, in seconds, between flushing the in-memory counters to the database. The default is 90.
commitTimeout	The time, in seconds, to wait before aborting the database command that writes the counters. The default is 60.

The <pagesToCount> element details which pages will have counter information logged. This supports wildcards, so a value of * indicates all pages, for example:

```
<pagesToCount>
  <add path="*" />
</pagesToCount>
```

Wildcards can also be included as part of the path, for example:

```
<pagesToCount>
  <add path="/*/default.aspx" />
</pagesToCount>
```

This ensures that only the default.aspx page is tracked, but only if one level down from the application root directory.

Only ASP.NET pages (.aspx) are supported and tracked by the Site Counters Service. All other pages are ignored.

Configuring the Counter Database

You don't need to do anything specific to start using site counters, even though they are logged to a database. Because the default provider is Microsoft Access, when you first hit a page with site counters enabled, a new directory called DATA is created under your application directory if it doesn't already exist. Then a template database is copied into this directory and called ASPNetDB.mdb.

For SQL Server there is no automatic installation, but a SQL Script, called InstallSiteCounters.sql, is included in the .NET Framework's installation directory.

Web Resources

Along with their assemblies, control developers often have to supply additional static files, such as stylesheets and images. With ASP.NET 2.0's new resources model, these static files can now be embedded into assemblies as resources. This is achieved through the addition of the Web ResourceAttribute (from System.Web.UI), as shown in the following example:

```
<assembly:WebResource("MyImage.gif", "image/gif")>

Public Class MyControl
  ' control code here
End Class
```

This simply enables the image to be available as a Web resource. Within the control code, the resource can be accessed like this:

```
Protected Overrides Sub CreateChildControls()

  Controls.Clear()

  Dim img As New Image()

  img.ImageUrl = GetWebResourceUrl("MyImage.gif")

  Me.Controls.Add(img)

End Sub
```

At compile time the resource can be embedded into the assembly:

```
vbc /t:library /out:MyControl.dll
    /r:System.dll,System.web.dll
    /res:MyImage.gif,MyImage.gif
```

The Web resources feature is not limited just to images. For example, to embed JavaScript for client-side support, you could add:

```
<assembly:WebResource("MyScript.js", "text/javascript", True)>

Public Class MyControl
  ' control code here
End Class
```

The third parameter for this attribute indicates that the Web resource parser should be invoked for the resource (which it isn't by default). This ensures that the embedded resource is parsed and will be correct when used by the client. You might notice that this technique is used for JavaScript by ASP.NET pages and certain controls, such as the `TreeView`.

Embedded Web resources can also be accessed from within ASP.NET pages. For example:

```
<script runat="server">
  Sub Page_Load()

    img1.Image = Page.GetWebResourceUrl(GetType(MyControl), _
                                        "MyImage.gif")

  End Sub
</script>
```

Note that this example uses a second form of `GetWebResourceUrl`, which applies to the `Page` object. Here the type of control for which the Web resource is being fetched is also required. Notice that the control type is the custom control, not `Image`, as the resource is part of the custom control itself.

SUMMARY

In this chapter we summarized the range of new server controls included with ASP.NET 2.0 and looked at the more significant changes to existing controls. In general the changes are concentrated on the controls from the `System.Web.UI.WebControls` namespace, and there is a conscious move away from the use of the controls in the `HtmlControls` namespace. This follows from the new control architecture and adaptive rendering advances, and the few gaps left in the `WebControls` range (such as the file upload and hidden controls) have also been filled with new controls in that namespace.

While we haven't covered every change to every control nor demonstrated all the possibilities of the new controls (mainly through lack of space), we have provided you with a good foundation to become familiar with using the new controls and the new architecture that supports them. Bear in mind that the current release is only a Technology Preview, so there are almost definitely going to be more changes and additions during coming months as we move through the beta stages to a final release.

Now it's time to take a look at how administration and configuration of ASP.NET have been improved.

13

Configuration and Administration

Y OU'VE SEEN THROUGHOUT THIS BOOK that building Web sites with
ASP.NET is easier than ever. Not only have more features been added,
but also there's much less code to write, with more use of declarative properties. However, when it comes to administration, the features are split—
it's more complex because there are more features to configure, but at the
same time it's easier because there is a Web-based administration tool and
an API to support it.

For the last chapter in this look at the new ASP.NET features, we'll explore a variety of configuration and administration topics. We'll start by
looking at the configuration files, seeing which sections have changed and
what the new sections are. Some of this material has been covered elsewhere in the book in more detail, but this chapter provides the definitive
reference for the changes in ASP.NET.

We'll then take a look at the Management API, which is the underlying
set of classes that provide easy management and configuration. Having a
consistent API means that it's easy to build custom configuration routines.

We'll briefly cover the Web Administration Tool, although the only features completed for the Technology Preview release are those for security
administration, which were covered in Chapter 6.

Application Configuration Files

The application configuration files (`web.config` and the site-wide `machine.config`) have had a number of changes, including new attributes added to existing elements as well as new elements to support the new features. The changed sections of the configuration files cover the topics listed below:

- Client targets
- Compilation
- Web proxy
- HTTP modules
- HTTP runtime
- HTTP handlers
- Globalization
- Pages
- Session state
- Web request modules

The new sections cover the following topics:

- Anonymous identification
- Code DOM
- Connection strings
- Data
- Caching
- Image generation
- HTTP cookies
- Membership
- Site maps
- Site counters
- Personalization
- Protocols
- Role Manager
- Mail servers
- URL mappings
- Web Administration Tool

Changed Sections

The text in this subsection details only the changes made to the configuration files and the changed attributes.

Client Targets

The `<clientTarget/>` section identifies browsers by their user agent string and provides a mapping to a simple alias. For the `downlevel` alias, the user agent has been changed from `Unknown` to `Generic Downlevel`, as shown below:

```
<clientTarget>
  <add alias="downlevel" userAgent="Generic Downlevel" />
</clientTarget>
```

Compilation

The `<compilation/>` section has been enhanced to allow for automatic compilation of source files and pre-compilation of applications. For this there is a new `<codeSubDirectories/>` element that indicates which directories contain code that should be automatically compiled. This section contains a collection of relative directory names where code is placed. The syntax is shown below:

```
<compilation
  urlLinePragmas="[true|false]"
  >
    <codeSubDirectories>
      <add directoryName="String" />
    </codeSubDirectories>
  </compilation>
```

There is also a new `Boolean` attribute on the main compilation section, `urlLinePragmas`. This indicates whether or not pragmas use URLs. The default is `false`, which means that pragmas use physical paths.

The `<compilers/>` section has been moved to the new `<system .codedom/>` section, which is covered later in the chapter.

Build Providers

The `<buildProviders/>` section identifies which files are part of the dynamic compilation process. The syntax for this section is:

```
<buildProviders>
  <add
    extension="String"
    appliesTo="String"
    type="String" />
</buildProviders>
```

The attributes are described in Table 13.1.

TABLE 13.1. buildProvider Attributes

Attribute	Description
extension	The file extension (e.g., `.resx`) of the file to be built.
appliesTo	The directory (e.g., `Resources`) where the files reside.
type	The type name of the build provider class used to invoke the compilation.

This section is for files that aren't part of the `compilation` section (those files are automatically built). Compilation and build providers were covered in Chapter 2.

Web Proxy

The `<defaultProxy/>` section defines how the `System.Net` classes access the Internet and has been enhanced to include the following settings:

```
<defaultProxy
  automaticallyDetectSettings="[true|false]"
  autoConfigurationScript="String"
  scriptDownloadInterval="Integer"
  scriptDownloadTimeout="Integer"
  />
```

The attributes are described in Table 13.2.

TABLE 13.2. defaultProxy Attributes

Attribute	Description
automaticallyDetectSettings	Indicates whether or not discovery of the proxy server is automatic.
autoConfigurationScript	Indicates a URI that points to the proxy server configurations script.
scriptDownloadInterval	Defines, in seconds, the time that elapses before the configuration script is refreshed.
scriptDownloadTimeout	Defines, in seconds, the time allowed for the configuration script to download.

HTTP Modules

Several new HTTP modules have been added to the pipeline.

- `SessionID` allows generation of `Session` ID values to be factored out by programmers. This enables developers to easily provide their own `Session` ID values.
- `RoleManager` provides support for the Role Manager.
- `AnonymousIdentification` provides support for identification of anonymous visitors.
- `Personalization` provides support for Personalization.
- `PageCountersModule` provides support for the page counters.

A full description of these is beyond the scope of this book, but details can be found in the SDK documentation.

HTTP Runtime

The `<httpRuntime/>` section has been enhanced to cater to application domain shutdowns and buffered uploads, with the following new attributes:

```
<httpRuntime
  enable="[true|false]"
  idleTimeOut="Integer"
  requestLengthDiskThreshold="Integer"
  requireRootedSaveAsPath="[true|false]"
  />
```

The attributes are described in Table 13.3.

TABLE 13.3. httpRuntime Attributes

Attribute	Description
enable	Indicates whether or not the current application domain (and those below it) is enabled. The default value is `true`.
idleTimeOut	Indicates the life, in minutes, of the application domain before it is shut down (unless a debugger is attached to the application). The default value is `20`.
requestLengthDiskThreshold	Indicates the threshold, in kilobytes, for buffering the input stream; should not exceed the `MaxRequestLength` property. The default value is `256`.

TABLE 13.3. httpRuntime Attributes (continued)

Attribute	Description
`requireRootedSaveAsPath`	Indicates whether or not the path for Save As operations must be a rooted path. The default value is `true`.

The `enable` attribute allows an entire application domain to be disabled, perhaps in a hosting environment. Any requests to that application will result in a 404 error.

The addition of automatic shutdowns is useful for sites that are hit infrequently (such as personal sites, maybe a photo album), where keeping the application active wastes resources. The `idleTimeOut` figure indicates the number of minutes since the last request was received.

The `requestLengthDiskThreshold` and `requireRootedSaveAsPath` attributes are for file uploads. They define the maximum size of uploaded files and the path to where they can be saved, respectively.

HTTP Handlers

The `<httpHandlers/>` section has been enhanced to cater to the following new handlers:

- `WebAdmin.axd`, for the Web Administration Tool
- `WebResource.axd`, for Web resources
- `CachedImageService.axd`, for cached images
- `Counters.axd`, for site counters for URL redirection
- `Precompile.axd`, for site pre-compilation

In addition, the following file suffixes are handled by the forbidden handler (`System.Web.HttpForbiddenHandler`), stopping them being served directly:

- `.master`
- `.skin`
- `.browser`
- `.mdb`
- `.vjsproj`
- `.java`
- `.jsl`

Globalization

The `<globalization/>` section has one new attribute, to allow automatic setting of culture depending on the browser.

```
<globalization
  enableClientBasedCulture="[true|false]"
  />
```

This attribute indicates whether or not the `uiCulture` and `culture` will be based on the `accept-language` header sent by the client browser. This overrides culture settings in configuration files, unless the client cultures cannot be mapped to a specific culture. The default value is `false`.

Pages

The `<pages/>` section has been enhanced to add Personalization, master pages, and theme support. Additionally, there is a subelement that allows automatic addition of namespace references to each page (see Listing 13.1).

Listing 13.1. pages Configuration Syntax

```
<pages
  enablePersonalization="[true|false]"
  personalizationProvider="String"
  master="String"
  theme="String"
  >
  <namespaces>
    <add namespace="String" />
  </namespaces>
</pages>
```

The attributes are described in Table 13.4. Both the `master` and `theme` attributes can be overridden at the page level.

TABLE 13.4. pages Attributes

Attribute	Description
enablePersonalization	Indicates whether or not Personalization is enabled. The default value is `false`.
personalizationProvider	Defines the name of the provider for Personalization.
master	Defines the site-wide master page. This allows a master page to be applied to all pages without adding the `master` attribute to the `Page` directive.
theme	Defines the site-wide theme. This allows a theme to be applied to all pages without adding the `theme` attribute to the `Page` directive.

For the `namespaces` subelement, the namespace is the full namespace to be included as a reference. For example:

```
<namespaces>
  <add namespace="System" />
  <add namespace="System.Collections" />
</namespaces>
```

The following namespaces are included in `machine.config`:

- `System`
- `System.Collections`
- `System.Collections.Specialized`
- `System.ComponentModel`
- `System.Configuration`
- `System.Text`
- `System.Text.RegularExpressions`
- `System.Web`
- `System.Web.Caching`
- `System.Web.SessionState`
- `System.Web.Security`
- `System.Web.Personalization`
- `System.Web.UI`
- `System.Web.UI.Imaging`
- `System.Web.UI.WebControls`
- `System.Web.UI.HtmlControls`

Session State

There are several changes to the state handling mechanism, which are covered in detail later in the chapter. Here's the new syntax for the `<session State/>` section:

```
<sessionState
  mode="[Off|InProc|StateServer|SQLServer|Custom]"
  sqlCommandTimeout="Integer"
  customType="String"
  cookieName="String"
  createEmptySession="[true|false]"
  allowCustomSqlDatabase="[true|false]"
  />
```

The new attributes are described in Table 13.5.

TABLE 13.5. sessionState Attributes

Attribute	Description
mode	Indicates how session state is being managed. Can be one of the following values: • Off: Indicates session state storage is disallowed. • InProc: Indicates the session state is stored in the executing ASP.NET process. • StateServer: Indicates that session state is stored in the external Windows Session State Service. • SQLServer: Indicates that session state is stored in SQL Server. • Custom: Indicates that session state is stored in a custom manner. • The default value is InProc.
sqlCommandTimeout	Indicates, in seconds, the timeout for a SQL command when the mode is SQLServer. The default value is 30.
customType	Indicates the full data type name of the class when the mode is Custom.
cookieName	Defines the default cookie name used to store the session ID.
createEmptySession	Indicates whether or not to create a new session even if it is empty.
allowCustomSqlDatabase	Indicates whether or not a custom database name can be specified in the Initial Catalog attribute of the SQL Server connection string.

Mobile Devices State

In addition to the session state changes, there is also a <sessionPage State/> element, which details the number of pages of session state stored on the server:

```
<sessionPageState
  historySize="Integer"
  />
```

This works in a way similar to the session state management for mobile controls in the MMIT from ASP.NET 1.x. This is required because the session state is stored on the server, and without the history it would be possible for the session state to become out of sync with the displayed page. The default value is 9.

Web Request Modules

When using the `WebRequest` class to access Web resources, you have the option of using HTTP, HTTPS, or FILE as the protocols. The `<webRequest Module/>` now has FTP added to provide file transfer support:

```
<add prefix="ftp"
  type="String"
  />
```

The `type` attribute identifies the full type of the class implementing the service.

New Sections

The configuration files contain many new sections to cater to the new features in ASP.NET 2.0. These new sections are described briefly below.

Anonymous Identification

The `<anonymousIdentification/>` section deals with how identity is assigned to users who are not authenticated (see Listing 13.2). It is used by the Personalization services.

Listing 13.2. anonymousIdentification Configuration Syntax

```
<anonymousIdentification
  enabled="[true|false]"
  cookieName="String"
  cookieTimeout="Integer"
  cookiePath="String"
  cookieRequiresSSL="[true|false]"
  cookieSlidingExpiration="[true|false]"
  cookieProtection="[None|Validation|Encryption|All]"
  cookieless="[UseCookies|UseUri|AutoDetect|UseDeviceProfile]"
  />
```

The attributes are described in Table 13.6.

TABLE 13.6. anonymousIdentification Attributes

Attribute	Description
enabled	Indicates whether or not anonymous identification is enabled. The default value is false.
cookieName	Specifies the name of the cookie. The default value is .ASPXANONYMOUS.
cookieTimeout	Specifies the value, in minutes, before the cookie expires. This cannot be 0 or less. The default value is 100000.
cookiePath	Specifies the path, which is case-sensitive, used to write the cookie. Using '/' allows applications within the same domain to access the cookie. The default is '/'.
cookieRequiresSSL	Indicates whether or not the cookie requires an SSL connection in order to be written to the client. The default value is false.
cookieSlidingExpiration	Indicates whether the cookie timeout resets upon each request (a value of true) or expires at a fixed time (a value of false). The default value is true.
cookieProtection	Specifies the protection scheme used to store the cookie. Can be one of the CookieProtection enumerations (from System.Web.Security): • None: Indicates no protection is used. • Validation: Indicates that the cookie is hashed and validated. • Encryption: Indicates that the cookie is encrypted. • All: Indicates that both validation and encryption are used. The default value is None.
cookieless	Specifies the cookie scheme to use. Can be one of the following: • UseUri: Forces the authentication ticket to be stored in the URL. • UseCookies: Forces the authentication ticket to be stored in the cookie (same as ASP.NET 1.x behavior). • AutoDetect: Automatically detects whether the browser/device supports cookies.

TABLE 13.6. anonymousIdentification Attributes (continued)

Attribute	Description
	• UseDeviceProfile: Chooses to use cookies or not based on the device profile settings from machine.config. The default value is UseDeviceProfile.

Code DOM

The `<system.codedom/>` section has been introduced to centralize the configuration of compilation features across all aspects of the .NET Framework, rather than having them be part of the Web configuration. The `<compilers/>` element has been moved into this new section (see Listing 13.3).

Listing 13.3. system.codedom Configuration Syntax

```
<system.codedom>
  <compilers>
    <compiler
      language="String"
      extension="String"
      type="String"
      warningLevel="Integer"
      compilerOptions="String"
    />
  </compilers>
</system.codedom>
```

The attributes for each listed compiler are the same as the previous version, but with one addition, compilerOptions, which allows default compiler options to be set.

Connection Strings

The `<connectionStrings/>` section allows database connection strings to be stored. Previously these were often stored in the appSettings section and thus used to get mixed in with general application settings. Now, however, they have a specific section, allowing database details to be stored either at the application level or for the entire machine. This also allows the connection string details to be protected (perhaps by encryption), thus keeping them secure. Although this functionality isn't part of the current release, it is planned for future releases.

TABLE 13.7. connectionStrings Attributes

Attribute	Description
name	The name of the connection string.
connectionString	The full connection details. No validity checking is performed.

```
<connectionStrings>
  <add name="String"
    connectionString="String"
  />
  <remove name="String" />
  <clear />
</connectionStrings>
```

The attributes are described in Table 13.7.

Like the application-specific settings, the connection strings are exposed through the ConfigurationSettings class. For example, we could define our database details as:

```
<connectionStrings>
  <add
    name="MyData"
    connectionString="server=.;database=MyData;Uid=;Pwd=" />
</connectionStrings>
```

Then we could use these details in our page or class:

```
Dim cs As String
cs = ConfigurationSettings.ConnectionStrings("MyData")

Dim conn As New SqlConnection(cs)
```

Data

The <system.data/> section allows configuration of data provider factories, allowing for abstracted access to data stores (see Listing 13.4).

Listing 13.4. system.data Configuration Syntax

```
<system.data>
  <DbProviderFactories>
    <add
      name="String"
      invariant="String"
```

continues

```
      support="String"
      description="String"
      type="String"
      />
   </DbProviderFactories>
</system.data>
```

The attributes for `<DbProviderFactories/>` are described in Table 13.8.

TABLE 13.8. DbProviderFactories Attributes

Attribute	Description
name	The name of the data factory.
invariant	The namespace of the data factory.
support	The level of support supplied by the provider. Can be a combination of items in the `DbProviderSupportedClasses` enumeration.
description	The description of the data factory.
type	The full type of the class that handles the factory.

The supplied data factories are for:

- `Odbc`
- `OleDb`
- `OracleClient`
- `SqlClient`

Caching

Caching is an area of ASP.NET that can bring great performance improvements, but one thing missing from ASP.NET 1.x was the capability to base the cache on a database. This capability would enable the cache to expire when the data it is caching changes, thus ensuring that out-of-date cached values are never used.

The new `<cache/>` section allows the cache dependency to be set and based on databases (see Listing 13.5). Initially only SQL Server is supported, but the architecture allows for others to be added in future releases.

Listing 13.5. cache Configuration Syntax

```
<cache>
  <sqlCacheDependency
    enabled="[true|false]"
    pollTime="Integer"
    >
    <databases>
      <add
        name="String"
        connectionName="String"
        pollTime="Integer"
        />
      <remove
        name="String"
        />
    </databases>
  </sqlCacheDependency>
</cache>
```

The attributes are described in Tables 13.9 and 13.10.
For more details on caching, please see Chapter 11.

TABLE 13.9. sqlCacheDependency Attributes

Attribute	Description
enabled	Indicates whether or not the SQL cache dependency polling is enabled. The default value is `true`.
pollTime	Defines, in milliseconds, the poll time. The minimum value is `500`. The default value is `60000`.

TABLE 13.10. databases Attributes

Attribute	Description
name	The name of the database.
connectionName	The name of the connection string from the `connection Strings` configuration section.
pollTime	The time, in milliseconds, between polls. If not specified, the `pollTime` from the parent element is used.

Image Generation

The `<imageGeneration/>` section allows configuration of the dynamic generation of images. The syntax is shown below:

```
<imageGeneration
  storageType="String"
  storagePath="String"
  storageExpiration="Integer"
  />
```

The attributes are described in Table 13.11.

TABLE 13.11. imageGeneration Attributes

Attribute	Description
`storageType`	The type of storage to be used. This can be one of the `StorageType` enumerations from `System.Web.UI.Imaging`: • `Disk`: Indicates storage on disk. • `Cache`: Indicates storage in the cache. The default value is `Cache`
`storagePath`	If `Disk` storage is being used, this specifies the path where generated images will be stored. If not supplied, the `ASPNET ImageStorage` directory is used, in the `Temp` directory of the ASPNET account.
`storageExpiration`	The default length of time, in seconds, before an image expires. The default value is `300`.

HTTP Cookies

The `<httpCookies/>` section controls whether certain HTTP headers are sent to the browser. This enables more secure storage of cookies and ensures that user-supplied code cannot access the cookies from the browser. Here's the syntax:

```
<httpCookies
  httpOnlyCookies="[true|false]"
  requireSSL="[true|false]"
  domain="String"
  />
```

The attributes are described in Table 13.12.

TABLE 13.12. httpCookies Attributes

Attribute	Description
httpOnlyCookies	Indicates whether or not the HttpOnly cookie attribute is added to the page, to ensure that cookies cannot be accessed client side.
requireSSL	Indicates whether or not the secure cookie attribute is added to the page.
domain	Defines the domain to which the cookie applies, which sets the domain cookie attribute for the page.

Membership

The <membership/> section defines the configuration for the supplied Membership schemes. It follows the standard providers pattern, allowing custom providers to be supplied (see Listing 13.6).

Listing 13.6. membership Configuration Syntax

```
<membership
  defaultProvider="String"
  userIsOnlineTimeWindow="Integer">
  <providers>
    <add name="String"
      type="String"
      [providerSpecificSettings]
      />
    <remove name="String"
     />
    <clear>
  </providers>
</membership>
```

The attributes are described in Tables 13.13 and 13.14.

TABLE 13.13. membership Attributes

Attribute	Description
defaultProvider	The name of the default provider. There is no default value.
userIsOnlineTimeWindow	The time, in minutes, since last activity when the user was deemed to be online. The default value is 15.
providerSpecificSettings	The settings specific to the provider.

TABLE 13.14. providers Attributes

Attribute	Description
name	The name of the membership provider. The default value is AspNetAccessProvider.
type	A string containing the full .NET type of the provider.
providerSpecificSettings	A name/value collection detailing provider-specific settings.

SQL Server and Access Membership Providers

Two providers are supplied with this release, giving support for SQL Server and Access databases. These are named AspNetSqlProvider and AspNetAccessProvider, respectively, and both have the same syntax for the provider-specific section:

```
connectionStringName="String"
enablePasswordRetrieval="[true|false]"
enablePasswordReset="[true|false]"
requiresQuestionAndAnswer="[true|false]"
applicationName="String"
requiresUniqueEmail="[true|false]"
passwordFormat="[Clear|Hashed|Encrypted]"
description="String"
```

The attributes are described in Table 13.15.

TABLE 13.15. SQL Server and Access Membership Provider Specific Attributes

Attribute	Description
connectionStringName	Specifies the name of the connection string, from the connectionStrings section.
enablePasswordRetrieval	Indicates whether or not the provider will allow retrieval of passwords. The default value is false.
enablePasswordReset	Indicates whether or not the provider will allow passwords to be reset. The default value is true.
requireQuestionAndAnswer	Indicates whether or not the provider enforces a question-and-answer method for retrieving forgotten passwords. The default value is false. Valid only when the passwordFormat setting is not Hashed and enablePasswordRetrieval is true.

TABLE 13.15. SQL Server and Access Membership Provider Specific Attributes (continued)

Attribute	Description
applicationName	Defines the scope of the application. The default value is `/`.
requiresUniqueEmail	Indicates whether or not the provider enforces unique e-mail addresses. The default value is `false`.
passwordFormat	Defines how the passwords should be stored. Can be one of the following: • `Clear`: For clear text passwords. • `Hashed`: For hashed passwords. • `Encrypted`: For encrypted passwords. The default value is `Hashed`.
description	Defines the description of the provider.

Membership is covered in detail in Chapter 6.

Site Maps

The `<siteMap/>` section allows configuration of site map providers, providing menuing and navigation features (see Listing 13.7).

Listing 13.7. sitemap Configuration Syntax

```
<siteMap
    defaultProvider="String"
    enabled="[true|false]">
  <providers>
    <add
      name="String"
      description="String"
      type="String"
      [providerSpecificSettings]
      />
    <remove name="String"
      />
    <clear>
  </providers>
</siteMap>
```

The attributes are described in Tables 13.16 and 13.17 on the next page.

TABLE 13.16. siteMap Attributes

Attribute	Description
defaultProvider	The name of the default provider. This should match one of the names supplied in the providers section. The default value is AspNetXmlSiteMapProvider.
enabled	A Boolean value indicating whether or not site maps are enabled. The default value is true.

TABLE 13.17. siteMap providers Attributes

Attribute	Description
name	The name of the site map provider.
description	A description of the provider
type	A string containing the full .NET type of the provider.
providerSpecificSettings	The provider-specific settings.

AspNetXmlSiteMapProvider

The supplied site provider is for XML files and has a single attribute, siteMapFile, which defines the name of the site map file. The default value for this is app.SiteMap.

Site Counters

The <siteCounters/> section defines the configuration for the site counters service, allowing tracking of navigation from server controls (see Listing 13.8).

Listing 13.8. siteCounters Configuration Syntax

```
<siteCounters
  enabled="[true|false]"
  defaultProvider="String"
  handlerPath="String"
  handlerType="String"
  rowsPerDay="Integer"
  type="String">
    <providers>
      <add
        name="String"
```

```
      type="String"
      [providerSpecificSettings]
      />
    <remove
      name="String" />
    <clear/>
  </providers>

  <pageCounters
    enabled="[true|false]"
    defaultProvider="String"
    rowsPerDay="Integer"
    trackApplicationName="[true|false]"
    trackPageUrl="[true|false]"
    counterGroup="String"
    counterName="String">

      <pagesToCount>
        <add path="String" />
        <remove path="String" />
        <clear/>
      </pagesToCount>
    </pageCounters>
</siteCounters>
```

The attributes are described in Table 13.18.

TABLE 13.18. siteCounters Attributes

Attribute	Description
enabled	Indicates whether or not the service is enabled. The default value is true.
defaultProvider	Indicates the provider to use if no explicit provider is named. The default value is AspNetAccessProvider. If no default provider is specified, the first provider in the collection is used as the default.
handlerPath	Indicates the URL used to handle click-throughs. The default is ~/counters.axd, which is an HttpHandler that intercepts page clicks and tracks the data.
handlerType	Defines the full name of the class that handles the site counter data. The shortened default is System.Web.Handlers.Site CountersHandler—full class details can be found in the configuration file.
rowsPerDay	Defines the granularity with which data is logged to the provider. The maximum value is 1440 (1 row per minute). The default value is 1.

There are two supplied providers for site counters, `AspNetAccess Provider` and `AspNetSqlProvider`, both of which have the same provider-specific attributes, as shown in Table 13.19.

TABLE 13.19. Access and SQL Server Site Counters Attributes

Attribute	Description
name	The name of the provider.
type	The full class name of the provider.
connectionStringName	The name of the connection string, from the `connection Strings` configuration elements, that defines the connection details for the tracking database. This property is specific to Access and SQL Server.
description	A description of the provider.
commitInterval	The interval, in seconds, between flushes of the in-memory counters to the database. The default is `90`.
commitTimeout	The time, in seconds, to wait before aborting the database command that writes the counters. The default is `60`.

The `<pageCounters/>` section allows configuration of how pages are tracked as part of the site counters service. The attributes are shown in Table 13.20.

TABLE 13.20. pageCounters Attributes

Attribute	Description
enabled	Indicates whether or not page tracking is enabled. This is ignored if site counters are disabled. The default value is `false`.
defaultProvider	Specifies the default provider to use for tracking pages.
rowsPerDay	Defines the granularity with which data is logged to the provider. The maximum value is `1440` (1 row per minute). The default value is `1`.
trackApplicationName	Indicates whether or not the application name is tracked with the site counter details. The default value is `true`.

TABLE 13.20. pageCounters Attributes (continued)

Attribute	Description
trackPageUrl	Indicates whether or not the URL of the current page is tracked with the site counter details. The default value is true.
counterGroup	Defines the group name to use for tracked pages. The default is PageCounters.
counterName	Defines the counter name to use for tracked pages.

The `<pagesToCount/>` element contains a collection of page names, meaning that the add and remove elements do not behave like ordinary add and remove elements that have a key. For the add element, the default value is *, which indicates that all pages recursively are included. Under default conditions, therefore, the remove element indicates the pages to exclude.

Personalization

The `<personalization/>` section allows configuration of the Personalization service (see Listing 13.9).

Listing 13.9. personalization Configuration Syntax

```
<personalization
  enabled="[true|false]"
  defaultProvider="String">
  <providers>
    <add name="String"
      type="String"
      [providerSpecificSettings]
      />
    <remove name="String"
      />
    <clear />
  </providers>
  <profile>
    <property name="String"
      readOnly="[true|false]"
      serializeAs="[String|Xml|Binary|ProviderSpecific]"
      provider="String"
      defaultValue="String"
      type="String"
      allowAnonymous="[true|false]"
      />
```

```
  <group name="String">
    <property />
  </group>
 </profile>
</personalization>
```

The attributes are described in Tables 13.21 and 13.22.

TABLE 13.21. personalization Attributes

Attribute	Description
enabled	A `Boolean` value indicating whether or not site maps are enabled. The default value is `true`.
defaultProvider	The name of the default provider. This should match one of the names supplied in the `providers` section. The default value is `AspNetAccessProvider`.

TABLE 13.22. personalization providers Attributes

Attribute	Description
name	The name of the site map provider.
type	A string containing the full .NET type of the provider.
providerSpecificSettings	The provider-specific settings.

The `<profile/>` section allows definition of custom types, such as a shopping cart, that can be stored with the Personalization details.

Table 13.23 shows the `personalization profile` attributes. Only the name attribute is required—all others are optional.

TABLE 13.23. personalization profile Attributes

Attribute	Description
name	Specifies the name of the profile.
readOnly	Indicates whether or not the property is read-only. The default value is `false`.
serializeAs	Defines how the property is serialized. Can be one of the items from the `SettingsSerializeAs` enumeration (from `System.Configuration.Settings`):

TABLE 13.23. personalization profile Attributes (continued)

Attribute	Description
	• `String`: Indicates the property is serialized as a string. • `Xml`: Indicates the property is serialized as XML. • `Binary`: Indicates the property is serialized in a binary format. • `ProviderSpecific`: Indicates the property is serialized in a provider-specific way. The default value is `ProviderSpecific`.
`provider`	Defines the name of the property.
`defaultValue`	Defines the default value for the property.
`type`	Defines the type of the property.
`allowAnonymous`	Indicates whether or not values can be stored for anonymous users.

Page Personalization

The `<pagePersonalization/>` section details the Personalization providers available for individual pages (see Listing 13.10).

Listing 13.10. pagePersonalization Configuration Syntax

```
<pagePersonalization
  defaultProvider="String"
  />
  <providers>
    <add name="String"
      type="String"
      [providerSpecificSettings]
      />
    <remove name="String"
      />
    <clear />
  </providers>
</pagePersonalization>
```

There is only one attribute for `<pagePersonalization/>`, which is `defaultProvider`. This defines the name of the default provider and defaults to `AspNetAccessProvider`. The attributes for the `providers` element are described in Table 13.24.

TABLE 13.24. pagePersonalization providers Attributes

Attribute	Description
name	Defines the name of the provider.
type	Defines the data type of the provider.

There are two supplied page Personalization providers, `AspNetSql Provider` and `AspNetAccessProvider`, both of which have the same two provider-specific attributes, as described in Table 13.25.

TABLE 13.25. Access and SQL Server Page Providers Attributes

Attribute	Description
connectionStringName	Defines the name of the connection string, from the `connectionStrings` configuration section.
applicationName	Defines the name of the application to which the page provider has scope.

Protocols

The `<protocols/>` section defines the protocols available to the system and the protocol handlers that process them. Here's the syntax:

```
<protocols>
  <add
    id="ISAPI"
    processHandlerType="String"
    appDomainHandlerType="String"
    validate="[true|false]"
    />
</protocols>
```

The attributes are described in Table 13.26.

TABLE 13.26. protocols Attributes

Attribute	Description
id	Specifies a unique protocol identifier.
processHandlerType	Specifies the full name of the type that handles the process. This attribute is optional; if unspecified, the protocol does not require a protocol handler.

TABLE 13.26. protocols Attributes (continued)

Attribute	Description
appDomainHandlerType	Specifies the full name of the type of the application domain.
validate	Indicates whether or not processHandlerType and appDomainHandlerType should be validated as proper types. The default is true.

Role Manager

The `<roleManager/>` section allows configuration of roles for use in authorization (see Listing 13.11).

Listing 13.11. roleManager Configuration Syntax

```
<roleManager
  defaultProvider="String"
  enabled="[true|false]"
  cacheRolesInCookies="[true|false]"
  cookieName="String"
  cookieTimeout="Integer"
  cookiePath="String"
  cookieRequiresSSL="[true|false]"
  cookieSlidingExpiration="[true|false]"
  cookieProtection="[None|Validation|Encryption|All]"
  >
  <providers>
    <add name="String"
      type="String"
      [providerSpecificSettings]
      />
    <remove name="String"
      />
    <clear />
  </providers>
</roleManager>
```

The attributes for the `<roleManager/>` are described in Table 13.27.

TABLE 13.27. roleManager Attributes

Attribute	Description
defaultProvider	Indicates the name of the default role provider. The default value is AspNetAccessProvider.

TABLE 13.27. roleManager Attributes (continued)

Attribute	Description
enabled	Indicates whether or not the Role Manager is enabled. The default value is `false`.
cacheRolesInCookies	Indicates whether or not cookies are used to store role information. The default value is `true`.
cookieName	Specifies the name of the cookie. The default value is `.ASPROLES`.
cookieTimeout	Specifies the time, in minutes, before the cookie expires. This cannot be `0` or less. The default value is `100000`.
cookiePath	Specifies the path, which is case-sensitive, used to write the cookie. Using `'/'` allows applications within the same domain to access the cookie. The default is `'/'`.
cookieRequiresSSL	Indicates whether or not the cookie requires an SSL connection in order to be written to the client. The default value is `false`.
cookieSlidingExpiration	Indicates whether the cookie timeout resets on each request (a value of `true`) or expires at a fixed time (a value of `false`). The default value is `true`.
cookieProtection	Specifies the protection scheme used to store the cookie. Can be one of the `CookieProtection` enumeration values (from `System.Web.Security`): • `None`: Indicates no protection is used. • `Validation`: Indicates that the cookie is hashed and validated. • `Encryption`: Indicates that the cookie is encrypted. • `All`: Indicates that both validation and encryption are used. The default value is `None`.

Role Manager Providers

There are three supplied Role Manager providers:

- `AspNetSqlProvider`, which uses SQL Server to store and retrieve role information

- `AspNetAccessProvider`, which uses Access to store and retrieve role information
- `WindowsToken`, which retrieves role information from the Windows authenticated token

The SQL Server and Access providers have the following attributes:

- `connectionStringName`, which defines the name of the connection string in the `connectionStrings` configuration section
- `applicationName`, which defines the application to which the provider has scope

All three providers also have a `description` attribute.

Mail Servers

The `<smtpMail/>` section allows configuration of a mail server for use with the SMTP `Mail` class (see Listing 13.12).

Listing 13.12. smtpMail Configuration Syntax

```
<smtpMail
  serverName="String"
  serverPort="Integer"
  from="String">
  <fields>
    <add name="String"
      value="String"
      typeName="String"
      />
    <remove name="String"
      />
    <clear />
  </fields>
</smtpMail>
```

The attributes are described in Table 13.28.

TABLE 13.28. smtpMail Attributes

Attribute	Description
serverName	Defines the name of the SMTP server. The default value is `localhost`.
serverPort	Defines the port used to send mail. This must be a positive number; the default value is `25`.
from	Defines the `from` tag to use when sending mail.

Field Settings

The `<fields/>` section allows definition of custom fields for the SMTP mail server. The attributes are described in Table 13.29.

TABLE 13.29. smtpMail fields Attributes

Attribute	Description
name	Defines the name of the field.
value	Defines the value of the field.
typeName	Defines the data type of the field. The default value is `String`.

URL Mappings

The `<urlMappings/>` section allows configuration of URLs that will be rewritten, thus allowing the actual URL to be hidden. Here's the syntax:

```
<urlMappings
   enabled="[true|false]">
  <add
    url="String"
    mappedUrl="String"
    />
  <remove name="String"
    />
</urlMappings>
```

The attributes are detailed in Table 13.30. For removal, the `url` attribute must contain a relative URL starting with `~/`.

TABLE 13.30. urlMappings Attributes

Attribute	Description
enabled	Indicates whether or not the URL mappings service is enabled. The default is `true`.
url	Specifies the displayed URL. This must be a relative URL starting with `~/`.
mappedUrl	Specifies the actual URL. This must be a relative URL starting with `~/`.

Web Administration Tool

The Web Administration Tool (see Chapter 6) is configured with the `<webSiteAdministrationTool/>` section (see Listing 13.13).

Listing 13.13. webSiteAdministrationTool Configuration Syntax

```
<webSiteAdministrationTool
  defaultUrl="String"
  physicalPath="String"
  enabled="[true|false]"
  errorPage="String"
  localOnly="[true|false]"
  >
  <authorization>
    <allow
      [users|roles]="String"
      applicationPath="String"
      />
    <deny
      [users|roles]="String"
      applicationPath="String"
      />
  </authorization>
  <categories>
    <category
      title="String"
      navigateUrl="String"
      imageUrl="String"
      selectedImageUrl="String"
      />
  </categories>
</webSiteAdministrationTool>
```

The attributes are described in Table 13.31.

TABLE 13.31. webSiteAdministrationTool Attributes

Attribute	Description
defaultUrl	Defines the URL of the Web Administration Tool, and is used by the `HttpHandler` to redirect requests to `WebAdmin.axd` to the correct URL. The default value is `/aspnet_webadmin/default.aspx`.
physicalPath	Defines the physical location of the Web Administration Tool. The default value is `%SystemDrive%:\inetpub\wwwroot\aspnet_webadmin\default.aspx`.

TABLE 13.31. webSiteAdministrationTool Attributes (continued)

Attribute	Description
enabled	Indicates whether or not the Web Administration Tool is enabled. The default value is true.
errorPage	Defines the page to use for displaying errors.
localOnly	Indicates whether or not the tool can be used only from the local machine (i.e., http://localhost).

Authorization Settings

The <authorization/> section allows configuration of which users or roles are allowed access to which parts of the administration interface. The attributes are described in Table 13.32.

TABLE 13.32. authorization Attributes

Attribute	Description
users/roles	Specifies the collection of users or roles defining who is allowed or denied access to the Web Administration Tool.
applicationPath	Defines the application that the users or roles are allowed or not allowed to administer.

Categories

The <categories/> section defines the categories that appear on the main administration page. The attributes are shown in Table 13.33.

TABLE 13.33. categories Attributes

Attribute	Description
title	Defines the category title.
navigateUrl	Defines the relative or absolute URL that will be requested for this category.
imageUrl	Defines the relative or absolute URL that represents this category.
selectedImageUrl	Defines the relative or absolute URL that represents this category when it is selected.

The default categories are:

- Home
- Security
- Personalize
- Reports
- Data Access

For the Technology Preview, only the content for the Security tab is implemented; the other tabs are simply placeholders for future implementation.

State Management

As Web applications are transmitted via HTTP, we have to carefully ensure that any state we require is kept between postbacks to the server. In ASP most state was handled by the `Session State` dictionary, but in ASP.NET controls intrinsically handled their own state via the `viewstate` mechanism. However, the problem with this is that `viewstate` can become large, especially when dealing with grids.

One of the goals of ASP.NET 2.0 is to add flexibility by introducing three new state handling mechanisms:

- **Control state**, allowing controls to store specific state that they require between round-trips
- **Page state**, where a history of state is kept, ensuring that state for mobile browsers is synchronized with the state held on the server
- **Session state plugability**, allowing custom state modules to replace the existing session state module

As part of this support for session bases, state persistence is also supported. This allows state to be stored server-side when dealing with mobile browsers, where large pages can be a limiting factor for both memory and bandwidth reasons.

Control State

In ASP.NET 1.x, controls save state as part of the viewstate. However, viewstate is really intended to store state set by the application, not individual controls. Additionally, if viewstate is turned off at the page level, several controls break (e.g., the current view of a multiview or the sort order of a sortable data grid). The only solution is to reset the properties on every request, which is not always practical because the controls themselves decide what state they need.

To solve this problem, a new state has been created, called control state, to store control-specific state. Control state is stored in a hidden field (called __CONTROLSTATE) in the same way as viewstate, but it is completely separate from viewstate and thus works when viewstate is turned off. For example, consider a `Pager` control:

```
<asp:Pager runat="server" />
```

This would normally require viewstate, but under the new model its viewstate is 0 and the control state is 12 bytes. This can be found by looking at a new column when tracing is enabled, as shown in Figure 13.1.

Implementing Control State in Custom Controls

When creating custom controls, control state can be implemented by the following three steps:

1. Calling `Page.RegisterRequiresControlState()`
2. Overriding `SaveControlState()` and returning the control state
3. Overriding `LoadControlState()` and processing the control state

Control Tree

Control UniqueID	Type	Render Size Bytes (including children)	Viewstate Size Bytes (excluding children)	Controlstate Size Bytes (excluding children)
__Page	ASP.foo_aspx	694	24	0
_ctl0	System.Web.UI.HtmlControls.HtmlForm	694	0	0
_ctl1	System.Web.UI.LiteralControl	6	0	0
Gridview1	System.Web.UI.WebControls.GridView	0	0	0
_ctl2	System.Web.UI.LiteralControl	6	0	0
SqlDataSource1	System.Web.UI.WebControls.SqlDataSource	0	0	0
_ctl3	System.Web.UI.LiteralControl	12	0	0
Pager1	System.Web.UI.WebControls.Pager	25	0	12
Pager1 $_ctl0	System.Web.UI.WebControls.LinkButton	0	0	0
Pager1 $_ctl1	System.Web.UI.WebControls.ImageButton	0	0	0
Pager1 $_ctl4	System.Web.UI.LiteralControl	0	0	0
Pager1 $_ctl2	System.Web.UI.WebControls.LinkButton	0	0	0
Pager1 $_ctl3	System.Web.UI.WebControls.ImageButton	0	0	0
Pager1 $_ctl5	System.Web.UI.LiteralControl	0	0	0
_ctl4	System.Web.UI.LiteralControl	8	0	0

FIGURE 13.1. Page trace showing control state

Listing 13.14 shows an example.

LISTING 13.14. Implementing Control State

```
Public Class MyControl
    Inherits WebControl

  Private _myProperty As Integer

  Protected Overrides Sub OnInit(E As EventArgs)
    Page.RegisterRequiresControlState(Me)
    MyBase.OnInit(E)
  End  Sub

  Protected Overrides Function SaveControlState() As Object
    Return CType(_MyProperty, Object)
  End Function

  Protected Overrides Sub LoadControlState(State As Object)
    If State <> Nothing Then
      _myProperty = Convert.ToInt32(state)
    End If
  End Sub

End Class
```

It is important to remember that control state is designed for critical private storage of state, so storage should be kept to a minimum.

Page State Persistence

ASP.NET 1.x persisted all viewstate to a hidden control on a page. As mentioned earlier, this can be inconvenient for some devices (such as phones), where the reduced bandwidth means slower loading speeds and reduced memory means a limited page size. Under these circumstances it's sensible to store state on the server.

In ASP.NET 2.0 the page adapter architecture allows for page state to be implemented by an object that inherits from a page state persister. This lets the page abstract the storage of state into a separate class, which the adapter can implement, allowing different state mechanisms to be implemented depending on the adapter.

The framework supplies two page state persisters:

- `HiddenFieldPageStatePersister`, which stores server-side hidden form controls, such as viewstate and control state
- `SessionPageStatePersister`, which keeps a history of viewstates and control states in session state

The latter of these is implemented in a way similar to the viewstate persistence in the MMIT from version 1.x.

Session State Plugability

By default there are three ways to store session state:

- In-Process, stored within the ASP.NET worker process
- State Server, stored in the Windows State Server service
- SQL Server, stored within a SQL Server database

These provide most users with what they need, but session state handling in version 1.x isn't extensible. ASP.NET 2.0 allows session state to be completely unplugged and replaced with a custom module. In addition, there is a new Session State ID module, allowing just the creation of IDs for session state to be replaced. Both of these allow custom data stores or even just custom handling of the session data.

There are two ways to provide custom session state handling. The first is to author a completely new session state module; the other is to just replace portions of the existing system. The first of these is the most flexible solution but is the most complex, whereas the second is simpler because you can replace only those bits that need to be changed. For example, you could just implement an Oracle session provider.

To replace the session state system, you can do any of the following:

- Replace `SessionStateModule` with one that implements `IHttpModule`.
- Replace `HttpSessionStateProvider` class with one that implements `IHttpSessionState`.
- Replace `SessionIDModule` with one that implements `ISessionIDModule`.

Only the first of these is required to implement your own method of handling session state. Optionally you can implement your own `HttpSessionStateProvider` to provide your own storage mechanism for session state or implement `SessionIDModule` to provide creation of session IDs. As mentioned, you don't need to implement these—there's no requirement for a custom session state module to implement ID handling at all. In fact, you don't even need an `HttpSessionStateProvider`, although your custom class has to return an object that implements `IHttpSessionState`.

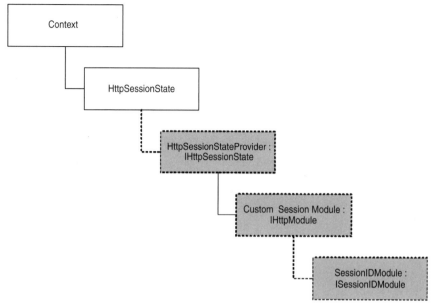

Figure 13.2. Session state object hierarchy

Together the three of these provide a complete implementation of session state. The hierarchy of objects is shown in Figure 13.2.

Once session state is implemented, you can simply replace the existing module with the new custom module by editing the `httpModules` `configuration` section (see Listing 13.15).

LISTING 13.15. Configuring Your Own Session State

```
<configuration>
  <system.web>
    <httpModules>
      <remove name="Session" />
      <add name="Session"
         type="AW.MyStateModule, MyStateModule" />
    </httpModules>
  </system.web>
</configuration>
```

The second approach to customizing session state is to use the existing session state module but to replace portions of it, such as:

- `ISessionDictionary`, which is the interface for the class that manages the session data

- `SessionStateStoreItem`, which represents the data retrieved from the session data store
- `SessionIDModule`, which represents the handling of IDs for the session
- `ISessionStateStore`, which is the interface for the class that provides the interface to the actual data store

Only the session state store (`ISessionStateStore`) is required to customize session state—replacing other classes is optional, allowing the existing functionality to be preserved while customizing just selected sections. The hierarchy of these items is shown in Figure 13.3.

If implementing a custom state provider class, this can be configured by modifying the `sessionState` section of the configuration file:

```
<configuration>
  <system.web>
    <sessionState mode="Custom"
      customType="AW.MyStateModule, StateModule"
      />
  </system.web>
</configuration>
```

A more detailed explanation of customizing session state is beyond the scope of this book.

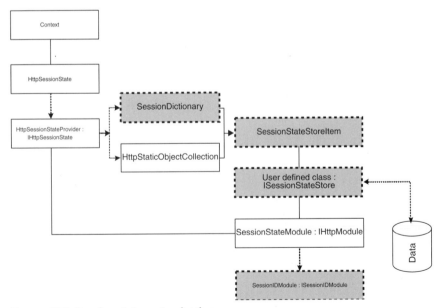

FIGURE 13.3. Session state customization

The Management API

There's no doubt that the Web Administration Tool is a great utility to help administer an application, but some administrative tasks either aren't suited to a Web interface or need to be run before the application is created (or as part of the application).

ASP.NET 2.0 provides a comprehensive Management API, which allows complete manipulation of the XML configuration files as well as integration with IIS. In particular, the following configuration tasks are supported.

- View configuration data merged from all levels of an application hierarchy.
- Allow configuration changes to specific configuration files.
- Import and export configuration sections.
- Create new configuration sections.

These features allow you to set up and configure not only local machines but also remote machines.

IIS Integration

The Management API has been integrated into the IIS Management Console, so when you view the properties of a site or virtual directory, you now see an additional ASP.NET tab, as shown in Figure 13.4.

FIGURE 13.4. IIS ASP.NET configuration

On this screen you can see the current ASP.NET version, with a drop-down list allowing you to select other versions to use for this application (if other versions are installed). You can also see the full path to the application and the dates and times the configuration file was created and changed.

Figure 13.5 shows the screen that appears when the Edit configuration button is selected. Here you can see tabs for the major configuration sections. We won't go through them in detail because they just map the properties from the XML file. Any settings that don't appear to have a tab themselves are on other tabs—Membership and Roles are on the Authentication tab, and things like Tracing, Compilation, HTTP Handlers, and so on are on the Advanced tab.

There are two things to note about this interface.

- It shows a merged view of the settings and thus includes settings from all levels of the hierarchy.
- Sections can be locked, thus preventing any changes at a lower level in the application hierarchy. When locking a section is allowed, you'll see a padlock icon next to the section.

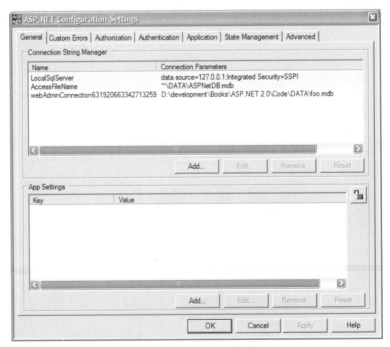

FIGURE 13.5. ASP.NET Configuration Settings window

Management Classes

The management classes reside in the `System.Web.Management` and `System.Configuration` namespaces. There are too many classes to detail here, but essentially each class provides a strongly typed interface to a `configuration` section, with properties representing the individual attributes of the XML file. For example, listed below are a couple of the classes.

- `WebApplicationServer` maps to a Web server.
- `Configuration` maps to the configuration file.

The `Configuration` class provides access via properties to the various sections. For example:

```
Dim server As WebApplicationServer
Dim cfg As System.Configuration.Configuration

server = WebApplicationServer.OpenServer("localhost")
cfg = System.Configuration.Configuration.GetConfigurationForUrln("App")
```

At this stage `cfg` contains references to the configuration details for the selected application, and these are accessed via properties such as `Web` (for the `system.web` section) and `AppSettings` (for the `appSettings` section). The configuration details are a merge of all settings from the current node back up the hierarchy.

Updating Configuration Settings

To update settings you simply use a property. For example, it would be possible to turn off custom errors with the following lines of code:

```
cfg.Web.CustomErrors.Mode = CustomErrorsMode.Off
cfg.Update()
```

Updates are always written back to the currently open node and cannot be written to a node higher up. However, before writing settings, you need to ensure that you are allowed to do so because the section might be locked. Check the `IsLocked` property:

```
If Not cfg.Web.CustomErrors.IsLocked Then
  cfg.Web.CustomErrors.Mode = CustomErrorsMode.Off
  cfg.Update()
End If
```

Note that the ASP.NET process needs write permissions on both the `web.config` file and the application directory. This is because a copy of `web.config` is created during the update process and removed once the update is complete.

SUMMARY

Although left to the end of the book, this chapter certainly doesn't contain the least useful material. In fact, in many ways it contains some of the most useful information because the increased administration facilities reduce the time (and potential for errors) that inevitably get tied up with administrative work. Simplifying the tasks required, adding an API to allow custom administration, and providing a Web-based administration tool make our jobs much easier.

That may not seem that important, but consider what the bulk of this chapter has been about—documenting the changes to the configuration files. There are many changes and new sections, so anything that enables us to administer them more easily is a boon.

Now it's time for you to come to grips with all of the new and exciting features. Install the Framework and start playing. You'll soon be wondering how you lived without the new features that ASP.NET 2.0 offers.

Index

Microsoft .NET Development Series

.NET Web Services
Architecture and Implementation

Keith Ballinger

0321113594

Essential .NET
Volume 1
The Common Language Runtime

Don Box
with Chris Sells

0201734117

Graphics
Programming
with GDI+

Mahesh Chand

0321160770

The C#
Programming
Language

Anders Hejlsberg
Scott Wiltamuth
Peter Golde

0321154916

A First Look at
ADO.NET and
System Xml v 2.0

Alex Homer
Dave Sussman
Mark Fussell

0321228391

A First Look at
ASP.NET v.2.0

Alex Homer
Dave Sussman
Rob Howard

0321228960

The
Common Language
Infrastructure
Annotated Standard

James S. Miller
Susann Ragsdale

0321154932

Essential ASP.NET
with Examples in C#

Fritz Onion

0201760401

Essential ASP.NET
with Examples in Visual Basic .NET

Fritz Onion

0201760398

Building Applications
and Components with
Visual Basic .NET

Ted Pattison
with Dr. Joe Hummel

0201734958

Windows Forms
Programming in C#

Chris Sells

0321116208

Windows Forms
Programming in
Visual Basic .NET

Chris Sells
Justin Gehtland

0321125193

Programming
in the .NET
Environment

Damien Watkins
Mark Hammond
Brad Abrams

0201770180

Pragmatic ADO.NET
Data Access for the Internet World

Shawn Wildermuth

0201745682

For more information go to www.awprofessional.com/msdotnetseries/

Register
Your Book

at www.awprofessional.com/register

You may be eligible to receive:

- Advance notice of forthcoming editions of the book
- Related book recommendations
- Chapter excerpts and supplements of forthcoming titl
- Information about special contests and promotions throughout the year
- Notices and reminders about author appearances, tradeshows, and online chats with special guests

Contact us

If you are interested in writing a book or reviewing manuscripts prior to publication, please write to us at:

Editorial Department
Addison-Wesley Professional
75 Arlington Street, Suite 300
Boston, MA 02116 USA
Email: AWPro@aw.com

Addison-Wesley

Visit us on the Web: http://www.awprofessional.com